THE
POWER
OF GOVERNANCE

EMMA KNIGHTS

Together we unlock every learner's unique potential

At Hachette Learning (formerly Hodder Education), there's one thing we're certain about. No two students learn the same way. That's why our approach to teaching begins by recognising the needs of individuals first.

Our mission is to allow every learner to fulfil their unique potential by empowering those who teach them. From our expert teaching and learning resources to our digital educational tools that make learning easier and more accessible for all, we provide solutions designed to maximise the impact of learning for every teacher, parent and student.

Aligned to our parent company, Hachette Livre, founded in 1826, we pride ourselves on being a learning solutions provider with a global footprint.

www.hachettelearning.com

To order, please visit www.HachetteLearning.com or contact Customer Service at education@hachette.co.uk / +44 (0)1235 827827.

ISBN: 978 1 0360 0528 3

© Emma Knights 2026

First published in 2026 by
Hachette Learning,
An Hachette UK Company
Carmelite House
50 Victoria Embankment
London EC4Y 0DZ

www.HachetteLearning.com

The authorised representative in the EEA is Hachette Ireland, 8 Castlecourt Centre, Dublin 15, D15 XTP3, Ireland (email: info@hbgi.ie)

Impression number   10 9 8 7 6 5 4 3 2 1
Year   2029 2028 2027 2026

Cover photo Rebecca Taylor.
Illustrations by DC Graphic Design Limited, Hextable, Kent
Typeset in the UK.
Printed in the UK.

A catalogue record for this title is available from the British Library.

MIX
Paper | Supporting responsible forestry
FSC
www.fsc.org
FSC™ C104740

Emma Knights OBE was chief executive of the National Governance Association from 2010 to 2024, growing its services and the understanding of school and trust governance. She had the privilege of representing the voices of school governors and academy trustees across England. Before NGA, Emma worked in third sector organisations, always aiming to support people from disadvantaged backgrounds with advocacy, access to civil rights and entitlements, and by tackling child poverty or encouraging early education. She continues to govern and now chairs a local environmental charity, Action21.

Acknowledgements

The introduction shows I have huge numbers of people to thank for sharing their experiences with me, but there are a few people who contributed most to my learning about governance. My two deputies at NGA were the best you could possibly have: Gillian Allcroft and then Sam Henson. Clare Collins MBE who led NGA's consultancy service until 2023 made me think. I must also thank NGA's chairs of trustees who encouraged me to embark on this endeavour: Ian Courtney MBE, Maggi Bull MBE and Lynn Howard. I would like to thank John Catt Educational and Meena Ameen in particular for their patience when I took so long to get going while leading NGA and then ended up writing a lot!

Last a huge thank you and many hugs to my lovely family – Mark, Sam and Caitlin – who believed I could finish this when I didn't, and a special mention to my son Sam who removed some excess words when I was struggling to.

Contents

Introduction

It was an absolute privilege to serve as the chief executive of the National Governance Association (NGA) for 14 years from 2010 to 2024. I arrived as a school governor, but a relatively recent one. It was my second chief executive post, so I already knew something about reporting to a board of trustees, but apparently, I was largely appointed for my experience of having saved another third sector organisation from the rocks of insolvency. At that time, NGA was small and arguably unsustainable, so the trustees were primarily looking for someone with the skills to grow a relatively new membership organisation. This job at NGA enabled me to learn so much about governance, and after departing from a much larger and sustainable organisation last year, I wanted to share that knowledge.

There are many in the sector who are extremely knowledgeable about what good governance looks like and how to improve practice, not least my former colleagues and the more than 60 National Leaders of Governance that NGA recruited and deployed for two years on behalf of the Department for Education (DfE). This book is absolutely not a guide on 'how to govern': that is NGA's bread and butter – and I, of course, commend NGA's resources.

The book is an attempt to bring the knowledge about the parts governance and those who govern play out of the shadows and into the sunshine to ensure our children get the best possible education. There is a real gap in the research literature over the past 10 years, and while I do try to summarise the key findings from previous decades, this book doesn't pretend to be in any way academic. I do however hope it stirs some interest in academia and stimulates some research.

I am a creature of the third sector; the not-for-profit sector. I was proud to describe NGA as a social enterprise where we aimed to keep prices as low as we could for schools and plough any surplus into improving our services. NGA also champions a volunteer community and civic engagement: those who volunteer to govern are citizens engaged in supporting a crucial public service.

So, as a true believer in collegiate enterprise and collective wisdom, it goes a little against the grain that this book is not an NGA publication; but it would have been impractical to make sure every nuance fitted with the organisation's consensus positions. And, of course, I have my own passions, a few I was careful to rein in as the figurehead of the governance community, but most I had the opportunity of building on in that role, such as: getting the best possible deal for disadvantaged children; equity, diversity and inclusion; the importance of place, parental engagement, environmental sustainability and ethical leadership.

I took great care at NGA to try to represent the full range of views of the huge group of people who govern our schools. It is sometimes difficult to reconcile all viewpoints and not disregard the minority, but it is a challenge I relished: it makes for a more interesting world, sustained by a belief that pretty much everything benefits from a multiplicity of views and experiences. It is important that the voices of those who govern are heard. I know that is often said by leaders, to the point that it can become trite, but in NGA I really did try to act on these principles, and I know that continues.

The stands we take – as individuals and as parts of bigger groups – build on our values and beliefs as well as our knowledge and experience. We all have baggage and, in the spirit of good governance, I should declare mine. I wholeheartedly embrace the mission of our state schools. My father was the headmaster of an independent school, but when we arrived in England after living overseas, he allowed me at the age of 15 to choose to go to the local state school in Liverpool, on the edge of Toxteth. Having been at a state school in Bermuda, it perhaps felt more familiar and more diverse in terms of class, although not race. It was a girls-only school, which did seem odd: in Bermuda, all state schools were co-educational.

As an undergraduate at Oxford University, I coordinated the student union's Target Schools scheme, which encourages state school pupils to apply to the university. Sadly, the project still needs to exist today, 40 years later. On graduating, I volunteered in community advice centres along the ring road – a whole different world from the dreaming spires in the city centre, but one which cemented my commitment to those families who had not had the advantages I had. It shaped the next 20 years of my career, largely spent in citizens advice, legal advocacy and anti-poverty work.

Almost 20 years ago, I began an application to train as a maths teacher, but it would have necessitated me being away from home during the week to brush up my maths knowledge. That wasn't an option I was going to choose while I had school-age children. I became a school governor, and a few years later, I applied for the job at NGA. In effect I was a campaigner and policy geek who fell into leadership and governance.

NGA is unique in the school sector; there is no other organisation that represents the governance community. There are many selling services to governing boards, but they are not attempting to speak on their behalf. This allowed me much access to conversations with DfE – ministers and officials – and to be part of the relatively small group of organisations who often work together, sometimes in tension, to try to influence policy on schools. There are many partners from whom I have learned so much, but the two leadership unions, ASCL (Association of School and College Leaders) and NAHT (National Association of Head Teachers) stand out as super collaborators; there were many times we laughed when we could have cried. At national level, we tried to emulate the relationships we expect governors and trustees to have with school leaders and trust executives, built on trust, respect and honesty.

Recent governance experiences in a time of significant change are not thoroughly documented elsewhere, and the specific academic literature is paltry, apart from a few small-scale studies, whereas research from earlier decades provided a treasure trove for which I am truly grateful. I've also plundered governance literature from other sectors. NGA publishes a series of policy and research reports every year, from which I draw heavily. I aim to knit them together to illustrate the bigger picture. The story of the development of governance in the English school sector needs to be told.

I did not achieve the fundamental change I would have liked to at NGA in terms of the position of governance within the sector, its visibility and the buy-in from others, including policymakers. I'm still saying many of the same things that I did over my whole period of leading NGA. I had wanted to move school governance from the niche it currently occupies into the mainstream, from the periphery of the system into the centre of school leadership and, perhaps most ambitious of all, the centre of the accountability system.

I thought we'd been fairly loud and insistent, but outside our world of governance, with the exception of some allies, the message of the importance of governance wasn't remembered at crucial points. Lots of people of course understand its role intellectually, but that isn't enough to become an advocate for governance. I became embarrassed to be repeating myself so much; blogs, articles and presentations at events clearly not penetrating the fortresses of power sufficiently. So I felt I couldn't sign off completely without trying one last approach: this book!

The history of the past 20 years shows that governance of the English school sector did not feature sufficiently in the minds of policymakers redesigning the system. It was an afterthought, a sideshow to the real business of structural change, rather than an element that needs to be right to ensure the best possible schools for children and young people. Hence we now find ourselves in a muddle in terms of the variety of school structures and their accountability. I hope to make the case that if governance is given respect and its rightful place in the story even at this stage, it would go a large way to making accountability more intelligent.

A complex ecosystem has been created for England's state schools, while the world around them has changed dramatically. The system is regularly characterised as fragmented, and sometimes chaotic. I suggest it would be more accurate to call it fragile and under strain. That is not to say our school system is failing: it is being held together by a huge amount of commitment, energy, talent and goodwill. It can be argued that it is achieving more for its pupils than in any time in its history, and there are more officially 'good' schools than ever before.

Tensions are caused by a long list of familiar challenges: funding, staff recruitment and workload, the rising needs and numbers of pupils with SEND (special educational needs and disabilities) and mental health issues, more families in poverty, the continuing legacy of the pandemic and, as if that wasn't enough, the fear of Ofsted. There is a constant pressure on schools to alleviate problems that arise elsewhere in society.

Is the glue provided by the people in the system strong enough to continue sticking it all together, and even to strengthen it further? Will our governance ensure this happens?

My various jobs have placed me on the periphery of Whitehall and Westminster for a long time; my first bilateral meeting with a Secretary of State was with Peter Lilley MP, more than 30 years ago. I hope that joining up my lobbying experience with governance theory and school leadership practice may add something to the debate about where next for the school system and where next for our pupils.

I would like to thank all those who have shared their ideas with me over the years and taken the time to debate. I have enjoyed our conversations, and the arguments I make here have been all the better for being stress tested. I have learned so much from NGA colleagues, members and education leaders. Yet this book is my take, my analysis, my emphasis and, on occasion, my obsessions. And no doubt my mistakes too.

Most of all, I want to document and acknowledge the enormous work of school governors and academy trustees. Having been embedded in their world for so long, I have not lost the faith. Despite having heard every scenario there is to hear on governance disasters, I am not jaundiced. I remain in awe of the commitment and tenacity of volunteers. Wherever I go I see the effort, the care, the thoughtfulness and the desire to challenge constructively and to support school leaders and staff in the interests of children. There may be no statues to committees, but the work being done quietly, often behind closed doors, should be more visible and valued properly. This book is dedicated to the nearly quarter of a million people who are governing state schools now, those who have in the past and those who will follow in your footsteps. I hope it does their gift justice.

Emma Knights

June 2025

Part A:
The fundamentals

1.
What is governance?

'Governance determines who has the power, who makes the decisions, how other players make their voice heard, and how account is rendered.'

Many people have come up with definitions of governance, most revolving round three dimensions, authority, decision-making and accountability, though a whole range of similar words are used, such as control instead of authority and oversight rather than accountability. I adopted this one from the Institute on Governance in Canada a decade ago, not only because its elegant use of language hits the nail on the head, but also because of its universal applicability. Governance applies to all countries, systems and institutions across the globe, clearly not something particular to schools or to England. Governance is how society, or groups within it, organises to make decisions.

Governance systems can be interlinked, overlapping, hierarchical in part and horizontal in others. There is much literature on the nature of those systems and the principles underlying them, and it would be presumptuous to pretend I've analysed it all in depth. Instead, I offer some examples that I think are of most relevance and interest to the school sector.

Governance – processes, mechanisms and relationships through which decisions are made – is related to government, the formal institution or body that holds the power to make and enforce their decisions. This leaves governance also entwined with the field of politics. This is where language can start going round in circles, as politics refers to both the way power is exercised in a country or institution as well as policymaking as distinguished from administration or law.

Another definition worth quoting is UNESCO's from 2017 on the concept of public sector governance, which 'refers to norms, values, structures and processes designed to ensure accountability, transparency, rule of law, stability, equity and inclusiveness, responsiveness, empowerment and broad-based participation'. This definition also refers to the subtle nature of governance, meaning it is often not observable.

While many of the concepts recur, governance is a very contested territory. To govern is usually thought not to include delivery, but to ensure or enable delivery of those decisions by others. Some consider governance in its present form in the Western public sector to be instrumental, normative and performative. Many commentators, particularly academics, take this to be a negative distortion of the higher aims of a more democratic form of governance, rather than as an extension of it.

Over the past 50 years, some power has been devolved away from traditional structures of government towards non-state organisations and at least notionally local communities. Some of that governance remains top-down, through accountability mechanisms that I look at in the next chapter, but some represent a shift towards decision-making by local organisations or horizontal networks. The state is exercising its power and control through other agents, governing more at a distance; the expression 'arm's length' is often used.

The question now in dispute is to what extent is the state – central government – truly devolving power? Or is it just as interested as ever, possibly even more so, in ensuring control, shaping services and managing expectations by mandating responsibilities and setting rules that must be followed? There is an argument made that those who have had governing powers granted to them, such as school governors and academy trustees, are mere agents of the state, acting out its will. While it is true that they are actively engaged in continuing the work of a democratically elected government, my experience of the past 15 years suggests this does not have to be done in a slavish fashion. Such an intimation doesn't pick up on the nuances of governance; it's a distortion of reality that does a disservice to those who volunteer and the professional leaders they work alongside. That is why I am so keen that current practice illuminates the theoretical; it is only with a confluence of theory and practice that complexities will be fully understood and conclusions made that reflect and improve the actuality.

There are many models of governance developed for different situations and sectors, which give power to a person or, more usually, a group of people. The model chosen will vary depending on the nature and purpose of the system or organisation, the values and ideology of those making the choice, and the voices they think are important to listen to. They evolve over time as society and its expectations, values and culture change, and new possibilities are created by the law or technology. Norms and assumptions of the past become not just indefensible, but often downright astonishing. Not so long ago we celebrated the centenary of universal women's suffrage in the UK; it is hard now to understand that decision-making limited to 'one man one vote' was so deeply engrained.

Ensuring a system performs well is only one of the principles underpinning governance; others identified in the international literature can be described as legitimacy and voice, direction and vision, accountability and fairness. Applying these principles is complex; they overlap and sometimes conflict. How they play out in practice varies according to the context and to how well power is exercised. I will return to those concepts in the following chapters.

One of course cannot fully consider the governance of one school, or even a group of schools, without considering its place in the wider system. I am going to come on to governance of the state school system as a whole at the end of the book, but I am concentrating in the main on institutional governance within the sector. Another phrase sometimes used is 'corporate governance', which some assume refers to the for-profit sector, even though governing bodies of schools maintained by local authorities have long been referred to as corporate bodies – corporate in the sense of being shared by a whole group.

Theories of governance

There is a huge amount of literature covering a number of disciplines about the phenomenon of governance, with some intense debates about its nature and practices. Political scientists write about those who hold power (for example, at national state and local government level), how much decision-making they are taking away from others in society and how influenced they are by the voices of others. There is also considerable classification of different structures or mindsets of governance and their evolution. In practice, governance systems tend to be complex hybrids.

Given that democracy is the central principle of our Western governments at many levels, this begs the question of the role of democracy in governance of other institutions and networks. How do we keep the power with the electorate while decisions are made by others on their behalf or supposedly in their interest?

There are both hierarchical and horizontal models of governance. The latter is often called network governance, involving the collaboration and coordination of independent actors. Networks may be based at local level. There may be rules or a framework, either designed and imposed from the centre or agreed between themselves, which are likely to cover the way in which decisions are made for and within the network. The consent of the others in the network will be needed in most arrangements to reach collectively binding decisions, whereas in a hierarchical structure, decisions can be made without the consent of others being required. A network involves an element of interdependence, but in a very specific remit. It can be more precise or tailored governance, and more adaptive to experience, given that it is nearer the user and likely to have more efficient feedback loops. The independent individuals or institutions within it may bring different attitudes and different levels of power, and I will return to networking in chapter 14.

The state, central or local government can apply different types of control with carrots and sticks, information and other forms of influence to achieve certain societal outcomes. Some literature presents governance as a contest between hierarchical and horizontal structures, but those structures could also work harmoniously with the right conditions, including meaningful delegation of power and decision-making. I appreciate this is difficult to achieve in a culture where the methods of accountability are heavy-handed. I will also touch on the role of the market, which can be classed as a third form of governance; however, I suggest in the school sector the relevant debate is to what extent markets influence the decision-makers, rather than the markets taking decisions in place of institutions.

What I attempt to do in this book is apply the governance principles and theories from other places to the state school system in England in a way that practitioners – whether volunteers or educational professionals – may find helpful. In particular there are two relevant theories of governance applied in all sorts of contexts: the 'principal-agent' and the 'stewardship' theories. I will return to these ideas when looking at how those that govern are held to account.

The first is where the principals (sometimes owners, but in our case governing boards) assign various tasks or responsibilities to the managers or executives (agents) to undertake on their behalf. Three problems are identified in these arrangements. Firstly, conflict can arise due to differences of the two parties' interests. Secondly, there can be differences of attitude to risk taking, and thirdly, differences due to the information held and valued by principals and agents.

Under the alternative stewardship theory, there is no conflict of interest between managers and the shareholders. The interests of the two parties are aligned as managers are employed to handle operations in a way that improves the performance of the organisation and thus provides reward to the owners.

In practice, both can play out on a board at different times or even at the same time on different issues, which serves to illustrate how complex and nuanced the relationship between a board and its executives is. Both theories narrow the relationships to the interests of owners and managers, whereas the board and management have responsibilities to a wider group of stakeholders. Furthermore, in the public service, the Nolan principle of selflessness expects holders of public office to act solely in terms of the public interest. I am more convinced by the stewardship theory with its emphasis on relationships, shared goals, trust and collaboration.

A collective endeavour

An institution gains from having a group of committed people serving on a board who bring a range of experience, skills, knowledge, backgrounds and outlooks to help achieve the organisation's purpose. The governing board exists to prevent one individual – the headteacher or the chief executive – from having unfettered powers of decision, as the White Paper *The Importance of Teaching* reminded us in 2010. A board helps management keep an appropriate sense of perspective; some executive leaders, even successful ones, can become convinced of their own infallibility. In common parlance, power corrupts.

My preferred definition makes it clear that governance concerns the executive as well as the non-executive. Executives have power and take key decisions too. Where one set of decision-making stops – that of the board – and the other starts needs clarity if governance is to function well; schemes of delegation might sound dull, but they contain vital information as to who makes which decisions.

The governing board's role is to focus clearly and solely on the purpose of the enterprise, which in the case of state schools is the education of its pupils for the public benefit. The board defines the ethos, expectations and direction, and employs staff to deliver that operation.

Executives are the employees of the organisation, and non-executives are those who are recruited from outside to play a role in governance without being paid to do any other role. Academy ambassadors (the scheme funded for some years by the DfE to headhunt trustees for the larger academy trusts) adopted the language of non-executives, mainly because they were recruiting from the private sector, and this is the language they recognised. In the private sector, non-executives are paid roles, as they are in many parts of the public sector and occasionally in the larger institutions in the third sector.

Learning from other sectors

As with any area of practice, it makes sense to look at and learn how institutional governance works in different sectors, particularly in the charity sector given academy trusts are charities, although with different regulation. Even before academy trusts with company directors became common place, 'non-executive director' was an analogy used for the work of the school governor; in 2001, almost half the governors (44%) surveyed viewed their role in this light (Adams, 2001).

Comparison is interesting, but direct adoption of specific practices from other sectors is more complicated and needs to be done with reflections on different contexts, purposes, values, models and legal responsibilities. For example, far too often the members of academy trusts (much more on trusts later) are likened to company shareholders, and sometimes shareholders are compared with stakeholders more generally. Neither of these comparisons work at all well: shareholders are the company owners unlike either trust members or stakeholders. Furthermore, the desire of shareholders to make a profit and be paid dividends drives decision-making in a very particular way that does not transfer to our sector.

No sector has a monopoly on best practice. Organisations with good governance do not fail: the right people are making the right decisions. This is thoroughly reinforced by the literature. There are high-profile failures in every sector, and stories from different sectors show remarkable similarities. Other sectors are much better than ours in reviewing and documenting governance failures, and that learning informs my thinking.

I am not summarising here the full range of public sector forms of governance as to do it well would take far too much space in a book about school governance. I therefore concentrate here on those that are most discussed as comparators.

Corporate sector

Private companies in the UK have a different model of governance from the public and not-for-profit sectors; they tend to have integrated boards where executives and non-executives sit together. The board has both independent and insider members, all of whom are paid. It is responsible for ensuring that the business has the necessary framework within which to function.

In the United States, a chief executive officer can also be the chair of the company board, but this is increasingly rare. Boeing is an example where this contributed to devastating consequences: in 2018 and 2019, two crashes of Boeing's best-selling airplanes took the lives of 346 passengers. It was concluded that not only was there dereliction of duty by the board but that deaths could have been avoided if its senior managers had had adequate supervision from an independent chair. In addition, a poor corporate culture was said to be responsible for leading to negligent engineering practices and substandard aircraft taking to the skies despite significant flaws.

On the other hand, the private sector in some European countries, such as the Netherlands and Germany, have two levels of board: one of executives who report to another board of non-executives, who are often drawn from shareholders and other stakeholders, such as unions.

In the UK, there is a senior independent director who supports the chair in their role and tends to lead the non-executive directors in the review of the chair. They can act as a trusted intermediary for other non-executive directors when necessary. This role should be fulfilled by the vice chair in the school sector.

In the UK, the board of directors' responsibility to the shareholders is not disputed. On paper, control is separated from ownership by shareholders. Yet in practice there is evidence (for example, from the Association of Chartered Certified Accountants) that company directors regard their duty as being to maximise short-term shareholder interests. The attention on the payment of dividends can provide perverse incentives and is seen by some as a fundamental flaw in the system. When we discussed scoping a piece of work with Bayes Business School (then Cass), we were advised that corporate governance would not have anything to teach us. At one of NGA's national conferences, in a session on learning from other sectors, the contributor from Cass Business School stated what company boards monitor – the bottom line – is much simpler than in the public sector, which must also look at the effects on beneficiaries. They were clear that private sector governance needs reform. There are many suggestions for such reform, one from the Trade Union Congress who campaign for workers on boards.

Much has been written about the operation of company boards and the role of non-executive directors. I found it interesting to see one example state that non-executive directors have a number of similarities with school governing bodies, in that they 'normally don't get involved in the daily running of the business but they monitor performance, provide wider experience to assist in longer term strategic planning and become involved in areas of specific interest or aptitude' (Whyatt, 2002).

At times of considerable corporate failure, significant reviews have been commissioned to investigate the reasons, such as the Cadbury review in the 1990s after a whole series of disasters. The Cadbury report had a significant effect not just in the UK but also abroad in improving governance. This was helped by the London Stock Exchange recognising the report's significance and insisting on listed companies adopting the Cadbury recommendations. It set out the responsibilities of boards with clarity, but not in a mere technical way, based on ethics, transparency and accountability. It introduced the concept of 'comply or explain', which gave companies the flexibility to adopt alternative practices as long as they could justify their decisions to shareholders.

In 2009, the government commissioned another independent review of corporate governance, this time into the banking sector after catastrophic failure throughout the banking system. The resulting Walker (2009) report quotes Larry Scanlon, president and chief operating officer of the Hunter Group: 'I have never seen a distressed organisation that could not be traced back to ineffective governance.' A well-functioning board should help executives keep an appropriate sense of perspective, which can be invaluable in a crisis.

The review's emphasis is on the need to improve corporate governance behaviour, rather than rules and frameworks. Walker argued for a culture change, particularly a culture of challenge. He made a number of recommendations including induction and a formal external review of governance every second or third year. Induction and reviewing board performance were not new ideas: for example, the Financial Reporting Council had published good practice suggestions in 2006 after the previous review of corporate governance, the Higgs report. The Institute of Directors was disappointed not to see a move towards a structure more akin to a traditional profession, with training and continuing professional development (CPD) requirements and an ethical framework. The UK Corporate Governance Code expects the evaluation of the board of FTSE 350 companies to be externally facilitated at least every three years.

Different language is used not just between sectors and counties, but also by many experts and consultants, but they generally cover very similar territory. Patrick Dunne (2021) uses very accessible language to describe three things that a corporate board must do:

- 'Ensure the right strategy is in place and that it is being followed;
- Ensure there are the right resources in place to fit with the agreed strategy. The most important of these are human and financial resources;
- Keep out of jail. By this I mean that the board needs to ensure that the company complies with all the appropriate regulations relating to its industry and the countries within which it operates.'

Others include risk management as a fourth function and scrutiny of performance as a fifth. Sometimes 'people' will also feature, given that non-executive directors are responsible for determining appropriate levels of remuneration of executive directors and have a prime role in appointing, and where necessary removing, executive directors. They also have a role in succession planning and leadership talent development. An advisory function is also noted by others.

The DfE – and its predecessor – has talked much about recruiting volunteers from the business sector and needing business skills on school and trust governing boards, which I will return to in chapter 7. This privileging of the private sector could suggest a hierarchy of expertise or even success. However, even a cursory study of different sectors shows each has had its own disaster stories. With very little research on the impact of good governance, most learning from published sources comes from failure.

Charities

The third sector model of charity governance has been adapted for academies, with trustees and company directors. Individuals on academy trust boards have both those roles. NGA, and now the DfE, default to the word 'trustee', as this not only emphasises that non-for-profit legal role, but also 'directors' is often a job title given to executives, which can blur the distinction. The Roman Catholic sector instead chooses to use 'director' and often calls multi-academy trusts 'MACs' (the 'c' stands for 'companies') to distinguish them from diocesan trusts who appoint most of the directors of MACs. But the choice of language does not alter the legal responsibilities of those volunteering.

In the UK third sector, unlike the corporate sector, there is almost always complete separation between executives and non-executives, and permission is required from the Charity Commission for this to be otherwise, even for a temporary period. As a chief executive of two different charities, at neither have I been a trustee, and I experienced the benefits of this clarity between roles. I argued for years that the academy sector should look more to charity governance for ideas given it is squarely and inarguably part of that sector. However, overall charity governance is probably no better than school and trust governance, which I will argue has improved over the last 15 years. The challenges are very similar and NGA does keep a close eye on practice, development and debates in the third sector in order to inform the school sector.

The literature on charity governance is fairly extensive. There isn't the equivalent of NGA for the charity sector, so rather than libraries of resources, the space is filled by a number of books, some of which I include in the bibliography. I particularly like this from *Governance as Leadership* by Chait, Ryan and Taylor (2005), which underlines the added value of the board: 'Trustees are typically situated at the edge of the organisation, close enough to understand the organisation's aims, operations and cultures, yet far enough removed to have some perspective, distance, and detachment. Board members usually embrace the institution's mission but have little at risk personally or professionally. From this vantage point, trustees can see the larger picture, overall patterns and tell-tale anomalies.'

The Charity Commission – the charity regulator – produces guidance but is much more hands off than the DfE is for schools; it would have to be, given the enormous number of charities in England and Wales and their diversity of objectives. As a result of a legal challenge, the Commission recognised that it had no power to require trustees to fetter the future exercise of their fiduciary duties. The Commission has had cuts in its funding, which has resulted in less activity. They describe themselves as 'a small organisation, compared to the vast size of the sector we regulate' (Charity Commission for England and Wales, 2023); although they have over 500 members of staff, that's to regulate almost 170,000 registered charities. It has also had some governance difficulties of its own in recent years. One newly appointed chair had to stand down after it came to light that, during the recruitment process, he had not reported an allegation made against him by an employee at a charity he had chaired.

Independently from the commission, six bodies developed the charity governance code, which has seven key principles: organisational purpose; leadership; integrity; decision-making, risk and control;

board effectiveness; equality, diversity and inclusion; and openness and accountability. The code sets out how each of those is met and evaluated. All of this fits entirely with the good governance principles set by NGA, and indeed they were used as the starting point for the academy trust governance code developed last year.

There is much concentration in the charity sector in the distinction between the role of the board and that of management. For example: '[Governance] is about ensuring that the organisation is well managed, but not about managing it … Governance is ultimately concerned with providing insight, wisdom and good judgement,' as expressed by Mike Hudson (2017) in *Managing without Profit*. Not only am I fond of the word 'wisdom' here, judgement is very much overlooked in the discussions of governance. The exercise of power absolutely requires good judgement.

Independent schools

Another near example to consider is the governance of independent, fee-charging schools in England. NGA has swapped practice with the Association of Governing Bodies of Independent Schools (AGBIS), and there is much similarity. But although it was occasionally suggested that state schools should emulate the independent sector, this was said without any comparative study. Our discussions with AGBIS very much confirm that learning is not one way and that the context in which state schools operate can increase the range of challenges for their governing boards.

Indeed, it has been acknowledged at some AGBIS events that state schools probably have the edge on good governance, particularly regarding financial oversight. Independent schools have the option of putting up their fees and, given the level of past increases, it's arguable many revert to doing that too quickly instead of accepting alternatives, which would prove more difficult for those running the school. The standard of governance practice is less critical when resources – money and staff – are plentiful and efficiencies are not paramount. The imposition of VAT on school fees in 2025 will have been testing boards, both those used to looking closely for efficiencies and those for whom it had not been a necessity.

Independent schools have a history of using alumni to govern more than state schools have; but in recent years more state schools have successfully been approaching this source of volunteers. They have the advantage of not just already knowing the school, but also knowing it from a different perspective. They tend to be younger than other volunteers and nearer the education system, sometimes even still in higher education.

Independent schools also often use governors to fundraise, an additional role familiar to some charity trustees, but not routinely expected in the state sector. They are also more likely to use the services of governors pro bono. This is a contentious area at best and potentially poor practice. If one provides services to an institution, one cannot then monitor those services too. One could of course leave the room, but that rather defeats the point of governing. For example, a lawyer on a governing board provides legal advice to the headteacher who acts upon it; the issue then comes to the governing board, and the governor who might otherwise be best equipped to comment has to excuse themselves. I come onto the related area of conflicts of interest in chapter 9.

Further education colleges

Further education (FE) and sixth-form college corporations are the legal entities that operate one or more colleges, and they are also exempt charities regulated by the DfE. FE colleges have been governed in this way for significantly longer than academies, having been taken out of the local authority control in 1993. There are far fewer FE colleges than schools, and they are much larger institutions, more equivalent to multi-academy trusts (MATs). Sixth-form colleges being smaller have in some cases joined MATs.

Colleges had a 20 year start on developing corporate governance and have all the familiar trappings of other sectors, such as a code centred round six principles, which offers assurance to stakeholders, helps ensure boards fulfil their regulatory requirements and provides a standard for external reviews. In particular they grew a governance profession earlier than schools.

The 2013 Association of Colleges' (AoC) publication *Creating Excellence in College Governance* gives many messages relevant to schools and trusts. Some lessons are repeated from even earlier publications: for example, the challenge of 'polite consensus and a wish to avoid conflict and a search for harmony which militates against challenging the status quo' and 'frequently good, free discussions take place but rarely the powerful debate over the big issues that research shows is a key feature of high performing teams'. The AoC notes that: 'Although this seems innocuous it can lead to devastating results. Governors at recent failed Colleges have commented that they knew something was wrong but did not feel able to speak up and were therefore unable to hold the senior leadership team to account. They were not able to challenge effectively and did not have the data and information to underpin their position.'

The report concludes that serious failures by a college, whether education provision or sustainability, are always ultimately attributable to failings in the leadership provided by the governing board.

Core functions of governing boards

To return to the sector I suspect readers are involved with: the school sector in England has had a formulation of the functions of governance set out by the DfE, and its predecessors. In maintained schools, the core functions of the governing body are set out in legislation and include, but are not limited to, ensuring:

1. That the vision, ethos and strategic direction of the school are clearly defined;
2. That the headteacher performs their responsibilities for the educational performance of the school;
3. The sound, proper and effective use of the school's financial resources.

Some years ago, I added a fourth core function of engaging with stakeholders, something often spelled out in other literature and central to our definition of governance: 'determining how other players make their voice heard'. I will return to this topic in chapter 16. A second addition I toyed with was adding the responsibilities of being the employer as these aren't spoken about enough. They are slightly complicated by the fact that most maintained schools act in the place of the local authority who is the employer in law, but I think my contention still stands.

Those same three functions were also used by the DfE for academy trust boards until recently. Even though the regulations don't apply to trusts, they provided a perfectly good description of what the trust's board of trustees was there to do (once you've swapped headteacher for the chief executive). However, the DfE published a separate guide for academy trust governance in March 2024 and summarised the functions as strategic leadership, accountability and assurance, and strategic engagement. It was pleasing to see that engagement role included as that additional emphasis from the DfE might be enough to promote better practice.

Conclusion: so what?

There is much contested territory across many sectors and jurisdictions on what is needed to govern well, which I will come back to in chapter 3. I have challenged myself with my description here of governance, its key principles and core functions to check I'm not in danger of getting too comfortable with what has now been largely established as the conventional wisdom in the UK. It will, of course, continue to evolve. As I review my conclusions, the Labour government has just announced the abolition of NHS England having experienced it as a duplication of the department run by the Secretary of State. A secondary argument is that NHS delivery will be nearer the democratic mandate, an interesting comparison with education where one often hears the lamentation that educationalists should have more input into policymaking. I will return to that conundrum later.

A few challenges are being made in the financial sector to the emphasis on what is known as ESG (environment, social and governance), provoking healthy debate, until we get to the next governance disaster and the next report brings us back to the fundamentals. State school and trust failures don't have investigations that are publicly reported as many other sectors do. I have tried to suggest this to the DfE on numerous occasions: having thoughtful, analytical reports of governance failures would be hugely useful.

Governance is much more than the work of boards. It is about who makes the decisions that affect the rest of us, how they make those decisions, and above all else, how good the decisions are that they make. Good decision-making is a necessary prerequisite to success. Organisations lacking meaningful checks and balances against flawed or reckless decision-making are acutely vulnerable to human fallibility. If missteps or bad behaviour go unchallenged and uncorrected, such organisations should be viewed as accidents waiting to happen.

If there is a problem with governance, it is not necessarily confined to the board and its non-executive members, but it comes back to the board's responsibilities to decide on the delegation of power and set the culture. A governance failure means something fundamental has gone wrong at the heart of the organisation, involving the abuse of power or its ability to assess performance well. There has been a failure in decision-making, which may be due to the people, the process or the culture in which the people and processes are operating, and that failure – even if not the board's own – still lies with the board as its very existence is to prevent a lead executive and their team from having unfettered power and running amok.

It should be self-evident therefore that good governance is fundamental to the success of a school or trust, but is our sector convinced of that? All my experience of pushing this argument for the past 15 years suggests that generally this theory is accepted, in large part because of its inclusion in DfE guidance and Ofsted frameworks. However, in practice, not enough time and thought is given to governance by those paid to lead our schools and trusts. Leaders should be debating the issues surrounding power, decision-making, consultation and influence. The acknowledgement of power, and the discourse around it, tends to be shied away from. Despite the relentless work of NGA and others, the knowledge of what governance is has not been embedded in the sector. Sometimes it is thought of as a necessary evil for compliance purposes, something that others – those well-meaning amateurs – do. It is so much more. The role of school governance is to ensure the education of our young people is fit for purpose, safeguarding their future and this country's.

2.
The web of accountability

The Committee on Standards in Public Life (1995) stated in its first report: 'Holders of public office are accountable for their decisions and actions to the public and must submit themselves to whatever scrutiny is appropriate.' In all my many conversations on the topic, I have never heard practitioners dispute being responsive to the public and submitting to scrutiny, so I start from the point that those who practise in the system accept the need for accountability.

Tim Brighouse and Mick Waters (2022) discuss the rise of the language, culture and practice of accountability from the 1980s in their book *About Our Schools*, quoting Steve Munby: 'Internationally our heads face the fiercest accountability system with direct consequences of any; and the direct impact of that is felt further throughout the school. Accountability has grown from being a "general expectation" rather like the other Nolan principles to being a process of increasing specification and regulation.'

The malign consequences of the out-of-kilter accountability system for schools in England have been particularly and more publicly evident in the last couple of years, since the suicide of headteacher Ruth Perry in January 2023 after a negative Ofsted inspection. The accountability system does of course shape the work of public sector professionals and their modes of thinking, feeling, speaking and acting, and then in turn the governance volunteers that work with them.

There is also much academic literature critiquing the neo-liberal performative approach to accountability and governance, arguing that those in power who set up accountability frameworks exert harmful pressure and excessive control, and that this has been increasing over the last 50 years. The Labour government elected in 2024 has accepted some changes need to be made.

The very difficult question is how should accountability manifest itself? We make it harder to design an appropriate accountability system by limiting understanding of how it can be demonstrated in different ways for different audiences. Sadly, the academic critics tend not to suggest what healthy, proportionate school accountability should look like, but I am going to have a go here.

We have a fundamental problem in the terms of the state school system in England in that accountability has concentrated on only two dimensions: inspection and published measures of pupil outcomes. This is deeply unhelpful, a far cry from healthy, intelligent accountability. In the last decade as other pressures have risen in schools, it has become downright dangerous in all sorts of ways. This needs to change with more weight given to the profession, institutional governance, the involvement of stakeholders and performance across the locality.

Five to 10 years ago, there was even more focus on holding schools to account via numbers: published pupil performance data. The way it was done became a tyranny, introducing perverse incentives, some junk data, and much over-engineered and time-consuming data practices. These were reinforced by the then Ofsted framework and the introduction of the coasting school targets by Education Secretary Nicky Morgan MP on top of the existing targets.

A rather overlooked Education Secretary, Damian Hinds MP, instigated a piece of work to clarify school accountability and 'trust school leaders to get on with the job': a noble aim. Although his service in that position lasted only 18 months in 2018 and 2019, he did manage to remove some of the duplication. In 2024, he returned to the department as schools minister in the last few months of the Conservative administration, and at the time of writing is serving as the shadow Education Secretary.

The Covid-19 pandemic stalled the ability to report pupil performance data publicly, and although this data should ordinarily be interrogated by leaders and governing boards to inform discussions, it has not returned to that all-consuming pitch it was before Covid. Rightly so, as the numbers are crude and do not provide the breadth and nuance necessary to get the best out of schools for their pupils.

This downplaying of pupil data in the accountability stakes was reinforced with Amanda Spielman's 2019 inspection framework that promoted a focus on the curriculum. This was welcomed at the time, but a downside has been that since the end of the pandemic it has left Ofsted entirely in the spotlight of school accountability.

One measure to judge such a complex and important public service is doomed to failure. Also, inspection then takes centre stage in a way that has become damaging, negatively affecting the culture of school leadership and the climate for all school staff and pupils. The ubiquitous use of the phrase 'high stakes' exemplifies this. Dame Christine Gilbert in her independent learning review for Ofsted in 2024 also concluded that 'the accountability system has reached a crisis point and to focus on just the reform of Ofsted is too narrow'.

Seven years ago, Damian Hinds MP (2018) identified that there can be 'confusion about the different actors within the system … who has the power to do what and on what basis, the exact circumstances that could lead to enforced structural or leadership change at a school'. He was correct to the extent that there was very little data on the consequences to leaders of having an inspection below 'good'; this is still the case. There is a widely held belief that a poor Ofsted judgement is career ending, and this can become self-fulfilling with the shame and stress leading to a headteacher walking away, rather than continuing to worry about whether their job is in danger. For example, in 2020 a large-scale NGA survey of governors and trustees found that 15% of MAT respondents reported that their last head or CEO left with a settlement agreement. The same was true for 9% of maintained schools and SATs (single-academy trusts). The question did not mention Ofsted, and I couldn't find how these figures compare with managers in other public sectors.

Even if the consequences of an Ofsted inspection, such as job loss, are fairly low – and it remains an 'if' – the perception of high stakes is widespread, spawning a huge level of fear alongside the culture of mistrust, which is corrosive among the profession. I have tried over the past decade to move that culture by encouraging governing boards to promote the importance of doing the right thing and not what leadership think Ofsted want. Making any difference to this culture of fear has turned out to be a much harder job than I anticipated. It is so deeply entrenched that governors and trustees from outside the school sector soon become indoctrinated by school leaders about the all-important status of Ofsted, even though the consequences are sometimes in the hand of boards.

That reduction of accountability to inspection also limits the discourse and thus potential reform. There has been much agreement across the sector for years that we need a more intelligent system of school accountability, and some of us have continued to talk about how to achieve this since Hinds' changes. However, no subsequent Conservative Education Secretary was brave enough to return to this difficult issue, despite the hiatus caused by the Covid-19 pandemic and subsequently the death of Ruth Perry. The first year of a Labour Education Secretary suggests she has slipped into shoring up Ofsted rather than checking the power of the Chief Inspector.

Interventions following an inspection or data suggesting poor pupil outcomes by the primary regulators – local authorities and the DfE – are not well documented. The ultimate action is to academise underperforming maintained schools and re-broker underperforming academies. There is an interesting discussion to be had as to whether the regulators have the right interventions at their disposal and use the best ones, and I will come back to this in chapter 17.

There is often confusion between methods of accountability and those of school improvement. Clearly, the accountability system should contribute to school improvement, not just by diagnosing weaknesses and encouraging improvement, but maximising it by instilling a culture of organisational learning, as opposed to blame. Here, I am going to limit myself to how we hold organisations and leaders to account, and I'll return to school improvement in chapter 14.

The shape of intelligent accountability

To achieve a mature, nuanced system of ensuring schools are the best they can be and that pupils are getting a great education, we need to look across the full range of what accountability of public services encompasses. The aim is to ensure that public officials and public bodies are performing ethically to their full potential, providing value for money and being responsive to the individuals and community they are serving. The word accountability is derived from the practice of financial accounting, whereas now we have much broader expectations.

The sector has some shared language, for example, on ethical leadership, but more discourse is needed on other aspects, in particular the purpose of education. The national network FED (Foundation for Education Development) has for the past five years provided a platform for discussion so that solutions for long-term local, regional, national and global educational challenges can be found. FED has involved as many groups as possible: students, parents, employers, teachers, leaders and governors. Some argue that public trust will be only established when all the different participants reach a shared understanding, but that is highly unlikely to happen. I think the same end can be achieved by reporting different things in different ways to different constituencies, so each gets what they want to hear about; what they consider most important.

There are many ways for citizens – or the state on their behalf – to hold public services and those who lead public authorities to account. They interrelate and overlap. There is no universally agreed set of the various dimensions of public accountability, let alone those that apply to state schools. Different tasks are undertaken by different people in different ways for accountability purposes.

An understanding of accountability located merely in the hierarchical practices of bureaucracy and management is a dangerously limited one. Of course, institutional governance and leadership operates within the constraints set up by the state, but we need to develop a system that expects not just slavish compliance, but a dialogue of accountability at every level. This dialogue should take place between those who govern and those who are governed, so that includes between the funders and the institutions receiving funding, between trusts and their schools, and between schools and their communities. Accounting for present performance and the negotiating and agreeing of future, possibly improved, performance are interrelated processes in the aim of achieving excellence, or school improvement as it is often called.

I suggest this list covers the range of main accountability methodologies:

- Legal, including legislation, statutory guidance, case law and, by contract, the regulator.
- Inspectorates, audit and scrutiny processes, such as Ofsted.
- Professional accountability, including with peers and managerially.
- Organisational governance.
- Accountability to users, in particular parents and carers, and ensuring voices are heard.
- Democratic and social accountability.
- Media: mainstream and social.

I do not mean this to be a hierarchy or an order of importance. Understanding how the different dimensions of accountability interact is complicated. They are also different in terms of how they manifest themselves. Being accountable in one case may mean no more than having to answer questions about what has happened or is happening within one's jurisdiction. Giving an account to different audiences will be different events, some more structured than others; for example, compare giving information to the parent body and answering questions publicly to discussing the same information at an employee's appraisal discussion or in a court of law. Each audience will have different expectations of what is appropriate and sufficient. With published information and larger meetings there is likely to be more than one expectation and many interpretations of what the audience hear.

The different forms of accountability can work in concert, holding each other in balance and with some of these dimensions producing information; for example, inspections, data sets and journalists, which are then used by decision-makers such as governing boards and the regulator. Some dimensions are more relevant day in, day out, and others become more relevant when problems arise, acting as that check. The Centre for Public Scrutiny (CfPS – now the Centre for Governance and Scrutiny) developed the useful concept of the 'web of accountability' in which public life operates.

I have been tempted to add whistle-blowers to that web but decided that although the information provided by them can be enormously useful in holding an institution to account, it is an ad hoc mechanism, a route by which the decision-makers can learn, rather than a fundamental method of regular accountability. While we must make the conditions for whistle-blowing – usually by staff – as easy as possible, we really shouldn't be relying on whistle-blowers for systematic public accountability. Until the recent ITV drama on subpostmasters and the Horizon scandal, I was considering the same argument to regulate the media, and so perhaps whistle-blowers should feature in the web too. They certainly feature often in the uncovering of fraud.

There are many in the school sector – both the regulator and the regulated – who argue for frameworks and standards of all sorts, who want everything tied down so there is something to point to. I was surprised when I arrived in the sector to find this and still do not fully understand it. I prefer to keep such specifications to the essential and for the profession to have confidence in its ability to determine the right thing to do and to report.

Trust and control

In 2002, Professor Onora O'Neill who coined the phrase 'intelligent accountability' gave the Reith lectures on the question of trust. Her third lecture, 'Called to account', considered the public's stated reduction in trust of our public services and the people who run them, and the suspicions of their motivations, pointing out that there was no evidence that people or institutions now are less trustworthy. Yet the 'accountability culture aims at ever more perfect administrative control of institutional and professional life'.

Accountability is not just about policing public servants, but there is an element of that. Academic Julian Le Grand (1997), one of the architects of New Labour's reforms of public service, considered the dangers of treating public service professionals wholly as knaves: 'Evidence suggests that people who work in public services are more altruistic than those working in the private sector ... But if you treat people as though they were knaves, they often turn into knaves. Disastrously, knaves can serve their own ends at the expense of the user – and of the government. They neglect anything where there is no target; they fiddle the figures.'

So, how far can we rely on the professionalism and personal morality of public servants and how much should they be following instructions from their political masters? How much should be guided by parents and the local community, who are after all both taxpayers and users? Modern citizens are generally more assertive and less likely to defer to professional judgement.

Accountability is derived from being part of a profession; it accepts responsibility for outcomes and acts with competence and honesty. It should play an important role in that web. There should be much space in which a professional can exercise independent judgement, guided by the needs of children and acting before the regulator needs to regulate. Further space is made for the board acting first to hold the lead professional to account, placing trust intelligently, based on evidence of that competence and honesty, not on blind faith, bureaucratic compliance or externally imposed targets. Professionals are not just rule followers.

As we will see in chapter 5, many have argued that the age of trusting professionals was superseded over the past 40 years by performativity and corporate accountability alongside parental choice and the fulfilling of quality and contract specifications. Professor O'Neill (2002) argued, 'If we want a culture of public service, professionals and public servants must in the end be free to serve the public rather than their paymasters.' This is as true now even though the context in which public servants are operating has changed, as explored by the 21st-century public servant project at the University of Birmingham: professionals must be even more now, including navigators of complexity.

Some of these dimensions are vertical – upwards accountability – and others horizontal when professions and those governing institutions adhere to their codes of conduct or to their societal mandate and work together in partnerships. Despite much rhetoric otherwise (which I will return to in chapter 17), vertical accountability has dominated the thinking in the school sector. To create a healthier, more intelligent system, we need to give more priority to the horizontal. Wiser people than me have said the same thing.

What about the market?

Consumer choice is generally considered to provide another distinct form of accountability for public services; a market-based accountability being a key part of the move to a neo-liberal approach and 'performativity'. This features heavily in academic literature at a theoretical level; for example, it is common to be told that with the advent of academies this mechanism has grown in importance, and some go as far as asserting that the market principles have become crucially important in school governance and other forms of control of public servants. There is little evidence provided, and I have not generally seen this borne out in practice. Clearly there is a market in the provision of services sold to schools, but that is completely distinct from accountability.

Parental choice of schools for their children – more accurately described as parental preference – creates a dynamic that could – and does – affect the decisions of those in power in schools. It's a spur especially to less popular schools with falling rolls to make changes or risk closure. Of course, leaders and governing boards pay much attention to the state of the school roll, which is crucial to funding levels, and consider how to market their schools. But this does not seem to me to make school 'choice' a form of holding them to account. Falling rolls do not correlate fully with school performance, as many primary schools are experiencing now with the falling birth rate.

Many parents do not place a large weight on what the sector is measuring in terms of performance. They may for valid reasons not necessarily always choose what the regulator or the professional would consider the 'highest performing' school. While parents on the whole do value their children's schooling and are concerned about matters of quality such as school academic performance and discipline, these are typically balanced against a preference for a local school and consideration of the child's wishes. A 2023 ParentKind survey found that when choosing a school, parents prioritise aspects like curriculum breadth (60%), reputation (43%), proximity (39%) and peer opinions (35%) far more than Ofsted reports (8%). DfE research also laid out socioeconomic differences and the consequences exacerbated by parents who value the presence of children like their own.

A quasi-market is not feasible everywhere, particularly in rural areas where travelling to another school may not be practical. It also does not work for families who have to move at a time of year that doesn't coincide with primary and secondary entry: only some schools have spaces. Schools are not elastic; it is often difficult and expensive to expand to accommodate more children. Finally, when schools are in danger of closing, local communities almost always fight to keep them open. Should politicians allow the school to continue as it was, or ignore the community's wishes and let the market dictate? Elected representatives quite often do bow to the electorate in these circumstances, so we have re-emerged in another part of our web: democratic accountability.

I have therefore concluded that the quasi-market is not worthy of being promoted to a dimension of accountability in its own right. It is, of course, one of the contexts schools work with; it shapes their intake as does their local community. I return to the role of parents as an extremely important part of accountability to users in chapter 16.

The need for transparency

Transparency – the proactive publication of information relating to services and decisions – is needed to allow local people, and others, to understand how their schools are doing. On its own it won't be transformative: research suggests that making information available does little to increase direct accountability to the public. Transparency is not a replacement for other methods of accountability, but there needs to be a willingness for useful information to be published and used well. That culture of openness is important for all acting in the web of accountability.

Professor O'Neill mentioned three critiques of indicators used for accountability purposes: that they can be misleading due to inaccuracy; that comparative rankings do not reveal anything fundamental about education quality; and that the information generated is not understandable for the general public. We need to find ways of measuring what we value, and not simply value what we can measure easily. This a fundamental part of getting accountability right. The academic literature sometimes suggests that measures manufactured and imposed on the sector are typically 'fabrications' of performance. This is indeed a risk, and ownership of the measures is important. A more intelligent system would provide the ability to influence what is being reported. We need a system where dialogue is really taken seriously and professional judgement is valued when crafting measures.

The school sector has created an industry out of collecting data, some of which may have been totally unnecessary. Even the more useful data is not always used well. It should be the start of the conversation, not an end point in accountability. Attainment data does not reveal what it is about the lives and educational experiences of particular groups of children and young people that leads them to underachieve at school nor indicate what needs to be done. Discussions should involve soft data as well as hard data, a balance in all things. The Labour government's proposal to develop a school report card with a range of measures presented a real opportunity to better showcase what a school and its pupils achieve, while reducing the 'high stakes' consequences. However, having it as the output of inspection, rather than an input, and leaving its development in the hands of Ofsted is a major mistake, confusing two different methods of accountability and entrenching the power of inspection.

It would also be interesting to show results of all schools in the locality with joint accountability, so that schools could not be rewarded if their success is at the expense of other more challenged schools or even just in isolation from other schools. There is rightly much talk about collaboration needed between schools and trusts, and this would provide an incentive that is currently lacking in the system despite warm words. After all, we want all children to have a good education and a good local school.

There is also information over and above 'measures'; there needs to be more transparency in some of the decision-making processes within the system; for example, local parents and the wider community surely have the right to see who is bidding to run their local schools and potentially influence the decision. I will return to this issue later.

The law and legal instruments

The legal framework is extensive and along with statutory guidance sets many of the rules against which schools are to be judged. For academies, these are added to by articles of association and funding agreements. The main body of the law can be a way to control the behaviour or limit the actions of public servants, setting the boundaries for accountability and the rules of the regulator. Yet there is more freedom in practice than this array of legislation and associated paraphernalia might suggest.

Legal disputes are not always a good lever by which to hold the powerful to account. And I say that as someone who spent more than a decade in the legal advice sector, in one role, looking for cases to test propositions that could then set precedent as case law. Money and time are not the only barriers; a win in court can be overturned fairly easily by subsequent amendments to regulation. Legal challenges of course have their place in providing a check in the system; for example, when a case blew open the practice of removing children from sixth forms, which many had known about for a long time, but ignored. This serves as a warning that the self-improving, school-led system, apparently awash with moral purpose and expertise, had not taken it upon itself to tackle the issue. Sometimes poor practice can become entrenched if not challenged by someone outside the system.

The DfE is the principal regulator of academy trusts, not the Charity Commission as they are exempt charities, whereas maintained schools are answerable in the first instance to the local authority. Some of the duties held by the boards of academy trusts belong to local authorities for maintained schools. Local authorities also have more powers of intervention with governing bodies, governors and headteachers than the DfE has with boards, trustees and chief executive officers, something they have been trying to unsuccessfully correct for some years without a relevant bill.

Academy trusts also have a contract with the regulator in the form of their funding agreement. The accounting officer – the lead executive appointed by the board of trustees – has personal responsibility for ensuring the trust is acting according to its articles, funding agreement and the *Academy Trust Handbook*. It's interesting to note the term: accounting officer. This responsibility on paper is to Parliament as well as to the regulator – another example of the web of accountability containing an overlap with democratic accountability. However, in practice parliamentary oversight has not been a conduit for holding errant accounting officers to account. As this is also the role of boards of trustees, perhaps direct parliamentary accountability is an unnecessary addition; after all, the trust is accountable to the Education Secretary and the Education Secretary is accountable in turn to Parliament. Surely the system should minimise the need for MPs and peers to act as a first line of accountability as that is not a practical solution given all their other roles.

Regulation has brought with it much compliance activity requiring record keeping with provision of information in specified formats, and often conformity to procedures and protocols. Leaders and boards comply for fear of the consequences, even if they may perceive them as illegitimate and lacking in credibility or utility.

The law can act as a deterrent, and it can punish. However, for the law to be effective, it must be clear and unambiguous. In 2020, the Law Commission identified shortcomings in the offence of misconduct in public office, which it found was outdated and confusing, and recommended replacing the current common law offence, which has existed for hundreds of years, with two offences – an offence of corruption in public office and an offence of breach of duty in public office. The government announced in the 2024 King's Speech that it would legislate to introduce a duty of candour for public servants, and the Prime Minister has said that the law will include criminal sanctions for those who breach it.

Audit and scrutiny

Central government can delegate specific regulatory functions to non-departmental regulators who undertake investigations, some on a cyclical basis and others via a risk-based approach, prioritising areas where violations are judged to be most likely or severe or where users or whistle-blowers have raised issues. Enforcement action aims to deter and punish non-compliance by naming and shaming those who break rules, imposing financial or legal penalties, or barring offenders from regulated industries or professions, as the Teaching Regulation Agency (TRA) does.

There are sometimes blurred lines between decisions that are properly for ministers and those that are properly for officials or agencies. Clear instructions should be found in regulators' remit letters, and although some powers are statutory, others may be added by the government and the remit expanded. The agencies have operational but not strategic independence. Ofsted sometimes calls itself a regulator, but its remit for schools is limited to inspection and it helps to avoid the language of regulation.

Parliament has a role in overseeing institutional performance – regulating the regulators, as it were – rather than just scrutinising rules made either by Parliament, the Education Secretary or those institutions. The Institute for Government states that most parliamentary committees do not conduct proactive scrutiny well, for a combination of reasons: it is not as politically interesting to committees; the mechanisms for sustained and consistent scrutiny are not formalised; committees have limited bandwidth and more urgent work takes precedence; and the volume and expertise of supporting resources that would be required does not exist.

Other than inspection, external scrutiny of the school sector at national level is more directly focused on oversight of central government by the National Audit Office (NAO) and House of Parliament committees. Gareth Davies, comptroller and auditor general, said in 2024: 'Every piece of our work has an improvement objective as well as an accountability objective, so, as people become experienced in that kind of role, they become helpful in encouraging the teams that we are working with and that we are auditing to make the most of the opportunity. It can sound a bit counterintuitive, but it is a big learning opportunity as well for them and for us. It is helpful to have that mindset in that relationship.'

Good scrutiny, according to the CfPS, is led by independent people, needs constructive 'critical friend' challenge, amplifies the voices and concerns of the public, and drives improvement in public services. A local government scrutiny committee gathers evidence on issues affecting local people and makes recommendations to influence the policies and decisions made by the council and other organisations delivering public services in their area. The way scrutiny is practised varies widely, and local government has generally not had the bandwidth to develop its scrutiny of education.

There is now much support across the sector for safeguarding audits to be carried out separately from Ofsted's inspection of education provision. There are other audits and compliance checks, particularly external annual financial audits of trust accounts. These, however, did not prove to be the driving force for holding trusts to account for some of the early financial scandals. Instead, a high proportion of financial probity issues seemed to arrive from tip-offs. In the meantime, much has been done to improve financial governance and oversight by the DfE, until recently through an agency.

Diocesan schools – both Church of England and Roman Catholic – are also subject to specific diocesan inspections with a particular focus on ethos and vision, religious education, collective worship and how the Christian mission is embedded in school life.

There are also other forms of scrutiny such as the Office of the Schools Adjudicator and the Local Government Ombudsman, but only very specific limited decisions end up there. It would be helpful for there to be a thorough review of the redress, and I return to the issue of complaints later.

Professional accountability

Professionals holding themselves to account by taking personal ownership of the results of one's decisions and actions is an incredibly important feature of any functioning public sector. It must be coupled with high aspirations, ethics and good judgement. There are many organisations in the sector devoted to ensuring this happens well. The Chartered College of Teaching, superbly led by Dame Alison Peacock, stands out; it also has the advantage of being independent of government. Professional accountability is unlikely to be visible to the public by nature of being a reflective activity in a personal space or in a professional network. On the other hand, the chair of a governing board would want to know that an executive leader was participating in such practice.

Secondly, peers can add hugely to the knowledge that aids professional accountability, but it is easy to fall into the trap of giving too much credibility to peers holding each other to account in a formal way. I remember Professor David Hargreaves losing the audience at a governors' conference about a decade ago when he asked who held school leaders to account and was quite perturbed by the universal and confident answer 'we do'; the answer he wanted and insisted upon was 'they hold each other to account'. That debate shouldn't have been binary: professionals or governing boards. They are both part of the web of accountability. I will return to this issue of partnerships between the board and senior leaders in depth in chapter 4.

Collaboration with peers is an important source of learning and support. There is also an industry of formal peer review, which can have benefits, depending on the quality of the peers and the culture in which the review takes place. Is challenge really part of the process? When push comes to shove, outside their own institution, leaders can walk away from partnerships and collaboratives: there aren't mechanisms for holding them to account for the results of their decisions. I am also not aware of cases where peers have been the whistle-blowers of malpractice, failure or even underperformance, although this might happen behind the scenes. A formal accountability role would surely not be the right and proper use of peers, distorting these important relationships.

There is a third and rather different element of professional accountability: employed professionals are also held to account through line management. Line management is an underrated and underdeveloped part of the school accountability system. We do not invest enough in it, in ensuring our managers are equipped to do this well in a way that both develops staff and holds them to account. Appraisal has sometimes been rendered less than effective, contributing to the stress of staff by the crass use of objectives and a heavy reliance on numbers. There is a line of argument that subjecting professionals to performance management denies them agency and suggests a lack of trust, but this objection is usually made by those who have not experienced appraisal done well. As both a professional being managed and as a manager of staff, I have found it to be an important route to development.

Performance-related pay was introduced by Michael Gove when he was the Education Secretary, but it is now removed as a consequence of the last government's taskforce on workload that I was involved in after agreement it had added bureaucracy without discernible benefits.

Governance as accountability

Professor O'Neill (2002) in her Reith lecture on trust also concluded: 'Serious and effective accountability, I believe, needs to concentrate on good governance, on obligations to tell the truth and needs to seek intelligent accountability. I think it has to fantasise much less about Herculean micro-management by means of performance indicators or total transparency.'

Over 20 years later, we are still missing that very trick in the school sector. Governing boards are the accountable body for the school or trust. The legal status and structures of maintained schools and academy trusts are different, but the principles hold. There are also schools with religious and other foundations who have other legal frameworks; in particular the role of the dioceses cannot be underestimated in terms of their responsibilities for the many Church of England and Catholic schools, another addition to our web of accountability.

School and trust leaders as individuals of course have a range of attitudes to their relationships with their governing boards, but as a sector they have not embraced thoroughly the power of governance. The board should be the first place they look for accountability after their own professional accountability – I know it was for me as a chief executive of a charity with my own board of trustees. Building mutual trust and respect with your trustees and governors should be a central part of being a leader, and it pays dividends.

Governance is now in theory better embedded into the high-level curriculum of leadership development programmes, but the knowledge of those who deliver those sessions is not always as deep or practical as it should be. It is sadly common for school leaders to take on their first headship or trust executive position without understanding what good board reporting looks like, let alone how to work well with their board, and this is not always rectified with experience or professional development. If the sector culture is not supportive of and knowledgeable about good governance, no amount of process design or structural change will fix that.

My long experience within the sector of representing both the governance community and the organisation whose governance expertise is second to none tells me without a doubt that governance has not taken its rightful place in leadership hearts, minds and CPD.

CfPS research suggests that accountability works best when it is carried out by people who: are not perceived as having a vested interest; have a clear reason for holding to account; and are adopting an open and evidence-based approach. These principles can – and should be – applied to institutional governance. Instead of being sidelined, it needs to be recognised as a powerful part of the system of accountability.

The governing board in turn must be held accountable for its decisions by those on whose behalf it exercises its powers. There are a number of ways in which this is done within democratic systems, even within the current structures. Local authorities have more mechanisms for doing that with maintained governors; dioceses have much power with their foundation appointments, but the DfE has fewer options with trustees as this is the domain of the trust's members. I return to oversight of governing boards in chapter 15.

Accountability to users

There have been some high-profile governance failures in other sectors where the role of users – and sometimes staff – was identified as key. For example, the Francis inquiry into Mid Staffordshire Health Trust's failure laid much of the blame on the board. Its members chose to rely on apparently favourable performance reports by outside bodies, such as the Healthcare Commission, none of which detected anything wrong, rather than effective internal assessment and feedback from staff and patients. The trust failed to take patients' complaints seriously enough, and Francis went on to chair the Freedom to Speak Up Review, which recommended a package of measures to ensure in future NHS staff are free to speak up about patient safety concerns.

In the school sector, users should involve both pupils and parents or other carers. We tend to use the language of consulting stakeholders; the discourse about accountability to users, even parents and carers, let alone pupils, is minimal. What happens to young people after leaving school as a consequence of the education provided should really be a key consideration, but it is extremely difficult to determine. I'm circling round to how success could be measured whichever from of accountability is being used, rather than direct accountability to pupils and former pupils in terms of what they consider to be success. The interest of pupils is at the heart of what professionals and those who govern want to achieve, but how is that determined? When dealing with any vulnerable users, the web of accountability must come into play, and there is more than one view of what's in a young person's best interest. Clearly, parental views and working in partnership with parents and students are crucial.

In 2019, the ParentKind Annual Parent Survey reported that half of parents thought their school should be more accountable than it currently was and only 17% disagreed, and they were not equating accountability with inspection. Three quarters (76%) of parents agreed that they want to be able to have a say at school level, and this has more recently gone up to 85%.

In that gap in the discourse, Ofsted has inserted itself as central to accountability to parents, to an extent that isn't justified. Both the last HMCI (His Majesty's Chief Inspector) and the current one, Sir Martyn Oliver, have used this to defend their approach in the face of criticism from the profession. Inspection reports are one source of information used by some parents: ParentKind reported to the House of Commons education committee in 2023 that fewer than a quarter (24%) of parents agreed that reports are useful to them. More parents (40%) agreed that reports are easy to understand than disagreed (36%). Very slightly more parents (39%) don't look at Ofsted reports at all when choosing a school for their child than do (38%), and a further 17% knew the Ofsted grade but hadn't read the report.

At NGA, I made accountability to stakeholders an intrinsic part of good governance, and this has been adopted by the DfE. Boards should be engaging with and listening to others if they are to govern well. Information gleaned from these dialogues will aid decision-making. Such customer insight should not be thought of as an inappropriate adoption from the private sector; it is a crucial way of understanding the performance of the school and its effect on people. This is not always easily achieved. For example, reporting to parents via an annual report at an AGM is supported in theory by a large majority of those who govern, but almost all those who have done it found it to be unproductive.

Secondly, complaint processes and other mechanisms of redress for wrongs, such as through the courts or ombudsmen, can be thought of as part of the accountability web for parents. Although these redress mechanisms focus on individual cases, findings and rulings can reveal systemic problems with implications for others. The complaints system is not functioning well with enormous time commitments placed on leaders and governance volunteers. It requires a thorough overhaul to ensure complainants do have access to redress in a workable way. There is work currently ongoing at the DfE to streamline the myriad of avenues for complaints in order to reduce the pressure and workload on staff, leaders and governors/trustees, but not, it appears, with the urgency needed given that the current system is not working for anyone.

Thirdly, the pandemic has changed for some the contract between schools and families with pupil attendance falling, pupil behaviour deteriorating, mental health issues rising and more children arriving in reception unready to learn: I will return to this in chapter 13.

Democratic and social accountability

In a democracy, at least in theory, the people are ultimately in control with accountability existing through the ballot box: voting is the primary way we hold our politicians to account. Electing representatives at both local level and Westminster provides an opportunity for citizens to register their approval or disapproval of local state schools.

There are not many examples where education policy or performance has been the driving force in the choices citizens make in the voting booth. Schools are not traditionally high on the list of issues that make a difference to election outcomes; the general election in 2017 was unusual in that a school cuts campaign begun by the teacher trade unions pushed education into the top four issues of concern to the electorate. But not many seats, in Westminster or even in local councils, change hands because of underperforming schools.

The second aspect of democratic accountability is through the day-to-day work of those elected representatives, scrutinising relevant draft legislation and holding the executive (in other words, the government) to account. This can operate at the level of the system as a whole or of performance of individual schools, and in a number of ways, for example, taking up the cases of constituents or being on the receiving end of a lobby. This day-to-day aspect is downplayed by some commentators who consider that the exercise of democratic accountability only really occurs through the ballot box. However, the activities of elected representatives once in post should not be overlooked; for example, the school funding increases in 2018 were a direct result of the cases made by backbench MPs.

Locally elected representatives also get involved in concerns and complaints made by individual families on a huge range of topics – from admissions to special educational needs – and at a community level when, for example, a school is threatened with closure. This aspect of having to hold on to your seat at the next election would not apply to trustees of a multi-academy trust considering that school's future.

Thirdly, civic engagement – contributing and working to make a difference in the public life of our communities – can add value to the performance of public services through both political and non-political processes. These might take the form of collective action – perhaps a protest of some sort, the voicing of public concern – and this needs to be engaged with in a meaningful way.

Another good example of civic involvement is volunteering as a governor or trustee, including as a parent governor. Once elected, they don't represent that group or place, but they provide a legitimacy and instil confidence in the wider community. Nicky Morgan felt that strength when, as Education Secretary, she tried – and failed – to reduce the involvement of parents in school governance. Their knowledge and perceptions are vital. There is an argument sometimes put forward that democracy – elections – should be the route onto governing boards, and that it should form a key plank of democratic accountability, something I will return to later.

Conclusion

Accountability of public services deserves championing, even celebrating: it is essential to the functioning of our democracy and civil society, but incredibly hard to get right. The specifics of accountability need to be considered legitimate and proportionate. They seem to be most effective when perceived as useful by all concerned. We are very far from that now in the school system in England. Accountability has been morphing over the decades with increasing pressures on those working in our schools.

We now have diminishing returns from the onerous school accountability system to the point it has become not just burdensome but positively damaging. A fundamental rethink is needed, and that must go well beyond amending the inspection system. Now is the time to move without more delay to a less distorting, less distracting and less distressing web of accountability. It is currently a very tangled web; although the interweaving could not disappear completely, more clarity and more balance is needed. We need to value the dimensions of accountability differently.

Labour's school report card manifesto commitment provided the new government with an excellent opportunity to steer a debate about the essential elements of the wider school accountability system. By giving it to Ofsted to own, they have totally undermined the reform, also giving a credibility to data that it does not deserve. At the time of writing in May 2025, the plans for Ofsted to provide a school report card with many scores at five different levels is counter to the aim of reducing the power and dominance of the inspectorate. It falls at the first hurdle of improving the intelligence of the system.

A report card generated by the DfE in partnership with the profession and parents could be useful information for all other dimensions of accountability; the beginning of the conversation, including with the inspectorate. Ofsted could then consider those issues where performance appeared to be away from the norm on the report card; inspectors could have a specific professional conversation about those, considering why that might be. It could help in the limited time inspectors have to provide a focus on the issues likely to be most critical at that institution and potentially most relevant to their pupils.

Instead of inspection being in the driving seat, governance should sit at the centre of that accountability web, alongside a renewed commitment to parent and community participation. This follows Professor O'Neill's recommendation that we trust institutional governance to bear the brunt of public accountability. This would act against undue weight being given to inspection or performance tables. It would simplify the system considerably and should help reduce the fear of potential consequences of a visit from Ofsted. Looking outwards, more than upwards, needs to be interwoven into all aspects of the sector's work.

An important part of making an accountability mechanism credible is the perceived independence and objectivity of those doing the holding to account: governors and trustees should be just that. They have no skin in the game apart from the interests of the children and communities being served. Institutional governance can provide both the clearest and the most responsive form of accountability, most relevant to and knowledgeable about the local context, and is able to adapt as circumstances require.

Boards can work with leaders in a way that is intelligent, practical and proportionate, and that eradicates perverse incentives. They provide the challenge that is needed, but in a supportive environment. They can also encourage networking – horizontal contributions to improvement for their own institution and others. They can be another antidote to top-down accountability that I will consider in chapter 14.

If we – governance volunteers and educational professionals – can together show it works, other accountability modes will not need to be so heavy handed. Ethical leadership must take centre stage. Values and the behaviours that flow from those are so important in building and retaining the trust and respect that are so crucial to our public services – and those that work within them – thriving.

The pandemic gave us a glimpse at a world of accountability without inspection and league tables: governing boards can attest to the fact that leaders worked incredibly hard during the lockdowns to make sure everyone was as safe as possible and still had some access to learning. We now know that the periods when schools were closed to many had adverse effects still being felt today, but it also demonstrated that professional accountability did come to the fore. Just as there was a moment when it looked as though the country valued 'key' workers more, there was a moment when that rebalancing of accountability was tried and not found wanting.

Clear, relevant information needs to be provided to government, parents and the public, but in a way that ensures that school evaluation and the dialogue that surrounds it is dynamic and inclusive, building trust, confidence, professionalism and better practice.

The governing board needs to achieve an appropriate balance between its own internal accountability with a strong internal focus on its agreed strategic priorities for student learning and support for high-quality professional development, with the demands of external accountability, performance expectations set by the wider society and the government. If schools and trusts are governed well, then other forms of accountability could – and should – be lighter than they have been in the past. In the next chapter, I will examine what constitutes good governance.

3.
Good governance

Having established that good governance is vital to any school successfully fulfilling its purpose and that it also has a part to play in ensuring proper accountability, what does good governance look like? Good governance is composed of ethical governance, effective governance and accountable governance. The use of the word 'good' had absolutely nothing to do with Ofsted's previous expectations for 'good' schools. They aren't experts in governance and shouldn't be looked to for the first word, or the last word, on the topic. The broader understanding of governance I am laying out here has not yet fully infiltrated Ofsted's framework.

Figure 3.1 The three pillars of good governance.

I came up with these three pillars – ethical governance, effective governance and accountable governance – because I was concerned that the English school sector only considered effectiveness with a focus on process and compliance over the substance of decision-making. I took reassurance that those other two other concepts – ethics and accountability – ran through the literature from other sectors. They were even writ large in the thinking behind the Cadbury review of the corporate sector in 1992, 10 years before Professor Onora O'Neill introduced these features into the understanding of intelligent accountability.

The foundations of good governance

A focus on mission, values, culture and diversity is essential, alongside exhibiting the behaviours needed for good governance. The four Ps of governance – people, purpose, processes and performance – are used in some other fields; and although memorable through alliteration, they are not all of the same order. Performance is a function of governance, but not a building block for ensuring good governance. However, a strong sense of purpose or mission and agreed values guide decision-making first and foremost. It also helps the organisation to tell a positive story and make a positive impact on stakeholders. If everyone involved works by those values, they can be reminded of the mission when decision-making becomes contentious – it is an extremely uniting force for the team involved in this collective endeavour.

Across the world, we have principles, codes and competency frameworks galore to refer to, but there is much less said about the complexity of putting those into practice. Governing well requires knowledge, skill and experience. It takes courage, integrity, commitment and good judgement to make good decisions. And it takes much dialogue and teamwork too.

Culture of governance

On arrival in the world of school governance, I heard interminable conversations about process and detailed procedures, but there was not enough time left for the topics that mattered most. The Centre for Governance and Scrutiny (formerly the Centre for Public Scrutiny) stated that good governance is as much a matter of culture and attitude as it is one of having systems and processes in place, and that too much time has been spent on compliance at the expense of culture.

Three governance modes were developed by Chait, Ryan and Taylor for the charity sector almost 20 years ago: the fiduciary, the strategic and the generative. I adapted them to encourage our sector to understand what being strategic really meant and to embrace the generative: being supportively inquisitive in and searching for ideas to make sense of the world that the school and pupils are operating in. This mode is not commonly seen. It also reminds me of one of the seven Cs – don't we love a bit of alliteration – the personal attributes the DfE wanted to see all those governing exhibiting: committed, confident, curious, challenging, collaborative, critical and creative. Curiosity is very much one of my favourites as it lacks antagonism while being absolutely essential to governing well, as was noted in CSPL's (Committee on Standards in Public Life) 2025 report.

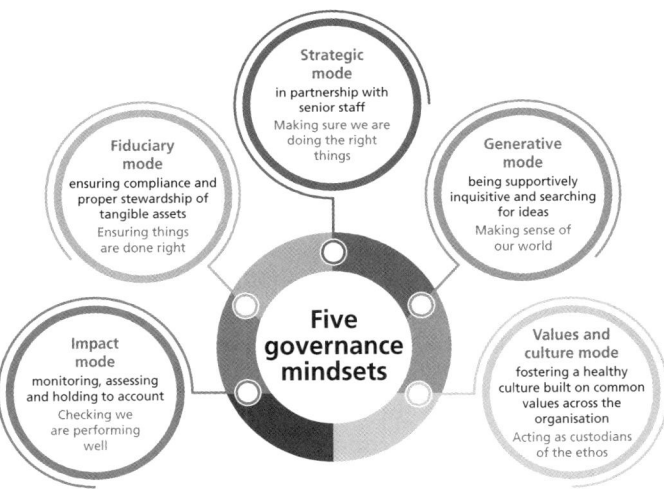

Figure 3.2 The five governance mindsets.

The fourth mode of governance – assessing the performance of the institution – is well established. I called this the 'impact' mode: monitoring, assessing performance and holding to account. This is, in fact, probably the other mode most often in evidence in school and trust governing boards along with the fiduciary.

I then added a 'values and culture' mode: acting as custodians of the ethos and fostering a healthy culture built on common values. The recent CSPL report (2025) devoted a whole chapter to board culture, concluding it is 'a crucial factor in its effectiveness and will be heavily influenced by the quality of the relationships between and among the executive leadership and non-executive directors. … An open and trusting relationship will support the exchange of ideas and perspectives and allow risks to be exposed more quickly, even though conversations will not always be comfortable.'

This mindset also recognises the role of the board in creating an organisational culture in which people flourish: I come back to the topic of cultivating culture alongside school and trust leaders in the next chapter.

Behaviours

Rules and processes on their own don't get you to where you need to be: they set the parameters, the boundaries, for good governance, but no more. There is much common ground between sectors on the necessary behaviours. Reviews into public service failures consistently identify patterns of contributing behaviour. The phrase 'the patronising disposition of unaccountable power' comes from the Hillsborough disaster report in 2017. The 2025 report *Recognising and responding to early warning signs in public sector bodies* from CSPL highlights that the behaviours of individuals and the cultures of organisations are at the heart of good public service. CSPL identifies the barriers to addressing and learning from problems in public sector bodies. As well as the quality of the governance by boards who failed to identify the red flags, it is also about: institutional defensiveness; prioritising reputation over redress; groupthink; poor relationships; and the failure to build a speak-up culture.

When I joined the school governance sector, behaviour was barely mentioned in training and guidance once the code of conduct was signed; yet behaviours and the consequences on relationships constitute a significant portion of the queries from governing boards seeking advice when experiencing troubled waters.

Codes are a staple to setting out the expectations more specifically than the Nolan principles, and that has been so in the school sector for some time. In 2012, when we first asked about codes of conduct in the annual NGA survey, 83% of respondents had such a code, and the last time we asked the question it was 85%. Generally, it was only brought out when there was a problem to find a route for redress; a process to undertake. Conversations about behavioural changes to improve their practice were not usually had at any earlier stage.

Codes of conduct do not do justice to the care, reflection and sometimes courage that is needed from individuals to govern well. The expression 'crooks, cronies and cowards' taken from the corporate sector describes what must be avoided. Board members are not always brave enough to question each other and their executives; a worry about rocking the boat or being seen as impolite prevents questions being asked. Governance should be rocking the boat sometimes, but with the tone and spirit that empowers, enables participation and extends the conversation. Thoughtful dialogue with colleagues on the board, senior executives and other important constituencies is crucial, in part to ensure good board governance in their circumstances and in part to think ahead, balance issues and make difficult decisions.

Boards should also cultivate members who can think creatively about which governance practices make the most sense for their specific situation, and who can balance encouraging and supporting executive leaders with providing a healthy dose of perspective. Boards shouldn't be trying to cultivate a uniform set of behaviours; each individual should be able to make their point in their own way, as long as it is respectful and fits with the agreed values. The people who govern care about the pupils and their institution; there will be times when, with differences of viewpoints, discussions may become tense, and the board under the leadership of the chair has to navigate that conflict. This requires skill, emotional intelligence, a range of personal qualities from patience to perseverance, and knowing when to bring each to the fore.

Codes of governance practice

In the last 20 years as the understanding of the importance of good governance to organisations has grown, almost every sector has designed and adopted a code of governance. Most differ from a code of conduct concerning behaviours; they generally include principles for good governance and tend to also cover functions. Almost all aim to help boards to continuously improve and meet high standards. The charity code was amended for the academy sector in 2023, a topic that I will come back to in chapter 12.

As well as formal sector codes – some of which run to many pages – there are many different writers and consultancy firms who offer their own slightly different versions, usually shorter, sometimes alliterative, which they invariably use as the basis for their evaluation services. Very few other sectors have an organisation equivalent to NGA, which specialises in governance for that sector, so there are often large numbers of consultants reinventing wheels.

There is one main way in which school and trust governance practice differs from other sectors where it is common to have mandatory term limits for service on boards. NGA has suggested for many years that it is good practice to serve at one school for no more than two terms of four years, and for chairs to step down from the chair before serving more than six full years. We have met resistance to this idea from some – but by no means all – of our long-serving members. Relationships tend to get cosy after a period of time. Longstanding colleagues become comfortable with each other and with their practice: 'this is how we do things round here'. The axis between a long-serving chair and the senior executive can become too strong, with others not getting enough of a look in. The power dynamics may have changed in an unhelpful way without the two players noticing. We do not want to lose this experience from the sector, and we can't afford to, given how difficult recruiting volunteers has become. There will always be another school or trust very keen to have the retiring chair, and that movement of volunteers is an important way of sharing practice round the system.

Diversity

The diversity of boards has been a concern for me since I first joined NGA, initially as a result of walking into local governance conferences with very little visible diversity. For the first few years at NGA, I had to find partners to make campaigns work, on account of our limited capacity. Sadly, it was hard to get anyone involved; I had my first real go in 2014 to stir up some interest in a campaign to improve the diversity of boards, but to very little avail. At a group that the DfE convened to work on the recruitment of volunteers, the Inspiring Governors Alliance, I wanted to include an emphasis on ethnic diversity. This was not then seen as a priority by the DfE, and I was told NGA would have to find other ways of doing this.

So, did this really matter? Well, yes, diversity is important enough to be included as one of the foundation stones of good governance. The best decisions are not made by a group of like-minded individuals. Boards need people from a range of backgrounds, experiences, skills, knowledge, approaches and perspectives, who come together to work for a common mission. Literature from the private sector shows that companies with more diverse boards perform better.

Good governance requires the governing board to set a healthy culture with a commitment to diversifying itself and ensuring its behaviours are inclusive, and by doing so setting an example and acting as a catalyst for achieving diversity and equality at all levels of the organisation, including school leadership. The literature shows that celebrating difference and being inclusive enables organisations to better serve the people they want to make a positive difference to. There are additional benefits for schools serving communities. First, reflecting the community provides more legitimacy for the board and often buy-in, as I will explore in chapter 16. Second, in terms of equipping pupils for the wider world, seeing themselves and others reflected at board level can provide role models and shows them what is possible for everyone.

Over the last decade, more and more has been written about the need for diversity and difference to avoid groupthink. There have been many campaigns, from women on FTSE boards to NGA's Everyone on Board campaign set up in 2018 in collaboration with Inspiring Governance. We were supported by the emergence of grassroots campaigning networks, including BAMEed, LGBTed and DiverseEd. It has been a delight to work with passionate, innovative people who have access to educators that NGA didn't.

Although there have been many discussions in many forums about improving diversity, both at governance and senior leader level, hosted by a range of partnerships, campaigns and organisations, the learning had not been recorded. So in 2021, NGA carried out further work and made the case thoroughly for diverse boards in their report *Increasing Participation in School and Trust Governance: A State of the Nation Report on Recruiting and Retaining Volunteers*. I come back to this topic in chapter 10.

Effective governance

Within months of arriving at NGA in 2010, I was concerned about the amount of wordy guidance for governance volunteers from all sorts of places, including the DfE, which disguised what mattered most. So I set about defining effective governance in a shorthand way that captured its key elements in a more memorable way, and that became the eight elements of effective governance.

Figure 3.3 The eight elements of effective governance.

I checked the validity of the eight elements with a number of other organisations specialising in governance, and one memorable encounter was with Bob Garratt, the author of *The Fish Rots from the Head*. His first edition was subtitled 'The crisis in our boardrooms', but by the time I met him he had published his third edition, less dramatically subtitled 'Developing effective board directors' but still with the philosophy that 'the buck starts and stops in the boardroom'. Given his long experience of working with boards and my fairly recent arrival, I was reassured to get his endorsement.

Five years later, the DfE in its now mothballed governance competencies suggested that there are six features for effective governance: strategic leadership, accountability, people, governance structures, compliance and evaluation. Unsurprisingly, they are similar to the six principles in the governance code for FE colleges: determination of organisational aims and strategic oversight; responsibility and accountability; leadership and integrity; collaboration and stakeholder engagement; regulatory compliance; and board and organisational effectiveness. The Association of Colleges has reviewed it every couple of years, with these six sections a streamlined version of what went before.

I didn't see the need to change our definition of good governance or the eight elements in the light of the DfE's competencies that covered similar ground, just categorised slightly differently. For example, the DfE included ethical governance within culture rather than in the foreground, and parental and community engagement within strategic leadership, rather than accountable governance. The similarity was unsurprising as over the years NGA has always had close contact and extensive conversations with the DfE's governance team, usually being asked to comment on drafts before publication.

The DfE language was slightly amended in 2023 with the trust quality indicators, where the fifth pillar is governance and leadership. It took many versions and discussions to get to the DfE's published version that draws from and builds on this body of understanding. Having read a large number of reports, guides and event proceedings for different sectors from all over the world, the words vary and overlap, but the themes are universal. Everyone has their own emphases and tone as befits their context and its complexities. The differences in languages and format are not worth fretting about: they add up to a common theoretical understanding of what constitutes good governance.

I will now leave the eight elements be: quite rightly, NGA staff hadn't wanted me to mess about with them given how well embedded they are and how they have stood the test of time. If I had to identify an omission with hindsight it would be the importance of sound, objective, strategic decision-making and being able to judge when the main thing is the main thing. NGA encourages boards at the end of each meeting to consider whether their focus was on the mission: enabling pupils to thrive and what their deliberations would achieve for pupils.

Ethical governance

In the school sector there had been much talk of moral purpose. Sometimes the phrase was repeated so often – for example, in the Labour academy movement – that it began to ring hollow. I am from the third sector, which only exists due to moral purpose, to deliver a charitable mission; that is taken for granted and rarely paraded for display. We don't need to be constantly reminded of our moral purpose. When I arrived in the school sector, it seemed odd that this was happening so much.

Then it dawned on me that it was possibly to demarcate the good guys who had chosen to work in the most challenging schools from others who had chosen an easier route. And, of course, everyone defined their 'good guys' differently. For example, I remember being at an Independent Academies Association (IAA) conference in the very early days of the academy conversion movement. The tension in the hall erupted between those who were committed to leading tough schools in deprived neighbourhoods – the founders of IAA – and those who had recently chosen to leave local authority status for the promised autonomy and additional funding. The academy movement had indeed been changed dramatically with the Academies Act 2010 and the differences played out among its leaders. It was about territory: 'who do you want in your gang?' The battle for the high ground was unedifying and divisive. The discourse continued at this superficial level for some time, often managing to alienate those who led and governed in the maintained sector with the inference that the real moral purpose lay in the academy sector. On the other hand, many academy leaders were under attack for opting out of the local authority family.

Without that counterbalance of ethics, some accountability processes and measures can – and sadly have – provided incentives for arbitrary and unprofessional choices. The Nolan Principles of Public Life – selflessness, integrity, objectivity, accountability, openness, honesty and leadership – had framed my keynotes for a number of years, and I stopped being surprised by how often people looked blankly at me when I raised them. Heads and other school leaders were highly unlikely to recognise them at the time. That is no longer the case.

I wanted to change the discourse, move it from the debating platform to the boardroom in a way that was meaningful, and very fortuitously the Association of School and College Leaders (ASCL) set up an Ethical Leadership Commission, which I was pleased to be part of. It had concerns about the lack of guiding principles for ethical leadership in education and wanted to recognise that school leaders, including governing boards, are regularly faced with issues that test the moral compass of decision-making and leadership styles. The Commission and the dissemination of what resulted would never have happened without the leadership of the fabulous Carolyn Roberts, then a member of ASCL's council and a headteacher in London.

Although leadership is the seventh Nolan Principle, there was nothing further at that time on how to put that ethical leadership into practice. The Commission agreed that the language of values and virtues needed to become a part of everyday decision-making. 'The nation trusts us to form young people into the best that they can be. The public expects us to know what kind of example we should set them, but do we? We all have a duty to behave ethically, but the bar for school and college leaders is particularly high because they are setting the standards for the young people in their care and in turn the sort of society that we become in the future. That is why we embarked on the Ethical Leadership Commission which resulted in the publication of the Framework for Ethical Leadership in Education' (Carolyn Roberts, chair of the Ethical Leadership Commission, 2019).

The Commission produced the Framework for Ethical Leadership in Education to support and guide the profession and governing boards in their decision-making and their behaviour. It added seven virtues to the seven Nolan principles in order to establish a language for school leaders to use in their decision-making. It was not a policy, a tick list, a performance indicator, a code of conduct or a quality mark; in fact, I am not sure that it needed to be a 'framework' either, which perhaps brings with it ideas of performativity. Instead it was intended to be versatile, adaptable and engrained within school leadership.

At its publication at an Ethics Summit in 2019, it was hugely well received, including by DfE officials. It fitted the supposed zeitgeist of the self-improving system. A wide range of national organisations endorsed the framework, committing to promoting its use and its language and including it in training and development. How much was actually done by some is unclear. Minister Gibb was said to be sniffy about the idea; apparently he objected to people ascending the pulpit. Some previously loud supporters of the framework went a little quiet after that, which is rather ironic for an initiative that promotes courage as part of its virtues.

FRAMEWORK FOR ETHICAL LEADERSHIP IN EDUCATION

1. **SELFLESSNESS** | School and college leaders should act solely in the interest of children and young people.

2. **INTEGRITY** | School and college leaders must avoid placing themselves under any obligation to people or organisations that might try inappropriately to influence them in their work. Before acting and taking decisions, they must declare and resolve openly any perceived conflict of interest and relationships.

3. **OBJECTIVITY** | School and college leaders must act and take decisions impartially and fairly, using the best evidence and without discrimination or bias. Leaders should be dispassionate, exercising judgement and analysis for the good of children and young people.

4. **ACCOUNTABILITY** | School and college leaders are accountable to the public for their decisions and actions and must submit themselves to the scrutiny necessary to ensure this.

5. **OPENNESS** | School and college leaders should expect to act and take decisions in an open and transparent manner. Information should not be withheld from scrutiny unless there are clear and lawful reasons for doing so.

6. **HONESTY** | School and college leaders should be truthful.

7. **LEADERSHIP** | School and college leaders should exhibit these principles in their own behaviour. They should actively promote and robustly support the principles, and be willing to challenge poor behaviour wherever it occurs. Leaders include both those who are paid to lead schools and colleges and those who volunteer to govern them.

Schools and colleges serve children and young people and help them grow into fulfilled and valued citizens. As role models for the young, how we behave as leaders is as important as what we do.

Leaders should show leadership through the following personal characteristics or virtues:

a. TRUST | *leaders are trustworthy and reliable*
We hold trust on behalf of children and should be beyond reproach. We are honest about our motivations.

b. WISDOM | *leaders use experience, knowledge and insight*
We demonstrate moderation and self-awareness. We act calmly and rationally. We serve our schools and colleges and propriety and good sense.

c. KINDNESS | *leaders demonstrate respect, generosity of spirit, understanding and good temper*
We give difficult messages humanely where conflict is unavoidable.

d. JUSTICE | *leaders are fair and work for the good of all children*
We seek to enable all young people to lead useful, happy and fulfilling lives.

e. SERVICE | *leaders are conscientious and dutiful*
We demonstrate humility and self-control, supporting the structures, conventions and rules which safeguard quality. Our actions protect high-quality education.

f. COURAGE | *leaders work courageously in the best interests of children and young people*
We protect their safety and their right to a broad, effective and creative education. We hold one another to account courageously.

g. OPTIMISM | *leaders are positive and encouraging*
Despite difficulties and pressures, we are developing excellent education to change the world for the better.

FRAMEWORK FOR
ETHICAL LEADERSHIP
IN EDUCATION

Figure 3.4 Framework for ethical leadership in education.

Ethical leadership pathfinders

NGA ran a pathfinder scheme to explore how the framework was being used in practice in its first two years. Over 340 schools and trusts of all sorts of shapes and sizes across England signed up to review, reflect and report in 2019 and 2020, and many tested our resources to answer the main question: what kind of role models are we to the children in our care?

The pathfinders' experiences recorded in NGA's report *Paving the Way for Ethical Leadership in Education* are a good news story. For some, the framework provided more structure or a way to describe work that they were already doing. For others, it was the first time they had considered what they were doing through this ethical lens. Kindness, courage and optimism were the virtues most frequently mentioned, and leaders in particular appreciated the permission to be kind and that it wouldn't be seen as a bit fluffy and not 'leader-y' enough.

It was clear that the framework provided a common language and shared focus for ethical dilemmas and those complex issues that leaders and governing boards have to get their heads round at all times and in all contexts. Doing the best for pupils could be interrogated against the framework without relying on untested assumptions. It gave people confidence that they were doing the right things for the right reasons. It helped leaders to articulate that, first when making decisions and then when communicating the decisions well to a range of people, including parents. It helped governing boards and senior leaders make decisions that previously might have seemed tricky to defend.

The framework did not create more work for hard pressed staff. It informed decision-making that would have had to happen anyway. As the stories and blogs illustrated, it was used in all sorts of ways, including helping to bring schools into one multi-academy trust together with one set of values, and in one county, secondary schools worked together to ensure places for the most challenging pupils. Having a commonly held set of principles and virtues gave a solid basis for collaboration and innovation.

As well as shaping or reinforcing the culture of whole institutions, the framework proved valuable when reviewing the curriculum. Some teachers reported embedding the values into classroom practice, so that pupils were using them in discussion and testing arguments against them. A really significant area for pathfinders was in managing human resources (HR) and being an ethical employer. There were examples where HR processes were improved by considerations of the framework, including when restructuring or making redundancies. It also played a positive part in recruitment, especially of senior leaders, and in developing a real emphasis on staff CPD.

One of the early and often repeated comments was that the framework didn't just apply to leaders: pathfinders had used them with everyone. Perhaps it should be renamed more simply as 'the framework for ethics in education'. The framework helped embed ethical language and discourse in pathfinder schools and trusts. It was rewarding to hear the passion shining through from pathfinders who took the framework to their school's and trust's heart. To quote one: 'I think it's a hugely positive step forward and should become the standard for leadership in the education sector.'

The future of the framework

The framework has strength in that it was not handed down from on high with an instruction to comply. It was determined by leaders of sector organisations and then consulted on widely by the Commission and ASCL. Being sector-led was in theory the DfE's priority, but in practice at least one minister feared 'capture' by those with a different point of view. Unless an initiative was inspired by one of their favoured people or institutions, it was unlikely to be of interest. It remains to be seen whether the Labour government will change that culture.

Although the framework itself wasn't mentioned, ethics and professional conduct were placed at the centre of a graphic the DfE produced in October 2020 when it published the revised Headteachers' Standards, which are in turn enveloped by governance and accountability. It is pleasing to see the framework itself referenced in the 2024 edition of the DfE governance guides.

Figure 3.5 DfE graphic of the Headteachers' Standards in 2020.

Although the framework has not had the profile over the last couple of years that it deserved, an Ethical Leadership Alliance has now been revived by Carolyn Roberts and the Chartered College of Teachers to embed it further into the sector. There are very few issues that do not require an ethical consideration: for the pathfinders, a range of ethical dilemmas were posed that covered topics such as: exam malpractice; pupil behaviour and exclusion; breadth of curriculum; the best use of public funds; pupil wellbeing; the response to whistle-blowing; assessment; teacher workload; pupil grouping and attainment; and setting leadership pay. These are still available on NGA's website along with many other resources to support ethical leadership.

One of the issues that illustrated the need for a commission on ethical leadership in the first place was the rise of off-rolling: the practice of removing a pupil from the school roll without using a permanent exclusion when the removal is primarily in the best interests of the school, rather than the pupil. It may be done by pressuring a parent to remove their child from the school roll. These 'unexplained' exits were found by EPI (Education Policy Institute) to number 47,225 in the 2011 cohort of pupils, 49,051 in 2014's cohort and 55,309 or 8% of the 2017 cohort (Hutchinson and Crenna-Jennings, 2019), so a substantial minority of pupils moved to a different school or left the state school system entirely for unknown reasons. After the ethical framework was published, Ofsted made it clear that off-rolling is never acceptable and blogged about their approach to scrutinising off-rolling, but has not followed this up. For example, the

2023/24 Ofsted report had a detailed section on the children not attending school, but there was no mention of off-rolling. I had thought that perhaps off-rolling was a thing of the past until, at a recent governance conference, I heard the local authority speaker berating schools for their significant amount of off-rolling. These unexplained exits are exactly why boards exist: to ask the questions and scrutinise the answers.

In 2023, CSPL published a report – *Leading in Practice* – sharing examples and case studies gathered from public, private and charity sector organisations on maintaining ethical practices. The first of those case studies is one of the 'ethical leadership in education' pathfinders: the story of colleagues in Warwickshire collaborating to ensure places for all challenging pupils and avoid permanent exclusions in the county.

Accountable governance

As people worldwide have become more interested in the ethics of organisations from which they purchase their goods and receive their services, people power has acted alongside increased media activity to provide more of an external focus. Organisations are being expected to become more transparent in terms of their decision-making and operating practices. It's been good to see this – with lots of encouragement from NGA – making it into the 2024 DfE guidance, which says, 'It is important that academy trusts have a culture of transparency and welcome public scrutiny.'

There are several actors in good governance including the politicians, voters and taxpayers as well as those more intimately involved in organisational governance: the public servants and the non-executives. There are many different conceptions of governance in the political science literature, and even more understandings of different mindsets of governance at different levels. But here I am looking at the role of the governing board in accountability. The board is not the public space itself, but it has a duty to create a public space and then be an actor within it. This engagement happens at many levels for a multitude of purposes, right up to involving the community to help shape services to meet its needs. This active community participation will take schools beyond the narrow inward-looking agenda. I return to this in chapter 16.

Given the web of accountability, you won't be surprised to hear that accountable governance works in a number of directions and with a number of overlaps. First, the board is the organisation's accountable body: so there are a whole range of legal responsibilities that stop at the board.

Being an accountable body brings with it the need to report and explain to constituencies from the inspector to the regulator, the press and the public. The last is often overlooked and could perhaps be done better by many schools and trusts. I will come back to this later.

Second, DfE school governance guidance has for some time emphasised the role of governors – and then trustees – as holding senior leaders to account for the performance of the organisation, its staff and its pupils; indisputably this is a key part of the role, but absolutely not its entirety.

Third, there is that part of the governance that involves not just reporting to but also listening to the voices of stakeholders and considering those views in the decision-making process. This requires both having processes and information that enable stakeholders to influence decisions and to make complaints. This is very much mainstream governance thinking. For example, the Charity Commission has spelled that out for academy trusts, but attention hasn't always been paid to this to the extent it should have been in schools and trusts. Crucially, boards need to have information from a number of sources in order to truly know their school or trust.

Conclusion

It is now clear from a large amount of literature what is required to achieve good governance and deliver the mission. Good governance must be ethical, effective and accountable, and built on the foundations of agreed values, diversity, behaviours and a healthy culture. Governing can be a phenomenally challenging task, often harder to get right than the executive role, but there is now much guidance and training in the school sector. The framework for ethical leadership in education provides a compass to help exercise power and navigate decisions.

Good governance requires a board to work in five modes with different mindsets and behaviours: the fiduciary, the impact mode, the strategic, the generative, and values and cultures. Those first two have historically taken up too much board time, and more space needs to be found for the other three. Compliance has its place, but it should not be king. When I joined the sector, behaviour was barely mentioned once a code of conduct was signed, even though the consequences of behaviour on relationships constitute a significant portion of the queries from governing boards seeking advice when experiencing troubled waters. Better conversations happen more often now. I want the five mindsets to enter board parlance.

NGA's definition of good governance is not under dispute in the school sector. There is much agreement from other sources and sectors. Where

NGA led, the DfE has – after much discussion – followed in part. This can be seen in their reworked 2024 governance guides, in which they mention 'expected' behaviours but don't exemplify what they are. They said this is down to NGA and the rest of the sector.

Framing good governance in this way should help counter the very real objection found in the academic literature that the public sector has been mobilised by central government to consider only effectiveness: evaluating quality and ensuring standards with a narrow understanding curtailed by the accountability framework. This is a danger if conversations and challenges are limited by external authorities expecting risk and performance to be monitored only through an agreed prism of data measures. Being strategic, generative and values-driven prevents this from being the only lens of governance.

There is very little research on the impact of good governance, and in other sectors most learning comes from published reports of individual failures or the wider reviews set up after periods of failure. They invariably point to failures to listen to and act on concerns raised by employees and/ or the public, a failure to learn lessons from past mistakes or similar incidents, and a failure to identify and share emerging themes that might have alerted the organisation to a developing risk. While it is a shame to have to rely on just this deficit approach, even such review and analysis of failure has not happened in the school sector. At an individual institution level, boards should be asking: when things have gone wrong, how could the signs have been spotted and addressed earlier?

4.
Leadership and culture

This chapter was a late addition when I realised that one of the most crucial aspects of governing well – arguably *the* most important aspect – was in danger of being a sidenote in each chapter, not centre stage. My adopted definition of governance underlines that it doesn't exclusively concern the board but includes the power and decision-making of others too, and those others tend to be senior leaders. I want leaders – as well as those who govern as volunteers – to keep reading this book and know it is absolutely about their role too. They need to be convinced that governance is core to their business and that they aren't consumers of good governance, but very much participants and furthermore co-creators.

For too long, governance has been a secret garden, even in terms of leadership development where it is notionally on the curriculum, but not always in a meaningful or a challenging way. The usual approach is to ask a chief executive to talk about governance, and so often they – by definition – will talk from their own singular experience and not from a wide base of knowledge. I hope this book can provide a foundation for discussion of those experiences and for there to be challenges between peers.

The leadership of English schools is made up of school and trust executive leaders together with the governing board. The models of governance have changed with the introduction of multi-academy trusts (MATs), but the essence of successfully establishing those key partnerships does not change. Building relationships based on trust is one of NGA's eight elements of effective governance, and it forms a chapter in *The Chair's Handbook* in which I attempt to explore the subtleties of achieving that. Here, I want to do some of the same for leaders. When I say leaders, I am also referring to school and trust business leaders, not only headteachers and other executives leading teaching.

NGA aims to replicate at national level the trusting respectful relationships governors and trustees have at local level, a partnership devoted to meeting the needs and aspirations of their pupils. Governance should not be the periphery of what a senior leader does but guiding their day job. Others writing for headteachers and chief executives make the case well. Introducing his book *Being the CEO* to *Governing Matters* readers in 2019, Michael Pain said: 'The CEO should embrace the advice and guidance of a board of trustees who can bring a level of insight appropriate to the scale of the organisation and its influence; not having access to a good board is a real danger for a CEO and should be a big consideration when taking on the job.'

It is often used as shorthand in governance literature that the board sets the vision and strategic direction of the organisation, and hires – and, when necessary, fires – the chief executive who is paid to deliver the vision and strategy. This is a glib formulation of a much more nuanced relationship. Respective roles and responsibilities need to be known and understood by all, with accountability acknowledged and accepted. Then, negotiation of how the relationships will work in practice can be built on mutual respect and trust. It is fairly quickly noticed if the lead executive is dismissive of the board, or thinks their role is to manage, or 'deal with', the board. Sometimes when that view was expressed, I would occasionally retaliate with the question: 'who's the boss?' But I admit that response was born out of frustration, as even though technically true, it is not a helpful formulation for the collaborative working, which is very much needed.

The division of labour

The senior executive leader, whether a trust CEO or a school's headteacher, is not merely operational, and if they were that would be a problem. They are the professional whose judgement the board seeks and tests. Leaders have to think strategically too and, without that ability, they cannot give the board the proposals or advice that it needs.

The DCSF in 2010 published its report just before the general election and found that the distinction between the strategic role of the governing body and the operational management of the school was blurred in some cases. For a number of years when presenting to audiences, I had a slide with tasks listed as either operational or strategic. However, a better way of expressing the same thing is contained in one of my mantras: 'Governance is a thinking role; not a doing role.' This does not hold true in a couple of instances, the biggest being the recruitment and performance management of the senior leader. But very little else operational comes within governance.

Now, as a chair of a small charity, that phrase haunts me; we as trustees, with only three paid members of staff and a large team of volunteers, are undertaking some tasks that I spent my time at NGA frowning about. However, there is a difference between the sectors, the third sector with its history and ethos of volunteering and its unreliable funding, as opposed to a crucial public service funded by the taxpayer and fundamental to our society and its citizens' lives. We shouldn't be boxing and coxing when it comes to state education; services should be provided in a thoroughly professional and publicly funded way.

Sometimes those governing will also step in to volunteer in other ways, such as support on school trips or reading with the pupils. This separate role will no doubt provide more information on the school, but care needs to be taken not to confuse these roles, and making extra requests on volunteers already undertaking a significant role is best avoided. Occasionally, leaders will suggest these types of additional volunteering are required of governors when they are not.

There is also a danger that governance volunteers with other professional skills are asked to do pro bono work for the school/trust: this definitely should be avoided. Their knowledge needs to be used in the course of their governance duties, not in an operational capacity building in a conflict of interest and eliminating their ability to oversee that function objectively. I saw a charity use one of their trustees who ran a PR firm to undertake their branding review pro bono. The change proposed was not a good one, but the chief executive felt unable to dispute it and the board of trustees waved it through, leaving stakeholders puzzled by the new logo. Once that trustee left the board, there was a properly commissioned more successful rebrand.

Senior leaders do often appreciate free advice, and it may make the volunteer feel useful, but it risks preventing the board from dealing with the actual issue at stake: why doesn't the trust or school already have access to those skills or advice if that is needed? In small schools, but increasingly in others, the answer is often: 'We don't have the money to pay for it.' Although the volunteer is getting involved from good instincts, it's not sustainable and it blurs the role of the leader. Volunteers can undertake some advisory work unpaid if they are suitably qualified but not if they are on the governing board.

A board member interfering by actually doing things themselves should not be difficult to avoid. Acting as a sounding board is a legitimate role, as opposed to telling a senior leader how to do their job. Retired school and trust leaders tend to feel this temptation more often than volunteers from outside education. When there are real concerns about the performance of the leader, there are ways of addressing that which rarely involve direct instruction.

Although boards should not step over the line into the operational domain, they need a level of understanding of the operation of the organisation in order to determine whether it is succeeding in all sorts of ways. There's a real art in not becoming overly concerned with operational matters but knowing enough about the work of the organisation and especially the leadership team to be able to exercise judgement and make good decisions. Boards have to be clear when to get out of the way and let leaders lead, but sometimes boards have to take the initiative. A deep-dive may be needed to explore an aspect of school or trust business. The CSPL 2025 report underlined that in order for a board to prevent decline and ensure sustainability, there cannot be a substantial disconnect between its decision-making and its understanding of the operating functions; otherwise it is likely to be unable to identify risks and potential problems until it's too late.

The emphasis on holding to account, while important, is only part of the picture. As we have seen from the five mindsets of governance, the vision, ethos, culture and strategy need to be co-created with the testing out of ideas in both directions. Although everyone should know who has the ultimate power, very few conversations should be had in that spirit. If a board is operating in a command-and-control mode, that signals a problem. The governance structure, culture and practice must allow leaders to look beyond the day to day. Together, the governance and leadership teams build a sustainable future for their school or trust. If splits are appearing, reminding everyone of their common mission goes a long way to reversing them.

Many headteachers and some academy trust CEOs are governors and trustees in the organisations that they lead themselves: this is not good practice. In the charity sector, chief executives are not generally trustees of charities who employ us. Although an application can be made to the Charity Commission for an exception to be allowed, this is rare. There is occasionally a plea for the charity world to emulate the business world, but it's not gained traction. We understand that ultimately the trustees are the people holding us to account; in my view, being one of them would be an insurmountable conflict of interest. It does not just apply to performance and pay; almost every proposal put forward to the board by the executive leadership is there to be tested. This is an essential check and balance of power and decision-making, and working in this way is an expected part of bring a charity professional.

Charity chief executives also tend to understand that we are not passive recipients awaiting the instructions of our board, but co-creators of the vision and strategy, influential in most discussions in the board room. And yes, we are in the board room. In practice, it is rare for us to be asked to leave. It is not to say that charity governance is always sound in practice, but it makes sense to embed this obvious risk mitigation. Some early literature suggested that headteachers needed to be governors to allow them to legitimately play a part in setting the school's course, when in fact their role as headteacher alone gives them that legitimacy.

Mutual respect

The status of headteachers and CEOs is such that their job alone affords them some – often much – status and respect. That can be lost over time, but they begin new relationships from a position of power, often still felt by other adults as a leftover from their childhoods. Those who take on the role of holding the executive leaders to account may not feel as powerful, and this imbalance can be reinforced by the headteacher's and chief executive's greater knowledge of education and the organisation. This mismatch of perceptions is rarely spoken about but is rife and can be obvious when observing boards.

Furthermore, some educationalists struggle to accept a leadership role given to those from outside the profession. There needs to be respect for those who teach and those who don't. The latter bring other perspectives, knowledge and skills, but those are not always valued by the teaching profession.

I worked in the legal aid sector for some years and ended up with a senior and profession-facing role; not once was I asked if I was a qualified lawyer, but when I joined NGA, I was more often than not asked when I met someone if I had been a teacher (which I haven't). This is possibly a hangover from schools being that secret garden with professionals valuing their autonomy and not expecting other adults to step inside. A relationship that begins from a place of 'what are you really doing here in this school that I run' is going to be a bit fraught.

I was initially surprised to hear an educationalist directly stating that non-educationalists don't bring useful skills for school governance. 'What do you bring to the table' doesn't necessarily need to be said out loud for it to be evident. The questioning of the right to be in the room is much less evident now, especially from leaders who have worked with boards.

On the other hand, I've seen more than one MAT board made up almost entirely of trustees who were experienced educationalists and did not govern well; in two cases I remember they lost schools. There also were a few sponsored SATs with a list of eminent people who failed to govern well and had to be taken over by a MAT. Governance is a difficult business, and there are struggles for all sorts of reasons. However, being on the periphery of an organisation, rather than employed by it, can make for better sight of the bigger picture, the patterns of progress, the anomalies and for what really matters.

Arrival in the school sector with my fresh eyes felt a little like the experience I had returning to England having grown up overseas; some things that the majority hold self-evident seem questionable and others that are held dear feel odd. Four things struck me very quickly about the school sector from the periphery. The first was how hierarchical and compliant teachers and school leaders were, certainly by contrast with the sectors I had worked in. Advocacy and challenging the system is part of the day job for legal aid lawyers and those in the third sector supporting disadvantaged families, and being feisty is second nature.

Second, the school sector had little respect for human resources (HR) expertise, and as a result was behind other sectors in using many positive aspects of HR from performance development to flexible working. When the Headteachers' Standards were being reviewed in 2014, I had the most peculiar conversation with the chair of the DfE's advisory board, who in response to me arguing for school leaders needing more understanding of HR, asked: 'So you want me to be a lawyer as well as a headteacher?' This seemed especially strange as this super head was by then a MAT chief executive. This resistance to learning about managing staff well ran through the system from top to bottom. I commend two books in this area: Mandy Coulter's *Talent Architects* and *Putting Staff First* by John Tomsett and Jonny Uttley, both of which have helped to change the tide. Understanding the law and the rights it gives employees is not a replacement for good management and leadership; it is just foundation knowledge on which you layer your judgement and the human element.

My third observation was that everyone talked about leadership, while management was a bit of a dirty word. I subsequently learned that this had not been the case in the 1990s with government initiatives to improve school management. The move away from 'management' and towards 'leadership' as a key factor underpinning school success was fully realised when in November 2000 the National College for School Leadership was established. Despite middle leaders seemingly having a grander status, they got neither the time nor the training, and sometimes not even a job description or simple recognition that many of them were responsible for a team and its development. Research by Earley et al. in 2002 found that often those who seemed to us to be middle managers did not see themselves as managers, let alone leaders. I wonder how much this has changed.

My fourth observation was that the school sector seemed to be behind the third sector in terms of strategy planning, which I will return to below.

A professional relationship

I want to caveat this section with a comment on language. There is rightly much said about teaching as a profession, exemplified by the Chartered College of Teaching. It is indeed a noble calling. On the other hand, when the word 'professionalise' is used for school and trust governance, this raises the hackles of some who take it as evidence of moving governance from a democratic activity to a business-like activity inappropriate to the public sector. I don't think it does, and I positively wanted to claim the word 'professionalism' for those who volunteer to govern: they can do the role well as a volunteer, with the skill, good judgement and behaviours that are expected from a professional. The relationship between senior leaders at the school/trust and their board should be conducted equally professionally by both parties. While good boards value and thank professional school leaders, the paid professionals should also acknowledge the work of the volunteers and thank them for their contribution.

During their appointment process, prospective heads and CEOs talk with trustees and governors about building sound relationships. Candidates know what they have to say, but once in the job, with the myriad of other duties, some may not properly invest time or thought in developing relationships with the board. This may manifest itself in a range of behaviours, for example: not having papers ready for distribution in advance of meetings; failing to provide the requested information in the appropriate format; swamping boards with detail; talking at length in meetings; failing to act on governing board suggestions; sidelining trustees and governors; or involving the governing board in other pro bono activities rather than the core functions of governance.

Even when accepted intellectually, challenge can be resented in practice. When a chief executive myself, I could come over as defensive at meetings even though I completely bought in to the principle of being challenged. Dissent is a good thing as part of the decision-making process; the best decisions aren't always made when everyone agrees. Exploring differences of opinion without escalating into a conflict or damaging relationships is crucial. People becoming entrenched in their views must not stop a corporate decision being made and, although this is the responsibility of all involved, the chair will need to facilitate the process. Challenge should go every which way, across the board and also executive to non-executive.

The good boards are those that have an open relationship with the chief executive and senior team. There are no secrets, and the board can ask for any information they want so they can get under the skin of the organisation. When information is hidden from the board, things are likely to go very badly wrong. For non-executive directors to be able to provide constructive challenge to an organisation, they must have good access to information. The responsibility for ensuring this happens is two-way – the executive needs to provide accurate and candid information about the organisation's performance and any emerging issues that may stand in the way of the organisation delivering its objectives, but non-executives also have a responsibility to ask for the information they need. Both need to seek out and stay responsive to the needs of pupils, families and the local community. I will return to this issue in chapter 7.

Getting the balance right

In 2004, the Department for Education and Skills in *Governing the School of the Future* made it clear that: 'The governing body, headteacher and senior management team together constitute the leadership team of the school. Good headteachers recognise the importance of challenge and support from their governing bodies especially at a time when managing change has become a key role for all headteachers.' As I will return to in chapter 5, practice at that time did not always live up to this expectation. The following graphic that accompanied the original aspiration largely stands the test of time, although the term 'critical friends' should be archived. A variation on this for leadership is Mary Myatt's concept of 'high challenge, low threat', which is especially pertinent at a time when the accountability regime is almost always referred to as high stakes.

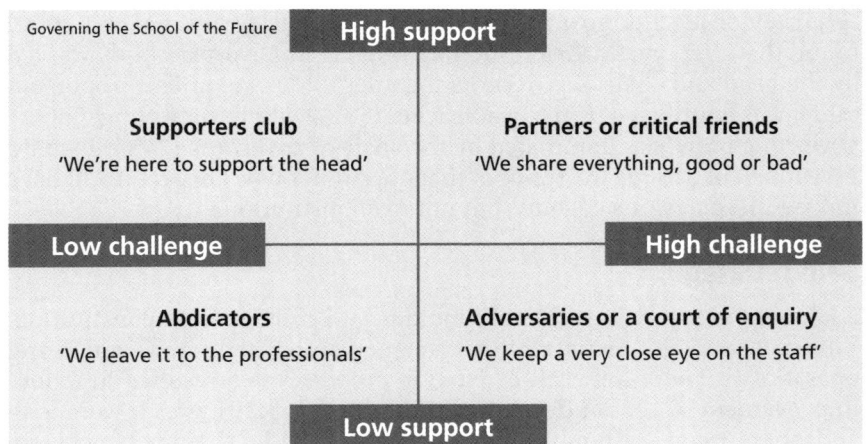

Figure 4.1 Types of challenge and support in school governance from 2004.

As I will look at in later chapters, there's now a higher proportion of governing boards – 90% – in the high support, high challenge quadrant. That is not just my wishful thinking, having run an organisation dedicated to improving school and trust governance: it's a research finding from just before the pandemic.

NGA's work over the Covid-19 pandemic saw relationships between governing boards and senior leaders tending to become stronger. There was huge respect reported by those governing for the way in which leaders dealt with the new and serious challenges presented by the pandemic. Almost all boards prioritised support, recognising the huge pressure on leaders who had never before faced this situation that hadn't appeared on risk registers. In the post-pandemic phase, governors and trustees had to carefully recalibrate the balance of challenge and support, knowing that new challenges continued for schools and that many leaders were exhausted.

Balance pervades so many aspects of governance: skills and knowledge on the board; support and challenge; when to take charge and when to get out of the way; loyalty to the organisation and the ability to be dispassionate in the analysis; helicopter oversight and diving down to explore potential areas of concern; measuring quantitatively and judging success in other ways; time for all five mindsets of governance, including generative discussion and culture as well as compliance and monitoring; working in partnership and holding to account.

A survey of teacher governors 25 years ago (Earley and Creese, 2000) found that over one third of respondents felt their governing body was led by the head and chair of governors together (35%). A similar proportion said it was dominated by the headteacher (38%) with fewer feeling that the governing body was dominated by the chair of governors (24%). I would very much like to see the result of that question today. I expect it will have moved more towards equality, but not in all institutions.

Being strategic

Each trust or standalone school should have a strategy for the institution. Fifteen years ago, being strategic seemed to be defined as not being operational. There were self-evaluation processes that resulted in school improvement or school development plans (SIP/SDP), which were long and operational. Although they were presented by the headteacher to governors as part of a crowded agenda, they were not in any way co-created. That is not necessarily wrong for a management plan: that is the business of the headteacher or the chief executive. A board might want to be aware that such a plan exists, or what alternative management process is being used, but to go through a plan line by line is not a good use of board time.

Time and space need to be made, ideally in the summer term, to hold a strategy session for both the board and the school or trust leadership. There is not enough time for the strategic and generative mindset in regular business meetings, and an external facilitator can be used to underline the change of mode and spirit. Leaving these important deliberations until September is likely to mean they don't get enough reflection in the hurly-burly of the new school year.

Strategy sessions need to take a very different format with far fewer papers, real back-to-basics open discussions with everyone participating, and stakeholder input heard and welcomed. In a MAT, local governors can be included alongside trustees, even though it's the trust board that will sign off the developed strategy. The environment outside the school/trust needs be considered, along with a debate as to what success looks like and how best to achieve it.

NGA has two very well-loved *Being Strategic* guides developed with the National Association of Headteachers (NAHT) and the Association of School and College Leaders (ASCL), one for single schools and the other for MATs that takes people through the process in more detail.

The resulting priorities should be central to both board business and the objectives of the lead executive for the coming year.

Making decisions

Business meetings and committees (when they are used) tend to have very full agendas; discipline is needed but not to the extent that it prevents useful discussion. It should be clear what items require a board decision, but how do we ensure proactive decision-making, compared with a 'rubber-stamping' of the headteacher/CEO's proposals? We must not assume that ratifying a headteacher's recommendation has no value: putting it through a process of consideration will be useful if it is not entirely passive. On the other hand, constant dismissal of executive recommendations would also signal danger. Again, a balance needs to be struck: endorsing executive plans can be quite right and proper as long as there is good discussion of options, an understanding of the reasons behind the propositions, a fit with the ethos and strategic priorities, and alternatives dismissed for good reason.

It can be frustrating for executives when no substantive issues are raised in a paper that took much time to come up with. On the other hand, the participation of the headteacher/CEO also needs to be appropriate. Too often they talk at great length through papers that have already been read by governors/trustees, wasting time and encouraging bad habits.

So what are 'big' decisions for boards after the strategy setting? The very biggest aren't usually frequent, such as the appointment of a new headteacher or CEO, changing school status (to become an academy, for example) or taking on additional schools into the trust. Other significant decisions include signing off the budget, staff restructuring, and agreeing to building work or other considerable procurement.

So many of the issues in this chapter interlink: the board culture and how decisions are made are very much affected by the relationship between the lead executive and the chair. Some governors and trustees feel they are at meetings to rubber-stamp decisions made by the headteacher and chair of governors, who enjoy a close working relationship, often called 'cosy', when in truth that is dysfunctional and should be recognised as such. It can fly under the radar as nobody is overtly excluded from making a contribution, but few feel able to challenge. The courageous conversations that need to be had are between board members as well as with their senior leaders, and a good chair is key to making this happen.

It is wise not to chair the same organisation for a lengthy period of time: at NGA, we recommended six years maximum for school and trust boards. Chairs should make it very clear when they are entering their final year. On the NGA board, we had a term limit of three years as chair, and so I got used to much change, working with eight chairs in my 18 years of being a chief executive. I will come back to succession planning and term limits in chapter 10.

Leading the board

A discussion about working in partnership as leaders would not be complete without including the role of the chair. Good chairing is another of the eight elements of effective governance, and arguably the most important as a good chair will make sure the other seven elements are in place too. This is no mean feat and takes considerable time, effort, reflection and skill.

The chair will usually have more involvement than other trustees and governors, and more contact with the senior leadership, but has very little power specific to the role. 'Chair's action' can only be used if a delay waiting for a board decision is likely to be seriously detrimental: this rarely is met in practice especially as key matters are excluded. The governing body or board of trustees is a corporate entity; the power and authority rests with the governing board as a whole.

The chair is sometimes described as 'first among equals'. They are not decision-makers; any power they hold comes from influence and presence. NGA's *The Chair's Handbook* provides a manual for new and aspiring chairs, but is also a useful introduction for heads/executives and aspiring heads. In 2020, NGA published research on leading boards that also points to the need for a vice chair and the sharing of tasks around the whole board. This very much rose again in research two years later on governance workload, which I cover in chapter 10.

The chair leads the governing board, with the support of the vice chair, ensuring it fulfils its functions well, and the lead executive runs the organisation. The culture of the board is often in practice shaped by its chair with the help of the vice chair and possibly a core group of others, for better or worse, but all members are responsible for this. A good chair will ensure the board's focus is on the strategic, while not overlooking compliance functions nor duties to staff. It is no exaggeration to say that the success or failure of a governing board depends heavily on the calibre and actions of its chair.

The relationship of the chair and the lead executive is absolutely key to ensuring the governing board and senior leadership team establish a vision and strategic priorities for the school(s). A good chair works well with executive leaders to advise on and shape proposals to be discussed at the board meetings. The chair's ability to build good, productive relationships with a range of different people is absolutely critical, but the same is required of the executive leader. A lack of communication between chair and executive leader is likely to create tension and certainly will create problems and disjointed leadership if it continues.

As well as a leader, the chair is at times a confidant, a manager, a sounding board, a catalyst, a cheerleader, an ambassador, an arbitrator, a negotiator, a networker, possibly a mentor or coach, and sometimes the first port of call for other agencies. The balance of these roles adopted by any chair will depend on the situation at hand, and also the experience and strengths of the lead executive. However, even this list can underplay the role a good chair plays in encouraging the lead executive to develop proposals that are fit for purpose and ensuring that the governing board is active in driving the strategic direction of the school/trust.

When the relationship is working at its best, it can provide inspiration as well as support to the headteacher and CEO. I experienced that very much with most of my chairs while a chief executive. It does require openness, one of the Nolan principles, but because they are also being held to account, some leaders struggle with that. The number of times I have heard words from an executive to the effect of: 'I couldn't tell my chair that as they might think I am not coping.' That was not my experience; I would use 1:1s with my chairs to discuss the things that were keeping me awake at night, things I couldn't usually discuss with staff. I think the honesty displayed strengthens the relationship and builds trust. I have been called naive for taking this approach, but I have never regretted it. Quite the contrary, I have always found it supportive and helpful to hear someone else's perspective and would commend it. So often there is talk of leadership being lonely: this is a very good way of changing that. There are two of you at the top of the organisation.

Being held to account happens in a myriad of ways; the 1:1s with the chair, but also the sheer act of regularly reporting to a board, both with preparing papers and in person handling questions. Quarterly board meetings were a discipline that improved my assessment of NGA's performance and my leadership of it. Having to convincingly explain a dip in performance or your rationale for improvement enforces a rigour of analysis that you might not otherwise demand of yourself or not make time to explore fully given daily pressing issues.

It is commonly said that the stakes for school leadership are very high. However, working with the chair, as with the whole board, can be protective. A good chair will move further into support when it is clearly needed. One of the main reasons employees leave jobs is due to their relationship with their bosses, so a good chair can help retain a lead executive, including by building their confidence. An anonymous headteacher blogged: 'I couldn't say to my Governors or academy chain that "I'm feeling a bit doubtful this term" because they're my bosses, and they might construe that as meaning that I'm not up to the job.' On the contrary, being able to be open with the chair could be transformative, and with a local chair within a MAT there is less at risk as they do not also act as the line manager.

The chair/executive dynamic does morph from the informal – friendly but not friends – to the formal. But there should be complete agreement that there are never surprises. Neither person should turn up at a board meeting to hear the other say something substantive they did not already know. It is of course fine to have disagreements behind closed doors, but when they are speaking from a public platform together there has to be unity; a single message, shoulder to shoulder.

Let's not pretend that every head/CEO and chair will always get on famously; sometimes it can become a real problem, not adding value but distracting from the business of running the school or trust. If that is the case, the pair need to sit down together and ask: 'what do we expect of each other?'

Chairs are an undervalued part of sector leadership. The level of attention given nationally to the role of the chair ebbs and flows, but sadly not from a very high point.

Performance management

I find the language of performance management (PM) uncomfortable, while at the same time, both as a manager and an employee, I found the process of six-monthly reviews enormously beneficial. I know that is not the experience or attitude of all executive leaders, especially headteachers who are sometimes frustrated by being appraised by non-educationalists. Some educational professionals are concerned PM could reduce their professionalism, narrow their horizons and squash their agency as a leader. Done well, it achieves quite the opposite. In the school sector, there has been too much dependence on tightly defining targets, which I hope now is a thing of the past. These conversations need to be nuanced and flexible, part of intelligent accountability and professional development.

I call the process D&A: development and appraisal. With any employee there must be dialogue about objectives when they are set. With the lead executive, these stem from the organisation's objectives and priorities. Objectives don't have to be monitored numerically; feedback from others and the telling of stories can be very illuminating. Dialogue and learning continue between the more formal six-monthly conversations, with issues arising dealt with openly and directly.

'With a volunteer board overseeing the work of a professional chief executive and constrained by the difficulty of agreeing appropriate performance measures, the relationship between the board and the chief executive is more subtle than in for-profit or public sector organisations,' David Fishel (2003) wrote in *Boards That Work: A Guide for Charity Trustees*. The same is true of schools and trusts. There is a difference in practice from charities; I hadn't come across external advisers for chief executive's PM in the charity sector. In fact, I was even surprised to have it proposed that my appraisal at NGA might be with three trustees; it ended up as two – the chair and one of the two vice chairs. Looking back, it could have been good to have a third trustee who changed each year and did not have one of the five key board roles to give a different perspective and to learn more about the organisation.

Maintained schools have to appoint an external adviser, and although there is freedom for academies not to continue with this, many have done. I am not convinced this is necessary given that the organisation's strategic priorities will generally become the objectives of the lead executive – after all, that is what they are employed to deliver. This should make the whole process far more straightforward if the strategy has been well constructed. Research for the DfE on PM of headteachers in 2014 identified the setting of objectives as one of the 'most challenging aspects of the process'; this fits with the situation that existed before the sector better understood the nature of a strategy and setting priorities. Linking pay rises to the PM process is unhelpful; it can change the nature of the conversation with the employee trying to prove they are worth a pay rise rather than honestly assessing their progress and achievements. I am pleased performance-related pay is no longer mandatory for other staff, and it does not need to be for trust executives.

I am not going to talk further about doing PM well here. NGA and the professional representative organisations have relevant resources.

It is worth mentioning that for heads within MATs the role of PM has transferred to executives, although it is good practice for the chair of the local governors to be included in the review meetings. In some MATs, it is still the chair who spends more time with the headteacher. In some cases, the local chair may even be seen as an ally; whether that is wholly appropriate is a discussion to be had, but it could be a positive dynamic in some appraisal rooms. I would be interested to see research looking at how PM has changed when carried out by an executive, rather than governors. Although new governance structures in MATs are talked about, the new leadership structures haven't had that level of scrutiny: I will return to that issue in chapter 12.

Little is known about the ways in which the PM of the headteacher and chief executive shapes overall school performance, or PM across the whole institution shapes teaching and pupil outcomes. Such knowledge would be extremely useful to ascertain whether it is playing its proper part in the web of accountability, and if so, it adds to the argument that other dimensions could be less relentless. I would like PM to become accepted as a force for good, lessening the need for external forces to apply other pressures.

Leadership dysfunction

There are occasions – let's assume and plan for them to be few and far between – when school/trust leaders struggle to perform the job. If, after all the support and development possible, the conclusion is that the role is not right for them or there is a case of gross misconduct, it is down to the governing board in a standalone school, either maintained or SAT, to organise an alternative, of course with HR support. Suspending a headteacher is a hugely difficult and stressful task on many levels. Even where those governing are used to the process from their own work experience, at a school the situation is a lot more public and yet of course must remain confidential. Parents often want answers where none can be given while an investigation is being held, and they may think the governing board is hiding problems. They almost always are, but transparency and HR processes do not tend to go together.

As I will look at in a later chapter, the level of central control varies from MAT to MAT, both in terms of what headteachers can control and the level of responsibility given to chairs of local governors. Unless it concerns the chief executive's performance, within MATs any capability and misconduct work will usually be carried out by the trust's executive team, but with the knowledge of trustees. This comes as a relief to most local chairs of governors as long as their view has been sought. Moreover, a disciplinary process is doing, not thinking.

Maintained schools have the support of the local authority to call on, and there is the option of an interim executive board if the governing body itself is part of the dysfunction: I will return to this in chapter 15.

Single academy trust boards are much more exposed. The governing board needs to be confident and capable, assessing when their headteacher is struggling, how to support them, and understanding when a different approach is required, which may include replacing them. Not only is this a difficult decision with difficult consequences, but it also requires a different decision-making model to the usual corporate board decision: not all of the board can be involved in what is one of the most important decisions that trustees could make, due to the need for some to remain untainted so that they are able to be involved with an employment hearing.

The role of the employer

Obligations come with the board being the employer of staff (or in the case of some maintained schools acting in place of the employer) and these include staff workload, wellbeing and development, as well as the compliance on such legal duties as health and safety. The board must exercise a duty of care, not just to help ensure that their leader can keep leading well, but also because this is part of being an ethical employer.

The board also needs to be assured that the organisation's HR policies and procedures reinforce their agreed culture. Replacing the language of HR with a people strategy for the school and trust can be an important way of reviewing how things are done and how it feels to be an employee. It may be more acceptable to the profession, easier to explain as a force for good, and not simply a set of legal rules.

There are a number of areas in which schools are different from some other modern workplaces, and some of those have been exaggerated during the Covid-19 pandemic and its aftermath. There has been a change of many expectations; for example, more homeworking and more flexibility requested. Schools had been slow to adapt before the pandemic, but some progress has been made since, with resources developed by a DfE working group as well as others. Staff recruitment and retention is one of the challenges for boards I will look at in chapter 13.

As well as the board seeking staff feedback more broadly, the chair should be raising and taking note of head/CEO's own work–life balance as part of their regular discussions.

Wellbeing

There is much written and said about wellbeing at the moment, and a long list of organisations are now devoted to support headteachers with EdSupport probably at the top of that list. NGA has worked with many of them to provide resources so that chairs and others on the board make sure they can have those conversations. We cannot and must not expect leaders to keep managing whatever the pressure and personal cost.

I've said already in a number of ways how essential it is for school governors, trustees and leaders to work together in a mutually supportive and respectful way. The leader has no legal duty to look out for the governance volunteers' wellbeing, but having one eye to this will strengthen that relationship and the commitment of the volunteers. NGA's research on recruiting and retaining volunteers in 2021 showed that the lead executive could make a significant impact on how governors and trustees felt about the role and their own place in it.

One example that can be a bone of contention is timing of meetings. I have heard leaders insist that board meetings should be entirely within the working day on the grounds of their own and staff wellbeing. This expectation overlooks that some governors and trustees are also employees and may not be able to take time off in the working day.

Cultivating your culture

A healthy culture is absolutely essential to the success of schools, as indeed it is for all organisations. Culture is the way things get done; it is culture that builds cohesions in groups, helping people maximise their efforts for the greater good, adding up to more than the sum of their parts. You are striving for a culture where the workforce is unified by a common purpose.

Anyone who has gone to a leadership conference session on strategy and culture will know the much-quoted axiom 'culture eats strategy for breakfast: a strategy that is at odds with a company's culture is doomed', attributed to Peter Drucker and popularised in 2006 by Mark Fields, president of Ford Motor Company. This does not mean to render strategies redundant but emphasises the essential need for a culture that supports the strategy, a synergy between the two. Similarly, if the culture is not supportive of good governance, no amount of process design will fix it.

The board should work with the leadership to foster a common culture, values and ethos across the whole organisation, ensuring it is reflected consistently in its policies, practices and people. The leaders and board need to be as one in creating a positive culture; the tone needs to be set from the top with the knowledge of the mood from the bottom. I am convinced that this is such an important but underplayed aspect of governance that I have added it to the mindsets of governance (see Figure 3.2).

Over the past decade, more and more has been said and written about organisational culture, something that can be pretty difficult to ascertain, let alone change. Culture is unlikely to be perceived or experienced in the same way by everyone. I am unconvinced by visitors who claim they can smell the culture as soon as they walk through the door; although some aspects of culture are clear from a walk-about, others remain undetected until conversations are had with a range of people. Just because we talk more about culture doesn't necessarily mean we have got the hang of making our schools places in which people want to work or be educated.

Much has been said over the years – particularly in the last two – about the culture of fear among staff, including leaders, created by the accountability framework, particularly inspection. Clearly, there are major sector-wide influences on school and trust culture. It would be naive not to recognise that, but let's not forget that the board also can have huge power and influence here working with the senior leadership.

The culture should flow from the organisation's values and ethos. But if the board and leadership have never sat down, taken stock and articulated the culture they are trying to instil, it will just have developed over many years. If culture hasn't been addressed openly, collaboratively and fully, the climate – the way things feel – at the trust or school will have formed in an ad hoc way. It will also be shaped by the worst behaviours leaders display or are willing to tolerate or ignore. Words are easier to forget than feelings: many have said over the past 60 years, people may not remember what you did, said or wrote, but they will remember how you made them feel.

For there to be any feeling of ownership, staff must be involved in a purposeful exercise. It is imperative that boards understand staff morale and consider what needs to be done to ensure the culture is aligned with their vision and strategy, not acting against it. It is the people and their behaviours that deliver the results envisioned in the strategy, and the culture that enables or inhibits them from doing so.

An ethical culture

Lord Evans, chair of CSPL, in his foreword to the *Leading in Practice* report in 2023 said: 'Senior leaders must ensure that values are understood and embedded into all aspects of how their organisations operate – from the way leaders communicate with employees, to the priority given to developing good decision-making, to the approach taken to recruitment and performance management. While the tone from the top is critical, leadership matters throughout an organisation. Leaders at all levels have a fundamental role in exemplifying and helping their teams live up to the Principles in their day-to-day behaviours. From the evidence we have heard, it is clear that there is no single right way to embed an ethical culture in organisations, but a range of possible approaches and measures. … We certainly do not have all the answers but we are clear that building an ethical culture does not happen by accident. We want to challenge leaders in the public sector to reflect on their own leadership and consider whether there is more they can do to support the ethical buoyancy of their organisations.'

Leaders should display the Nolan Principles and the virtues of the ethical leadership framework, modelling them for everyone else in the community. Leaders must be role models for the standards they expect of others, even when they are under pressure or exhausted. There is the well-known expression that the standards you walk by are the standards you accept. Leaders must address behaviour that is inconsistent with its values and expectations.

An open culture

Collaboration is at the core of every team. People are encouraged and success celebrated; mistakes become opportunities to learn and grow. Dialogue is encouraged, each contribution valued. There is a real openness to ideas, with the possibility of doing things differently. Concerns are heard, and conflicts, complaints and whistle-blowing are dealt with constructively, equitably and with empathy. Leaders feel confident and courageous to have the right conversations, with the right people at the right time. Governors and trustees listen and respond to the needs of their diverse stakeholders. As hard as that may be, there is no defensiveness.

Cultures where bad news will not be tolerated lead to disaster, as was well documented in Mid-Staffordshire Health Trust. Embracing the culture of learning at every level is key, and the board has an important role in championing CPD for all, from the board to non-teaching staff.

Once again, I am back to the importance of relationships, this time to changing and shaping culture. Mutual trust, respect, enthusiasm and that sense of shared mission all need to be built. Communication should be open, honest and two-way. Employees want to be heard, valued and empowered. Beginning with your agreed values and putting people at the centre should help develop a strategy and a culture that delivers for pupils, while breeding confidence in leaders.

Building an organisation where it is second nature for people to speak up is an art and not a science. There is no blueprint to follow, but leaders who are committed to advocating the benefits of an open culture and potentially doing things differently listen with curiosity and genuine interest, not irritation, when staff raise concerns and make suggestions for better ways of doing things. Leaders must be clear that they welcome potential problems being brought to their attention early and that everyone in the organisation has a duty to deal with each other and the public with openness and honesty. When employees speak, leaders – both executive and non-executive – must listen. It is not always easy to speak up; it often requires moral courage, especially as schools can be quite old-fashioned organisations with lots of rules set from the top and where challenging the status quo is not commonplace. Leaders need to be visible and available. Many are but not all.

A culture of accountability

Meaningful stakeholder engagement is an indicator of a healthy culture. An accountable culture means listening to feedback from all stakeholders and taking action, and if this is not yet the case, a board must convince the leadership that it's the way to improve. It is not generally easy as a leader to hear what others perceive as going wrong but those giving their views need to know that they will be considered seriously and fairly.

Dialogue with the parent community, or at least the vocal part of it, can become dysfunctional and disrespectful with parents being seen as the problem, not as crucial partners. In recent years, particularly since the pandemic, the attitudes of some parents towards school staff have deteriorated, leading to increasing numbers of complaints and problematic use of social media.

A defensive, controlling culture and set of behaviours adopted by those in leadership positions can easily outweigh formal good governance processes. Those that govern exercise power: hard power in that they make decisions and hold the executive to account, but also that all-important soft power when it comes to vision, ethos and culture. To ensure that there is an organisation-wide culture of learning, boards need to support leaders and encourage them to listen and respond. This cannot be led by a single person and needs to be embedded across the organisation.

Governing boards need to understand the climate of their institution and find ways of taking its temperature. Schools cannot become places where adults do not want to work and pupils do not want to learn. Most schools are happy and vibrant places, but this mustn't be taken for granted, especially with more pupils feeling pressure and missing school for longer since the pandemic. Wider society's culture will of course affect the culture of the school, but this mustn't happen by osmosis without the implications being considered by leaders. Culture and values are one of the five mindsets of governance, and that mode of governing is not just for the strategy day.

Culture is not fluffy, and it isn't a second-order consideration to the more hard-nosed aspects of fiduciary governance: ignoring it or getting it wrong can have very serious consequences. Poor corporate culture was identified as leading Boeing to negligent engineering practices and substandard aircraft taking to the skies with disastrous results; the board had failed.

The CSPL reviewed the reports of independent inquiries and concluded how, when the public has suffered as a result of action or inaction by a public sector body, it is often the defensive response of the body and its failure to admit where it went wrong and apologise that compounds the pain suffered by those affected by its actions.

Other ingredients of a healthy culture

As well as fostering that culture of aspiration, learning, improvement and development, I would want to ensure two other ingredients: a culture of diversity, equity and inclusion and a culture of belonging and wellbeing for all.

Other leaders may have their own essential ingredients. Innovation is often thrown into these conversations, but I'm a little jaded about that. In the third sector, we generally have to be entrepreneurial as our income is not as constant as in the public sector; we are always having to find new ways to deliver our services and generate income. Once, I was in charge of distributing £1 million of public money to innovative money advice services. During our tender process, we received all sorts of applications for delivering perfectly sound services in non-traditional settings, but there wasn't one that I as an experienced practitioner hadn't seen before. So I quietly ignored the innovation criteria and held my breath as the recommended winners were sent up to the treasury minister for sign-off. It was approved.

By contrast, schools are fairly traditional, hierarchical organisations with much unchanging practice and lots of rules. This might not be recognised by many teachers and school leaders who perceive themselves to be in receipt of a constant stream of change coming from on-high, but that is often internal and not necessarily perceived from outside. Recently, I heard two headteachers discussing conversations they had had with parents about whether school uniform, in particular ties, was outdated. Uniform is a custom many centuries old and a topic with a list of pros and cons, but neither headteacher wanted to have that debate with parents or consider any changes. Even the challenge to defend the status quo was discombobulating them. This summer, parents have been challenging headteachers who still expect pupils to wear blazers in a heatwave. Apart from IT (and even that is often adopted after other sectors), little has changed in the way education is delivered in classrooms. Most of us recognise the schools of our childhood in the current set-up, whereas treatments on offer by health services have changed enormously.

The bigger points are two-fold: is there an appetite and mindset for real and fundamental change? And is there the courage and confidence to push back against the changes from above if they are not well informed? My answer to the second is no, there is much conformity in the sector: yes sir, no sir, three bags full sir. So often trust leaders won't want to be seen by the DfE regional directors as troublemakers: they want to be in the good books so that they are in the queue when schools are looking for a MAT to join or for additional funding when it is being dispersed.

This makes the roles of the representative groups and trade unions even more important, although during Michael Gove's time as Education Secretary those groups were very much pushed to the periphery. He and his team – and to some extent the regimes that followed – were obsessed by organisations being 'captured' by the wrong people. It can even be seen in the architecture of the system with ministers quickly going off the Chartered College of Teaching when they found it was being led by an independent-minded woman with huge experience, rather than 'one of their own'. They tended to use a small group of teachers and leaders who were on the same page as they were: they certainly didn't want challenge as well as support. That approach reinforced the profession's natural aversion.

At present, the profession is often too tired by the day to day to have the time and space to consider the issues that are important to stakeholders or prevalent in society. It is, however, the role of leaders to engage in this sort of learning and reflection. Raising your head above the parapet requires energy, courage, an appetite for risk and a belief that it will make for a better education system. This requires the generative mindset of governance.

Professional leadership

There is a vast literature on leadership that I am not going to attempt to summarise here, but it is worth noting the move away from hero heads – the 'super heads' – to a range of leadership styles less about having charismatic presence and more about servant leadership and distributed leadership. If you're new to the sector and not already well versed in leadership literature, you may be interested to read these two books: John Dunford's *The School Leadership Journey* and Steve Munby's *Imperfect Leadership*. My recommendation isn't just because I know them both; their storytelling is engaging, authentic and grounded in experience.

There was a piece of research published by Hill et al. in 2016 that caused a bit of a stir as it linked leadership styles with the subjects taught by school leaders. It didn't gain credibility in the sector, possibly in part because it wasn't written by an education guru but by the Centre for High Performance, who observed 160 academies over five years, with unprecedented access to school information systems, enabling them to record pupil, teacher, management and financial performance. Moreover, the researchers didn't share their data and seemed keen to make some money from spin-offs from the work. Yet, I have to admit these findings spoke to me: 'The most effective leaders were the least well-known, least rewarded, and least recognized; although they did a great job, the results took time to show, allowing them to be overlooked. Yet they were the only ones who built a school where exam results continued to improve long after they'd left. … They're insightful, humble and visionary leaders who believe schools fail because they're poorly designed, or do not serve (and thus are not supported by) their local community.'

Without taking it all to heart, it is worth bearing in mind the spirit of this research when involved in the all-important job of selecting and interviewing that next executive leader. We shouldn't be looking for people who are showy. Leaders do of course need to align people to the school's or trust's ethos and vision, by gaining buy-in and inspiring and motivating people, but there are many ways of doing that.

Distributive leadership involves delegation to the executive team and beyond into middle leadership. This approach has been identified by many as beneficial, although not universally. The leadership approach of an institution should chime with its values. My belief in collective wisdom goes beyond the governing classes; tapping into the knowledge and collective intelligence right across the organisation is crucial. That means not only listening to staff, but moving away from centralised decision-making and recognising where else in the school or trust there is potential to make good decisions.

Research has underlined the importance of school leadership for the quality and development of schools, recognising that leadership is second only to classroom teaching in its impact on students and their learning (Leithwood, Harris and Hopkins, 2020). Acquiring leadership skills should not be left to chance. It's an important role of the chair to make sure the executive leaders are engaged in useful development and have access to a mentor or coach.

Leadership development

Over the last 40 years, there has been a growing emphasis on leading development, often with a corresponding infrastructure to develop leadership in private and public sector organisations. From 2000 to 2013, this was manifested in the form of the National College for School Leadership (NCSL), and then to a lesser extent in the National College for Teaching and Leadership, by then an executive agency that finally had its functions fully subsumed into the DfE. A suite of national professional qualifications (NPQs) have grown up with funding devoted to them, delivered by a range of organisations.

For years, NGA argued that NPQs did not adequately prepare leaders for the challenges of headship. For example, the topic of governance had not featured highly enough in senior leadership development programmes. As long ago as 2002, Peter Earley et al. concluded when researching leadership training: 'This unsatisfactory waste of opportunity and potential governor talent could perhaps helpfully be redressed if the training of headteachers gave even greater priority to how they can work strategically with governors.'

In 2020, NGA submitted some detailed evidence to the DfE on the areas that new heads and trust executives found particularly challenging and needed training in. These challenging areas were: financial oversight and budgeting; staff management and HR; working with parents and dealing with complaints; embedding school culture; and school improvement. These survey findings have been reinforced so often by anecdote. My argument was that the issues associated more closely with classrooms and educating pupils did not need to feature as much as at earlier stages of training. Almost all headteachers and most CEOs have been teachers and should have been trained on oversight of behaviour, curriculum development and assessment.

The so-called golden thread, although fairly popular with the profession, through all layers of training was being overdone. The repetition was at the expense of those areas new to teachers: organisational management, strategy development and partnership working. It seems obvious that these were generally gaps in prospective senior leaders' knowledge and experience and needed more time. The minister for schools Nick Gibb MP was very wedded to the golden thread. One of his special advisers sat in the room with the advisory group reviewing the HT standards and occasionally let it be known what the minister would and wouldn't support. Having been involved in this sort of capacity in a number of government departments for 30 years, I understood how special advisers worked, but this seemed rather more blatant than usual. Perhaps because of Nick Gibb's long tenure, his views and way of working had infiltrated. The advisory group claimed to be using evidence, but rarely have I seen evidence so evidently pushed to the periphery.

While I was pleased to be involved in the review of the HT standards, I wasn't completely convinced that they provide much value in addition to a job description. Their stated aims are to:

- Shape headteachers' own practice and professional development, within and beyond the school.
- Support the recruitment and appointment of headteachers.
- Provide a framework for training middle and senior leaders aspiring to headship.
- Inform the performance management of headteachers. (DfE, 2020)

The education sector does seem to love a framework and they didn't seem harmful. I was pleased that the standards graphic ended up with ethics in the centre and governance wrapped around the other domains (see Figure 3.5). But, rather more importantly, what effect have they had?

Governance and accountability was also one of the 10 elements in the frameworks of the NPQs published at the same time, although sadly their 'learn that' elements remained the same throughout the suite and were not at all ambitious. I was told not to worry about that as the programme delivery agents would add the substance. It's now five years later and, other than a review by Ofsted, we have still yet to see whether these latest versions will translate into better knowledge in the sector's leaders. There is a lack of transparency generally about the curricula of the programmes and not much quality assurance of the contracts evident. There has been a significant amount of funding attached, albeit scaled back considerably in 2024–25.

In 2025 the Labour government is conducting a review of NPQs to ensure that they are 'fit for purpose', which is likely to take 18 months. I was pleased to see its scope emphasises four issues, of which two very much chime with my earlier critique: 'Ensuring that areas that are repeated across the different NPQ frameworks genuinely support progression through different levels of leadership' and 'Best practice, particularly at executive leadership level, in operational aspects of leadership, such as how to manage a budget and deploy a workforce effectively'. We shall see what comes of this in the future.

Conclusion

Governance is an intrinsic part of leadership as the literature across sectors and countries makes clear: that is axiomatic. Governance, whether of an individual school or a MAT, should work as a partnership between the governance volunteers and the executive leaders, with mutual respect, trust and understanding of each other's roles and neither party dominating. Many factors affect the power balance at any one time, some systemic, some cultural, some behavioural, and some due to individuals' attributes and the organisation's context.

If this partnership is not working in any institution, it should be talked about, first perhaps between the lead executive and the chair, and if not resolved, then with the whole board. Being part of the same team with the same mission working with the same values is hugely uniting. The answer to 'whose side are you on?' should always be the children educated by the school or the trust. You have all signed up to the same thing, albeit in different roles.

At the same time as being a leadership partner, the governing board is the first line of accountability for the leaders of institutions and the institution itself. The board should be seen as a protection for the organisation and its mission by the executive leader; insurance against failure and an engine for success. The board must also recognise the duty of care that's owed to their leadership teams and the whole staff. Everyone involved needs to accept this and play their part in creating the culture and climate in which engagement, openness, learning and accountability will flourish. A spirit of support, challenge and development needs to be fostered. This is not often easy, and there is a need to invest in governance knowledge, time and above all else the relationships. This does not mean just the volunteers, but also the executive leadership. School leaders and executives who embrace governance understand that it does not distract them from the young people but concentrates minds on providing the best education possible.

Part B:
The recent history

5.
Where have we come from?

Governing boards are a longstanding accountability structure within the education sector. School governance has a rich history going back centuries when the first schools were set up by benefactors. The Education Acts of 1944 and 1968 provided for the existence of 'school governing bodies' in the case of secondary schools and 'managing bodies' that were designed to play a substantial role in giving each school identity and purpose in managing its affairs. However, what happened as a result didn't become substantial for a very long time.

I shall begin with James Callaghan's famous education speech at Ruskin College in 1976, very nearly half a century ago. This speech is usually presented as setting up the 'great debate' about the purposes of education and is still often referred to in current debates on core knowledge and vocational and academic routes. When I read the speech, I was surprised how much of it was setting out the need for public accountability. Callaghan makes a strong case for the right of the public to have a view on education: 'There is nothing wrong with non-educationalists, even a prime minister, talking about it again. Everyone is allowed to put his oar in on how to overcome our economic problems, how to put the balance of payments right, how to secure more exports and so on and so on. Very important too. But I venture to say not as important in the long run as preparing future generations for life. … There will be discussion. But let it be rational. If everything is reduced to such phrases as "educational freedom" versus state control, we shall get nowhere.'

This speech came at a time when the extent of professional autonomy was being questioned in a number of sectors, and Callaghan was reacting to the concern that education and particularly the curriculum had become a 'secret garden'. There are possibly still some educationalists all these years later who may not wholeheartedly accept Callaghan's view of this being a legitimate arena for the public. At the time, it set the scene for the restructuring of the governance of education.

The Taylor Committee had been set up the year before by Rt Hon. Shirley Williams MP, then Secretary of State for Education and Science, along with the Secretary of State for Wales. Its report *A New Partnership for Our Schools* published in 1977 tried to maintain the existing partnership between local and central government and the school, while making the governing body more representative of all those with an interest in the school. It proposed changes in the composition of governing bodies but made relatively few new points about their role. The relative power of the local education authority (LEA), the profession and the governing body continued to be hedged about with qualifications both about LEA policies and consulting the profession. For example, take the topic of recruitment of staff. Rather differently from today, the 1945 model articles had envisaged that the appointment of teachers other than the head should be made by governors in consultation with the head, whereas Taylor recommended that 'the selection of deputy heads and other teachers should rest with the governing body, who should give due weight to the professional advice made available through the LEA' (DES, 1977).

In the Education Act 1980, the new Conservative government aimed to end the situation in which governing bodies acted as an offshoot of the LEA and ensured the school was a force for good in the life of the pupils, their families and the community. It also gave parents and teachers representation on the governing bodies, alongside LEA governors and community governors. Parents elected by their fellow parents would be given the right to form the majority of the governing body in the case of a county school or maintained special school and, together with the foundation governors, to form the majority in the case of a voluntary controlled school. But the exact role of the governing body working in cooperation with the LEA was still unclear.

Governing bodies were given the functions of strategic oversight, holding the leaders to account, financial management, staffing decisions and community engagement. The academic literature talks about vague and imprecise phrases in official documents. For example, the 1945 model articles had given governors 'the general direction of the conduct and curriculum of the school', whereas the 1980 Act often replaced 'direction' with the term 'oversight'. Research noted that the governors might mediate between the school and the community, both of which they were knowledgeable about, but they were not truly accountable. The governors were described in 1984 by Brooksbank and Ackstine as 'sandwiched between the head's responsibility for controlling "the internal management and discipline of the school" and the local authority's right "to settle the general educational character of the school"'. Curriculum matters were delegated nominally to governing bodies but it appears in practice to the profession.

Further changes on the balance of power followed that heralded a shift towards more localism and more power for parents in their children's education, sometimes called market accountability. Legislation introduced provisions to allow parents to express school preferences and establish a formal appeal process against school admission decisions. It also allowed for the provision of more information from LEAs and encouraged parents to serve as governors. A Green Paper in 1984, *Parental Influence at School*, and a White Paper, *Better Schools*, the next year formed the basis of the 1986 Education (No. 2) Act, which, among a wide range of issues, broadened membership of governing bodies to include co-opted governors and introduced the four-year term of office we are still familiar with.

Local management of schools

The introduction of local management schools (LMS) in 1988, when governing bodies became responsible for the conduct and direction of schools and overseeing the performance of headteachers, was a much more significant change. LMS, as the name suggested, shifted local authorities to being regulators, only intervening when there were problems, rather than being the bodies 'running' schools. Governing bodies were still accountable to the local authority, but with so much more delegated to governing bodies and then, in turn, to school leaders. LMS was revolutionary in that 90% of schools' budgets were delegated from the local authority to schools.

This may come as a surprise to some; there is an urban myth that responsibilities only increased for governors in more recent years. Actually, the legal role of governing bodies of schools maintained by a local authority has barely changed in the past 37 years. Some national commentators and even some at the DfE never quite understood the full significance of what this had meant – or should have meant – in practice. I would often have to explain to policymakers what maintained governance actually involved, and I don't think I was always believed. The language used even in the last decade was local authority (LA) 'control', and I'm not sure how they thought this was achieved. Did they suppose LA officers attended every governing body meeting to give instructions about what to spend money on and make staffing decisions? Clearly not. That is not to ignore the important role of the LA: to keep a watching brief on maintained schools, and to support, challenge and intervene should the need arise. I will come back to that in chapter 15.

Theory and practice

Going back to our definition of governance, LMS on paper was a considerable shift of power and decision-making from local authorities to governing bodies, giving a large amount of freedom to individual schools. The word 'autonomy' springs to mind. This represents a more devolved system than exists in many other countries today.

The basic responsibilities of governing bodies laid out by the then Department for Education and Science would look familiar to governors – at least of maintained schools – today. It is not so much the law, but the way governance is practised, that has changed considerably over the intervening four decades. The culture and customs of governance initially developed under LMS didn't tend to live up to those legal responsibilities.

The academic literature shows two very different versions of this past period. Some appear to consider it to have been the heyday of school governance when our schools were safe in the hands of elected stakeholders who had the community's interests in their hearts. They compare this with what they consider to be a subsequent takeover by professional types who are only interested in a narrow understanding of the performance of schools and act on behalf of the government. Effectiveness was often defined at the time as promoting the school as a force for good in the life of the pupils, their families and the community, which fitted more with the philosophy of governance by stakeholders.

As part of the web of accountability, governing boards of any decade act within the various parameters set by government and other relevant central bodies. How much space governing boards have to innovate within the frameworks and policies set by government is an important consideration, and is why stressing the generative and strategic mindsets is important. It is a particularly live debate at times of funding constraints. Balancing budgets has never been optional, but having more funding available indisputably makes that responsibility easier to deliver. This characterisation of governing boards who were independent years ago and now simply do the government's bidding is a crude one that needs much unpacking and will appear at other points in this story.

The alternative view, often from school leaders of the time, is that governors – during the initial period after LMS – turned up to have cups of tea and the odd biscuit at meetings and school events to support the school (and sometimes the headteacher) and say well done. Many governors seemed happy to limit their role in this way, or perhaps many did not realise that they were limiting themselves. There were of course other volunteers who were committed to being trained and carrying out the role more fully.

Those two standpoints, on the surface diametrically opposed, have some common ground in a reluctance to believe that 'lay people' (as volunteers were often termed in the literature of the time) would actually have the wherewithal to govern well. On one hand, there was the view raised in chapter 4 held by some leaders that only educational professionals could have the knowledge to make the correct decisions. And on the other, those coming at this purely from a theoretical perspective with a purely democratic lens were reassured that the local authority with its elected councillors was the real power.

Both groups understood the arrangement as notionally satisfying the democratic dimension of accountability, rather than having an understanding of – and buying into – the need for institutional governance in its own right. This was bound to lead to a confused general understanding of what constituted governing a school well. Luckily, there was a period of about 15 years when a considerable number of studies looked at this question of what governing bodies were actually doing and what decision-making they were engaged in post LMS.

Governing in the nineties

Several empirical studies of governing bodies built up a consistent picture: in practice, governing bodies tended to be more supportive of headteachers than challenging. Even a decade after LMS, research was making it clear that the contribution of governing bodies was largely contained by what the headteacher was prepared to allow, in part driven by the profession's concern of having 'lay' people in their domain. The job of headteachers also changed considerably, and there was much that they needed to be doing more of and differently. The work with governing bodies was sometimes described as 'a burden'. Although there was work in preparing papers for meetings, there was still support from local authorities in terms of the processes required.

Although the local authorities in most cases remained the employer of staff, the governing bodies – and their headteachers – were able to take the human resources and budget decisions necessary to lead and manage an organisation. An analysis of the empirical studies by Professor Peter Earley

(2003) concluded that 'governing bodies are more or less at the mercy of the headteacher and other senior managers' and that 'even when lay governors have opinions they wish to express, it seems that they face great difficulty in making their "voice" heard, let alone in having their views taken seriously'. In practice, the head's position had been considerably strengthened by LMS.

Earley also reported that: 'Headteachers and senior staff value a range of governing body roles: a critical and informed sounding board; a support for the school; a help breaking down headteacher isolation; a link with parents and the community; a provider of direction and vision for the school in partnership with the staff; a forum in which teachers could explain their work; and a provider of non-educational expertise and experience.'

A survey of members of the Secondary Headteachers' Association coupled with case studies published by Dingle in 2000 found that senior staff were influenced by governors both in their day-to-day operation and in their thinking.

The difficulty of recruiting volunteers has been mentioned in research over the decades, and in 1999, SGOSS – then School Governors One Stop Shop, now Governors for Schools – was set up with government funding to recruit volunteers from business, so this was already very much part of the discourse.

Governing at the beginning of the 21st century

Regulations in 2000 specified the strategic responsibility of the governing body and contrasted this aspect of their responsibilities with those of the headteacher as follows:

'The governing body shall exercise their functions with a view to fulfilling a largely strategic role in the running of the school.

(2) The governing body shall establish a strategic framework for the school by

(a) setting aims and objectives for the school;

(b) setting policies for achieving those aims and objectives;

(c) setting targets for achieving those aims and objectives.

And the head teacher shall be responsible for the internal organisation, management and control of the school, and the implementation of the strategic framework established by the governing body.'

I quote it to underline the similarities with today. This level of clarity still did not result in culture or practice focused on meeting these objectives. The stakeholder constitution, which ensured parents, staff, people from the community and others nominated by the local authority governed, may have contributed to the confusion about the role of the governing body; perhaps it felt more like a stakeholder forum than a decision-making body with power and responsibilities.

This role was spelled out further the following year by Derek Twigg, then the Labour Parliamentary Under Secretary of State for Schools, in DfES's *Governing the School of the Future* (2004): 'The role of the governing body has changed beyond recognition over the past twenty years. With the introduction of local management of schools and further reforms, governing bodies have become the strategic leaders of schools. They are rightly responsible and accountable in law and in practice for major decisions about the school and its future. Governing bodies are equal partners in leadership with the head teacher and senior management team. We want to see them taking a full part in driving the improvement and culture of the school.'

Twigg also wrote that the aim was to 'make it easier for governing bodies to play their key role in accountability, a role that includes responsibility for the school's performance management policy and for managing the headteacher's performance'.

With the exception of the extended schools programme, much of the government rhetoric and guidance would still be familiar to today's governors and trustees: the aim was described as more flexibility for innovation, increasing collaboration with schools and with other partners, and a more intelligent accountability system with less red tape. There was also a promise of three-year budgets, which would be extremely helpful to achieve, but have yet to materialise a quarter of a century later.

Governing the School of the Future also provided the reminder to remain strategic and focused on school improvement: 'In all they do, governing bodies need to focus on their strategic role and on how they can support the school to raise standards. We know that governing bodies do a good job: the Ofsted report *"The Work of School Governors"* indicates that the quality of school governance has been improving at a time when governing bodies have taken on more responsibilities, such as the performance management of headteachers. The same report indicated that 90% of schools have governing bodies that are satisfactory or better in fulfilling their responsibilities, and that about 60% of governing bodies were graded good to excellent.'

Developing the board's leadership role

Insight into how this strategic role was put into practice can also be gleaned from the academic literature. Much of the research demonstrated a clear gap between the desired state provided by the rhetoric and the practice on the ground, and it also highlighted the considerable variation among governing bodies and the way they worked.

There were some consistent conclusions. First, the finding that governors rarely took up the role of challenging the headteacher or changing headteachers' decisions continued to be largely confirmed. Second, there were few references made to operating strategically or sharing leadership with the head; rather the head most often persuaded governors to accept their proposals. A significant study by Ranson et al. (2005b) concluded that most governing bodies could be characterised as deliberative, consultative, reactive and unable to question the authority of the headteacher. In another study by Ranson et al. (2005a), one third of headteachers (35%) thought that their governing body played a 'minor role' or 'no role at all' in the strategic leadership of their school, and only 22% of heads agreed that governing bodies should play a major role in the strategic.

It was suggested that governors felt more comfortable giving support and offering advice than they did in helping to decide the school's strategy and direction. For example, a survey of governors by Punter, Adams and Lang in 2003 recruited from the business community by SGOSS found that a majority (71%) felt that supporting the headteacher was one of the things they found particularly satisfying in governance, as well as being invited to use their skills (71%) and being welcomed by the headteacher (84%) and fellow governors (70%). Headteachers commented that these governors from a business background have 'the ability and confidence to ask challenging questions' and that they 'listen to ideas in a non-threatening way and hold things together'. As every survey of governance volunteers has ever shown, their principal motivation was that of 'putting something back in the community' or 'making a contribution'.

By comparison, change was afoot in governance in further education, with governors maintaining a certain distance from the principal of the college and aiming to operate at an appropriately strategic level. For example, PWC in 2007 found that 'the importance of good governance as a source of support and challenge for leaders was mentioned by several stakeholder interviewees in relation to the further and higher education sectors'.

Third, governing bodies were rarely involved in shaping school strategies, although chairs of governing bodies, who tend to work more closely with headteachers, may have been involved informally as a sounding board. When the University of Hertfordshire asked governors about the roles they adopted, being a 'strategist' scored the lowest of nine given roles and only 35% of respondents placed value on that role. It was suggested that the lack of involvement in strategy was because governors tended to focus on their areas of specialism, such as finance and accounting, and then take on more specific tasks. The use of committees with specific responsibilities may have strengthened this tendency.

A minority of governing bodies were found to be in executive board mode where there was a division of labour with the headteacher. Governors had 'overall responsibility for the business aspects of the school: the budget, staffing, and the infrastructure of the building', and headteachers assumed 'overall responsibility for curricular and pedagogic aspects of the school'. In this case, 'there is likely to be a strong structure of subcommittees with considerable delegation of responsibility' (Ranson, 2011). This fits with the concept that many educationalists subscribed to at the time that headteachers are just that – the chief teacher – and not organisational managers. The training teachers received was not preparing them for these management roles. In effect, governing bodies were stepping into the gap and undertaking the functions of administrators or even business managers, remembering that at this time, especially for primary schools, business managers were not ubiquitous. Much work had to be done to convince smaller schools to invest in a part-time or shared post.

In 2003, Professor Peter Earley stated, 'There was a view expressed by some training provider interviewees that many governing bodies were ineffective as "strategic leaders" and became over-involved in the detailed running of individual schools. LEA respondents, too, generally did not consider governors to be effective in terms of their role in helping to raise standards or improve schools – only about one in eight rated them as effective.'

Headteachers viewed effective governing bodies as those that: communicate well; are supportive of the head; take a pragmatic approach; and demonstrate commitment to the role with an active chair. In one study by PWC in 2007, one fifth (21%) of the participating headteachers described their governing body as quite or very ineffective. In the same study, secondary heads (68%) were slightly more likely than primary heads (63%) to state that their governing body was quite or very effective. For those heads who described their governing bodies as ineffective, the main reasons given were inexperience, insufficient skills and knowledge, and a low level of practical assistance. Governors wanted more training in order to better support school leaders. Headteachers generally found governing bodies to be supportive, but with caveats sometimes about governors not having the 'experience, information, time or commitment to support the school fully'.

The fourth common finding was that headteachers had a limited understanding of governance and the role of the governing body. Many, however, welcomed governors and did want them to play a leadership role, but we are back to the lack of clarity as to what they meant by that. The relationship with the headteacher was rightly considered as fundamental, and in the main governors were reported as welcoming better and closer working relationships with their headteachers. Despite the deficits on both sides, research by Earley et al. in 2002 commissioned for DfES showed 'the clear value of effective governing bodies, especially chairs of governing bodies, when the relationship between headteachers and governing bodies is successful'.

Ofsted and governing bodies

The Office for Standards in Education (Ofsted) was created by the Education (Schools) Act 1992 in a bid to secure school improvement and enable parents to make informed choices about their children's education. This was another element of central government's move to increasing accountability to compensate for the increased autonomy granted by LMS.

In 2001, Ofsted set out the central responsibilities of governing bodies as strategic direction, critical friendship and accountability. Ofsted also stated that governing bodies should establish 'a strategic framework for leadership development', champion 'continuous professional development for all school staff', and 'make creative use of resources'.

Its unpublished report the following year, *The Work of School Governors*, stated that governors in about 90% of schools have a satisfactory or better understanding of the strengths and weaknesses of their school, but they are less effective in shaping the direction of the school. Where governors did contribute well, this was often through their involvement in the development of the school improvement plan, whereas those who did not 'often have little knowledge of the school's main development priorities, agree plans and policies unquestioningly, and rely too much on the headteacher as the source of their information about the school'. Ofsted reported that governors who had a good understanding of the school gathered information from a range of sources; as well as headteacher's reports, they visited the school, received data analysis and had presentations from other senior managers and subject coordinators.

Ofsted reported that a common failure of governors was meeting statutory requirements (more commonly for secondary than primary schools). This was most frequently in relation to the act of collective worship in secondary schools and to aspects of the national curriculum, as well as health and safety issues and sending the annual report to parents.

This internal Ofsted report drew together evidence from inspections, reports and visits to schools in 1999–2001 and found the following:

- Where governance was good, standards of attainment were likely to be higher than in other schools. The behaviour of pupils, the quality of teaching and the leadership and management of schools were also more likely to be good.

- Where leadership and management was good but governance weak, this failure was due to a number of factors including governors not being well informed about the day-to-day running of the school, overdependency on the headteacher to provide information on how the school is performing, failure to meet one of its statutory requirements (such as lack of strategic management and forward planning) and/ or a lack of training with the governing body being unaware of its responsibilities.

- Governors in areas of socioeconomic advantage, measured in terms of the proportion of pupils taking up free school meals (FSMs), were effective more often than other schools. Overall the quality of governance was found to decline as the proportion of pupils with FSMs rose. Schools in inner-city areas in particular had difficulty in recruiting the full number of governors (vacancy rates in these areas were 30% compared to the national rate of 5–10%).

- Grammar schools were found to have the highest levels of effective governors. Over three quarters of these schools were found to have good or better governance, and none had unsatisfactory governance.

- Schools put into special measures often had governing bodies not fulfilling their responsibilities. They were supportive and gave enormous amounts of time, but were not offering any real challenge.

There were also a number of exceptions to the findings above; good governance alone does not guarantee that a school is successful. There were, and of course still are, other factors that interact to make some schools more effective than others. Schools in advantaged areas, for example, generally had less difficulty in recruiting teachers. Then, like now, pupils in these schools were likely to have more access to educational resources at home, and parents of pupils in these areas were more likely to provide additional opportunities for their children.

The Ofsted Inspection Framework in 2003, rather than seeking to ensure the governing bodies' legal responsibilities were understood and performed well, reinforced the custom and practice that had developed by describing the governance role in terms of:

- Contribution to the school self-evaluation.
- Supporting and challenging school management teams.
- A leadership partnership between the governing body and the headteacher and senior managers.

The Ofsted 2007 annual report summarised evidence from nearly 7000 inspections conducted in 2006 and concluded that the majority of schools' governing bodies carry out their duties well.

Twenty years of LMS

There were a number of reports published in 2007 and 2008 that give us some idea of how the self-management of schools was progressing. They noted the considerable investment in developing the leadership and management capacity and expertise of headteachers and other senior staff in schools, which had not been seen on the governance side. The state of school governance was often now being assessed through the views of those volunteering.

A small-scale study by Dean et al. in 2007 of 14 schools in three disadvantaged areas is typical of the conclusions being drawn: as well as finding once again that many governors found it difficult to challenge the headteacher with some simply offering uncritical support, governors also often did not feel able to challenge decisions made by local authorities. Although most governors preferred to work collaboratively with headteachers for common goals, some reported that headteachers limited their access to information to minimise the opportunities for effective challenge. Researchers noted that in schools stuck on a plateau of performance, questioning was either weak or absent.

In some cases, the governing body was perceived as a vehicle for scrutiny only in terms of financial management. Governors did however have a strong sense of acting in the interests of the school and their pupils. Their support for the headteacher was therefore conditional on the head also acting with regard to this 'common interest'.

Another study by James et al. in 2011 considered governing bodies under pressure and compared schools in richer and poorer areas. The more affluent school governing bodies under less short-term pressure tended to include medium- and long-term planning as part of their role as well as representing community and parental interests and financial management. They had higher levels of participation in induction and mentoring of new governors; governors from different stakeholder categories were more likely to work well side by side; attendance was more likely to be good; and governors were more likely to feel able to speak their minds. Yet the researchers observed high-quality governance in both low and high socioeconomic settings, so they concluded that the quality of school governing and socioeconomic context did not appear to be direct and causal.

No significant difference between the functioning of governing bodies of high-attainment schools and those with low attainment was found. It was recognised by governing bodies of the former that if 'the school is doing well already … it would be easy to sit back and be complacent'. Headteachers often understood, as one participant put it, that 'there's not enough questioning of what I say or do'. Another headteacher felt that in the past 'the governors trusted the school [that is, the headteacher] too much; they could have asked more searching and critical questions'. Another felt the school's governing body could be stronger: 'They are all very nice people but they don't challenge me enough.'

Business in the Community published *Governing Our Schools,* alongside a research report of the same name by University of Bath, which characterised school governing as 'overloaded, overcomplicated and overlooked' (Balarin et al., 2008). In his foreword, Barry O'Brien, a partner at Freshfields Bruckhaus Deringer LLP and a school governor, says: 'I am particularly pleased that the study makes clear that school governors already make a substantial and high quality contribution to the work of schools. Any changes therefore will be built on extensive existing good practice. Many of their responsibilities could be assigned directly to the headteacher. Governing bodies have a high workload and strategic management, scrutiny and other responsibilities. Governing bodies' extensive responsibilities may prevent them discussing the kind of school we want.'

The report compared and contrasted effective and ineffective governing bodies, and concluded these aspects needed to be in place so the governing bodies can work well:

- Clarity of understanding of role and responsibilities.
- A shared common vision.
- The provision of good-quality relevant information to the governing body.
- An effective chair.
- Governors are able to speak their minds.

The research also reported governors generally frustrated at the extent to which operational matters crowded out strategic considerations; this is a bit of a progress from the previous decade in that the role was now at least recognised as a strategic one.

In Ofsted's 2010/11 Annual Report, Miriam Rosen, the chief inspector, said that 'inspections identified considerable variations in the quality of governance across different types of school'. Governance was judged good or outstanding in 58% of schools inspected this year overall, but this varied between 53% in pupil referral units and 55% in primary schools, to 64% in secondary schools and 71% in special schools.

Impact of governance

The first major national research on the contribution of governance to school improvement based on primary empirical study was undertaken by Scanlon, Earley and Evans in 1999 and found a strong association between inspection assessments of a school's effectiveness and the assessments of its governing body. A study undertaken by Ofsted a couple of years later also argued that where governance is good, standards of attainment are more likely to be higher than in other schools. Research by Balarin et al. in 2008 concluded that 'generally school governing functions well, can be very resilient at times of acute stress for a school, and can have a positive impact on school quality', and an overview of research by the Department of Children, Schools and Families (DCSF) that same year concluded that governing bodies do make an indispensable contribution to school effectiveness and school life.

Different structures

Voluntary aided (VA) and voluntary controlled (VC) schools were established as part of the Education Act 1944 to allow existing church schools to retain their religious character while receiving state funding. By 1988 when the school sector was further reformed, there were approximately 4600 VA and 4000 VC schools being maintained by local authorities in England. VC schools were largely Church of England primary schools, whereas VA schools were split between Roman Catholic and Church of England with other religions very much a minority. In 2008, we know approximately 22% of primary schools and 17% of secondary schools were voluntary aided, including all Roman Catholic schools, and in 2010 the numbers were very similar with 700 of the VA schools secondaries.

VA schools, which are both the employer of staff and the admissions authority, give more power to the foundation with a majority of foundation governors on their governing body and less to the local authority. VC schools have some foundation governors, a minority on the governing body and less autonomy from the local authority. Although the school's land and buildings are often owned by the founding organisation, usually the Church of England, the local authority is responsible for maintenance and funding. The local authority manages the admissions process and is the employer of staff for VC schools.

The foundations tend to be charities with their own trustees, but in practice the power broker is usually referred to as the diocese. In Roman Catholic schools, the bishop makes some decisions that foundation governors are expected to follow, one of which is to disallow formal partnerships with schools of other religious authorities. Generally, the sector does not talk enough about the power of the churches and the role of the dioceses, and I have fallen into that trap too in this book. This is perhaps partly because it is a bit of a secret garden and difficult to influence, especially the Roman Catholics. Even as a previous foundation governor of a VA school, I was still frequently treated with suspicion. The DfE also tends to leave the churches be, the power being too great even for the Education Secretary!

City technology colleges (CTCs) were a new type of state-funded secondary school introduced by Kenneth Baker as Education Secretary in the Education Reform Act of 1988. The primary aim of CTCs was to provide high-quality technical education to students aged 11 to 18, although they followed the national curriculum, and the BRIT school, which still exists, specialised in performing arts. CTCs were particularly targeted at disadvantaged areas of cities, but were independent of local authorities, some of whom did not prioritise finding city sites for them. The majority of their governing body was filled with representatives of the sponsor – usually a business or voluntary group – and the school had control over staffing and admission decisions. CTCs represented a very small share of secondary schools and nearly all have now converted to academies.

Grant-maintained status for schools was also introduced under the Education Reform Act 1988, which removed the remit of local government and made them directly accountable to central government. Ten years later there were almost 1200 grant-maintained schools, accounting for about 19% of secondary schools, 3% of primary schools and 2% of special schools in England. The Labour government under Tony Blair abolished grant-maintained schools, and instead introduced 'foundation status' in the School Standards and Framework Act 1998. This was a compromise where the schools were formally maintained by their local authority but the governing body was given more control than other maintained schools. Schools that had been grant-maintained were given the option to transition to other statuses, many becoming foundation schools to retain some autonomy.

Foundation schools had greater autonomy from the local authority compared to community and VC schools and from their foundation than VA schools. Foundation schools have a more balanced governance model than VA schools as their foundation governors do not need to outnumber other governors. Foundation schools often own their land and buildings, whereas VA school buildings are generally owned by the religious authority. Like VA schools, foundation schools set their own admissions policies and employ staff.

The Labour government then in effect rebranded one type of foundation school as trusts (but not academy trusts), but there were no incentives offered, or pressure exerted, to encourage schools to become trust schools, so there was very little uptake. All in all, in 2010 there were 1464 foundation schools in England and that included about 200 trust schools.

Labour's academies

The sponsored academy programme was introduced by the Labour government in 2000 to replace severely underperforming secondary schools in disadvantaged areas, and the first eight academies were opened in September 2002. This programme built on the success of the CTC model and was driven in quite large part by Andrew Adonis, first as education adviser to Tony Blair at No. 10 and then as a schools minister in the Lords. Adonis describes in his book *Education, Education, Education* the power he acquired by taking action and how he indulged in micromanagement.

Adonis insists the change in governance was key: 'Governance can seem tedious and irrelevant to the work of schools. Educationalists often think so and it almost never features in their discourse. But without strong and effective governance an institution rarely performs well, whether a school, a company, a charity or a government. This is a central insight of the academy movement: that governance matters fundamentally.'

I find it fascinating how strong this statement is, when there is then a lack of consideration of the governance structures he was setting up and what seems to be a misunderstanding of the structure that they landed on as a vehicle for academies.

That change of governance was to make academies both trusts and companies limited by guarantee, as I will cover in more detail in the next few chapters. That is not how it is described by Adonis, who does not use the word 'trustee' at all, but continues with the language of governors. When he discusses chains, he fails to distinguish between the role of board of trustees and local governors of individual academies. He wrote twice: 'there are no statues to committees'. Yet boards of trustees are very like committees in that they are a group with responsibility, whereas Adonis very much sang the praises of individuals who had a successful business career. That's a different model and a different philosophy of governance. Adonis disparaged the collective decision-making of 'committees' while setting up an organisational structure with such a 'committee' at the top.

Adonis explains that the independence of academies was essential to their success. By that he meant governors and headteachers 'need to be unambiguously in control of their schools without managerial interference from local or national bureaucracies'. But that independence from local authorities he believed had to categorically, without exception, go hand in hand with sponsorship. So actually the independence and the power was vested 'into the hands of a managing sponsor with control of the school, subject to a contract with the Education Department'. Adonis expected the sponsor to ensure the governing body is effective through appointing competent professionals and either chairing the board himself (I don't think I have to say 'or herself' as I can't remember an original female sponsor) or appointing an external chair. This has left us with the role of trust membership, which has caused a lot of confusion and questioning over the years. I will come back to this in chapter 15.

The formation of charitable trusts seems to be by the by; simply the vehicle chosen to achieve this independence and sponsor involvement. Adonis says nothing about this decision, which I find extraordinary. I have tried to meet up with him a couple of times to check this but with no luck. Any consideration and debate about governance and the move to trusteeship was missing in the design phase of the academy system by the Labour government. Perhaps the government's mantra of 'standards, not structures' made them reluctant to think about governance models.

Adonis makes it very clear that they wanted a change of mindset and culture, which he clearly didn't think would be possible while a school was maintained by the local authority. This was underlined by Prime Minister Tony Blair in the foreword to the 2005 White Paper *Higher Standards*: 'What is important to these schools is their ethos, their sense of purpose, the strength of their leaders, teachers and support staff, the motivation of their parents and pupils. And much of that comes from the can-do attitude of their principals and staff, and the drive that their business and educational sponsors bring to their development – backed by their willingness to innovate and use their freedoms imaginatively' (DfES, 2005).

While we know how important those with power, including the governing board, are in setting the ethos and culture, the connection between legal structure and leadership mindset has never been tested in the move to academies. That gap in our knowledge might not have been crucial when academies were a very small part of the education system, but it is frustrating now that it's the majority structure in the system.

Many of the first wave of academies were subsequently successful in turning round very poor schools and providing children with qualifications where their predecessors had left school with little. This often led to a change in the intake of pupils, but even when controlled for parental income, pupil attainment had improved. Some trusts became chains – or as we now call them, MATs – and I come back to those in chapter 6.

In 2006–2007, the academy movement became embroiled in the 'cash-for-honours' scandal, with allegations of wealthy businesspeople who 'sponsored' academies being rewarded with knighthoods. As well as a different way of thinking and working, another of the original purposes of sponsorship was to bring money into the state school system, initially £2 million per academy. In fact, many of those original sponsors did not pay up in full, and the expectation to give funds was subsequently quietly dropped. Although a few successful sponsors do donate, New Labour has turned out to be wrong on this – support from philanthropists and businesses was not a successful revolution.

Increasingly, the successful academies were being set up by educational institutions or charities, rather than business people. This was seen to be a more scalable approach, leading to a shift in emphasis under Gordon Brown's premiership with a wider variety of sponsors, including faith institutions and universities. By the time Labour left office there were 203 academies, all secondaries or all-through schools.

Federations

In 2002, the Labour government introduced legislation to allow for two types of federations, each a group of schools maintained by local authorities. The first was overseen by a single governing body, while in the second, each school retained its own governing body, but established a joint committee tasked with overseeing shared responsibilities and making decisions in specific areas of collaboration. As well as agreed delegation to the joint governance committee, the schools were expected to formalise their collaboration through an agreement containing its scope. Sometimes the former were referred to as 'hard' federations as opposed to 'soft' federations, but 'soft' ended up encapsulating a whole range of collaboratives. Not distinguishing properly between the three structures was deeply unhelpful as it impeded the sector's understanding of the real difference brought about by federating under one governing body: that the schools became in effect one organisation with a range of advantages.

Some very respected consultants muddied the waters for several years talking about federations – and then MATs – at the end of a continuum of collaboratives, coining the term 'deep partnerships'. There are indeed partnerships that are deeper than others, but a school collaborative or partnership is about different independent organisations coming together for a common aim: each of those individual schools can decide to disengage. That is fundamentally different from a single organisation – federations or MATs – governed by one board. This is not just being a pedant about language. They are different creatures, and because that continuum didn't acknowledge this, it confused the system about lines of accountability and governance for some time. I remember a very distinguished headteacher, a knight of the realm, who was understandably furious with an unexpected decision to remove him as the executive headteacher of a second school that he'd been improving for a couple of years; it turned out this could be done incredibly easily as it was not a federation at all, but an informal collaborative arrangement.

Federations with a shared governing body did not catch on in big numbers in most parts of the country. It was clear that schools were potentially giving up some freedom, their governors were giving up their power and parents felt that they lost out with an executive head leading more than one school, rather than a headteacher entirely dedicated to their school. Federations tended to be small with a couple of usually local primary schools coming together under one governing body, and almost always the individual schools gave up their own individual governing bodies. Many of the original governors might have ended up on the joint governing body, but even though their constitution ended up with larger boards, there wouldn't be room for all.

Federation was generally used in time of crisis when there was no perceived alternative, primarily when a school was unable to recruit a headteacher, in special measures or so small that financial sustainability was a concern. There was no big push from central government for schools to federate, although some local authorities did promote the option, even for successful schools. The percentage of federations therefore was greater in some parts of the county, such as the South West, compared with other rural counties in the North, largely due to the level of information and support provided by local authorities.

In 2007, the DfES published with PWC *Independent Study into School Leadership*, and it considered federated models of all varieties. It showed federated models to have a number of key benefits that ultimately impact positively on pupil performance, which included: greater leadership capacity; improved development and progression opportunities for the school workforce; a broader curriculum and extracurricular activities; smoother transitions of pupils between phases; shared resources from staff expertise to facilities; and economies of scale.

The support for smaller schools allowed them to remain viable by sharing administrative and operational costs. Federations with a single governing body across all the schools tended to show stronger improvements in leadership, learning outcomes and resource allocation due to clearer accountability, more streamlined decision-making by the governing body, and a single headteacher or leadership team providing consistent strategic direction and fostering collaboration. There were suggestions, including from headteachers as well as local authorities, that this model should be used more, and this was repeated in a DCSF report in 2010. Small rural schools welcomed the protection and that the number of governors was more realistic given the size of their communities. It was suggested that federations would suit the future with more executive headteachers supporting more than one school.

Public service reform

These governance changes were carried out as part of a wider programme of reforming public services and how they were held to account. The Conservative government in the 1980s had a particular focus on increasing parental involvement, including the introduction of a quasi-market. At the same time the practice of measuring performance had been an increasingly important feature of public services; this had required the introduction of national testing of pupils.

This approach was built on by the subsequent Labour government, which expressed its intention to move from a basic and standard public service for all to one that fitted the needs of the individual. At Stockwell Park School in 2002 Prime Minister Tony Blair said this approach required schools to be responsive to individual pupils' needs. In *Governing the School of the Future*, school governing bodies were invited 'to join a national conversation about how personalised learning can be used to drive success in every school' (DfES, 2004). A promise to make public services more accountable to parents led to a greater focus on performance targets, school inspections and intervention in underperforming schools.

By 2003, a parliamentary committee report – *On Target?: Government by Measurement* – recommended, among a number of things, 'ensuring greater local autonomy to construct more meaningful and relevant targets, and making sure they are as few as possible, and focus on key outcomes'. This was particularly pertinent as the government has recently advocated a 'new localism', which aimed to strike a balance between central control and more local autonomy and accountability.

A 2008 Cabinet Office White Paper *Excellence and Fairness: Achieving World Class Public Services* outlined a vision of self-improving systems, a phrase that has become embedded in the school sector. The aim was to reduce reliance on central direction and programmes by empowering leaders to innovate and collaborate at local levels. It spoke of the need to 'unlock the creativity and ambition of public sector workers' through a 'new professionalism'. There was concern about 'producer capture' where the interests of a public service reflect those of its workforce rather than the people being served.

Parental choice

Parental choice in schools in England was introduced as part of the Education Reform Act 1988 under the Conservative government led by Margaret Thatcher. This legislation aimed to create a quasi-market in education by allowing parents to state their choice of schools for their children, fostering competition among schools to improve standards. It also required schools to publish more information for parents, and introduced appeals for school admission decisions and a complaints procedure.

In the 1990s, Prime Minister John Major emphasised the importance of consumer choice and voice as tools for improving public service quality. The Labour government continued to promote parental choice, for example, by introducing choice advisers, although there was a debate within the party as to whether a good local school should take priority over attempting to create a market. Adonis in fact argued primarily for good local schools.

However, by 2006, there were growing concerns about the relationship between school admissions and social segregation as more advantaged families were better equipped to navigate the system and afford higher house prices, thus benefitting more. A House of Commons education select committee report highlighted that 'fair access' should take precedence over choice and diversity. The report also stressed that schools must recognise their responsibility not only to the students they admit but also to the wider community. It recommended placing a new duty on schools to promote social inclusion and community cohesion through their policies and procedures, particularly admissions.

I will come back to the role parents can play in the shaping of the school system and how they might be able to hold schools to account in chapter 16.

Collaboration and competition

It is often argued that cooperating and competing are not mutually exclusive, but trying to do both at the same time is likely to involve a bit of dancing around each other.

The Labour government attempted to change the framing to encourage schools to collaborate with each other in order to improve and to emphasise the need to create a community of practice with families. This leaves two modes of governance developing in parallel: hierarchical accountability (which encourages competition) and horizontal networks. A number of interschool collaborative arrangements were established, with various degrees of formality and structure and very often in different places.

Conclusion: the system inherited in 2010

The 30 years skated over here were a time of both decentralisation – with power delegated to the governing bodies of schools – and central government increasing its levers of accountability.

The research was invaluable: this chapter could not have been written without the insights from a whole range of academic studies that are missing for more recent times. The bibliography doesn't do justice to the full range of all I read, but I want particularly to acknowledge Professors Ranson, Earley and James who produced with colleagues a large body of work that I have drawn on significantly. As well as providing a foundation of knowledge, it's stimulated lots of thought for which I am deeply grateful. This richness does not exist for the current decade, and this is part of the reason I felt compelled to write this book. I appreciate I am not supplying what they did, but there is a gap to be filled.

LMS was the first revolution in England's school governance. The Education Reform Act 1988 radically transformed the local governance of the school sector with governing bodies delegated powers for budgets and staff as well as responsibility for the strategic direction of the school. It prepared the way by reconstituting governing bodies to ensure all stakeholders were around the table, a model that survived in maintained schools to 2010 and beyond.

The strategic and leadership expectations set by LMS that should be familiar to practitioners today were not generally met in practice, although there was much variability between governing bodies. In the 1990s, the power and decision-making was largely in headteachers' hands, and the value of governing bodies was seen by senior leaders as primarily that of a sounding board and a support for the school in the community. A decade later, practice had matured with both academic and government reviews concluding that most governing bodies carry out their duties well.

Individual schools, albeit in a multiplicity of forms, remained the bedrock of the English education. Federation offering benefits to groups of schools has begun in a small way. The second revolution in governance had begun, which reduced the power of local authorities, transferring it to the governing boards of grant-maintained schools at first and then city technology colleges and academy trusts. The architects believed governance change would be transformational, but because the sponsors – initially from industry – would drive innovation. That the trust structure invented was misunderstood even by its creators and greatest advocates underlines just how much the sector has in the past got governance wrong, often as a result of just not bothering to spend any time thinking and learning about it. It helps explain why there was rather a lot of unnecessary muddle and changing of plans during the next 10 years.

Accountability change without due consideration or full understanding of governance has happened under governments of all colours. There is a chance it might be about to happen again.

6.
What changed in the school system?

Since I joined NGA just before the coalition government came to power, 2010 provides a good starting point for my review of the more recent structural changes to the sector. Those of you who were already part of the English school system will remember these changes that I'm considering through the lens of governance: 'who has the power', 'who makes the decisions' and 'how account is rendered'. Governance was an important consequence of the structural change. Ideally it should have been considered as intrinsic to the change at the time of planning new structures, not subsequently as happened.

As with the setting up of Labour's first academies, the debates at the time were rarely discussed in terms of governance. I have never got to the bottom of whether this was a lack of knowledge or a lack of interest; after all, discussions about structures don't usually incite much passion, and talk of power makes us English folk uncomfortable, a bit like discussing salaries used to. It is also deeply political, and professionals tend to avoid the political sphere, while politicians wouldn't have wanted to emphasise the transfer of power to the central state.

So, instead of a debate about who should have what power and make which decisions, freedom and autonomy were the buzzwords. These terms had been around for some time in school system discourse. For example, Freedom and Autonomy for Schools National Association (FASNA), the predecessor to the Confederation of School Trusts (CST), even had those two words in their name. But they were turbocharged by Michael Gove's arrival as Education Secretary at the renamed DfE.

Giving individual schools more autonomy was central to his vision. The arguments used were all about freedom from the local authority, and freedom on curriculum, staff pay and the length of the school day. If discussion went beyond that headline, freedom and autonomy for headteachers was generally mentioned, rather than the institution's accountable body: the governing board of the trust. The experience of the Innovation Unit under the previous government has been that schools did not appreciate how much freedom they actually had; they often sought permission that they didn't need to make changes.

While it was clear Gove wanted to reduce the power of the local government, the significant move of power and decision-making to the Education Secretary – as the DfE became the direct regulator of more and more schools – was far less well understood. Many also missed that the decision-making powers of academy trusts largely mirrored the responsibilities already seen in voluntary aided schools and foundation schools.

Even if the structural changes were a genuine attempt to devolve as much as possible to school level, there was inconsistency in the government's adherence to this plan. In particular Nick Gibb MP, the minister for schools for much of the 14 years of coalition and Conservative governments, was often keen on dictating policies and even pedagogies to the schools while continuing to talk about school autonomy and freedom for leaders. The misuse of the language of autonomy confused the understanding of responsibilities in the new structures and demonstrated how easily a sector can begin parroting buzzwords when it comes to structure and governance without fully interrogating their meaning and purpose.

Academisation

The Conservative manifesto for the 2010 election included a promise of a significant expansion of the academies, to be achieved by:

- Extending Labour's programme of giving more underperforming schools to a sponsor.
- Allowing good and outstanding schools to convert to academy status.
- Allowing parents and other sponsors to apply to set up new 'free schools'.

Gove set about this with enormous speed when the Academies Act 2010 was rushed through parliament. The 2010 White Paper followed the act in the autumn, a rather unusual order for significant change. It acknowledged that: 'Academies ... have been securing improvements in standards well above the national average, turning around some of the worst-performing secondary schools in the country. Schools which had become sink schools with chronically low aspirations, poor behaviour and a culture of failure are now centres of excellence and engines of social mobility.... Twenty-six per cent of Academies this year were judged to be outstanding by Ofsted, compared to 18 per cent of all maintained schools.'

The National Audit Office (NAO) reported in 2010 that most academies were achieving greater rates of improvement in pupils' attainment than their predecessor schools but warned that performance up to that point could not accurately predict how conversion of many more schools under the new legislation would succeed.

Converter academies

The Academies Act 2010 came into force in time to enable the first converter academies to have undertaken the process by September 2010. It allowed individual schools maintained by the local authority to become an academy if they were rated as 'outstanding'. This was swiftly extended to 'good' schools with 'outstanding' features and the following year to all 'good' schools. It was their school governing bodies' role to decide to become an academy, although of course they took advice from their headteachers, some of whom had strong opinions, one way or another.

Year (Jan)	Sponsored academies	Converter academies	Net increase (sponsored)	Net increase (converter)
2011	271	137	68	137
2012	338	1194	67	1,067
2013	602	2015	264	821
2014	997	1616	395	601
2015	1314	3090	317	474
2016	1555	3540	241	450
2017	1754	4216	199	676
2018	2030	4966	276	750
2019	2248	5630	218	664
2020	2363	6098	115	468
2021	2465	6351	102	253
2022	2515	6641	50	290
2023	2595	7045	80	404
2024	2682	7387	87	342

Table 6.1 This table was provided in response to HL329, a House of Lords written question tabled by Lord Watson of Invergowrie and answered by Baroness Barran on 31 May 2022. The data for 2023 and 2024 was retrieved from other government figures.

The boom time for conversions to single-academy trusts (SATs) was the first three years after the 2010 act. Conversion was more prevalent among secondaries than primaries during that time: for example, 45% of secondary schools were either open or in the pipeline to become academies by January 2012. By April 2013 half of secondaries were academies but only 6% of primary schools, and three years later when a quarter of schools were academies, 19% of primaries were academies compared to 65% of secondaries.

From the beginning, NGA was advising governing bodies on the processes for conversion. We did not advise our members whether they should or should not convert; we wanted them to have all the information they needed so that they could make the right decisions for their school and community. No parent ballot was needed before the governing body came to a decision, which made it easier for schools to leave the local authority family than it had been in the grant-maintained era. During the passage of the bill, NGA had argued unsuccessfully that engagement with parents should come before a decision was made.

NGA's work with maintained schools considering conversion revealed that frustration with their local authority or the quality of the support they received was often the initial reason for embarking on the process. The performance of and the stances taken by the local authority to academies explain in part the very different rates of academisation that occurred in different places. Many, including a significant number of Conservative authorities, made an effort to keep as many of their schools maintained as possible. The NAO reported that the proportion of schools that were academies in different local authority areas in January 2018 ranged from 9% to 93%. This patchwork is still in evidence today, although not quite to that extent, with the highest proportion of academies at the start of the 2023–24 school year in the South West (61%) and the lowest in North West (29%) followed by London at 39%.

Research showed the freedoms were not used to the extent the government expected or wanted. For example, in 2014, trustee respondents to NGA's annual survey reported 46% of academies were making use of pay and conditions freedoms, 29% of curriculum freedom and 24% on length of school day and terms. DfE research provided slightly different figures with 55% saying the curriculum had been changed. Ten years later, TES reported 592 of 625 trusts surveyed still paid in line with national pay scales. Just 12 exceeded pay scales, while others had smaller differences, such as providing additional benefits.

Another argument made by the DfE and other academy advocates was that the mindset was different in academies: more entrepreneurial, more ambitious, with greater moral purpose. Suggesting other school leaders and governors lacked such qualities and were less interested in pupil outcomes was not a good way of winning allies; when it was suggested at one NGA conference in 2013, many maintained school governors understandably took umbrage.

A much more persuasive factor was the additional money academisation brought to the school at the point of conversion. Gove was on record a few times saying funding was a level playing field between academies and maintained schools. The additional element of funding academies received (then called LACSEG – local authority central spend equivalent grant) was to cover services they were not getting from the local authority. The DfE produced a school-specific calculator that made it clear what a school would gain. The DfE argued that academies did better financially because they sourced cheaper contracts, but while there were savings in some places, this was by no means universal or immediate. It was rather more complicated than that. The LACSEG equivalence payment was generous, and there was a rather peculiar period when academies were indeed being paid over the odds, but it was not acknowledged officially. We advised governing bodies that the bonus was not guaranteed to continue, but they were happy to proceed just on the basis of what they could see for the next couple of years. In due course, as local authority funding reduced, so did academies' LACSEG equivalent.

Some conversions were, however, very much driven by charismatic headteachers or those given the less flattering epithet empire builders. While this may have had benefits in a time of spreading best practice across a number of schools, as the government hoped, there was no guarantee that those ambitious heads had what it took to run a larger organisation.

Despite the work that was being done by the National College for School Leadership (NCSL) to develop business leadership, in 2012 NGA, alongside the National Association of School Business Managers, was raising concerns about the competence of the sector to deal with operational change and deliver efficiencies and good human resources. In some primary schools, the lack of the requisite skills or experience within the staff team was masked by governors, misguidedly but almost always with the best of intentions, stepping in on a pro bono basis to undertake management or basic finance work. We pointed out the greater risk with academies for poor financial management and suggested great moderation was required by the DfE, emphasising the need for public accountability.

After a year or more of working alongside the new academies, I amended our purist stance of never advising on whether to convert and began to suggest that small schools (at the time, those with fewer than 200 pupils or smaller than one-form entry primaries) would be better off forming a federation first, or if they were wedded to converting, joining a multi-academy trust. This went against all the advice being given at the time in public, although behind the scenes there was a consensus with our position. I was deeply disappointed that senior executives who appeared on platforms or were invited into the DfE would not repeat that in public or with officials, another example of the deeply compliant nature of some senior leadership.

Free schools

The Conservatives drew much of their inspiration from the charter school movement in the USA, and they also looked to another model: new types of private school in Sweden called 'free schools'. The New Schools Network was founded in 2009 by Rachel Wolf, a former campaign adviser to Conservative mayor of London, Boris Johnson, and education adviser to Michael Gove, the Conservative shadow children's secretary at that time. A mixed school economy will, Wolf said, 'allow new energy to explode into our system and force existing schools to up their game,' giving more choice to parents, including in deprived areas (Wilce, 2009).

During the election campaign, I debated Toby Young on television about whether free schools set up by parents would become a substantive part of the English system. Having recently spent a couple of years setting up an afterschool club employing staff at my children's middle school, I knew just how long that had taken with the support of a voluntary management committee. I argued most parents didn't have time, the inclination nor the professional experience to set up a successful school from scratch. Toby Young thought I was lacking in ambition, and after the election, he wrote in NGA's magazine about looking forward to having 'hundreds of thousands of energetic defenders' and 'mobilising that army in a battle to defend free schools'. Few of the free schools that exist now were set up by parents.

Initially, free schools were set up by a range of organisations, but over time MATs have become the most common instigators of free schools. It is rather ironic that a route designed to stir things up by bringing in new people – not educationalists – to add energy and innovation to the school sector ended up being the route for the more powerful educational professionals to grow their trusts. Research by NFER et al. in 2022 commissioned by the

New Schools Network found that on average free schools 'have gained in popularity relative to their nearest neighbours, which suggests that they have been successful in providing greater school choice'.

As he stepped down from being CEO of the West London Free Schools Trust six years after beginning its first free school, Toby Young admitted to *The Evening Standard*, 'I was very critical of England's public education system under the last Labour government, and I hadn't grasped how difficult it is to do better, and to bring about system-wide improvement.' He added: 'As someone coming into education from the outside, the bits you see of other schools are only the tip of the iceberg. You think, "well, I could do better than that", as you are pointing to the tip of the iceberg, without realising how much more there is to it' (Davis, 2016).

The new Labour government is conducting a review of the 44 pending free school projects having said: 'Under the last administration, substantial funds were allocated to the free schools programme, often resulting in surpluses in school capacity. The National Audit Office set out in 2017 that of the 113,500 new places in mainstream free schools due by 2021, an estimated 57,500 amounted to spare capacity in the new schools' local area. Not only is this poor value for money, the oversupply of places can be detrimental to the other, more established schools in that area – who might lose pupils, as well as teachers, to their new competitor' (Baroness Smith of Malvern, 2024).

Academy sponsorship

As covered in the last chapter, sponsorship was extremely important in the design of Labour's earliest academies, central to changing the thinking in and the control of England's most challenged secondary schools. There are a number of those original philanthropists who remain in the system, such as Harris, Dixon, David Ross and Future Academies, founded by the John Nash who served as government minister for the school system from 2013 to 2017. There were some charitable organisations that got involved early and remain sponsors to this day, most notably Ark and Oasis.

Other sponsors failed – the governance of their trusts clearly not strong enough to prevent this – and their schools generally transferred to successful MATs. In quieter cases, there were no published lessons learned, possibly to save the faces of certain sponsors and some of their heavyweight trustees. As an example: of the first 15 academies, six are still SATs, and of the nine in MATs, six founded them and three had to join a MAT after low performance. Currently two are 'outstanding' and three are 'requires improvement', which is lower performance than the national average, but that is hardly surprising when these are a group that replaced failing schools.

Sponsorship changed after the Academies Act 2010. From that point on, a sponsored academy was one that was forcibly converted to academy status, as opposed to voluntarily converted. Other academies applied to the DfE to be sponsors. The DfE separated the application to be a sponsor from the process of matching with a school that needed sponsorship. This left the system with significant numbers of empty MATs (i.e. one academy waiting for others to join its trust).

It took some time for the DfE to accept that other sponsors were unlikely to be forthcoming. Independent schools were targeted from the beginning to support existing schools or open new state schools. There are a couple of foundations of independent schools – United Learning Trust and Haberdashers' Aske – that sponsored academies early on, with ULT growing to be the biggest MAT with 90 academies at the time of writing. However, independent schools did not consider academy sponsorship their role. Wellington College was an exception, taking over Wellington Academy in 2009. In 2014, it was judged to be requiring improvement and Dr Anthony Seldon, the well-known headmaster of Wellington College, acknowledged that he may have been a bit 'naive' to think it was enough for an independent school just to sponsor a state-school academy and watch it thrive. Dr Seldon then became the executive principal of the Wellington Academy for a short period with a term's sabbatical from the college while rolling up his sleeves at the academy. He claimed by its next inspection in 2016 that the academy would be judged 'outstanding' – possibly more naivety. The academy did achieve 'good' in 2016, but it was by then part of Ascend MAT.

For over a decade, government ministers courted universities to sponsor academies, sometimes very publicly. Most universities turned down the request to sponsor struggling schools, although at its high-point in 2016 there were 71 university-sponsored academies. Research in 2017 confirmed it had been often less prestigious universities who answered the call to sponsor, while others considered investing in academies a financial or reputational risk. A few opened a free school and a few others got involved with a UTC (university technical college). The establishment of UTCs was also enabled by the Academies Act 2010, part of the coalition government's education reforms to provide specialised technical education for students aged 14–19. Many universities preferred the lower-risk option of using their expertise through partnership arrangements with local schools or over a larger area through schemes for disadvantaged pupils.

Their fears turned out to be well-founded: as the decade progressed, university-sponsored trusts did often get into difficulties, sometimes educationally and even more often financially (Camden, 2015). The following year 57% of university-sponsored academies were found by Ofsted to be less than 'good'. Yet at the same time in 2016, Theresa May's government was consulting on 'asking universities to commit to sponsoring or setting up new schools in exchange for the ability to charge higher fees' through *Schools that Work for Everyone*, a proposal that seemed lacking in understanding of the issues and did indeed come to nothing.

A number were disbanded, such as the University of Chester Academies Trust, a MAT which, in its early days, had been allowed to expand. The Education Central MAT sponsored by the University of Wolverhampton ran 13 schools in the West Midlands when it received a damning focused review from Ofsted in 2017. Its chief executive combined the role with that of director of the university's Institute of Education. The secondary schools, none of them rated 'good', were transferred to other MATs, and its 10 primary schools remained together in a reconstituted and renamed trust. In February 2025, it appears from GIAS (Get Information about Schools) that 10 universities remain as sponsors, although some are SATs.

Although sponsorship remains part of the language of academies, it no longer makes much sense. The phrase 'sponsored academy' now denotes a school that had no option but to join a MAT because of its poor performance. The original Labour aim of sponsorship of bringing new resources, knowledge, innovation and entrepreneurship into schools had a very marginal impact.

Continuing to use the phrase 'sponsored academies' for some individual schools within trusts, including on the DfE's GIAS directory, seems inappropriate. If a trust now has a number of good schools, what relevance is it that one or two were underperforming and originally forced to convert a decade or so ago? The label for each school suggests some sort of hierarchy of schools, which is completely not the case. Once a MAT is formed, no additional legal power is provided to any school; they are all governed by the same board of trustees. Local governance might vary between academies but the criteria for that will be laid out.

When MATs were initially being formed from a group of local schools, it was quite usual for those trustees disproportionately, and most probably the initial chief executive, to be drawn from the 'lead' school as the DfE termed the 'good' or 'outstanding' school that applied to be a sponsor and set up a MAT. This lead school concept was reinforced when the MAT was named after that initial high-performing school.

Those trusts where there is another external organisation providing resources will usually have this represented in the legal structures in some way, not just by the sponsor being one of the trust's members and appointing some of the trust's members, but often with the involvement of other structures; a foundation, for example. The most usual external organisation involved in a trust is a diocese, and both the main Christian churches have model articles tailored for them.

Opposition to academies

The anti-academies movement was very active during the coalition government to the extent that Michael Gove devoted a large proportion of a speech in 2012 to dismissing them. Much of that opposition came from the teaching unions, who organised locally to encourage parents to express their opposition during conversion consultations.

The Anti Academies Alliance, with strong links to the teaching unions, supported local campaigns. They argued that the conversion process lacked genuine accountability and transparency, which was likely to be the case if the governing body did not make this an aim. It was not mandated. Criticisms were made about the accountability and transparency of MATs themselves. Campaigners were worried that academy status opened up the public sector to private interests and fractured the local family of schools. A number of financial scandals involving MATs provided some credibility, although the argument that the schools had been 'privatised' should have floundered once it was made clearer that trustees could not profit from their association. I will return to the topic of excessively high pay for executives.

The Local Schools Network was set up by four individuals to celebrate local state schools and to provide counterarguments to the prevailing government ones, as they termed it 'dispelling the myths'. They interrogated the national data in depth, publishing evidence as well as opinion, such as considering the effect of any changes of intake. They thought that comprehensive schools might be under attack, but this did not happen, apart from a short-lived proposal when Theresa May was prime minister. Melissa Benn and Janet Downs set out their case in 2016 book *The Truth About Our Schools*.

In *Schools Week* in 2020, Leora Cruddas, CST's chief executive, argued that the narrative needed wrestling away from organisations like the Anti Academies Alliance, which she described as an influential voice. There is little evidence to show that over the last five years that the public conversation has changed. Some MATs invest in marketing, but the general public still often seem to consider academisation equivalent to corporatisation despite the not-for-profit status of trusts.

Grassroots Labour Party members were generally anti-academy and pro-local-authority as can be seen by the motions passed at their annual conferences. This led most shadow education spokespeople to avoid the topic of structures, especially as parents tended not to care as long as their children's school suited their child.

Schools Week looked at 21 voluntary conversions that sparked Change.org opposition campaigns and found 14 ended up in a trust, of which one improved its Ofsted rating, six remained the same, two got worse ratings and one is waiting for inspection. One school of the remaining seven that didn't convert improved, two received the same rating and four haven't been inspected.

Schools Week also found another 16 Change.org petitions, some with thousands of signatures, against the academisation of failing schools: 'All 12 that went on to become academies were improved by the trust that took them over. Ten were rated "good" at their next inspection, and one "outstanding"'. Similarly, 'the three schools at the centre of protests that did not academise also improved to 'good'' (Dyson, 2025).

The rise of MATs

After that initial rush to convert, there was a slowing down of single academy conversions; in NGA's annual survey in 2012, 15% reported having converted in the previous year, but this was down to 3% in 2016. On the other hand, the number of MATs was rising.

Some MATs, such as Ark, Dixons and Harris, had existed for some time, previously called chains by most, including, for example, the 2013 Academies Commission. Chains had had a quick mention in the 2010 White Paper: 'And a real success has been the establishment of powerful Academy chains supporting schools to improve even more rapidly.' Sam Freedman, a senior policy adviser to Gove closely involved in the development of the 2010 White Paper, argues that 'the expansion of academies, and specifically multi-academy trusts … was set in the 2010 *Importance of Teaching* white paper, in the context of a wider agenda to build a "self-improving system"'. Rereading the White Paper to find the promotion of MATs confirms this is largely wishful thinking.

Gove's time in charge was all about promoting school autonomy and single conversions. Collaboration wasn't a significant theme in that White Paper. One of the few references to it is: 'Our direction of travel is towards schools as autonomous institutions collaborating with each other on terms set by teachers, not bureaucrats' (DfE, 2010). Why does this matter? Because it should be recognised that such an enormous change to the structures of the school system in England – MATs – came about almost by accident. They were in part a response to the impractical and chaotic position that had been thousands of schools – SATs – having to be regulated by an ill-prepared DfE. We were promised autonomous schools and we ended up with autonomous MATs.

This move from SATs to MATs – governing or leading an institution comprising a group of schools, not just one – is a really significant change that began under the radar. There was no momentous speech or government publication announcing this change of direction, let alone a consultation. However, it was resisted by very few players in the sector, possibly only by FASNA who truly believed in autonomy over and above collaboration.

On the other hand, it took some time before the sector was ready to have honest, transparent public conversations; this was highlighted for me when I took part in a Chatham House event at the then National College for School Leadership (NCSL) in 2012, where there was unanimous support for primary schools joining groups of schools, rather than converting to a SAT. Yet, that very afternoon at an Academy Show main stage panel, I caused a stir by saying exactly that in answer to a specific question, and a MAT CEO who had been part of that same NCSL conversation said the contrary. I was frowned upon by some officials for a while, who never actually admitted that this was correct all along. It became official government policy in the 2016 White Paper.

Nicky Morgan, replacing Michael Gove as Education Secretary in July 2014, brought about a change of approach with MATs more consistently publicly promoted as the preferred structure. By then, about one quarter of state-funded schools in England were academies, but already just over half of them (53%) were in MATs. This rose to 65% a year later, when 91% of academies that opened in 2014/15 did so as part of a MAT, up from 73% in 2013/14. Her 2016 White Paper stated, 'We expect most schools will form or join MATs so proven educational models can spread and grow, and the best leaders can extend their influence by running multiple schools.'

NGA preferred the potential of collaboration, support and oversight offered by the MAT structure compared to the isolation of a SAT. We were an early adopter of the benefits of formal families of schools, learning from our work on federations. NGA's *Road to Federation* research, published in 2013, reported on governors' and headteachers' experiences, and in every case bar one, federation had proved to be mutually beneficial. Failing schools had improved measurably, often moving out of special measures to 'good' or 'outstanding' within the space of a few years. Reported benefits for stronger schools included the ability to attract and retain better staff, more specialist skills, sharing good practice, economies of scale and access to new funding. All of them were locally based.

The report also identified the common barriers, in particular initial opposition from parents and staff, and that had to be overcome by good honest communication. There was no one route to, or set model for, federation with a range of school sizes, phase and type, but they were all closely local, allowing easier collaboration between leaders, staff and pupils. Achieving a federation required commitment, time, trust, common purpose and due diligence, and could stretch both headteachers and governing boards.

In 2015, with Association of School and College Leaders (ASCL) and our legal partners Browne Jacobson, we published the first edition of our popular guidance on forming or joining a group of schools. We presented it at the Houses of Parliament with a positive response from then-minister, Lord Nash. Its original title, *Staying in Control of Your School's Destiny*, resonated across the sector. The DfE for some years kept using the phrase 'group of schools' or 'family of schools', which we had used to cover both federations and MATs. This phrase seems to have been resurrected since the election of a Labour government.

The guidance tried to change the perception that MAT status was only a punishment for failing schools. Instead, it argued that it is a choice to work together within a disciplined framework, holding schools to account and, more importantly, with the trust shouldering the accountability for all their school's performance and sustainability. NGA used the language of 'forming or joining a MAT' for a number of years, until it became clearer that the DfE were no longer allowing new MATs to form in most parts of the country.

Other forms of collaborative structures

Before MATs became the clear favoured structure, there were and still are a huge range of partnerships. There were also a few other more formal forms of collaborations available for groups of schools. The word 'chain' was used to describe all sorts of group structures. It was mainly just a precursor for MATs and was fading out by 2017.

Co-operative trusts

Co-operative trusts were very much a schools-led initiative, although they did gain the blessing of the final Labour Secretary of State in 2009, Ed Balls, also a Co-op sponsored MP. At that point, there were only 26 co-operative schools, but by 2016 there were 656 usually in local partnership, making it the third largest network of schools in England. That was especially significant given the lack of any fundings or incentives, and the support of a tiny team at the Co-operative College.

Co-operative trusts built on the foundation school model and were seen as a mutualisation of schools, working strategically together and with strong community links. They were often a way of formalising an existing partnership, sharing expertise and CPD but adding the ability to purchase services and potentially to become the provider of services. The ethos emphasised collegiality, self-responsibility and stakeholder engagement. They were seen by some as an alternative to the more corporate approach of existing MATs, especially as the schools within the trust kept their own independent entity. While this was appealing to many, it did mean that when member schools got into difficulties, there was nothing to stop them turning inwards, away from the partnership.

The Co-operative College also worked with the DfE to obtain a set of academy trust articles for co-operative academies as early as 2012. The most striking difference was the stakeholder engagement where various groups had a voice on the governance structure: more on that in chapter 16. The hope was for this to extend to MATs being formed, but that did not gather the traction that the maintained trusts did, perhaps in part because the Co-op College did not have the capacity to pursue this agenda.

Umbrella trusts

An umbrella trust was an overarching charitable company or incorporated organisation set up to offer services to individual schools or MATs, and as a vehicle for collaboration. Some included maintained school members or independent schools as well as academies, and some were set up by dioceses to support their schools and promote their Church character. Some umbrella trusts acted as sponsors for academies and through that have a role in appointing trustees for member academies. The DfE had no relationship with the umbrella trust; each individual academy trust remained fully accountable to the department, whereas the umbrella trust is regulated by the charity commission.

By 2017, the DfE's *Governance Handbook* emphasised that the board of each academy trust is fully empowered to deliver its charitable object with a single clear line of accountability for its performance to the department. The department would, therefore, no longer allow new or existing academies to join an umbrella trust that had governance or intervention powers over its constituent academy trusts. It made clear that 'the department's strong preference is for academy trusts to collaborate within a MAT in which there is robust shared governance arrangements and clear lines of accountability'. By the 2020 edition of the handbook, there was no mention made of umbrella trusts at all. Unfortunately research for the DfE on sustainable improvement in multi-school groups, published in 2018, did not cover umbrella trusts.

Federation first

I have discussed the emergence of federations and their advantages, very similar to small MATs, although without the financial windfall. During this period, I failed to persuade Lord Nash that maintained schools wanting to form a federation should be entitled to a grant from the DfE; at that time, £25,000 was being given to each school joining a MAT. Despite favouring smaller boards, the DfE refused even to simplify the constitution for maintained federations, which is unwieldly and results in large boards.

NGA suggested that maintained schools who were unconvinced by joining a MAT could consider forming a federation first in order to improve the education of pupils without incurring legal costs. Instead governors and school leaders can focus on forming relationships between schools first and introducing joint leadership, governance and business management. The federation could apply to become a MAT at any time in the future, so it wasn't an alternative route, but a step with reduced workload. A few new federations formed and many more become MATs.

Federations remain a small part of the school sector. NGA's surveys suggest they may have fallen from approximately 7% of all schools in 2013 to 4% 10 years later. There is no data on federations kept centrally, although 719 federations come up on GIAS in April 2025.

For a few years, NGA had federation champions as part of a Federation First information campaign to supply governing bodies with options. One champion was the then-chair of NGA, Ian Courtney, also the chair of a large federation at the time – one secondary and several primaries. He and I debated the pros and cons with Lord Nash in 2014, trying to tease out the additional advantages to becoming a MAT. The minister's only argument – that a MAT is forever and a federation is temporary – has not stood the test of time given the re-brokering of MATs. In subsequent years, it was clear that the only way their federation would be able to have another secondary school join the group was if they complied and became a MAT.

The '100% academy strategy'

The coalition government's position was to offer academy 'freedoms' to all 'good' schools with compulsion only applying to 'failing' schools. Although the Conservative Party 2015 general election manifesto was silent on the issue of full academisation, Prime Minister David Cameron's '100-days' article in the *Daily Telegraph* in August 2015 contained the first indication that the newly elected Conservative Government was going to take the school system to the next stage. 'We will make local authorities running schools a thing of the past' was then a phrase used by a number of cabinet ministers.

The government aimed to accelerate the academisation process by compelling local authorities and governing bodies to actively progress the conversion of failing schools into academies. The government claimed that its Education and Adoption Bill that year would remove 'roadblocks which previously left too many pupils languishing in underperforming schools'. This was an overclaiming and the bill's passage was far from smooth. For example, in December there was a stand-off between the Lords and the Commons on issues such as parental consultation. The bill also introduced the category of coasting schools, a short-lived and misguided complication to the accountability system.

In March 2016, Nicky Morgan announced in her White Paper *Educational Excellence Everywhere*: 'We will move to a system where every school is an academy' by the end of 2022. It set out the theory of how, by the end of 2020, all remaining maintained schools would be academies or in the process of conversion. There were a number of other announcements and themes in the White Paper (including an attempt to reduce the places reserved for parents on governing boards, which I will return to in chapter 16), but forcing academisation was the most controversial.

There was opposition from many directions, including some Conservative local authorities. The chief inspector of schools, Sir Michael Wilshaw, who had been the head of Mossbourne Academy, wrote to the Education Secretary reporting the seven focused inspections of MATs, highlighting some 'serious weaknesses that were contributing to poor progress and outcomes for too many pupils', saying that 'despite having operated for a number of years, many of the trusts manifested the same weaknesses as the worst performing local authorities and offered the same excuses' (Wilshaw, 2016).

NGA was against the change, our line being that the governing body is best placed to know what is right for that school and their community. Even internally at the DfE there were concerns, including about how the sheer volume of conversions would be managed, especially as many might be contested. I was speaking at the same event as the national schools commissioner, Sir David Carter, on the evening of the White Paper's launch; he followed civil service rules on confidentiality, but his anxiety was apparent. He wasn't his usual affable and passionate self.

NGA's annual 2016 survey came just after the publication of the White Paper, and its results showed that the issue of academy conversion was back on the agenda of many governing bodies: three quarters of maintained governing bodies reported being in discussion about conversion. Respondents who had decided not to convert gave a range of reasons, of which the common ones were: not considering there would be educational benefits for pupils; concern that it would change the ethos of the school; valuing the support the local authority provides; and already having strong links with other schools in the area.

That weight of opposition, in some cases downright anger, probably combined with recognition of the sheer difficulties of moving the unconvinced to becoming academies, led to a U-turn within two months. Nicky Morgan (2016) announced that she had listened to MPs, teachers, school leaders and parents and that there would be no compulsory academisation for 'good' schools. No mention of the people from whom the decision would have been removed – the governors. Instead, the DfE claimed: 'The academy programme puts control of running schools in the hands of teachers and school leaders – the people who know best how to run their schools.' Of course pedagogical and educational expertise sits in their hands, but how much agency they are given in practice very much depends on the culture and ethos of the trust they work for: I will come back to that in chapter 12. There is so much in that DfE statement of

May 2016 that could be quibbled with as it is not backed by evidence, but I don't think that my dissection would make for a riveting read.

The government reaffirmed its 'continued determination to see all schools to become academies in the next 6 years' but accepted 'that it is not necessary to bring legislation to bring about blanket conversion of all schools to achieve this goal' (ibid.). The Conservative government did not try to repeat this mandatory approach in their next eight years of governing. There was a considerable amount paid to support conversion and capacity building of the academy sector. We are now nine years further down the track and of nearly 22,000 state-funded schools, 49% of these are maintained by local authorities.

The role of the DfE

With the numbers of schools converting, as many commentators had predicted, the DfE was becoming overwhelmed. As well as the academisation programme itself to manage, it now had a significant number of academy trusts to oversee. The first schools commissioner, Dame Elizabeth Sidwell, had no team to speak of, but during the term of her successor, Frank Green, in 2014, eight regional schools commissioners (RSCs) were appointed. Most were former executive heads/MAT CEOs.

The following October, the Secretary of State told the House of Commons Education Committee (2015) 'that each Commissioner would have six staff and would be responsible for the oversight and monitoring of those academies which are in special measures, currently 112 schools across the country. The RSCs have no responsibility in respect of maintained schools at the moment but the Secretary of State confirmed that the "direction of travel for the Conservative Party" is for RSCs to oversee all schools: academy and maintained. It remains unclear whether the RSCs have any responsibility for promoting school-to-school support.' The staff teams grew substantially over the years.

The RSC role included taking decisions on: the creation of new converter and sponsored academies; matching schools to sponsors; ensuring there are enough high-quality sponsors to meet local need; and monitoring academy and maintained school performance and, where necessary, intervening. Where formal intervention was required, this could be commissioning support for the school, issuing warning notices, terminating funding agreements and identifying a new sponsor to take on responsibility for the academy.

Each RSC was advised by a headteacher board (HTB) of between six and eight people, four of whom were academy headteachers elected by their peers. Oddly, the election process didn't even fit with the MAT system they were constructing as it ignored CEOs and other executives of trusts while allowing executive heads to have a vote for each school they led. Headteachers were not the decision-makers for structural change, while trust boards who were didn't play much of a part; it proved hard to ensure each HTB had even one chair of trustees on it.

The House of Commons Education Committee in its report on RSCs noted that the balance of power between RSCs and HTBs was unclear. If an RSC ignored HTB advice, they had to report this to their line manager, the National Schools Commissioner and the minister, but the whole decision-making process lacked transparency. It was never clear how much HTBs were truly influencing decisions or just rubber-stamping the RSC's position, or whether they did actually supply geographical information not known by the RSC team.

Education Funding Agency (EFA)

Alongside the RSCs and their education oversight was financial oversight carried out by the EFA, which went through a number of names, roles and statuses until being closed in 2025, absorbed into the DfE's Operations and Infrastructure Group. Having experienced the disjoint between the information known by the two organisations, NGA had been asking for this integration of financial and educational oversight. This was particularly dysfunctional for governance issues, which of course cover both those arenas.

Since its inception in 2012, the EFA improved its functioning significantly, in part in response to financial scandals and mismanagement. The House of Commons Public Accounts Committee (PAC) did a good job holding the DfE to account, arguably bringing about more practical change than the House of Commons Education Committee. The chief executive of EFA in 2014 recognised the role PAC had played in changing the requirements of trusts, including when it came to publication of information. The EFA took much effort to ensure its handbook was fit for purpose, and it published useful investigation reports.

The role of local authorities

The rise of the trusts has had huge implications for local authorities (LAs) as the number of schools they maintain gradually reduced, alongside significant budget reductions and growing demand for many of their core children services. Their capacity to support schools has reduced but to varying degrees depending on the local rate of academisation and the way in which they provide services to schools. Often academies purchase LA services. Many LAs are also facilitating networks of schools. Schools will be working with LAs on SEND and with their specialist services, such as education psychologists, although there is much competition for the multi-agency support necessary for vulnerable children.

The *Importance of Teaching* 2010 White Paper recognised LAs 'as champions for parents, families and vulnerable pupils. They will promote educational excellence by ensuring a good supply of high quality school places, coordinating fair admissions'. Similar words were used by the following Conservative governments. The duty to ensure sufficient places are available was not straightforward given LAs were not allowed to open schools or force academies to take more students. They were left with soft power and their power to persuade.

Role of dioceses

Dioceses are much more powerful than I have given them credit for so far. Because the majority of schools are not diocesan schools, we think of them as a minority issue – just one of our many different school structures. But almost one third of all state schools in England have a religious character, with the overwhelming majority being Catholic or Church of England (CoE). CoE schools are the largest family of primary state schools (about 4500 of their 4630 schools), and Roman Catholic schools are the largest family for secondaries (about 500 of their 2100 schools) representing more than one in eight in England.

Dioceses have significant power and influence, playing a pivotal role in guiding, supporting and inspecting faith schools, including through the academisation process, with their consent required before a school joins a MAT. They are also involved in developing a publicly available strategic plan. There are 42 CoE dioceses in England and 19 Catholic ones, and their approach is by no means uniform. Although this varies considerably across the country, as of 2024, approximately 44% of all faith schools have academised, compared to 52% of their non-faith counterparts.

At first, church schools were slower to convert than other maintained schools; most dioceses were cautious. Many CoE schools are small rural primaries that are least likely to convert singly, and many Catholic schools were voluntarily aided, which have many of the advantages of SATs without their more onerous financial reporting.

Many Catholic dioceses from about 2015 onwards began setting up MATs, sometimes called multi-academy companies (MACs) to distinguish them from the diocesan trusts that own the land and buildings of their schools. Diocesan trusts at that point represented the largest and fastest growth in the MAT sector. Some dioceses expect governing bodies to join a particular MAT, causing controversy with foundation governors having to follow this lead and consider their position if they don't support it.

Sometimes the objections from governors have been to the size of the MATs proposed. There was an early cautionary example of the Plymouth diocese creating a diocesan-wide MAT from 34 schools in 2014. Its struggle was documented both in a focused Ofsted inspection – finding the trust lacked capacity for school improvement, with weak systems and poor strategic leadership – and by an EFA notice to improve citing weak financial management and inadequate governance in 2017.

Most Anglican dioceses, unlike Catholic ones, allow their schools to enter trusts that are not universally CoE schools; these trusts are termed 'mixed MATs'. They may be majority or minority CoE, and their number of members and foundation trustees vary accordingly. Mixed MATs have been welcomed often by governing boards wanting to work with local schools, irrespective of their faith status.

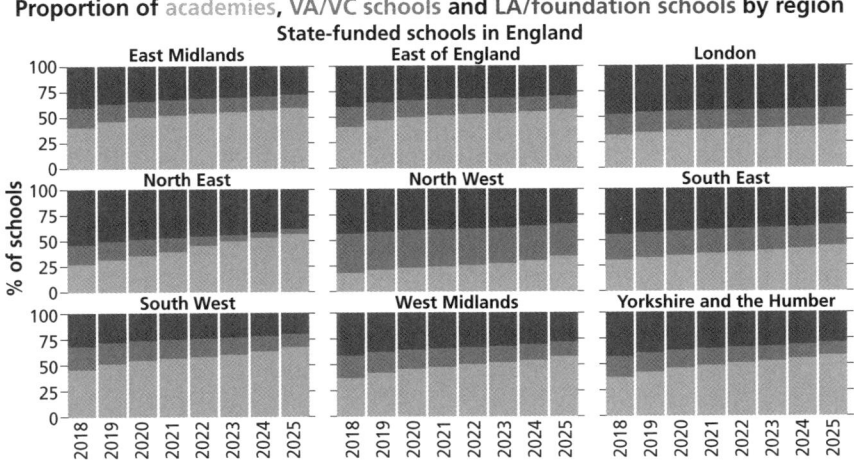

Figure 6.1 Proportion of academies, VA/VC schools and LA/foundation schools by region (supplied by FFT Education Datalab).

Taking the decision to join a MAT

With the exception of underperforming schools, just as with academy conversion, it was governing boards up and down the country who decided whether or not to join a group. They had to weigh up the evidence in the interests of the pupils they were educating then and in the future. The evidence was never presented well; this was reinforced by the House of Commons Education Committee in 2017, who recommended more guidance and research.

For a decade this question was dealt with regularly by most maintained governing bodies and boards of SATs. A large amount of leadership and governance time was being taken considering the options: NGA's surveys showed approximately half of GBs were considering this every year, and some still are. For example, in 2017, 14% of respondents were in the process of joining or forming a MAT, and in 2024, 17% had decided to join a MAT in the near future. Over eight years of NGA asking single schools whether they are going to join a MAT, on average just over 18% say they considered it in the last year but decided not to. The national data shows how many do join.

The DfE under the Conservatives talking about their vision had an effect on the numbers of boards looking at this, even though there was no change of law or even policy. It was a message that didn't go away, repeated again and again in all conferences. NGA members – both SATs and maintained schools – had heard the arguments for MATs on many occasions but had not been convinced by what they had heard. Even the evidence paper published alongside the White Paper in 2022 was not very convincing, which was surprising given the number of MATs that could be drawn from by that time.

For a number of years, NGA spoke directly with our SAT members regularly, including after the DfE began encouraging them to merge or join MATs. Many told us firmly that the SAT structure worked well for their schools and emphasised the benefits it offered, including that they could collaborate closely with other local schools in all sorts of ways and across phases, from the informal to more substantial, such as running a Teaching School hub. The majority were keen to conserve their SAT status until they had no option, although a smaller number did feel isolated. Some trustees acknowledged that they felt a lack of support, for example, on very specific HR and legal compliance available compared with MATs or maintained schools.

Both trustees and leaders tended to be concerned about the irreversible nature of joining a MAT and the potential loss of their school's identity and control; they wanted to keep their school values, ethos and community links. SAT leaders and trustees did not want to risk being expected by a MAT to collaborate in one way when preferring to continue their existing local collaborations: their school's context and the pupils across that place really mattered to them. Time and time again, they told the NGA that joining a MAT meant losing control of their destiny without any recourse if they were unhappy about the new trust's actions.

As available standalone schools were reducing, some thought that it was best to act now than face a poorer choice in a few years when mandated. Some leaders of leaders and maintained schools had explored options that were put aside for a range of reasons, including the DfE being unwilling to approve a new MAT, diocesan preferences and the inability to find schools to join.

We carried out a piece of qualitative work in early 2022 to inform the forthcoming DfE White Paper. Sam Henson and I spoke individually at length to chairs of governing boards of standalone schools, primarily maintained schools, as to why they had not joined a MAT. These very much confirmed our work with SATs. First, they did not find the evidence on the benefits to pupils of being in a MAT persuasive, from neither the DfE nor MATs with whom they'd had exploratory conversations and sometimes extensive negotiations.

Second, there is a huge attachment to locality and the importance of local collaboration, and third, there was a fear of being 'taken over' by a large distant organisation that would not have the interests of 'their' school and their community at the heart of their decision-making. Boards did not want to risk having carefully crafted a group of local schools or painstakingly negotiated with a local small or middle-sized MAT only to find in later years those trusts outgrow their locality or are subsumed into a much larger trust. They felt they would be taking a leap of faith with no way of withdrawing from the MAT if their promises didn't live up to expectations. The chairs expressed arguments about participation, connectedness, understanding of the context, risk and in effect who 'owns' our state schools, which I will come back to. More on local governance within MATs in chapter 9.

These three factors are nuanced and overlapping, and the strength of feeling differs from place to place and school to school with their history, context and past relationships. The views of headteachers usually carry a lot of weight with boards. The change to leadership positions, especially heads of school in MATs, can be very substantive and unappealing for some; experienced headteachers were often particularly concerned about joining an existing MAT with very little ability to shape it. Their leadership role was at risk of being diminished. The resignation of a headteacher is a time when governing boards are more likely to consider joining a MAT or a federation.

These reasons led to some boards and leaders being unwilling to prioritise the work of negotiating to join a MAT, especially when leadership capacity is needed for other current pressures. There is also another level of issues faced by smaller schools and those with financial stress, the schools sadly dubbed SNOWs (schools no one wants), where most usually it has been the MATs who have not wanted the conversations.

The growth of MATs

Here, the growth of MATs refers not to the number of trusts but the size of individual MATs. Externally sponsored MATs, the ones often called chains, formed the minority of the trusts and still do. Most MATs were homegrown, composed of a few local schools, and even now in February 2025, just under 30% of MATs have 10 or more schools. In the early days, diocesan MATs had yet to take off, but more recently they are often the larger trusts.

GIAS, the DfE's database of schools, has become a useful tool, although its numbers possibly need to be taken as approximate, but it's telling me that there are today 984 academy sponsors, 1036 SATs and 1379 MATs, which are a slight overestimate, given at the time of the 2025 general election, there were 2263 trusts, of which 960 are SATs and 1303 are MATs. You would expect the numbers of each to reduce as SATs and MATs merge.

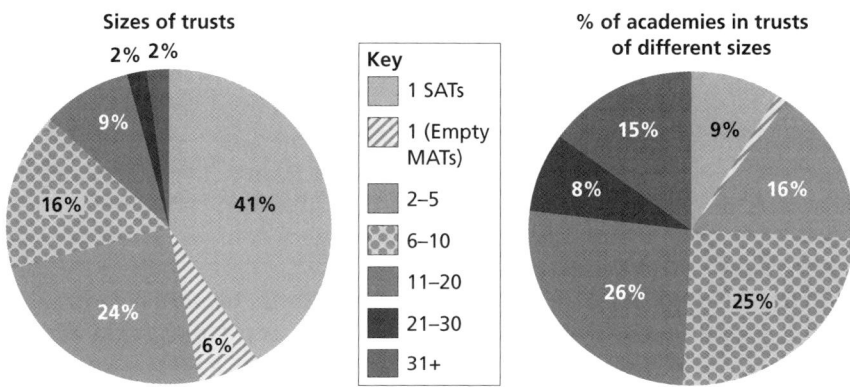

Figure 6.2 Percentage of trusts of different sizes, and percentage of academies in trusts of different sizes (May 2024).

Growth of MATs has been the order of the day from the DfE for more than a decade now. The DfE had been putting pressure on certain MATs to expand for some time when in December 2016 they spelled out the strategy in published guidance on their expectations of MAT growth. Given the difficulty of overseeing over 20,000 schools from Whitehall, or even from the DfE regions, there is an administrative benefit for the DfE with fewer but larger MATs to regulate.

Sir David Carter, national schools commissioner from 2016 to 2018, was very clear on every platform that MATs would need to grow to be sustainable, talking about starter trusts (1–5 schools); established trusts (6–15); national trusts (16–30); and system leader trusts (30+). That language didn't catch on, but Carter was open and thoughtful about the issues, focused on the needs of pupils and school improvement.

Trustees have a legal obligation to ensure that their trusts are sustainable and solvent, a going concern, and so should consider how big they want or need to grow their group of schools. In the early days, not every board did that well and some took on more schools than they had the capacity to cope with. Others took a risk and expanded the central team to support, advise and manage schools yet to be recruited. Not all sources of support have to come from a central team; some MATs deploy staff from better schools to contribute to the improvement of others.

The House of Commons education select committee report on MATs in 2017 pointed out there had been too much of a rush to growth, and cautious expansion was better. The DfE had by that year put nearly 60 academy chains onto a pause list in order to stop their growth, though a *Schools Week* investigation found several trusts were able to duck the pause list and expand. Ofsted also had raised concerns that expanding too quickly can lead to poor performance in schools and identified weaknesses in due diligence leading to a few MATs taking on too many challenging schools. In response, David Carter introduced 'health checks' to look at a trust's history before granting expansions.

Optimum size of MATs

When looking at the 2016–17 accounts, the Public Accounts Committee (PAC) was already saying that some MATs were so big that any failure would have a negative impact on the education of a large number of children. Many have continued to grow since.

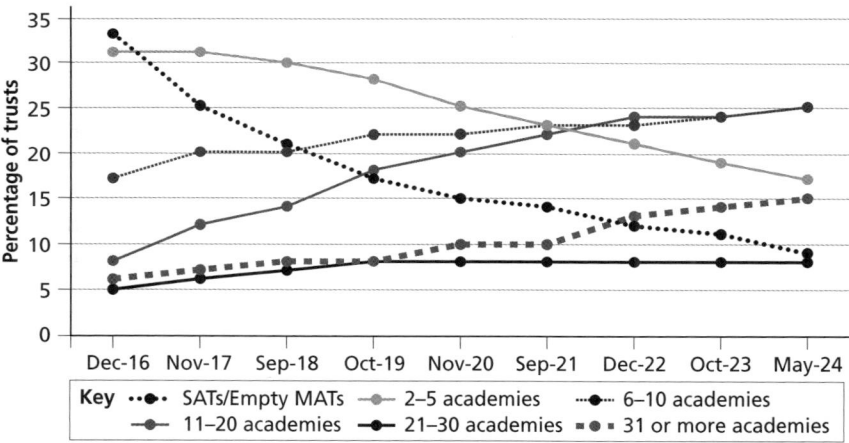

Figure 6.3 Trusts of different sizes over the years.

I have been frustrated about the lack of a well-rounded debate as to what constitutes a large MAT and whether a MAT can become too big. The DfE ran a couple of projects to ascertain the optimum range of size of MATs, but they floundered and were never published. I was involved in two such inconclusive attempts. As well as the operational issues of financial viability and impact on educational performance, there is also the bigger picture issue of how many trusts we want or need in the system, an issue that surely should be at the heart of a vision for England's schools. Conservative Education Secretaries avoided this question, and the new Labour government does not appear to be grappling with it.

The 2016 White Paper suggested that MATs develop the centralised systems that deliver financial benefits at a size of around 10–15 academies or 5000–6000 pupils. The following year, Lord Agnew, the minister responsible for the school system, suggested at a conference that 'the sweet spot for a MAT is perhaps somewhere between 12 and 20 schools, or something like 5000 to 10,000 pupils'. Both he and his predecessor, Lord Nash, were interested in 'human-sized trusts' that people could relate to, where they would know each other and could foster a sense of belonging, rather than being a 'faceless bureaucracy'. Lord Agnew was very interested in the efficient use of resources, but he mentioned being able to get 12–20 headteachers around a table to collaborate. In the 2022 White Paper *Opportunity for All*, the government's suggestion was taken one step further with the expectation that MATs should aim to be at least 10 schools or 7500 pupils.

Bernadinelli et al. in 2018 found that in terms of MAT size, primary pupils in small and mid-sized MATs tended to perform better, on average, than their peers in comparable standalone academies, and secondary school pupils in larger MATs (with 16+ schools) tend to do worse. The authors argued that 'these findings suggest that the economic drive for MAT growth promoted in contemporary policy may well be in tension with an educational argument for smaller groupings of schools'. However, they did underline that this was only indicative as they hadn't had the funding to undertake additional analysis by academy type and size of MAT controlled for relevant pupil characteristics.

Geography

Many of the advantages of being in a group of schools rely on staff, and to a lesser extent pupils, being able to travel between schools. The House of Commons Education Committee report on MATs in 2017 confirmed this: 'In its early enthusiasm for MATs, the Government encouraged trusts to expand too quickly over too large geographical regions. Schools which operate within close proximity to one another are best able to share resources and expertise and subsequently can most successfully take advantage of being part of a MAT.'

This was even more so before the Covid-19 pandemic made virtual connections the norm. Yet, for several years before that, the RSCs were giving schools to MATs spread across the country; at the same time Lord Nash was saying schools within a MAT should be no more than half an hour away from each other. Lucy Heller, the CEO of Ark, said to the education select committee 'there appears to be three common aspects to all the best performing trusts – a strong vision, high expectations and a geographic focus', emphasising that geography was 'hugely' important in Ark's decision-making. That is the case for many other MATs too. Not even every large trust is spread far and wide; some have taken decisions not to.

In a speech in 2014, Lord Nash said, 'In our view it is absolutely clear the local school to school support model is the only one that will really work', but this was also done by encouraging successful MATs to set up clusters of schools in other regions. Ark was persuaded to set up clusters in three areas where the RSCs were looking for more sponsors.

The choosing of sponsors could be controversial with some trustees saying that their MATs were being overlooked by the RSC who chose executives they were close to or were a safe bet. In 2016, DfE guidance for RSCs was published, and there were a number of geographical issues to consider: potential isolation of individual schools within a MAT; the development of geographical clusters; regard to how geography may impact on governance, school improvement capacity and overall performance; the need to avoid a single MAT running all or an overly significant proportion of schools within a local area; and how to avoid individual schools, especially small ones in rural areas, becoming isolated outside a MAT.

Mergers

Given that some empty MATs and small MATs were finding it hard to attract schools to join, it left them needing to merge if they couldn't otherwise achieve financial viability. Undertaking a merger involves a considerable amount of work. The ethos and relationships need to be compatible or the process might flounder.

Other changes

While all this structural change was going on, so many other aspects of the English school system were also changing during that decade from 2010, in particular the curriculum and assessment in both primary and secondary. The SEND system was reformed. There were changes to the routes into teaching and in 2019 an Early Career Framework was introduced. I am not an education expert, so I am neglecting the details of all those, but will come back to the challenges for governing boards in chapter 13.

School funding

The way in which school funding is calculated also changed during this time. First the coalition government introduced the pupil premium for disadvantaged pupils, and then the national funding formula (NFF) to reduce local variations was introduced very slowly with transitional protection from 2018/19. This was an important change to make as previously allocations had been built over past allocations and past formulae leading to much confusion and inconsistency.

The NFF brings more transparency to the situation, although it was a hard thing on which to consult members. Those in urban areas usually with more deprivation lost out to the underfunded counties who were in extremely difficult situations with austerity funding levels. It is likely to be a full 10 years before the DfE allocates funding directly to schools without any local adjustment, although it is unclear whether by then the funding system will recognise the existence of MATs.

Reducing bureaucracy

New governments tend to commit to removing the previous one's bureaucracy before inventing or even reinventing its own; Gove was more passionate than most incoming Education Secretaries about this. I sat on a DfE working group tasked with identifying bureaucracy to cut, but the only result was a change of the guidance to downgrade the need for all governors to be CRB checked, which was overridden a year later when the new DBS system required enhanced checks for governors. Gove removed the requirement to complete Ofsted's self-evaluation form, and guidance from DfE was cut.

Leadership roles

The school system had been based around every school having a headteacher, and we saw in chapter 5 that LMS enlarged that role. Leadership of schools began to change further, particularly with federations where an executive headteacher had responsibility for more than one school. Executive leadership was not always welcomed by parents as it's less visible leadership than headteachers based at the same school every day.

There were also less-formal arrangements where a successful headteacher, often designated as a national leader of education (NLE), worked with a struggling school. There were different models for this. Often the school in crisis also had a headteacher with the NLE supporting them for between a fifth and half a working week. These new models of leadership were recognised by the National Association of Headteachers (NAHT) in 2011 as having the potential to raise educational standards, prevent school closures and solve recruitment problems.

With the arrival of MATs, these executive leadership roles became more common, but the system oddly lagged behind. Even with the number of executive headteachers rapidly increasing, their remit and responsibilities varied and were largely undefined. In 2016, NGA worked with Future Leaders Trust and National Foundation for Educational Research (NFER) on a quantitative and qualitative study *Executive Headteachers: What's in a Name?* There were 620 executive headteachers in the school workforce, working with at least 970 schools. We found the role differed from the traditional headteacher role in requiring higher levels of strategic thinking, a greater emphasis on coaching, delegating and achieving change through others, and capacity to look outward. We couldn't find funding to take the research on to the next stage.

The substantial changes to the role of headteacher have been barely documented despite the significant literature on school leadership. For some, headship has returned to what it was before LMS almost half a century ago, losing the organisational management role concentrating more fully on education. In almost all MATs, a central business team has the specialists who cover finance, premises, IT and HR advice. A range of business leadership roles have been introduced into the trust sector, including chief financial officer, sometimes combined with the chief operating officer.

No longer having to cover all aspects of running an enterprise should suit many, especially first-time headteachers who also have the guidance of more senior educationalists in the MAT central team. Whether this new type of headship appeals to more experienced heads depends considerably on their approaches being compatible with the MAT's culture. The headteacher loses being monarch of their castle but should gain from joining a team. On the other hand, some MATs dictate more on the expectations for teaching rather than delegating that leadership of learning to the headteacher who may not remain the main leader of teaching practice in their school. Different philosophies could cause problems.

Some issues were reported by Greany and Ehren in 2016, such as the cultural challenges and tensions where senior education leaders of single schools used to 'running their own ship' have to work in matrix-like structures with centralised services. They found headteachers and teachers feeling disempowered by having to work within centralised structures of scripted curricula and lesson plans, particularly in large MATs where the chief executive tried to ensure control over schools. There have also been discussions as to how central support is distributed across the schools in the MAT and whether it discourages headteachers from thinking independently and developing innovative solutions for local problems.

Initially some MATs, sometimes called Mates MATs, tried to pursue flatter models, emulating a collaborative rather than accepting the trust was a single organisation. RSCs expected a single post to provide accountability, and this became a chief executive as soon as size allowed. That role was comprehensively covered in Michael Pain's 2019 book *Being the CEO*.

As well as central business roles, there are a range of new posts covering education, such as (but not exclusively): director of education; director of school improvement or curriculum; subject or phase specialists; SEND lead; safeguarding lead; inclusion or pastoral leads covering behaviour, attendance and wellbeing approaches; and CPD leads.

How much the additional management and leadership provided within MAT costs is unexplored apart from a 2019 report on understanding the middle tier, which found MATs spent more on leadership and administration than local authorities did for maintained schools, and somewhat surprisingly, the per-pupil amount was more with large trusts.

Conclusion

The structural changes brought with them a reduction of governance – both power and decision-making – at school level and at local authority level. Far more decisions were centralised to the Education Secretary and taken on her behalf by the RSCs.

The movement of power from individual schools upwards to groups of schools – MATs – is a change arguably as fundamental as the Education Reform Act 1988 devolving local management to schools. However, this reversal was unannounced, carried out not by an act of parliament, but incrementally, out of the limelight, with very little public debate and insufficient understanding. It was completely contrary to the stated aim of the coalition and Conservative governments of increasing school autonomy. For those who weren't paying full attention the change may appear to have been achieved by stealth, and it is not yet universal.

The 2010 *Hidden Givers* research had a striking conclusion: a significant finding was 'our sense of the relatively fragile nature of schools as institutions'. Although schools may seem stable and secure, they are in fact potentially subject to a whole range of influences in both the short term and the long term that can significantly affect them and their work. Successful school governing should secure schools as institutions against these threats so that the staff can undertake their work properly and the pupils can learn and thrive. The movement to MATs has led to less fragility for some individual schools, in particular less financial stress.

What have pupils gained from the changes? Most commentators agree that there have been some real success stories for previously poorly performing schools, but overall there is as much variability among academies as there was in the maintained sector. Some MATs are fabulous and other struggle, and they can have very different approaches, cultures and sizes. It is probably not contentious to say that where MATs work well, governance and leadership are strong. There has been a lot of time and money spent creating new structures, and we do not yet know if that was money well spent. Researchers to-date have tended to conclude any assessment of impact is insufficiently empirical and robust. Although a further attempt to assess that would be useful, given the variables, it would take a lot of unravelling.

What else have we learned from living through the significant structural changes? First, bringing additional money into the state school system from external sponsors did not work. Some charitable foundations, such as Ark and Oasis, carry out charitable work in their school communities or incubate education initiatives, but this rightly is not funding for core public education.

Second, Gove's revolution of letting a thousand flowers bloom or progressing through creative destruction has not stood the test of time. Instead, the creativity unleashed was used to reproduce a source of support albeit in a non-strategic way. Some thought of this as recreating a middle tier, a structure between schools and central government, but it is more fundamental than that; a MAT is an institution encompassing schools, not a separate layer of the system.

The implications of and complications caused by this unplanned movement even now have not been fully considered. By that I mean much of the school system – such as the funding formula, inspection, school teachers' pay and conditions negotiations – still operate as though the school is the universal institutional unit of education.

Third, the promise to give individual schools freedom and autonomy has in fact resulted in 90% of academies, now within MATs, having less freedom and autonomy than they had as maintained schools.

Fourth, these significant changes had the potential to give more power to maintained governing bodies and boards of trustees to create the shape of the school sector. They were taking many of the key decisions. The Education Secretary's attempt to take that away from them in 2016 failed. Governing boards had arguably become the architects of the school system, though without any responsibility for achieving a coherence to the whole. Was it even possible when considering whether to join or form a group, or take on another school to have one eye on the bigger picture – the needs of the wider community? Was this even compatible with their legal responsibilities? Boards operate within the parameters given to them by government and their decision-making was within the prism of their own school or trust. They can't be held responsible for the muddle we are left with.

We've spent a lot of time and money in creating new structures, mostly new MATs. What this has meant for governance? I will look at that next.

7.
What changed for governance?

Having documented the structural changes to the system since 2010, what did that mean in detail for the expectation on and practice of governance? First, there was the spread of trusteeship, and second, the emergence of MATs gave us the biggest revolution in school governance since LMS. Governing a group of schools is a significantly different prospect from governing a single school. Federations of maintained schools with one governing board had existed and still can, but they are usually very small and always local. The range of size and geography of MATs required a new model of governance, which requires a few chapters of its own, starting with chapter 9.

Here, I am going to look at the development of governance in five sections:

1. Trusts and trusteeship.
2. Governance professionals.
3. Size of boards.
4. Changes in composition: stakeholders and skills.
5. Knowing your schools.

Just before the 2010 election, the Labour government published a report from the Ministerial Working Group on School Governance entitled *The 21st Century School: Implications and Challenges for Governing Bodies*. It recorded that: 'Governing bodies are an integral part of school leadership, setting the ethos of the school, driving continuous improvement, supporting, challenging and holding to account the head teacher and other members of the school leadership team by negotiating stretching targets for improvements in standards, and monitoring progress towards them.'

It had taken much time and debate for the working group's 20 members – of which NGA supplied two – to agree its findings, which were still not unanimous. There was a very long list that can be summarised as:

- The majority of governing bodies do a good job.
- Governing bodies need to be clear about their purpose and follow a defined set of principles for good governance of schools.
- There needs to be more clarity concerning the strategic management role of the governing body and the day-to-day management role of headteachers to ensure that neither party crosses over into each other's role.
- The principle of stakeholder representation on governing bodies is essential but needs to be balanced against a requirement that all governing bodies have the necessary skills to carry out their tasks.
- Improvements were needed in the training for governing body chairs, new governors and governing body clerks.

There were also sections on what constituted effectiveness, and they expected that better practice would lead to better use of governors' time as well as a better contribution to school improvement and the outcomes for pupils.

Another significant change since 2010 was the practice move from just largely compliance to strategy and culture combined with the mindset move from just effectiveness to ethics, diversity, listening to stakeholders and cultivating the right behaviours for good governance.

Language also changed over this decade. In the legislation, maintained schools have 'governing bodies'. However, the default noun gradually over this period became 'board'. At NGA, we made the change to this in 2016; it was helpful to have one name that fitted all, while of course using governing bodies for maintained schools when we needed to distinguish their practice from boards of trustees. It was not about copying language from the private sector; charities and many other parts of the public sector have boards.

The coalition government from May 2010

The lack of understanding and debate about trust governance continued into the subsequent coalition government. During parliamentary debates on what became the 2010 Academies Act, there was some questioning of the legitimacy of the academy model in terms of the removal of power from local authorities, but very little on the role of trustees. Proponents of the academies system focused, not on the issues of power and oversight, but on the so-called greater freedoms to headteachers and more autonomy for schools that would emerge out of the system.

More 'autonomous' school structures meant that the role and performance of governing boards become more critical to the success of schools, but this went largely unacknowledged by DfE until things began to go wrong, which I will return to in chapter 10. At the House of Commons education enquiry on the launch of their report three years later, the committee chair Graham Stuart MP said: 'Greater freedoms for schools mean we need more effective governing bodies.'

The Importance of Teaching White Paper from the DfE in November 2010 made the welcome statement: 'School governors are the unsung heroes of our education system. They are one of the biggest volunteer forces in the country, working in their spare time to promote school improvement and to support head teachers and teachers in their work. To date, governors have not received the recognition, support or attention that they deserve. We will put that right.'

Sadly, that bold commitment to make governance more visible was not seen through by that government or any of the following Conservative ones. Governance was still not threaded through the work of the renamed Department for Education (DfE). I spent the following 14 years having to remind the DfE to include governors and trustees when statements were made; they were so easily left off the lists of people being thanked. Budgets were invariably talked about as headteachers' budgets. Lord Nash did try to change that by challenging civil servants about their understanding of the role of trust members and trustees.

On the other hand, the role of governance in driving school improvement and challenging headteachers to achieve high educational standards was generally acknowledged, and when occasions demanded, ministers – particularly Lord Nash – would use platforms to make this point. For example, to the House of Commons education committee (2013a) on the role of school governing bodies: 'I think Government should be sending a message at every point about the importance of governors. That is certainly at the top of my list of priorities. ... Perhaps in the past we have underestimated the importance of the governing body to drive change ... We should talk about it a lot. ... At every turn, we should invite more people to become governors.'

There were two more specific changes contained in the 2010 White Paper, one on volunteer skills and the other on board size, which I will cover later in this chapter after the most significant change.

1. Trusts and trusteeship

In the last chapter, we saw the very significant structural change of the English school sector with power moving away from local authorities towards the national government, accompanied by a move of the governance of individual schools from a public-sector model in the maintained schools to a third-sector model in academy schools.

The big difference between governing a maintained school and a single academy trust (SAT) is that those that form the governing board in a SAT are trustees and company directors. While of course a significant change of legal status, this was for some years bigged up to be more different and difficult than it actually is for those governing a SAT: after all, charities have been operating in this way for years with the Charity Commission having been established in 1853. On the other hand, trusteeship was new to most in the school sector, and this caused some to be discombobulated by the change. Others who were only providing services to trusts liked to take advantage of overemphasising the differences. The lines of reporting are different, but the principles of governance are in fact very similar. Trusts also have members in addition to trustees, and I will return to them in chapter 15. Over the years, the confusion about their role hasn't abated despite much guidance.

This movement of the governance of state schools into the third sector was not managed well. DfE model articles of association could have been more straightforward than they were. Initially they even kept 'governors' in the articles as well as 'trustees' and 'directors', which caused widespread confusion, and in a few cases it continues to this day. There are still some SATs who today refer to their trustees as governors.

Several witnesses to that select enquiry on governance singled out converter academies (which then constituted the majority of academy trusts), suggesting that their governing boards 'do not understand their new role and do not change their governance arrangements to adapt to their new role, despite freedoms allowing them to do so' (House of Commons Education Committee, 2013a). There were no details about the misunderstandings, and while NGA experienced much confusion among those governing academies for some years, it was most often about the difference in the roles of the trustees and the local governors within MATs. It was true that some of those in SATs did not change their mode of governing – apart from the necessary reporting requirements. This perhaps underlines the point that the practice of governing a single school well – whether maintained or a SAT – was not fundamentally different, particularly when the move was made by a voluntary aided (VA) school.

I don't want to divert here into detailed descriptions of the law and guidance around trusteeship and company directorship. The Charity Commission provides some of this, although academy trusts are exempt charities, which means they are not regulated by the Charity Commission but by the DfE. Over the past decade, the guidance provided by the DfE has morphed a number of times. First their *Governors Handbook*, growing to accommodate academy trusts, was renamed the *Governance Handbook*, and then in 2024 was replaced by two separate guides, one for maintained schools and one for trusts. NGA of course has all the information and guidance needed by academy trustees, and its handbook *Governing a Multi Academy Trust* draws from the DfE documents, including the *Academy Trust Handbook* in particular, to show what the regulator expects.

Being a member of a trust board is a collective role as is that of a traditional maintained governing body, and those principles and mindsets of good governance discussed in chapter 3 apply. The different reporting requirements, particularly on the financial side, are very much processes and procedures that a competent governance professional, a company secretary, will see to, rather than requiring a considerable change in week-to-week governance practice. The change in legal status has certainly necessitated significant development for governance professionals.

To whom one reports – the DfE rather than the local authority – does not require a great change in how one governs. There was much nonsense spoken on this topic, in part due to a great misunderstanding of Whitehall about LA-maintained school governance since LMS. It was said schools were 'controlled' by local authorities and that governing bodies just did local authority bidding, when in fact, as we have already established, LMS had effectively shifted local authorities to being regulators and the providers of support, rather than running schools on a daily or even weekly basis.

There were some local authorities who were overbearing and patriarchal, and others whose services were not great quality. Some did aim to keep governing bodies rather reliant on them; for example, by issuing model agendas that straitjacketed thinking. However, there was nothing to stop any governing body taking the initiative, and many maintained governing bodies did exactly that: determined their own agendas while drawing on the various expertise available from local authorities when it was valuable and looking elsewhere when it wasn't. By 2010, not all maintained governing bodies understood and embraced their power – their decision-making role – and were in practice still very reliant on local authorities to function. However, in the years since, local authority capacity has diminished and the remaining maintained governing bodies have had to adopt a more independent mindset.

The model policies developed and issued by local authorities were generally found to be helpful; a way of not reinventing wheels. This can be viewed as a form of efficiency, and as these diminished in many places over time as local authority services were reduced, many other organisations, including NGA, were asked to provide them. Ironically, it is now a practice understandably adopted by almost all MATs; it is interesting that something that used to be decried as bureaucratic when local authorities did it is regarded as efficient in the world of trusts.

There were clearly times when local authorities made decisions – for example, on pupil numbers or new schools – that maintained school leaders and their governing bodies disliked, but unless there was some sort of crisis or concern about pupil outcomes, local authority staff weren't regularly present at governing body meetings. Their advice might be sought on tricky situations and their involvement in headteacher recruitment was usually seen as invaluable.

Employers

Academy trusts are the employers of staff, which brings with it a raft of legal responsibilities. This includes a 'duty of care', meaning they must do all they reasonably can to support staff health, safety and wellbeing. In recent years as the profile of wellbeing has grown in our country, so has the time spent by governing boards considering these issues, whether the legal employer or not.

In terms of governance practice, becoming the employer was not as substantial a change as might be first assumed. First, as covered in chapter 5, some schools maintained by local authorities were already the employers, particularly voluntary aided (VA) schools, so it wasn't entirely new to the English school sector. Second, even those maintained schools who were not legally the employers acted 'in lieu of the employers'. This leaves local authorities (LAs) in a very odd position with community schools and voluntary controlled schools, where the LA was legally the employer but another organisation – the governing body – made the week-to-week employment decisions for which the LA would be held accountable. Some years ago, leading members of the Local Government Association requested that this anomaly be changed to eliminate the risk that an LA could be left exposed by decisions they had not made, but this change didn't gain any traction. It would of course also have eliminated other anomalies, such as small community schools having to pay the apprenticeship levy as they are linked to the number of LA employees.

Whether legally the employer or not, the decisions the maintained governing body has to make on staffing are the same ones that SATs do, the main practical difference being who can be called on for support. When recruiting a headteacher, a maintained school has to involve an adviser from the LA, and a diocesan school, even where VA, is obliged to work with an adviser from the diocese. Those advisers, however, do not have a vote in the selection panel and can be a helpful source of support and expertise. On the other hand, a SAT is free to choose any adviser, and they do not have to have an external adviser for headteacher appraisal at all, but most do continue to have one. Custom and practice runs deep.

Having said that, I do not mean to minimise the board's responsibilities for staff: this is crucially important. I will come back to it in chapter 13.

Financial oversight

Fundamental differences after conversion to academy status were experienced by the school business management staff as financial reporting and accounting expectations are significantly different, and financial oversight was usually the area of biggest change when moving from governing a maintained school to a SAT.

It is not just the reporting that is different; there is no local authority acting as 'banker of last resort' although the DfE provide loans to some struggling trusts. The DfE requires academy trusts to produce a three-year budget and to balance it for the current year (taking into account carried forward funds). This has become increasingly difficult over the past decade as school funding has not been increasing at the same rate as many costs for most schools, a challenge I will return to in chapter 13.

Successive years of deficits will consume reserves and could theoretically lead to the trust becoming insolvent. The DfE doesn't sit by and let this happen without protecting the schools. This can mean moving the schools from the trust and terminating its funding agreement. Where the DfE has concerns about financial management or governance in an academy trust, a Notice to Improve (NtI) can be issued and published. These cover a range of issues from setting deficit budgets to poor financial reporting or lack of adequate insurance, and have been issued against all sort of trusts, from the tiniest of SATs to large MATs.

The publication of NtIs is a good exercise in transparency, but what is more obscure are the loans and other payments made to trusts who do get into financial difficulties – or indeed for any other specific situation – as well as the amounts and the reasons for these. Such rumours perpetuate the idea that help will be forthcoming, but relying on this as a solution would not be seen as good trusteeship.

I am also struck that the language of the third sector has not penetrated the world of trusts. As charity leaders we are very aware of the phrase 'structural deficit' to describe a deficit budget that builds in expenditure, which will be required year-on-year without an ongoing income to fund it in the coming years. This is very different from making a loss for one, or even two, years when investing from reserves for either a short-term project or one that will cover its own costs in future.

Personal liability

The liability of the individual volunteering is sometimes thought to be of a different order in trusts and companies limited by guarantee. Especially in the early days of trusts, this was talked about as a deterrent to volunteering. However, it is very rare for individual trustees to be held personally liable when things go wrong, including where a trust becomes insolvent. It is the trust as an entity that is responsible. Trustees would not tend to be individually liable provided they had acted in good faith and had taken action.

Where trustees carry out their duties in good faith, defined by the Charity Commission as genuine, honest intentions or motives, trying to do the right thing, in the interests of the charity, no liability will attach to an individual. The DfE (2024) guidance states: 'If academy trustees act reasonably in the course of their duties, they are generally protected from personal liability, with liability falling on the academy trust (company).' This includes decisions taken by an individual or a committee of the board provided each has been delegated that authority by the board in the first place.

2. Governance professionals

A very necessary and important change over the last decade has been the growth of the governance profession; those who are paid to clerk, support and advise governing boards. Having a good clerk or governance professional is one of the eight essential elements of effective governance; the importance of the role cannot be overstated.

Clerking services existed in many parts of the country well before 2010, often run by local authorities, and in some places, clerks were well trained and offering an excellent service. Elsewhere the role was more limited, a minuting service rather than a full governance advisory service. It was not unusual for governors to be minuting committee meetings or panels. The increasing understanding of both volunteers who govern and senior leaders of the need for a governance professional since then has been substantial.

In 2013, the Clerking Matters campaign was set up by NGA and SOLACE (Society of Local Authority Chief Executives) to:

- Increase the understanding of the importance of the work of clerks and what can be expected of a well-trained clerk.

- Help governing boards find good clerks where there is difficulty in doing this.

- Help clerks know where continuing professional development can be found.

- Encourage appropriate remuneration of clerks.

The House of Commons education committee report that same year made it clear that 'as professional bodies, school governors need professional support' and the recommended that 'the DfE should act upon the findings of the NGA and the SOLACE project exploring the professionalisation of the clerk's role'.

To inform the campaign and test progress, and provide content and context to the ongoing debates surrounding the evolution of governance professional roles, NGA surveyed clerks in 2013, 2016, 2021 and 2024. As a result of the legal and structural changes, governance professionals weren't all doing the same role; there were different levels of knowledge, skills and experience required, depending on the type of board(s) being supported.

NGA wasn't the only organisation championing clerking and clerks. National Coordinators of Governors Services has existed for some time and more recently both the National Association of School and College Clerks and Trust Governance Professionals were set up. The Chartered Governance Institute (CGI) exists for us to compare and learn from practice in other sectors. The great thing about working on this topic has been the input of so many organisations and individuals working towards these ends.

Some research reports highlighted the role. The Education and Employers taskforce in 2018 recognised the vital role, but found that 'despite the best efforts of a number of stakeholders it appears that the universal availability of qualified clerks remains an issue' (Judge and Kashefpakdel, 2018). NFER's report for the DfE in 2020 was still having to conclude: 'Clerks, when utilised properly, were seen as key to the effective running of governing boards, but not all boards were making the most of the resource clerks can offer.'

There was a difference of opinion on whether to move to the title 'governance professional'. This has been suggested by the DfE when developing the clerking competencies in 2017, but the majority of the profession consulted wanted to continue to be addressed as clerks, and there wasn't a significant cadre of trust governance professionals as that stage. By the time of NGA's Clerking Conference 2020, this had changed, and in our research published as *Governance Professionals: 2021 and Beyond*, a significant majority of respondents – 70% – wanted to be recognised as a governance professional.

The 2021 survey made it clear there was one profession serving both trusts and maintained schools, not divided in two by school structures, even though different governance structures clearly require additional or different knowledge. Only a very few trust governance professionals had come from other sectors as governance professionals; most had previously worked for maintained schools, a move that allows progress within the profession, and there were – and still are – many who work for both academies and maintained schools. Within the governance profession there are a portfolio of different roles reflecting the variety of governance structures, and one of the job titles likely to endure is that of clerk alongside newer ones.

Changing the language was not as simple as waving a magic wand, but it was a prerequisite for professional recognition. There were a few in the trust sector who wished to keep their distance from maintained clerks, but I argued it would be counterproductive to fail to unite around the need for professional appraisal, development, progression and reward.

The change of language was officially recognised when the academy trust model articles were updated in 2021, with 'governance professional' replacing 'clerk'. The DfE also strengthened its guidance in the *Governance Handbook* and the *Academy Trust Handbook 2021*, finally and belatedly requiring boards to appoint a governance professional.

NGA's 2021 report drew from the experiences of over 1200 governance professionals, and found:

- Governance professionals are still undervalued because their critical and valuable role is not well understood by the sector.
- Governing boards had been slow to implement the Clerking Matters expectations with the result that pay had not advanced sufficiently and CPD was not usually rewarded.
- The governance profession required a career framework linked to clear expectations, relevant qualifications and remuneration.

Development and a career pathway

Until the development of the career pathway, convincing the minister, Lord Nash, of the fundamental importance of the role was the most influential thing Clerking Matters achieved. As a result, from 2014 until 2021 the DfE funded – albeit at only £350 a head – a development programme for clerks. Although it's no longer DfE funded, NGA's Leading Governance legacy programme continues to offer a Level 3 certificate in the Clerking of School and Academy Governing Boards accredited by the CGI, who in turn offer a Level 4 qualification.

The DfE published its Clerking Competency Framework in 2017 as non-statutory guidance setting out in detail the four competencies required to deliver professional clerking to school and trust governing boards: understanding governance; administration; advice and guidance; and people and relationships. It has since been archived largely because of its length, rather than its content dating, with ministers in the last Conservative government taking the view that less from the DfE was more.

Working with hundreds of governance professionals across the country and led by Steve Edmonds, then NGA's director of advice and guidance, a career pathway was created. It defines three distinct governance professional levels: clerking, governance coordinator and lead governance level, and it was very well received.

In 2021, there was still insufficient focus on development within the profession. Over a quarter of respondents to NGA's survey had been offered no induction training, with significant variations in quality and scope where such training was offered; this has reduced to 18% with 2024 respondents. In NGA's 2024 survey, 70% of respondents were highly satisfied or satisfied with training and CPD opportunities, compared to 63% in 2021.

The take up of clerking-specific qualifications has significantly increased over the past three years, with 74% of respondents having completed or started NGA's Level 3 certificate in clerking (the most commonly pursued qualification), compared to 41% holding a clerking qualification in 2021. There were also 30% of respondents who had completed a Level 4 or higher qualification. However, it was reported that these qualifications did not always lead to improved pay or responsibilities with only 19% of professionals reporting career progression resulting from completing accredited qualifications. Barriers remained for some to obtaining qualifications, particularly time constraints and cost.

Governance professionals should receive an annual appraisal at which CPD is discussed, involving the chair of the governing board (even if the clerk's services are engaged from a third party). Though this is still not yet the norm with a third not having an annual appraisal at all in 2024, it is an improvement from just over half in 2016. And even more pleasing is that when appraisals do take place, 70% now involve a conversation about professional development, whereas just three years ago this was a shocking 27%.

After a recommendation from the DfE's National Leader of Governance (NLG) advisory group, on which I sat in 2020, governance professionals were able to apply to be an NLG from 2021–23. This was important recognition of their skills and knowledge, but this recognition and funding has now disappeared.

Supply of governance professionals

In 2024, only one third of governance professionals reported working full-time, of which more than half worked in only one setting with the remainder working full-time hours across a number of schools and trusts. In NGA's survey, almost two thirds (63%) of governance professionals were directly employed by their schools or trusts. The remainder were employed by local authority (21%), self-employed (10%) or employed by an independent clerking service (6%). Of those employed by schools/trusts, 61% of respondents also held another role at the institution; the nature of these roles varied considerably, but they were primarily in administration, finance and human resources. A second role in business management can be tricky when that member of staff needs to report to the board in their second capacity while attempting to minute it as the clerk.

The governance professional should be answerable first and foremost to the board who must have independent, impartial advice. Having another role in the school or trust can compromise that independence, especially when that role is as an assistant to the headteacher or chief executive. The power dynamic there is unhelpful and that combination of roles should be avoided. Anything that diminishes the loyalty to the board should be avoided. Some local authorities' services used feedback from clerks to ascertain how a maintained governing body was performing: while it is understandable that the LA would want to know more, there is potential for a clerk to have split loyalties. This is a question of ethics: what must be kept confidential to the board and does the clerk let the chair know about questions from the boss in the clerking service?

Despite 88% of respondents in 2024 reporting that they were satisfied with their relationship with the leadership team, and 86% feeling that the board had confidence in their advice, just over half (54%) confirmed their intention to remain in the profession, a reduction from 61% in 2021. Almost one fifth of respondents indicated that they did not plan to stay in the profession for long. Almost a third (30%) were dissatisfied with opportunities for career progression. This plus low pay and workload were the three top reasons for wanting to leave the profession, although others' lack of understanding of the role and anti-social hours were mentioned.

Appropriate remuneration

In 2020, NGA responded to the fact that a large number of governance professionals were not being paid appropriately for all the hours worked. With the help of an expert steering group and painstaking consultation, we provided a credible evidence-based recommendation for a minimum rate of pay in *Putting a Price on Effective Clerking*: £12.85 per hour to £14.74 per hour, depending on experience. In 2025, that would correspond to a range of £16.08 to £18.45.

Some higher paid governance professionals were understandably disappointed with this outcome as not recognising their worth, and it was difficult upsetting an important constituent of our membership, but the work was thorough. What's more, we discovered the next year that the majority of practitioners clerking at school level (58%) were being paid below what had become NGA's recommended minimum. There needed to be a sea change, and this range was a modest beginning.

In 2024, just under half of governance professionals were still paid below £16 per hour with roughly the same number between £16 and £30 per hour, and 10% of respondents above that. For those who clerk at level 1 of the career pathway, two thirds are still below the recommended minimum.

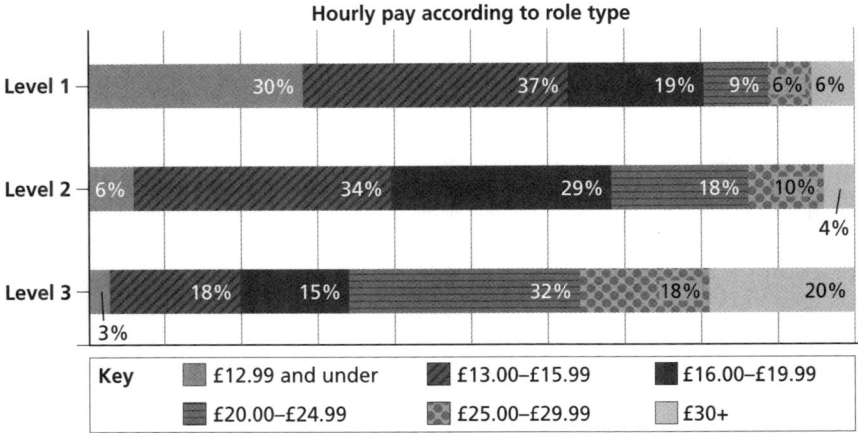

Figure 7.1 Distribution of pay across governance professional levels in 2024 (supplied by NGA).

The way in which governance professionals were employed and by whom influences their pay and working conditions. Those that can set their own pay as freelancers tend to do a little better. In maintained schools, 53% are earning less than £16 per hour, compared with 45% in SATs and 42% for academy committees. Even 32% of those working for MAT boards and extraordinarily 21% of level 3 governance professionals are earning less than £16 per hour.

There is scope for pay progression as professionals move from level 1 to levels 2 and 3. Perhaps this is why satisfaction with remuneration has increased: 58% of governance professionals were satisfied or very satisfied with their remuneration in 2024, compared to 46% in 2021.

3. Size of boards

The topic of the best board size has been debated over the years again and again, and was even mentioned once again by the minister Cat McKinnell at NGA's Summer 2025 conference. I could quote from almost every report published with one opinion or another on the matter, beginning with the Taylor Committee in 1975: '24 members shall normally be regarded as the maximum for efficient operation'. Fifty years on that figure has reduced hugely, more or less halved.

Andrew Adonis suggested about eight people and no more than 11 for Labour's first academies, based on a combination of his own experience of board discussions and the practice in the private sector. The Labour government's working group in 2010 discussed setting an expectation that governing bodies should not exceed 14 members. However, the consensus was that there wasn't the evidence to support that and that governing bodies already had appropriate flexibility to choose the right number of members for their local circumstances. It was felt that there needed to be a balance between the skill set and size of the governing body.

The coalition's 2010 DfE White Paper promised to 'make it easier for schools to adopt models of governance which work for them – including smaller, more focused governing bodies, which clearly hold the school to account for children's progress'. It claimed that 'many of the most successful schools have smaller governing bodies' but no evidence of this was given. There was none.

The 2008 Business in the Community study by Balarin et al. had found that there was 'no significant or substantive relationship' between the size of a governing body and 'aspects of its effectiveness'. Its lead author Professor Chris James wrote an article for NGA in 2011 on the evidence of board size and concluded: 'those who advocate smaller governing bodies fail to understand the practice of governing, and that size is not the issue. Ensuring effectiveness and stakeholder involvement are more important considerations.'

The vast majority of governors agreed with Chris: according to NFER's 2011 research, governors felt that the size of the board was the least important element of an effective governing body. The Academies Commission noted in 2013 there was much speculation about the optimum size of governing bodies, but judged that function, capacity and coverage of expertise remain the key criteria.

Regulations were changed to enable maintained boards to be smaller and initially the DfE did leave it to the discretion of governing bodies. This was changed due to the DfE's frustration by the slowness of change and maintained governing bodies were then expected to reconstitute. This meant that without equivalent compulsion, SATs often kept their original larger size while maintained schools had no option.

Bereft of evidence from the world of governance, I was an agnostic to begin with, but then my own experience influenced me. When I arrived at NGA, its board of trustees had 18 elected places and they were all filled. It took two consecutive chairs and an external review of governance to reduce the board to nine regionally elected trustees with the option of four co-opted places. Since then, it rarely had more than 10 members, and that was a more effective size for governing NGA: I say that as a former chief executive, but the trustees' views were similar.

Over the years, many governors already struggling with workload expressed concerns that if they downsized there would be fewer people to share the work with. The 2010 White Paper claimed 'smaller governing bodies with the right skills are able to be more decisive'. I have come to agree with this, not only from my own experience and the feedback from NGA members, but also because of the work of behavioural psychologists.

Big teams have been found to be less effective in terms of decision-making. This relates to time taken, dysfunctional conflict, cultural clashes, a perception of reduced responsibility, groupthink, free-riding and 'social loafing'. The latter refers to the phenomenon where individuals exert less effort in a group task than when working alone, often due to perceived reduced accountability, and is most evident where it is difficult to identify the contribution of an individual. Large teams show more dysfunctionality in decision-making, as the number of non-participating members increases. It is suggested that one disruptive person or 'bad apple' can harm morale and productivity.

The Walker review into corporate governance, commissioned by Prime Minister Gordon Brown after the banking crisis, did look at the behavioural evidence and suggested that views would probably tend to converge around an 'ideal' board size of 10–12 members, not least on the basis that a larger board is less manageable and inhibits the ability of individual directors to contribute. However, Walker didn't make a formal recommendation on board size but emphasised the importance of improving the behaviours of boards over structures and rules.

	2013	2014	2015	2016	2017	2018	2019	2021	2022	2024
Up to 10	17%	17%	25%	26%	37%	38%	40%	48%	47%	63%
11 to 15	54%	60%	58%	59%	52%	52%	51%	46%	46%	35%
16 or more	29%	23%	16%	14%	10%	9%	9%	5%	5%	2%
Don't know	N/A	N/A	1%	1%	1%	2%	N/A	2%	2%	N/A

Table 7.1 Board size: data from NGA surveys.

NGA survey data shows clearly that the average board in the school sector has reduced in size over time with one in five respondents in the last two surveys reporting that their board currently has eight or fewer members. Reducing the board to below eight members, not including the headteacher/chief executive, can begin to hamper board performance and adds to the workload of those remaining. Smaller boards also lend themselves to having few committees, which I will return to later, and to arrangements with other institutions to cover exclusion panels. Experience shows nine or 10 is the size to aim for.

Size varies with board type. Three quarters of MAT boards – both boards of trustees and academy committees – are now 10 or fewer places, compared to 44% of SAT boards and 54% of schools maintained by local authority. The reverse is true at the top end with only 5% of MAT boards having 14 or more places, compared with 25% of SATs and 11% of maintained schools. Looked at another way: a typical MAT board or academy committee is likely to have eight places, a SAT 11 and a maintained school 10.

The DfE (2024) doesn't give a number: it has for some time repeated words to the effect of: 'The DfE's preference is for smaller boards that help the board be cohesive, dynamic, and able to act more decisively on delivering its agreed strategic priorities.' I have been surprised by some senior officials wanting to return to the conversation about size and reduce boards further but largely to alleviate volunteer recruitment. This will cause far more problems than it solves. A board needs a certain number of members to function.

4. Changes in composition: skills and stakeholders

This – the move to recruit people with specific skills as opposed to reserving places for stakeholders – is probably the school governance change that has had the most written about it: my first draft of this section ran to pages and pages as I tried to record many of those interventions, but there were very few actual findings even though the topic was covered in depth for a couple of decades. What was under debate was something fundamental about the nature of governance of a public service, and the role of elected representatives. I have devoted a chapter to that crucial issue (chapter 16: Who owns our schools?). But here I will introduce the changes and the reaction to them.

The Taylor report of 1977 concluded that school governing bodies should be constituted on the stakeholder model, and the details of that form of governing body constitution were confirmed in subsequent legislation, beginning with the Education Act 1980. There was much concern that the increased flexibilities accorded to governing bodies by the Education Act 2011 were a move away from the stakeholder model. From September 2012, maintained schools could adopt a new approach with less prescription over the number of parent governors, and whether they were elected or appointed; a minimum of two parent governors was required but just a single local authority governor. Lord Hill, the schools minister, told the NCSL fellowship that he had wanted even greater flexibility, but the House of Lords wished to retain a degree of local representation.

First, the stakeholder model and the skills-based model were considered initially by almost all in the debate as alternative contrasting approaches. The underpinning assumption of the stakeholder model is that public sector institutions should be governed by those who have an interest in them, as opposed to the assumption that such institutions are best governed by boards made up of people with the requisite skills. This is unnecessarily oppositional. I, and many others with experience of governing boards in practice, argued that those models are not at odds. It is possible, and even desirable, to have both within the same board.

Many governors who joined boards as stakeholders had relevant skills: for example, in 2008 at the school where I governed as a parent before I knew of NGA's existence, the four parents (in elected places, although all elected without a contest) were a publisher, a senior leader in West Midlands fire service, a finance director at an NHS trust and me, a chief executive of a charity. This is a comprehensive secondary school serving a fairly affluent area, although with about one third of pupils eligible for free school meals. Chapter 10 will look at the national picture, which confirms the background of volunteers is much more likely to be professional managers than not. I fully appreciate that was not the case everywhere, particularly with small schools in disadvantaged areas.

Second, governing bodies had been considering the skills needed to govern and their gaps for years. Deem et al. in 1995 found that recruits with functional skills, such as financial or human resource management expertise, were welcomed by governors, but being able to participate made more difference than their knowledge. Balarin et al. in 2008 reported that governors considered the most important attribute of potential governors to be their support for the school and its ethos, followed by having relevant skills, functional and strategic capabilities, and specialist expertise, which were all seen as more important than community representation.

NGA's annual surveys show 72% of governing boards were conducting a skills audit in 2012, rising to a highpoint of 87% from 2017 to 2019. Only half were using it for recruitment purposes, as opposed to assigning people to committees, identifying development needs or planning succession.

There was a continuing conversation about what constitutes the required skills, knowledge, experience and attributes for governing. In 2017, the DfE published a very long set of competencies – more than 150 – for those governing, which has since been archived, but for some years the competency framework did cause a little bit of anxiety among volunteers who couldn't fulfil them. There were a further 60 competencies for chairs, which I did include in *The Chair's Handbook*; none of them were incorrect, but it was not clear how they should be used.

Introducing the huge number of expectations were the DfE's more accessible and memorable seven Cs: committed, confident, curious, challenging, collaborative, critical and creative. I was sorry not to see courageous there, already one of NGA's eight elements of effectiveness, and I don't really like critical, although it represents the analytical part of the role. So the legacy of the competency framework could be nine Cs: committed, confident, curious, challenging, collaborative, creative, connected, concerned and courageous. They certainly give the spirit of what's required to govern well, and they work fairly well for leadership too. Enough of the whimsy for now, but I wanted to illustrate the things that stick and help create change.

So, why did talk about skills worry many commentators and some practitioners? The language frequently used by the powers that be such as 'business skills' or 'business-like' made some commentators feel that too much notice was being taken of practice in the private sector and that a detachment from the community was being seen as a positive thing. It was an unfortunate perception to be reinforcing at a time when the academy movement was incorrectly being characterised as being 'privatised'. The third sector had been through a similar period a couple of decades earlier where we needed to move from being perceived as fluffy and not very efficient to growing and managing our limited resources well. At first, many noses were held until strategic planning and continuous improvement became second nature.

Some in the school sector and particularly academics also objected to the word 'professional' being used to describe governing bodies. This was largely due to globally circulating discourses of 'good governance', which saw the application of professional standards, technical expertise and performance evaluation as mechanisms for improving public service delivery as a sinister move. But no real alternatives for ensuring schools did the best for pupils were put forward. Plus, on the other hand, these approaches were not generally seen as objectionable by most governance practitioners who often had experience of them in their own workplace and who understood they had a part to play in holding schools to account. I mounted a defence of the language: that unpaid volunteers could do the role professionally. Being unremunerated was not a reason to do a role poorly, and I didn't want governors and trustees to be patronised or considered incapable, and for the same reasons, I objected to the word amateur being used.

There was rightly a common criticism that the emphasis on functional skills underplayed other crucial aspects, such as commitment, background and what are often termed 'soft skills'. *The State of School Governing in England 2014* report from the University of Bath and NGA showed that governors brought substantial expertise to the role and identified the kinds of capabilities respondents looked for in new volunteers:

- A readiness to ask challenging questions, which we contend is underpinned by assertiveness.
- A willingness to take collective responsibility for the conduct of the school.
- Commitment to the school, which we would argue needs to be tempered by a wider commitment to the success of other schools and high-quality education for all young people.
- The ability to work in a group, which is crucial for being able to contribute appropriately to discussions of complex issues.
- Specialist knowledge, such as financial or legal expertise, can be important for ensuring sound scrutiny of significant aspects of the school's work.

Most respondents also said their governing bodies seek to ensure that there is a balance of capabilities in the membership, and that this wasn't just a tick-box exercise in which we all end up with the butcher, the baker and the candlestick-maker (or the modern version: one lawyer, one accountant and an HR expert). Putting together the team that is the board is a more sophisticated affair, informed but not dictated solely by skills gaps. I return to recruitment and to the diversity of boards in chapter 10.

As the DfE was disappointed that not enough governing bodies took advantage of the new flexibilities, the changes in constitution were made mandatory. By September 2015, maintained school governing bodies had to reconstitute to conform as follows:

- One elected staff governor, although other staff members could be co-opted provided that the total number of staff governing does not exceed one third of the total size of the governing body.

- The headteacher (unless they choose not to be).
- One local authority nominated candidate, with the governing body making the appointment if they agree the candidate has the appropriate skills.
- Community governors were replaced by co-opted governors, although in many cases the governing bodies chose to appoint the same people.
- A minimum of two elected parents.

The flexibility with parent governors was largely welcome as some governing bodies had struggled to recruit parent governors and welcomed the opportunity to reduce to the minimum two elected places, knowing they could appoint more parents to the co-opted places if others came forward. Parent governors are important in providing legitimacy for governing boards, as I will unpack further in chapter 16 alongside other possible moves to improve the legitimacy of our governance models. Foundation and church schools retained foundation governors, which are usually required to be in the majority.

That mandatory reconstitution exercise required maintained schools only to review their structure, whereas SATs tended not to. Often they had transferred their maintained governing body structure into their academy articles when they converted, rather than considering first whether it actually was best suited to the functions and responsibilities of a board of trustees. Therefore, although many representing academy leaders and others argued that the new freedoms for academies placed greater emphasis on structures, which ensured effective, accountable and independent governance, in practice this did not happen straightaway.

5. Knowing your schools

This is another of the eight elements of effective governance and should have been happening well before 2010 too. It needs consideration here as not only did understanding and practice need to improve substantively, but I wanted to acknowledge the issue head on. Otherwise, it can be dismissed as all about data and the move to performative accountability. Rather than adding to the accountability weight on school and trust leaders, institutional governance can lift that weight. Those governing know the schools well in a very different way from inspectors who arrive for a snapshot of a day and a half.

Boards need to understand the day-to-day life of the school in order to be able to stand back and play a productive role at a strategic level.

Without some organisational and sector knowledge, the board's decisions will lack context and could be misguided. But the closer the board gets to the everyday operations, the greater the risk that some board members will start seeing only the trees and not the woods. They may get involved unnecessarily in the detail, which is easier than dealing with the bigger issues. Board members need to learn but not interfere. There are many ways of gathering useful information and they all need to be employed.

Data from *The State of School Governing in England 2014* tells us most governors (70%) visit to get to know the school, mostly to meet with staff, but also just over half visited to observe how a particular curriculum area or year group is taught. Governors' visits can also be to increase their visibility and support the school at events or listen to the views of different groups – parents, pupils or staff. For example, 45% of respondents visited the school to represent governors at parents' evenings. Governors also visited for monitoring purposes, especially progress towards a strategic target; how particular resources are being used in the school/lessons; how the values of the school are put into practice; or how a particular policy is being implemented. Although this is now 10 years old, I wouldn't have expected that to have changed much, apart from during the Covid-19 pandemic.

In 2014, one in eight governors reported visiting the school to judge the quality of teaching, which never was their role, but it is hard to argue against a headteacher who is claiming Ofsted expects it. There was an infuriating time when the system from governance trainers to inspectors expected governors to go into classrooms to look at books and judge teaching. Accompanying senior leaders on ambiguously named 'learning walks' blurred the question on who was doing the learning. A chair I met at an event was having a difficult time with a new head while the local authority's governor services were chasing her about going into classrooms to observe teaching: 'We don't need to walk round classrooms to know that our headteacher is struggling. We have a number of other sources. In fact, he was a good deputy head and is strong in developing teachers in the classroom. It is all the other things you don't do as a deputy head, budgets and difficult HR situations, he can't or won't manage.' I agreed at the time and she wouldn't be expected to do that now.

There is a skill in poking in the dusty corners and promoting a culture whereby staff help governors understand the school without there being interrogations. Simply saying to people, 'What is on your mind? How is it going?' can result in a wealth of information that will supplement other data. There is never just one source of truth and different things speak to different people on the board. The framing effect is a cognitive bias where people's decisions are influenced by how information is presented rather than the actual content itself. Essentially, the way a choice is framed, including in terms of a positive or negative spin, can alter decision-making. These different constituents together paint a picture, which is the start of the conversation. You may need to clarify the accuracy of data, but not to the extent that it dominates the conversation.

NGA did spend considerable time training governors on both the pupil attainment data and financial data. In 2012, we developed with FFT (Fischer Family Trust) an accessible data dashboard for governing boards. Very shortly afterwards, others did the same, including Ofsted, which I suggested at the time was dumbed down and underestimated the needs and abilities of governors. Ofsted's training didn't stand the test of time, whereas FFT developed Aspire. The DfE's education and financial information for schools has also improved over the period.

Some people who turn up on boards with a very particular view of accountability have a tendency to turn quantitative data into targets, and targets can then monopolise at every level. Board discussions and strategies need to be more nuanced and responsive. Otherwise, there is a danger that they and their leaders become more concerned with demonstrating the school is doing good work as defined by the data rather than concentrating on the whole range of good work as defined by the needs of the children.

Those entirely against the performative or 'datafication' approach to accountability and governance argue that schools are heavily prescribed by central government and that governing boards are therefore hamstrung as to what they have to monitor. While there are certain pupil outcomes it would not just be foolish, but negligent, to ignore, boards can in fact decide what else they value and wish to monitor.

Those that govern are not bystanders: they should be setting the agenda and have the confidence to take others with them. They don't need to be deferential and wait for the great and the good in the education sector to come up with all the ideas. Improvement is not all about those from outside education learning the school context. It also needs to be about educationalists looking to other sectors to question dominant education doctrine and to understand the experience of other sectors in achieving organisational change.

Conclusion

The first substantial change was trusteeship introduced into the sector on a widespread scale. Although the practice of governance is not that different from maintained schools, the law around trusteeship is. This transition to trust governance was not managed well by the DfE with articles using the term 'governors' incorrectly for quite some years and Ofsted not distinguishing the roles well. More thought and attention should have been paid to this considerable change. Given the large numbers of civil servants working on academisation, it is unfortunate that so little effort and learning was invested into the new form of governance, which could be characterised as the transfer of state schools into the third sector. There was a disdain to taking steers from the charity sector in terms of the roles of trustees or even the Charity Commission, which was odd and counter to learning from the huge experience of charity sector where trusteeship had existed for centuries.

Secondly, there was the move to undertaking the full range of governance activities. This applied to all boards, whether maintained or an academy trust, and could be termed 'modernising'. As I mentioned in chapter 3, there is much theoretical critique of an emphasis on risk mitigation, performance monitoring, financial probity and impact evaluation as part of officialdom increasing their own top-down control, accompanied by an assumption that the considerations will be narrow and result in standardisation. My response is that work largely corresponds to the fiduciary and impact modes, and the practice of the other three modes: the strategic, the generative and the cultural should go at least some of the way to allay the fears of governing boards being fully in the pocket of the powers that be.

Of course, those who govern state schools will always have to adhere to the law of the land – that is right and proper in a democracy. Yet a key question is whether during this decade the power has moved away from those who volunteer to undertake their duty as citizens to govern our state schools. If governing a single school, the answer is no: the wiggle room for unconstrained decision-making within the web of accountability is largely the same as in 2010. If governing within a MAT, the answer is affected by whether you are a trustee or a local governor, as I will explore in later chapters. I often argued that governors and trustees had far more power than they generally realised, but I failed to create a sea change in the levels of divergence from the prevailing views, wherever those originated. This is, I think, in large part due to the culture of the sector, and I do appreciate that is in large part determined by the governmental and accountability frameworks.

Better governance also required the development of governance professionals to support and advise boards, which is an absolute necessity of well-functioning governance. This is by no means a completed task: NGA's long-standing Clerking Matters expectations for the profession have not yet been universally achieved. Good progress has been made, but it continues to be a work in progress with more that can be done to value, reward and retain governance professionals in the school and trust sector.

Another reform since 2010 has been a move to smaller boards with fewer stakeholders. There is no credible voice making the case against the need to recruit skilled governors and trustees. I am also now much more likely to get support when I say nine to 10 board members works well, and eight is usually the working minimum. This really is a conversation that has run its course as the figures substantiate, but oddly it is one that both sides like returning to. I hope the Labour government does not spend time on this, when there are other more important measures.

Lastly, I suggest governing boards moved from concentrating largely on their compliance responsibilities – or as it is alternatively described, the fiduciary mode – to a more rounded practice of governance, balancing challenge with support and embracing the practice of the strategic, rather than simply paying lip service to it. In the next chapter on the state of governance, I will examine this further.

8.
The state of school governance then

So, have all the changes I detailed in the last chapter made any difference? I am looking here up to the onset of the pandemic in 2020. There is no official data or measure of governance. The separate Ofsted score for governance was dropped a long time ago in 2012, and anyway, I wouldn't want to have to rely on Ofsted for the last word on assessments of governance.

One thing I hope there is agreement on: with a nod to those nine Cs again, the first C of 'commitment' should be taken as read throughout the period as there are no dissenting voices on that score. For example, Ofsted (2011a) said: 'Governing bodies want to do the very best they can for their schools, pupils and local communities. That is why their members give so freely of their time.' Commitment, especially in hard times, is perhaps not acknowledged enough; the hard graft and persistence needed to govern well is often underplayed. But is that time and effort used to its best advantage? My contention is that, over the past 15 years, governance of our state schools in England has been improving. But having run an organisation devoted to making that happen, I'm not the most objective observer.

When giving oral evidence to the House of Commons Public Accounts Committee's (PAC) enquiry on school oversight and intervention over 10 years ago, I made the point that we didn't know enough about the standards on governance across the sector: 'We know that some governing boards are absolutely terrific and that some are pretty woeful, but what we don't really know is, do we have a bell curve? … And where are governing boards in our schools really placed?' But when pressed by MPs, I gave them my perception based on NGA's daily contact with governing boards that governance was improving. I probably shouldn't have been so reticent to commit, as NGA's experience of school governance across England was second to none and remains so in 2025.

Governance in 'outstanding' schools, especially those that have not been inspected for many years, can become complacent. As Ofsted's written evidence pithily stated 'some previously good or outstanding schools decline because governors have taken their eye off the ball', whereas some of the best governance happens in schools that have had to turn round their performance after a 'requires improvement' judgement where nothing is taken for granted.

Improving governance

There was a real push by the coalition government to improve governance, which continued into the next few years of the Conservative government. The first time I remember Michael Gove as Education Secretary addressing this issue publicly was at a FASNA conference in 2012 when he said:

'And there is another area where I need to drive reform faster: Governance. Good schools need good governors. And we have thousands of reasons to be grateful to those who give up so much time to help support school leaders in the work they do. It's because governance matters so much that the difference between good and bad governance matters so much.

We all know what good governance looks like. Smaller governing bodies, where people are there because they have a skill, not because they represent some political constituency. They concentrate on the essentials such as leadership, standards, teaching and behaviour. Their meetings are brief and focused; the papers they need to read are short, fact-packed and prepared in a timely way; they challenge the school leadership on results, and hold the leadership and themselves responsible for securing higher standards year on year – every year.

And, all too sadly, we also know what bad governance looks like. A sprawling committee and proliferating sub-committees. Local worthies who see being a governor as a badge of status not a job of work. Discussions that ramble on about peripheral issues, influenced by fads and anecdote, not facts and analysis. A failure to be rigorous about performance. A failure to challenge heads forensically and also, when heads are doing a good job, support them authoritatively.

We cannot have a 21st century education system with governance structures designed to suit 19th century parochial church councils. Ofsted, in their new inspection framework, will now be asking searching questions on governance – including assessing how well governors hold the head and senior leader to account. When it is our children's future at stake, we cannot afford the archaic amateurism of old-fashioned committee protocols – we have to be more professional.'

I put this here in its entirety to give the spirit of the political leadership under Gove. On the one hand, rightly exhorting all of us to use facts and analysis, while failing to do the same himself; this was several years before his famous quote during the Brexit referendum that 'Britain has had enough of experts'. His language was picked up by the press who showcased the villains of governance, not the heroes. *The Times* concluded that governors were looking for a badge of status and a chance to waffle on. Meanwhile, the Education Secretary had no evidence as to how much bad governance there was.

There was of course a grain of truth to his pronouncements. We had all heard of the local councillor who would become a school governor because it looked good on their election leaflets, but rarely graced meetings with their presence or would subvert the discussion to their latest local agenda. But political appointments had been in decline for at least a decade; they were rightly becoming an endangered species as local authorities sought local people with other skills and an interest in the school.

The Education Secretary hadn't gone out to meet governors to find out what goes on; he never even accepted NGA's invitation to speak to our members. He would have discovered, for example, that most governors were busy people with no time for rambling meetings. Given the 2010 White Paper's promise to put right the lack of respect given to governing bodies, this was a backwards step. Indeed, Gove stands out as the only senior figure in education who did not include a fulsome heartfelt thank you to volunteers when addressing an audience on governance. Luckily, the ministers with responsibility for governance took the issue more constructively and collegiately.

There's been much thought and effort in trying to work out how best to measure the quality of governance. The most significant attempt was in 2016–17 when the DfE commissioned the National Foundation for Educational Research (NFER) to undertake a feasibility study to look at defining and collecting metrics on the quality of school governance. Its objectives were to:

- Establish a set of criteria that, when combined, indicate whether a governing board is effective.
- Assess the quality of governance in a sample of schools of varying types by means of an external review of governance (ERG) carried out by NGA's team of expert consultants.

- Compare the results of the ERG and a survey of chairs and lead executives in order to test whether the survey using the criteria accurately measured the quality of governance.

Nine metrics were developed, but the scores coming from the surveys were too different from the ERGs. The metric that aligned least well was the one called 'cohesion', covering how well the governing board works as a team, the nearest to relationships and behaviours. Without seeing the board in action, it's so difficult to definitively judge. Metrics are unable to capture the art of asking the penetrating question, that simple question at the right time that changes the direction of a discussion. This fitted with NGA's experience of including questions on the quality of governance within the annual governance surveys: we stopped doing that as responses did not equate with our professional experience.

The conclusion had to be that this approach wasn't feasible, and this was not what minister Lord Nash had hoped. Every attempt to develop scalable metrics to assess the quality of governance has proved fruitless, but that's not a failure of imagination or effort. It is the correct conclusion for a difficult and nuanced activity. There has to be a balance between quantitative measures and valuing both professional judgement and the collective wisdom of our governing boards – those 'nine good people and true', to adapt the phrase applying to juries – and those who work alongside them.

The local authority role

At the beginning of the decade all local education authorities had a team providing governor services. They varied in size and services offered, but they usually included a training offer. They ran a volunteer recruitment service to supply a certain number of local authority governors for each maintained school governing body. NCOGS (national coordinators of governor services) represented local authority providers of services to school governors, as well as some diocesan and – increasingly as the years went on – some independent providers. In the early days, NCOGS supplied very useful data on such topics as vacancy rates, but this information reduced as governor support services in many places shrank.

A survey of coordinators carried out by NFER (McCrone, Southcott and George, 2011) provides a good starting point for the decade as their knowledge of governance locally was unparalleled. The survey found that governing bodies principally fulfilled monitoring and supporting roles. The two roles carried out by most governing bodies in the view of the coordinators were monitoring the performance of the headteacher (69%) and monitoring the school's progress against the school's development plan (61%). Moreover, only 13% of coordinators felt that most governing bodies 'provide strategic direction to the senior leadership team' and only 16% believed that most governing bodies 'are actively involved in self-evaluation of the governing body'.

Four coordinators suggested that primary schools tend to be less strategic. This can be associated with the perception that primary headteachers need greater support, especially if they have a considerable teaching commitment.

It is interesting that a large majority of governors either strongly agreed or agreed that their governing body provides an effective forum for discussion of school strategy and policy (87%) as at that time it was rare to find a school with a strategy. It was not unusual still to have agendas full of compliance, policy sign-offs, reports from committees and some monitoring usually carried out by reviewing the huge list of actions for staff on the school development plan.

The role of Ofsted

In her 2010/11 annual report, Miriam Rosen, the Ofsted chief inspector (HMCI) said that 'inspections this year identified considerable variations in the quality of governance across different types of school. Governance was judged good or outstanding in 58% of schools inspected this year overall, but this varied between 53% in pupil referral units and 55% in primary schools, to 64% in secondary schools and 71% in special schools. Although in the majority of schools the governing body acts as a critical friend, inspection findings show that where governance is less effective a lack of transparency and accurate information restricts the ability of the governing body to monitor the work of the school systematically.'

Although 58% strikes me now as low, this compares with 57% of schools inspected that year that were found to provide their pupils with a 'good' or 'outstanding' education overall. Around a third had improved, and nearly half achieved the same judgement, but nearly a fifth declined. Six per cent of schools inspected that year were judged 'inadequate', but with secondary schools most likely to be judged 'inadequate', at 8%. This was at a time when the challenges identified in the annual report by HMCI were tackling failure, raising aspiration, especially in stubbornly satisfactory schools, and improving the quality of teaching. Overall, the most recent inspection judgement showed that 70% of state schools were found to have been delivering a good or better standard of education.

Miriam Rosen's successor as HMCI, Sir Michael Wilshaw – not a favourite with the profession – was a great advocate for better governance and saw it as a priority, not something that can be said of very many senior educationalists. I had my policy differences with him, in particular he was interested in the payment of some governors and trustees (which I cover in chapter 10), but I was pleased to have such an influential voice raising the profile of governance. Ofsted's interest at that time was arguably and unsurprisingly the most influential lever for improving the quality of governance: I say that with sadness as it simply underlines that in the English school sector the inspectorate has such undue power.

A commission on the governance of charities set up by ACEVO (Association of Chief Executives of Voluntary Organisations) in 2013 compared school governance favourably, quoting NGA's view that 'Ofsted's investment in holding school governing bodies to account has helped to generate clear expectations of governors' responsibilities, and caused school governors to focus more on considerations of their own effectiveness and accountability. The stronger focus on school governance has also helped to raise the profile and visibility of the school governor role and contributed to more effective leadership.'

Although there was no longer a score specifically for governance, under Wilshaw's 2012 framework there had to be a paragraph in the Ofsted report on governance. From September 2012, the 'satisfactory' grade was replaced by 'requires improvement' (RI) and a pilot was undertaken to test whether schools graded RI for leadership and management should be expected to undertake an external review of governance (ERG). I remember that development well as HMCI rang me to test the idea out and ask whether NGA could provide reviews: he wanted to make sure there was a quality-assured supplier in the market. During the pilot over two terms, about 70 ERGs were recommended, some not until the monitoring visit, and most were provided by National Leaders of Governance. Of course I had said yes, and then I had a short period to set up a team of consultants. It was also a pilot, but both the Ofsted pilot and NGA's consultancy team were extended.

Learning from the best

In 2011, Ofsted published *School Governance: Learning from the Best* spurred on by its previous finding that, in just over a fifth of the schools inspected, governance was judged to be less effective than leadership.

The report looks at the principles and practices that contributed to an 'outstanding' governance grade in 14 schools, showcasing examples of highly effective governance that strengthened leadership and contributed to improved outcomes. Reading it again now, almost all of the identified good practice stands the test of time. One issue that needed a bit more exploration – and still does – was the role of committees, which in this report 'were typically seen as the "engine room of governance" where in-depth discussions, challenging questions and thorough debate of proposals took place'.

The danger with case study methodology is that the good practice of a particular school or trust does not stand the test of time, often as people change, and this appears to be the case for a significant proportion of these schools. Three of the six secondary schools have since had periods of being judged 'requires improvement' (RI), all after converting to be a single-academy trust. One remains RI, but the Ofsted report in 2022 barely mentioned governance other than incorrectly mentioning governors, rather than trustees. Good governance should be an insurance against this decline happening, but it is under-researched. Two of the secondary schools are now 'outstanding', but it is more difficult with current Ofsted reports to see if that extends to governance. One, now part of a MAT, had an inspection in 2017 that did still commend its governance at school level: 'the vision for a sixth form was finally realised in 2015 after many years of pushing by governors'.

Ofsted's survey on governance effectiveness

Sir Michael Wilshaw, frustrated by the DfE's lack of progress on tackling improvement in governance, decided in 2015 that Ofsted would carry out its own consultation. I gave a cautious welcome to Ofsted's spotlight on governance, while not being alone in questioning whether the inspectorate had the expertise to conduct such a review. During Wilshaw's regime, NGA was involved intermittently in training inspectors, especially in terms of MATs, which many inspectors did not have much or sometimes any experience of. Roles were often depicted incorrectly in reports. However, they did have knowledgeable internal leads on governance that were abandoned under his successor.

We had a healthy and constructive debate on what constituted effective governance, with much common ground. For example, HMCI adopted my mantra of 'eyes on, hands off'. He was concerned about governors who 'lack curiosity' and hold 'an overly optimistic view' of how their school was performing. Much of his analysis was correct, and his words on weaknesses have stuck with me: 'Governors devote too much time and attention to the marginal issues (like the school uniform, dinner menu or the peeling paintwork in the main hall) instead of focusing on the core issues that really matter – the quality of teaching, the progress and achievement of pupils and the underlying school culture.'

There was some truth in this characterisation, these being topics some governors felt more confident to contribute on, and it did result in NGA hesitating to forefront food in schools for a few years after.

The resulting Ofsted report *Improving Governance* published in 2016 began with the assertion: 'When inspectors judge the leadership and management of a school to be less than good, a common underlying weakness is the failure of governors to hold school leaders to account.' The final recommendations stayed away from the pay issue and were perfectly sound, featuring the well-rehearsed need for clarity of role, training, professional clerks, robust self-review and ERGs. Two factors were identified as crucial to making improvements possible:

- Schools becoming aware of the weaknesses in their governance arrangements: 'Too often, it is not until a school has an Ofsted inspection that leaders realise the weaknesses in governance.'
- The development of professional knowledge, understanding and insight within the governing board, although 'in some cases, this meant changing the composition of the board. In other cases, it meant accessing external professional expertise'.

The report concluded that schools showed that 'it is possible for weak governance to improve quickly. Neither the types of school nor the structure of governance were the reasons for the original weaknesses in governance'. This very much echoed NGA's experience and is in line with research from the previous decade.

Ofsted on governance since 2017

While Wilshaw was in charge, governance remained a theme. For example, when reviewing inspections of RI schools, Ofsted's annual report 2016–17 stated 'weak governance was a common feature' including:

- Not challenging effectively or holding leaders to account (for instance, by being too accepting of what they were told).
- Not understanding school performance or quality well enough.
- Not holding leaders to account for the use of additional funding (such as the pupil premium).

- Failing to act swiftly enough to challenge or support.
- Not checking the quality and impact of external support.
- Some governors lacked the confidence, skills and understanding to carry out their role effectively.

Ofsted used this slide, which wasn't in the report itself but is a powerful diagnosis.

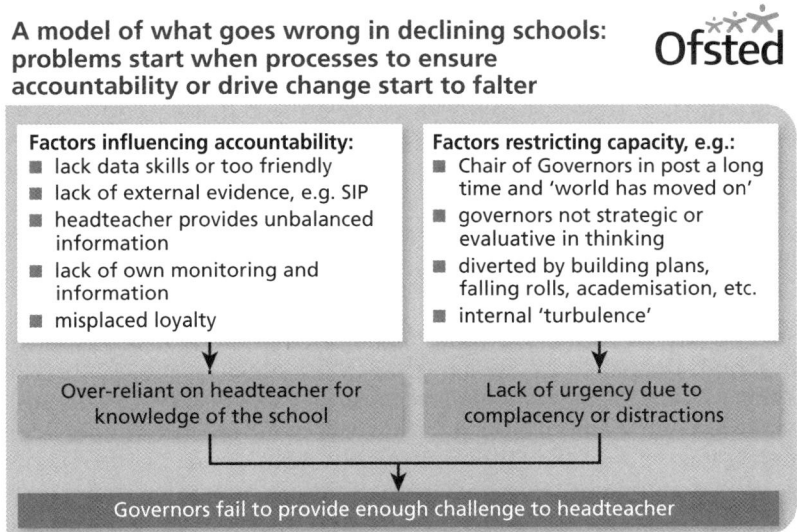

Figure 8.1 Ofsted's 2016 model of what goes wrong in declining schools.

Wilshaw's successor, Amanda Spielman, had little interest in governance, and it was clear from her 2019 framework and the resulting template reports there would no longer be a focus on governance. This marked the end of Ofsted as a driving force for the improvement of governance. For example, during 2014–15 inspectors called for ERGs in nearly 500 schools, approximately 15% of inspections, but these were no longer pushed by Spielman. Slightly surprisingly, the demand for ERGs didn't actually diminish as the DfE was also recommending them as good practice as a route to improvement – to be returned to in chapter 11.

Reviews of the decade

I have decided to include this summary here of reports on governance in chronological order for two reasons. First, to illustrate the range of other people and organisations involved in improving the practice of governing boards or in carrying out research. Second, the following six reports used different approaches and came from organisations with different roles but end up with a similar set of conclusions. From those with a good understanding of governance there was largely a consensus as to what would improve it. I will look specifically at MAT governance reports in the next chapter.

Just for full transparency, as well as being one of the authors of the University of Bath report, I gave evidence to the select committee and the National College fellowship; I was on the advisory group for the RSA project; I wrote a foreword for the Education and Employer's report; and I was asked to comment prepublication on the NFER's draft. But between the six studies, there were inputs from more than 10,000 people, mainly practitioners, both governance volunteers and education leaders: a very significant bank of evidence.

There were also two books during this time on school governance in England, both published in 2016: *Improving School Governance* by Nigel Gann and *Modernising School Governance* by Andrew Wilkins. Gann's book has elements of advice for practitioners. It's a second edition and, although it has a final chapter looking at the development of MATs, its tone is still very much grounded in maintained governance, but it is nonetheless a useful record of the decade completed, rather than one looking to future improvements.

Wilkins with his subtitle 'Corporate planning and expert handling in state education' examines the impact of market-based reforms on the role of governors in the English state education system. He also looks at how demands for 'strong governance' have been translated to mean improved performance management of senior school leaders and greater monitoring and disciplining of governors. He conducted a small-scale study of governing bodies over three years that enabled him to say he looked at the impact of these reforms on the day-to-day practices of governors.

However, Wilkins' main finding in terms of practice seemed to be that there was an inner core of governors who were more involved than the rest: this is often the case with boards and has been for a long time, as registered in earlier research. For example, as long ago as 1995, Deem, Brehony and Heath made the point that the participation of governors varies substantially: 'Governing bodies typically consist of a core of activists surrounded by a periphery of governors in varying states of inactivity.' The PWC study in 2007 included this quote from a headteacher: 'All are interested but they are busy people and commitment to the school can vary – the roles have changed and it can be the same teams who carry the burden – it's not the governors' fault.' I will come back to this issue in chapter 10 when we look at workload.

Most – if not all – of us involved in this field would like to see a more even distribution of power, influence and work among the members of boards, but this is often hard to achieve and little to do with an overbearing system. Wilkins considered the economic and political rationalities shaping the conduct of governors and is particularly interested in the diminished role of democracy in this context: I will come on to that topic in chapter 16.

2012: National College for School Leadership (NCSL) fellowship

NCSL used to bring together a group of national leaders of education for a couple of days to investigate a topic with eminent facilitators, advisers and witnesses, and in 2012 it was governance. They identified the importance of the right information being supplied to boards, though no mention of better papers from leaders. A tension existed for them between two of their recommendations: having a smaller board for effective decision-making and wanting stakeholder groups represented. They supported stakeholder engagement as a core function of governance, which I will return to.

The report underlines how poor the understanding of trust governance was even in a group including some academy heads and even a chief executive of a MAT. The word 'trustee' was not used, but they did rightly point out that there wasn't much change when single schools converted. Their reference to models of governance covering more than one school was a call for innovative examples.

2013: Commons Education Select Committee report

When publishing the House of Commons education committee report *The Role of School Governing Bodies* in 2013, the committee's chair Graham Stuart MP said: 'Greater freedoms for schools mean we need more effective governing bodies. At the moment, the quality of governance in many schools is inadequate. Accordingly, we are recommending a series of measures to boost governors' performance. These include introducing professional clerks, whose status should be similar to a company secretary. We also want to see greater training for governors – schools should be required to offer this to every new governor. Crucially, we want to encourage people from all walks of life to contribute as school governors.'

Lord Nash had put down a marker: 'The fact that Ofsted tells us that 26 per cent of our schools are not good or outstanding and that 44 per cent of our school governance is not good or outstanding clearly means that there are quite a few governing bodies that are not up to scratch … It seems to me that the two key pivotal decision points for a school are the head teacher and the governing body. Perhaps in the past we have underestimated the importance of the governing body to drive change, particularly in difficult situations' (House of Commons Education Committee, 2013c).

None of this was unexpected or revolutionary, but it was the bread and butter for a functioning system that supports those who govern. I would have been surprised if they'd come up with anything NGA hadn't already explored, but I was of course thrilled that the committee was recognising the critical voluntary role of governing bodies in England's schools and acknowledging that more should be done to ensure boards and their clerks have the support and information they need. However, there was a real push from a significant range of key stakeholders for mandatory training, including Sir Michael Wilshaw, and it was supported by almost all governors as well as NGA. The committee noted that with training being optional 'in weaker governing bodies it does not happen, and in stronger governing bodies it does'. They concluded 'government should require schools to offer training to every new governor'.

Instead, the committee took their lead from Lord Nash arguing that inspection would be the real driver of improvement: 'On being asked whether Ofsted would be resourced to take on so much responsibility for maintaining and raising standards in school governance, the Minister replied "Yes"'. There was a huge reliance by all concerned – the committee, the government and Ofsted – on the recently introduced role of ERGs to prevent school decline and improve governance.

The committee was also 'concerned at suggestions that few quality alternatives are emerging to the training traditionally provided by local authorities. We recommend that Ofsted and the DfE monitor the availability and quality of governor training in the light of greater academisation of schools and reduction of local authority services'. From that September, Ofsted would ask specific questions of governors regarding the amount and nature of training they are receiving, and how this was improving their ability to hold the school to account effectively.

The State of School Governing in 2014

This was a joint publication between NGA and the University of Bath, which we were encouraged to produce by the Education and Employers taskforce to coincide with the launch of Inspiring Governance Alliance, a collaboration aiming to raise the profile of governorship and have a positive influence on recruitment. The methodology was the same as NGA uses every year for its annual survey, and it's frustrating when some recent literature still refers to the figures in this report when NGA has since published updated ones. Publishing with the University of Bath under the leadership of Professor Chris James did give it more kudos and spurred us on at NGA to make our own reporting more thorough with a separate report from 2017 onwards. The 2014 report with Bath was more comprehensive than NGA's annual offering, which doesn't ask every question every year in an attempt to keep the time taken to complete it manageable. The 2014 survey also had the highest response level; 7713 individuals, which was quite an accomplishment. The largest response to NGA's annual response was during the first Covid-19 lockdown – 6864.

A large majority (84%) of respondents in 2014 reported that their governing body was working effectively, a figure more or less in line with the findings reported by the University of Bath in 2008 for Business in the Community in a similar survey. However, within the 2008 and 2014 figures, there were some detailed differences that indicated the school governing was moving in the right direction. In particular, more governors reported that they have a clear understanding of their role and responsibilities, one of the eight essential elements of effective governance. Secondly, governing bodies' self-evaluation processes had already begun to improve with 84% stating 'the governing body periodically reviews the way it is working'. Responses from governors (SAT trustees were still tending to call themselves that) of academies about the functioning of their governing bodies and their estimates of the overall effectiveness of their governing bodies were similar to those from governors of other types of school.

The study concluded that 'the data gives a strong sense that school governing overall is functioning well. Of course, such an assertion needs to be made with some caution. The data is self-reported… and the analysis has not explored governing bodies which are experiencing serious acute difficulties' (James and Goodall, 2014). NGA dropped the use of direct self-reporting of good governance in our own surveys; we would use questions about specific good practice and a range of proxy indicators.

Governors were invited to make suggestions about how the effectiveness of their governing body could be improved. The suggestions mentioned most frequently were:

1. Wider sharing of the workload among the members of the governing body.
2. Better/more training.
3. Governors with specific skills.
4. More governors.
5. Better chairs.

The launch of the Inspiring Governance Alliance and this research had taken much effort from a range of people with the aim of achieving some publicity to inspire more volunteers to come forward. The Education Secretary, Michael Gove, decided to subvert this celebration of the contribution of governance by including reference in his remarks to governors singing 'Kumbaya', hugging, and indulging in sherry and cake. There was much coverage of Gove's words, but little on the report findings at the time. Only twice at NGA did I write an open letter to the Education Secretary – and this was the first. He knew once again those words would be picked up by journalists, and I was livid that he had so little regard for those volunteering. But also turning the event into a farce epitomises the lack of seriousness with which he held governance of schools and ensuring we had people coming forward to take on this tough task.

2017: Who Governs Our Schools?

This report by Tony Breslin for the RSA in 2017 supported the focus on the need for better induction and training for school governors but emphasised that 'we need a better understanding of governance across the teaching profession and amongst others who work in and with schools, especially amongst school leaders and those who aspire to such roles'.

The report is much more than a stocktake of effectiveness of school governance, as its subtitle says: it looked at the 'trends, tensions and opportunities', largely brought on by the changes in structures I have covered elsewhere. Breslin underlines the need for rigour, excellence and better resourcing but cautions against the kind of clinical professionalisation that imports 'experts' onto boards while marginalising local stakeholders and weakening the connection between school and community. He is rightly very interested in the full purpose of governance, not just the more managerial aspects, and explores that pillar of good governance that I have labelled 'accountable governance', which I will come back to in chapter 16.

2018: Governing Our Schools: 10 Years On

Education and Employers, the charity that at the time was running the recruitment service Inspiring Governors, undertook research to update the 2008 report from Business in the Community (BITC). It looked at the high-level changes that have taken place over the last decade against the similar themes of: clarity of governing purpose; composition and skills of the board; governor recruitment and training; and the involvement of employers. In addition, they raised themes around governance not covered in 2008 – the impact of school funding changes, accountability changes and the rise of technology. They interviewed key players in the field.

The report concludes there has been progress and that despite the changes in structures, the different roles and responsibilities of governors and trustees are now much clearer. Governors and trustees are more informed and knowledgeable about their role, have a heightened sense of responsibility and are more focused on school strategy than they were 10 years ago. They highlighted that some governing boards were still not getting adequate information from the school's executive to fulfil their accountability function, something that hadn't really been embraced by leadership programmes.

2020: School and Trust Governance Investigative Report

In October 2020 the NFER released its report on school and trust governance commissioned by the DfE. The work, which involved a representative survey followed by interviews, had been carried out before Covid-19 hit the UK.

The research confirmed much of what we at NGA had thought, known and reported on for many years, but it's good to have those issues reinforced from another source. There was also a new finding that I have since used often as it gives the views of school and trust leaders: nine in 10 senior executive leaders (SELs) reported that their governing board was providing adequate support and challenge. Half (51%) of executive leaders 'strongly agreed' that they felt adequately supported and the same with being adequately challenged and scrutinised. Leaders interviewed by the NFER confirmed this with leaders noting that boards could be 'compassionate to staff' while they also offer 'a strong level of challenge'. It of course left 10% of boards not achieving this, but that is a level that is not too daunting to tackle.

In addition, the report confirmed:

- Clerks, when utilised properly, were seen as key to the effective running of governing boards, but not all boards were making the most of the resources clerks can offer: see chapter 7.

- The lack of diversity among those involved in governance, with regards to age and ethnicity, which means that boards are not necessarily representative of the communities they serve: see chapter 10.

- There are considerable challenges in the recruitment and retention of governors and trustees with the time commitment and workload seen to be the biggest barriers to recruitment: see chapter 10.

- The complexity of MAT governance presents a unique challenge in ensuring clarity in the roles and responsibilities of the different tiers of governance. The research found that there was confusion between the different tiers of governance as to where responsibility for certain areas of decision-making were held: see chapter 9.

Conclusion

I hope this wide range of sources and methodologies has convinced you that by the time the Covid-19 pandemic arrived five years ago, governance was no longer a weak point in the English school system. Nine out of 10 school and trust leaders think it's working. I am not saying all governing boards were functioning well, but the governance literacy and practice had generally improved. This is hugely to the credit of the volunteers who have embraced the role professionally even though its public profile does not do justice to it. When they get the occasional bashing in the press, they pick themselves up and continue on.

There was – and still is – more to do to spread the information and ambition to the minority of governing boards who do not govern well. Perhaps if they are without the support of a good governance professional and do not avail themselves of external training, they may not even be aware of their shortcomings. It was the role of the National Leaders of Governance to work with them and provide a further range of evidence as we will see in chapter 11. But first, let's see how governance of multi-academy trusts developed.

9.
MAT governance: the early days

By a long chalk, the greatest governance innovation in the recent past has been the shift from governing a single school to governing a group of schools. This revolution was not supported well – or even fully understood – by the powers that be who were unprepared for the change. It wasn't anticipated at the time of the 2010 Academies Act that almost all academies would end up being part of MATs. Perhaps if that had been the plan all along, the significance of new governance would have had more attention paid to it. So instead this was very much a case of the sector having to develop its practice, and I am exceptionally proud of the leading role NGA played in that.

For some readers, this period before the Covid-19 pandemic will be before their time in leadership or governance, whereas perhaps for others it will bring back memories of the Wild West days. There was no consultation, no fanfare; no official start date and very little official guidance on how to govern a number of schools. The system started to pay attention a little too late. I hope that this record of experimentation to solid good practice will be useful in terms of how to learn lessons and implement change.

I was initially convinced that other sectors would have something to offer: after all, the idea of a central overall board having oversight of service providers in different places wasn't that unusual. Charities often have structures that allow that, but when I looked at some, they weren't comparable. For example, Citizens Advice at a national level is a separate organisation from each local Citizens Advice Bureau with its own board. It has to live up to certain standards and periodic quality audits to use the CAB name. MATs are not franchises; they are a single organisation from top to bottom.

I asked The Institute of Chartered Secretaries and Administrators (ICSA) – experts on governance in most sectors in the UK and Ireland who later rebadged as the CGI (Chartered Governance Institute) – to see what other sectors could teach us. After all their research, for which I am grateful, including us attending their subsidiarity events, nothing transferable was found. So it really was a case of coming up with something new to put MAT governance into practice.

Clearly, there was no debate that the board of trustees had the power – and the responsibility – for the trust and its schools: that was the legal model. But the details of who made which decisions, how other voices were heard and how account was rendered had to be fine-tuned.

NGA's experience of working with MATs began in 2010, growing to become the majority of its work. At that point there were very few others engaged proactively in this work; as one CEO of a MAT said to me a couple of years ago: 'I was there in the front row at the Academies Show at the beginning when you were talking about trust governance and no one else was.' The NGA became the National Governance Association (as opposed to Governors') after our AGM in 2016 to underline that we spoke for and supported trustees too, and we worked with leaders and governance professionals as well as board volunteers. That year had seen NGA's publication of the first edition of its substantial and well-received *Welcome to a Multi Academy Trust*. By then, we had already had to produce other crucial guidance, such as model schemes of delegation.

NGA's early expertise was acknowledged by the IAA (Independent Academies Association) that styled itself as the voice of academies. Its origins were in the New Labour academies and City Technology Colleges; its president was Andrew Adonis. We ran the governance strands at their events, until they declared themselves insolvent in 2015. Being at IAA events underlined the fact that the academy movement was not one united band. There were palpable tensions between the original Labour academies – with their mission to improve the education in disadvantaged communities – and the converters, often from very different socioeconomic communities. Some of the leaders of early homegrown MATs, who were seen by some peers as empire builders who did not understand the benefits of autonomy nor possibly even sign up for the moral mission.

In the first few years after 2010, there was a complacent approach taken to examining MAT governance – still called 'chains' by most. By 2012, when there were 600 academies in chains, nine of which had 10 or more schools, the NCSL's fellowship commission heard from Robert Hill, author of a new report for the National College on effective academy chains that 'academy chain governance was mostly two-tier, with clear schemes of delegation and overlapping membership. They had small boards, with high calibre people and good training. There was also a focus on performance, using a standard data dashboard'. This suggestion that all was going well did not correlate with our experience, particularly the issue of clarity. The complacency and lack of challenge was surprising, but it may be that most participants had little knowledge of MAT governance at that point. Certainly, no one wants to wash their dirty linen in public, so difficulties or unknowns weren't shared, and no one else was carrying out thorough investigations.

This lack of rigour and curiosity was not helped by the then-minister for school structures, Lord Hill, favouring schools themselves deciding on the best form of governance as he confirmed to the NCSL commission: 'Government does not wish to direct schools (except those failing) on the best way to organise their governance.' This live and let live attitude should have been tempered by a little more realism and understanding of both the significant changes governing a MAT brought and the risks attached. Instead, the powers that be largely stood by until a few trusts began to implode, or should I say explode, into public awareness. Lord Hill's successor, Lord Nash, did speak often on governance, but without involving officials or commissioning anyone else to explore what worked well and what was to be avoided.

Even three years after the Academies Act 2010, there were few people who were experts on or even interested in MAT governance. At the House of Commons education committee enquiry, I said: 'I do not think there is enough talk about how we govern groups of schools, whether that is in multi-academy trusts or in federations maintained by local authorities. That is the real interesting discussion to be having: how can we do that well?'

The House of Commons education committee (2013a) report on the role of governing bodies report concluded, 'Lessons should be learned from the newer forms of governance appearing in academies, and greater consideration given to how groups of schools can be governed.' This was emphasised by the committee chair, Graham Stuart MP (2013): 'The Department for Education should play its part by explaining what models of school governance are now possible under the new regulations. They need to show how new arrangements can improve the ability of governing bodies to deliver their vital role to provide effective school leadership... Academies already have more freedom in how they constitute their governing bodies and – although not all academy governance is excellent – the Government should actively seek to learn lessons from the best approaches developed under these flexibilities in order to demonstrate what works best in the interests of pupils.' Once again, this never happened: instead, it was effectively outsourced to the sector, but without any funding or any public acknowledgement.

Finding good work to share is not simple. There is so often a request from the sector for case studies, but little appetite for schools and trusts to put themselves forward. When they do, there are almost always issues that they don't want in the public domain but would be good learning points. These often involve HR issues, executives recruited who struggled with the role or other sensitive topics. Also, they are not always strong practice. For example, the National College for Teaching and Leadership used a case study approach in 2015: one of the three trusts highlighted was Collaborative Academies Trust, which that very year was subject to an Ofsted focused review that found the MAT's impact on pupils' achievement was 'inconsistent and limited' (Bradley, 2015). The trust ended up being closed down, an abject failure for its sponsor, a well-known school improvement company. At NGA, we had a similar problem when one of the MATs who agreed to be part of our case study series in 2019 was closed down a couple of years later after terrible practice in one of their schools.

We found more useful learning happened in deliberative Chatham House forums where experiences could be shared by trustees. Once we gave up expecting the DfE to take the lead, in early 2016 – with Academy Ambassadors, the DfE-funded trustee recruitment service – we brought together 35 MATs at the DfE to discuss governance. A very thoughtful discussion confirmed the big themes coupled with a request to meet again. This spurred us on to set up NGA's MAT network, which met twice a year until it went online during the Covid-19 pandemic. As well as being an exchange of experience, challenges and successes, it served as a sounding board for new ideas. But before we consider those issues, I need to start with the governance scandals that cast a pall over those early years.

Mired by controversy

We have already seen that, like the Adonis era, the Gove acceleration of academies did not properly understand the need for a greater emphasis on governance to reduce the risk of trust failure. However, unlike in the Adonis era with smaller numbers and a very hands-on approach by the minister, after the Academies Act 2010 the consequences of a laissez-faire approach to governance and oversight began to be apparent with a series of trust failures, usually involving financial scandals.

Not all early MAT governance was poor, but the high-profile failures that could largely have been avoided also gave academies a poor reputation with the public for some time and aided the cause of the anti-academy campaigns. Stories of those in charge of schools profiting abounded when in fact those involved in trust governance are not paid and should not benefit personally from their connection. Opponents often referred to academies as 'privatised', rather than not-for-profit charitable trusts, but the financial impropriety exposed added to their arguments, while the hard work of the vast numbers of other trustees and local governors went unnoticed.

I will first consider the big issues behind these publicised problems and their elimination by better DfE oversight, and then go on to look at the much more common and garden practice that caused issues and had to be eradicated over the years, largely by NGA pointing out poor practice to avoid again and again. This is a deficit model of improvement, but it worked in practice.

Trust failures often, if not always, involve more than one deficiency. For example, take Wakefield City Academies Trust (WCAT), which had a lot of media coverage. There are many allegations and contradictory versions of what happened: the system needed more transparency to understand the pitfalls. It may be that the regulator didn't manage the situation well, which seems possible, but I can't be adamant without knowing the full situation, and there was no notice to improve issued. WCAT, a rapidly expanding trust, had been the subject of Ofsted's third focused MAT review in May 2015, which gave it largely a good bill of health, with most schools improving from a poor position. However, nine months later the CEO left under mysterious circumstances, and the chair, Mike Ramsay, was appointed as an interim chief executive. This would require permission from the charity commission as it is a risky situation that is avoided if at all possible, and it appears the EFA (Education Funding Agency) was aware of this. There were soon allegations of high pay for himself, a clerking contract for his daughter, poor use of funding and the removal of a critical trustee. A DfE-led investigation into WCAT in the summer of 2016 (leaked later that year) apparently found 16 breaches of official academy guidance by the trust, followed by a second leaked report from Ramsay's successor that identified a culture of fear and blame, dysfunctional governance and scant regard to HR and financial processes, although the police decided nothing criminal had occurred. Schools were brokered elsewhere in 2017/18, but not without delays for some and losses of funding. This illustrates the havoc an unethical chair turned chief executive can wreak and how fast things can go wrong for pupils if those governing or regulating do not carry out their roles well in those unusual circumstances. Either this decline happened extremely quickly or Ofsted, the RSC and EFA were not aware of the initial stages of the problems. In terms of accountability, the role of the media was important in shining a spotlight on the abuse of public office, but it was at the expense of the academy movement's standing.

Conflicts of interest

A conflict of interest has to be considered when a trustee's personal interests or loyalties could – or could be perceived to – prevent them making a decision in the best interests of the trust. There is a risk that the ability to exercise one's judgement could be impaired by another interest.

Conflicts of interest apply just as much to maintained schools and SATs, but I have included them here as it was in the early days of MATs that the issue came to a head and received much media coverage. Volunteering to govern a MAT appealed to those who sell services to the school sector: the need of MATs to source their own providers rather than relying on the local authority; the size of the organisation gave more opportunity for profits to be made; and probably a greater kudos associated with governing at the MAT. This was made worse by the unpreparedness of the sector to identify and deal with this change. Sometimes leaders would purposefully try to recruit those to the board who would provide services at a cheap rate or even pro bono. It would be completely wrong to assume malign motive of everyone in that position; some volunteers from education companies were of course just wanting to give their time and expertise. The crooks were very small in number compared with the cronies and cowards.

I have already touched on the unwillingness of the school sector – from the DfE to those leading trusts – to properly consider the practice in the wider charitable sector. Rather than begin from those principles and adapt if the business of education required it, the school sector expected to have everything bespoke. This form of exceptionalism does not fit well with learning from other sectors. There are of course some honourable exceptions; Forum Strategy, a not-for-profit organisation involved in the development of executive leaders in trusts, has been at the forefront of looking to other sectors.

Practice isn't perfect in charities, but the charity commission guidance on conflicts of interest for trustees (and company directors) is very clear and straightforward. Instead of adopting that with its mindset and behaviours, other more complicated rules were developed by the DfE, particularly as regards related party transactions (RPT). An RPT is a deal or arrangement between two entities or individuals that have a pre-existing relationship, which could influence, or be perceived to influence, the terms or outcomes of the transaction usually involving a transfer of resources, services or obligations. A trustee's company offering services to a MAT was expected to do it cheaper than anyone else, and the DfE argued that RPTs can be beneficial as schools could receive goods or services at reduced cost. The rules caused some confusion and possibly even added to the likelihood of a conflict existing.

Early on, conflicts of interest almost always concerned financial interests, involving board members who seemed to be making a profit from taxpayers' money. Scandals of this type diminished as oversight increased, arguably an example of where the accountability system has worked, albeit late in the day. In 2014, the House of Commons Public Accounts Committee (PAC), which had previously reported on problems with unmanaged conflicts of interest in schools, continued to have concerns.

The House of Commons PAC (2018b) recommended that the DfE should approve RPTs. The PAC was told by the DfE that 40% of academy trusts have RPTs that involve either the academy's headteacher or governors (it is unclear if that included trustees and executives), and that all RPTs are subject to a tendering process with trusts required to provide evidence that the service is being delivered at cost rather than making a profit. It is interesting to compare this assurance with a 2014 report commissioned by the House of Commons on the topic, which could not find evidence of whether or how the 'at cost' rule is assessed, but did find 'it is clear that very large sums of public money are being paid to trust Board members and their companies as well as the trading arms of academy chains via this route' (Greany and Scott, 2014). Trusts must now obtain the DfE's prior approval for contracts and other agreements for the supply of goods or services worth over £40k if a related party is involved.

In addition to financial interests, conflicts of loyalty were and still can be considerable, but initially overlooked. Many in the school sector – and not just leaders – simply didn't recognise that people who were related or friends posed a conflict of interest in other ways. I was astounded when defences were mounted for husbands and wives holding the position of headteacher and chair. Almost all of the DfE's financial investigations involved family members in some way or another, including appointing relatives or friends to jobs, sometimes at pay levels outside the usual process. Another conflict that became a crisis in 2014 involved religion in the so-called Trojan Horse case: I will return to that in chapter 15.

There is still some cronyism in the system, but usually of a much more benign nature. With the recruitment of volunteers, this is a heightened risk as often people have to be tapped on the shoulder with the suggestion that they would make a good trustee or governor. My advice is if you're trying to encourage a friend or relative to put themselves forwards to volunteer, point them to another school/trust, not your own. Cronyism also rears its head where senior leaders and executives invite friendly colleagues now at another institution onto their board to provide an overwhelmingly positive axis with the accounting officer. Taken to an extreme, this sort of groupthink leads to failure. We saw more than one MAT board full of eminent educationalists get itself into grave difficulties.

Even where a conflict was identified, there was often little rigour in dealing with it. Some people think the declaring of an interest is sufficient. Experience shows that most of us find it very difficult to consider how our own interests might be a problem, but also many boards find it difficult to discuss their fellow trustees' conflicts even if they are becoming a problem. This is where cowardice can come in. People don't want to rock the boat, so often saying 'so and so is a good guy; they wouldn't do anything wrong'.

I have devoted more paragraphs to this than I have for each of the other long list of issues that were carried out badly in the early days of the MATs, but it was the one seen most by the public, giving trusts a bad name.

Financial impropriety

As well as the risk of fraud, the potential for financial mismanagement and incompetence at governance or leadership level was exacerbated in the early days. This was due to the lack of experience on these matters in the first generation of executive heads and chief executives, combined with a greater commitment to school improvement in the sense of improving teaching and learning, rather than wider organisational development. Some chief executives recognised this and tried to persuade me that trustees should therefore major on compliance and budgets, which was counter to what the DfE and NGA were trying to achieve with the full range of core functions.

It was some years before all trusts could see the absolute necessity of a chief operating officer and development of a business team that had the knowledge and capacity to carry out these functions and HR activities well. For example, Education Funding Agency's *Final Notice to Improve* concluded in 2013 there was a 'lack of challenge and oversight over finance. One of the concerns received was that there was insufficient management challenge and that the CEO had too much power over the finance without proper checks and balances.'

There was quite a significant correlation between heads who were noticed nationally – often knighted or otherwise given the moniker 'super head' – and those who in the early days were found to be breaking the rules, perhaps suggesting an arrogance that rules are for the little people. Often, other people don't question their behaviour or are too intimidated to. One of those super heads heralded by both main political parties was Liam Nolan, head of Perry Beeches; one of his schools was very near NGA's office in Birmingham, so I knew him quite well. The trust he was chief executive of had four free schools granted so the DfE should have been looking at the trust's sustainability, leadership and governance over and over again. Nolan resigned in 2016 after a DfE investigation found that £1.3 million had been funnelled to a private company, connected with the chair of the trust, which paid Nolan a second salary, counter to proper procedures. The schools were not transferred until two years later, meaning a long period of uncertainty for staff and families of pupils.

Issues can, of course, arise in schools that are not academies: in this last example, the practice had begun while the school was a maintained foundation school, and staff reported it to the DfE once it was an academy. Jo Shuter, super head of Quintin Kynaston Academy, had been named headteacher of the year at the 2007 Teaching Awards and awarded a CBE in 2010, but was then found to be using school funds improperly. For example, funds were used on items for her personal use and significant payments for SLT food, presents and off-site meetings. There was also a question over some of her consultancy payments being made to her personally, although she was doing the work during school time: this was not that unusual at the time. A DfE audit in 2012 also identified lack of proper internal controls and poor financial oversight at governance level. And, once again, there were some payments made to family and associates. Jo Shuter resigned but was later able to overturn her teaching ban according to *Schools Week*.

Schools Week, which began life as *Academies Week* in September 2014, has proved itself invaluable as its investigative journalists do a public service, recording so many of the ups and downs in the school world. They are absolutely playing their part in my web of accountability. Other educational journalists do too, but I have noticed while accumulating the facts for this book and checking that I had got everything right, *Schools Week* comes up time and time again as leading the field.

Founder syndrome

This phrase coined in the charity sector captures the situation where the organisation's founder, often a charismatic individual whose passion was crucial to getting it established, has overstayed to the point they are no longer making a positive contribution. They see the charity as theirs and may not even have the skills necessary to lead a growing organisation. They risk becoming dictatorial as single mindedness becomes stubbornness. This can end up as unfettered power, with staff afraid to challenge or exhausted by trying to influence, while trustees are unaware of the management issues or inspired by the chief executive's commitment. Of course, not all founder CEOs behave in this extreme way.

The first generation of MAT CEOs tended to be the founders of the MAT; successful heads who sometimes brought a long-standing chair of their standalone school with them. Remember we were not yet completely out of the hero head era. Even though it was the trust members who signed the Memorandum of Association, the CEO was often the power behind the throne. Initially they were even allowed to be a trust member, something that is now ruled out. We saw a couple of cases where a CEO used their position as a member to get rid of trustees who were challenging them.

Improvements required

Trusts began to recognise more attention to governance was needed and were diligently and quietly cultivating good practice, often with support from NGA. Frustrated by the lack of informed discussion across the sector of what was working well and the lack of any leadership from the DfE on MAT governance, in 2019 NGA published *Moving MATs Forward*, aiming to broaden and deepen governance knowledge and practice across the sector. This work wasn't hidden behind a paywall: so much of the hard work in governance is done by people giving their time and experience for free. This was NGA's contribution to system improvement, sharing learning in our own area of expertise.

We identified the following interrelated issues:

1. Fragmented organisational identity, including an uncoordinated ethos and vision.

2. Issues with ethics, culture, behaviour and relationships across trusts.
3. Misunderstandings around charity and company law.
4. Misunderstanding around who should do what in terms of members of the trust, trustees and executive leadership.
5. Development of bureaucratic, over complicated structures.
6. Not using the local tier of governance effectively.
7. Lack of emphasis on stakeholder engagement and accountability.
8. Lack of connectedness to local community.
9. Poor communication and information management.
10. Misunderstandings around the importance of due diligence and risk.
11. Getting the right people around the table at a trust board and local level.
12. Lack of system leadership, with both a deficit of expertise and MATs failing to collaborate with and support others.
13. Confusion around growth, sustainability, optimal size and geographic span of trusts.

One organisation

There was often a lack of understanding that schools within a MAT were now part of one legal entity. A 'them and us' mentality could be heard and seen frequently. Perhaps both the DfE and some of the MATs recruiting schools preferred to obscure this information when persuading schools to join. The official language used was certainly unhelpful with never ending references to the 'autonomy' of academies, when in fact joining a MAT removed the school's autonomy. Also, much of the rest of the school system was built around single schools, such as inspection and funding, both topics that remain controversial and unresolved in 2025.

I tried to persuade the DfE to drop the phrase 'lead school', which was used for years to refer to the sponsoring schools but gave the wrong impression about the resulting organisation. For example, even an academic involved in the leadership programmes wrote 'MATs are generally led by a single academy which will take legal responsibility and accountability for the entire group'. So, if some experts were confused then it is no wonder that governors were too, after being told that 'nothing will change' when they moved from being maintained governors to local governors at an academy within a MAT. This was never going to be the case, but it was sometimes said to entice good schools to join.

There were indeed some trusts that formed seemingly to protect their status quo, choosing people they knew also wanted to preserve their independence; some didn't even buy into a collaborative ethos within the trust. In 2014, the DfE stipulated the accounting officer had to be a single person in order to prevent MATs rotating or sharing the role between all the headteachers.

It was alarmingly common for those at school level not to realise that the decision-making responsibilities in a MAT are held by the board of trustees unless they decide to delegate any. For many years, callers to NGA's Gold advice line would say, 'The board of trustees has just done such and such, but they can't, can they?' The answer was usually: 'Yes, they can.'

Understanding roles

Understanding roles and responsibilities is one of the eight elements of effective governance, and it's a fundamental first-order issue that leads to a myriad of confused practices and inefficiency. It felt as though this was made as difficult as possible with a lack of clarity over a number of roles, including that of trust members, which I will come on to later. Even the DfE kept calling trustees 'governors' for some time. Early articles of association were overcomplicated, ambiguous or otherwise badly drafted. The problem was identified by many sources for a number of years.

Schemes of delegation (SoDs) should have set this out, but their significance wasn't appreciated for some time. Initially many trusts confused SoDs with financial schemes of delegation, which the DfE had used the same phrase for. A lot of trusts used lawyers to draft SoDs, many of which ended up written in inaccessible language. Lines of accountability were lost in a long complex document, sometimes even containing contradictions. It was hardly surprising SoDs weren't owned by the people concerned or communicated well. A few MATs seemed unwilling to be upfront and transparent with the way their trust worked, especially when they were trying to bring more schools in.

From September 2015, MATs had to publish their SoD to comply with the Academies Financial Handbook, and this provided an impetus to review governance structures. Early structures were sometimes overly bureaucratic with multiple layers of committees, and a lack of distinction between board committees and executive groupings.

Separation of layers

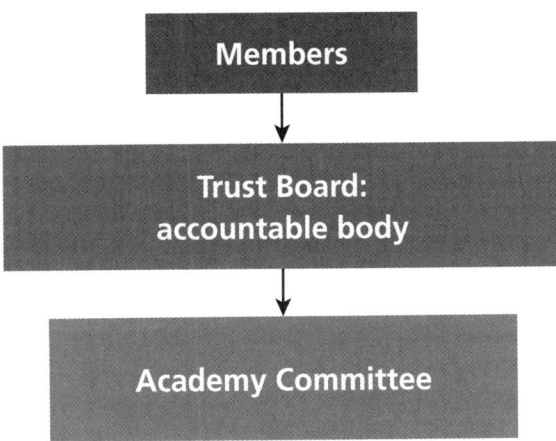

Figure 9.1 MAT structure.

The MAT structure with its three governance layers – trust members, trustees and local governors – unfortunately provides the opportunity for non-executives to undertake more than one role. It is poor practice to have the same individuals occupying more than one role in this structure. This builds conflicts of interest into the model as well as leading to less diversity of opinion and less challenge. Separation of function avoids anyone marking their own homework. It should be a basic tenet of accountability that you do not hold yourself to account. NGA had spoken and written about this fairly unremittingly, and it began to take some effect, but it could have been dealt with more swiftly if the DfE had taken a stand.

It is the trust members who hold the board of trustees to account for their governance practice, and yet it is possible to take both roles. The 2020 NFER et al. study found more than half of academy trust chairs also held the position as members of the trust, as did 20% of other trustees. This becomes in effect an oligarchy; presumably those individuals don't want to give up their power. The argument given is usually that having at least one person in common aids communication, which is nonsense as the chair of the trust board is perfectly able to communicate with the trust's members without being one themselves. The DfE goes no further than stating its 'strong preference' is for at least a majority of members to be independent of the board of trustees. A few years ago, it did finally prohibit employees from being members.

In the early years, the practice of chairs of academy committees or LGBs (local governing bodies) also having an automatic place on the main board was fairly common, and I still hear some suggestions of it today. However, these two roles do not work well together: a trustee has to consider all the pupils and schools across the whole trust, whereas a chair of an academy committee is representing that one school within the community and the trust. They often found that very hard to put to one side, not fully understanding the trustee role. In practice, we saw dysfunctional trust boards with trustees from different schools where local chairs defended their own school's interests, scrabbling for resources or influence, struggling to see the bigger picture and sometimes even blaming other schools. It can hold back the essential philosophy of the MAT being one organisation with one vision. Even if this model were a good idea – (which it isn't!) – it becomes less viable as a MAT grows; the trust board would swell to a size that would render it unwieldy and ineffective with every academy chair sitting on it.

Development of local governance

Because the need – or even benefits – for local governors was not spelled out by the powers that be, there was a period where this layer appeared to be optional. The trust board can delegate functions to the local level, usually the academy level, and has complete discretion over what is delegated to what is legally a committee of the trust board. For years, at NGA we were very purist about calling the local level 'academy committees', avoiding the more popular 'local governing bodies' (LGBs) as we emphasised the difference from maintained school governance. However, I have capitulated to the use of 'local governors' as this is recognised in practice, and we never came up with a good alternative. 'Academy committee member' is not only clunky but it uses the word 'member', which is a whole other thing in the life of an academy trust: more on them later.

First, it was not a foregone conclusion that local governance would survive. Not everyone was convinced, and 10 years ago there was real discussion on whether it added value. Often, the most questioning voices came from some of the bigger players and usually executives, whereas NGA members (who at the time tended to be the MATs that had grown out of local collaboratives) were very much in favour of local governors who knew the school and its community.

Second, the role has to be meaningful and contribute to the good governance of the trust. Knowing your schools (i.e. the organisation trustees govern) is another of those fundamental eight elements of effective governance. Trustees of MATs made it very clear to us that they needed local governors to be their eyes and ears. Local governors were seen to aid evidence-based governance by providing local knowledge of: the school's people, staff and families; its environment, local infrastructure, services, networks and employers; and the school and community's history, and the school's place in it. Equipping trust boards with school-level intelligence enables more strategic and robust trust decision-making that takes into account the needs of multiple communities. With that myriad of information, the board is likely to hear additional approaches and ideas.

Local governors should provide invaluable support and challenge to the board and the executive team, avoiding the groupthink that can set in on boards at a distance from schools and increasing the richness of discussion that is essential to good governance. They also add to the strategy development by being a point of consultation and representation, and assuring trustees that the school is operating by its values, ethos, strategic priorities and policies. By working with other local governors within the trust and outside of it, learning is shared and improvement encouraged.

It is a layer of visible governance that advocates locally for the trust and its vision, fostering a better understanding of the trust's role and, in turn, more support for both the school and the trust. It ensures active engagement of the school with its stakeholders and the wider community, providing a route for the trust to listen to parents, staff, pupils and others in the community and keeping the trust answerable to its stakeholders. Through this local collaboration, local governors help to anchor a school in its wider community and create a sense of place, belonging, connection and civic relationships. This local focus on accountability helps keep the trust grounded in the importance of place and understanding of the need to work with others locally. Some MATs stuck with local governance because Ofsted generally asked it to meet local governors, but they didn't appreciate its real value and therefore didn't always give the time and thought to developing it well.

I perhaps waited a little too long to spell out this out definitively as, in the spirit of the times, we didn't want to dictate to MATs. In the meantime, there were too many examples that either left governors confused and unsupported or rendered local governance meaningless, duplicating the executive function causing extra work for headteachers. Governance professionals were – and are – crucial to ensuring everyone knows their responsibilities and has the information to carry out their role well.

Sometimes the downgrading of local governance happened because executives wanted to save themselves work and challenge. It wasn't of much interest to many who had so much else to be thinking about, especially when they were trying to grow their trusts. Local governance wasn't seen as critical to the trust. Some of the practice was terrible. One example of an early 'innovation' was replacing LGBs with parent councils, and compensating by creating a large board of trustees that had members from every academy. That model didn't stand the test of time as the board proved too unwieldy, often divided by individual academy interests. Generally, there was a realisation that a trust board needed relevant input from academy committees in order to make good decisions.

Some MATs didn't necessarily downgrade functions in the SoD; they just ignored their LGBs. Before the Covid-19 pandemic, I attended governance conferences every other Saturday during term time, and that gave me the chance to have one-to-one conversations over cups of tea. One week, an accountant governing at a school in a large MAT was deeply frustrated by some poor decision-making by the board of trustees. When he contacted them, he was given short shrift; it was suggested that if he couldn't support the trust, he could leave. He was toying with exactly that; he was very committed to the school but wanted his time and skills to be used well, and his analysis was that the school was successful despite the MAT, not because of it. A fortnight later, I met the chair of a struggling school from the same trust but in a very different community; he was really worried about several issues that were not being dealt with and knew attainment would be falling. Everything I suggested to improve engagement with the MAT he had tried, and the LGB felt completely isolated. He said the only thing left to him was to contact the DfE, but despite the serious concern for the school and its pupils, he didn't want to throw the MAT to the lions.

Lots of different names have been used as well as LGBs – in particular academy councils, sometimes ambassadors – but the name is not as crucial as the role outlined in the SoD. There was a *Schools Week* story in 2016 and a bit of an outcry when one of the larger MATs, E-ACT, replaced LGBs with academy ambassadors advisory groups. This had not been the first MAT to reduce the functions of the LGB, but some hadn't underlined them with a change of name, and others had called their local groups something akin to advisory councils without this hitting the headlines. E-ACT made it worse by managing the change badly, in a way that was disrespectful to the local governors already giving their time. I am pleased to say that, like most other MATs who experimented in the early days with diluting their functions, E-ACT has since reviewed its model and not just returned to a fuller local governance remit but championed it.

We kept coming across people talking theoretically about potential other models, often under the flag of innovation, when those very models had already been tested by others and abandoned. They often involved both executives and volunteers, which bring problems similar to those discussed earlier on operating on more than one layer: it confuses roles, duplicates activities and reporting lines, builds in conflicts of interest and reduces challenge. Trust executives should not sit on LGBs; the headteacher will of course be there, but even the attendance of other executives can change the dynamic in the room. Executives attending occasionally for a specific purpose and encouraging challenge can be helpful, but that really should be at the LGB's invitation, not a decree from on high and definitely not routinely as a way of keeping local governors in line. One model since abandoned involved recently retired educationalists being paid to chair three LGBs each and being managed by a trust executive: this is a recipe for groupthink and top-down control.

Conclusion

We have seen that governance is not simple at the best of times, and the development of MATs brought with it more complexity for all involved. At the time, I was frustrated by the slow pace of change and understanding of what good looked like, but it shouldn't have been surprising given that governance had been overlooked, first in the design stage of the academy movement and second in the move to governing more than one school. Other considerations, such as growth of MATs, were dominating executive time.

The transition to MAT governance was not managed well by the regulator, largely leaving the sector to develop good governance. I appreciate small government was the order of the day under the Conservatives, but the lack of leadership on this crucial element of their own agenda – the system they invented and promoted ceaselessly – seems a dereliction of duty, especially given the scandals that haunted its early days. The minister for state for the school system simply stressing the importance of governance from platforms was insufficient. This was compounded by a lack of acknowledgement that academies are first and foremost charities; their exempt charity status seemed to lead to an undervaluation of charity practice altogether, and the DfE's work with the charity commission was pretty perfunctory.

After the demise of the National College for School Leadership, the DfE didn't provide routes to share learning, despite promoting it when in front of the House of Commons select committee. There was generally a closed-door culture around sharing between MATs. No one wanted to expose their flaws, and the continuing stream of understandably negative press stories added to this fear. We are all more willing to share our successful experience, but we probably all learn more from our failures. In this dearth of exchange, NGA had the advantage of spending day in, day out having confidential conversations with trustees, local governors, trust governance professionals and, increasingly, trust executives.

This lack of DfE involvement was despite the interest of most of the ministers for the school system, particularly Lord Nash from 2013 to 2017 and then Lord Agnew until 2020. A couple of times we convinced ministers to take a more strategic approach to developing governance, and each time it evaporated to no more than an update of the DfE *Governance Handbook* or rewritten role descriptions. Most of their time and energy went into dealing with the disasters. Even while governance disasters in the press pushed the topic up the political agenda, this did not focus minds on anything beyond very top-line principles.

The couple of times the DfE agreed to change the detail of governance policy, it struggled to enforce it. It is exceedingly difficult and bureaucratic to change every set of academy trust articles. For example, in 2014, the model articles for SATs changed to say that heads may be a trustee 'if their appointment is ratified by members'. As late as 2021, trustees operating with an older version resigned as their executive head insisted on remaining a trustee even after an EFA notice to improve recommended moving to the latest model articles. *Schools Week* reported that a source close to the school said that 'the DfE are basically sitting on the fence about this' and called for 'clear direction that this is not good practice' (Staufenberg, 2021). (GIAS now reports she is no longer a trustee, so slowly progress is made.)

Although governance structures are rather different from other aspects of education that are best left to the teaching profession, I really would not want the DfE to decide every aspect of good governance practice in the system. It was odd to see ministerial involvement in the teaching of reading and maths but a reticence to get involved in the MAT governance model when there were clearly issues. There was of course the DfE's *Governance Handbook*, which was an important resource but still left much to be developed in the field. The DfE needed to engage in a visible way and provide leadership when it was lacking, or publicly recognise where the expertise lay. There was little public acknowledgement given to those who were developing quality practice and guidance. There was no quality assurance at any level. I and other NGA staff often attended event sessions, even professional development ones, where executives or sometimes chairs with experience of one MAT would give their reflections: sometimes they were brilliant and sometimes they promoted poor practice.

Ofsted played no role in developing MAT governance, and as much as I hate to say it, I speculate that if MAT governance had been subject to inspection, there would have been more interest and a greater pace of change.

I have focused here on the financial scandals rather than the outcomes for pupils. Like everyone who has read the various evaluative reports over the years – from EPI, Sutton Trust and others – with the exception of Labour's original early academies, it is difficult to isolate the effect of structures on pupil outcomes. We still have to say there are some brilliant MATs, some brilliant SATs and some brilliant maintained schools, and some troubled schools of each type.

A MAT has the advantage of being able to offer more sharing of expertise and activities as well as backroom infrastructure, but we all know cases where that hasn't materialised. My children's former secondary school would have been described as a coasting school back in the day, but they worked enormously hard to get from 'satisfactory' to 'good' and maintain that. Sadly, after joining a MAT, it was judged 'requires improvement' by Ofsted. The promised magic hadn't worked. As most are, it was a complicated story, but part of the issue was a change of culture and leadership that didn't suit the staff or the local community. That is only one story among many, but in the absence of definitive data, it is stories that influence people at all levels in the system.

The Academies Commission was instigated by the RSA and chaired by former HMCI Christine Gilbert. They reported in 2013 and raised three main questions in relation to governance that needed addressing to realise the potential of academisation:

• How to secure better capacity of governing boards.

• How to encourage governors and trustees to support school-to-school improvement.

• How to ensure democratic representation and local accountability.

These still apply, and I explore them in the coming chapters and come back to the model of MAT governance that has been settled on.

Part C:
Governance now

10.
Who governs our schools?

Volunteers govern our schools and trusts. In my early days at NGA, I quickly grew used to governors being called 'amateurs' or 'do-gooders' by all and sundry, often prefixed by 'well-meaning'. It was not usually in the spirit of commending voluntary effort, but at best patronising or at worst dismissive with suggestions of incompetence.

I very much wanted to reclaim the high ground of volunteering. There are two definitions of amateur: one is engagement in an activity without financial gain, and the other is unskilled or inexperienced. 'Volunteer' is not synonymous with that second definition: governors and trustees can do a professional job – by which I mean undertake the role well – without being paid. The suggestion of governance being a paid role is made by educational professionals more than anyone else. This can appear to demonstrate a lack of respect for a role that doesn't bring with it remuneration. That is not something we experience regularly as trustees in the third sector, which arose from a philosophy of volunteering; it is part of our foundations and our ethos.

When I joined NGA, it was the era of the Big Society; David Cameron's 'great passion' featured heavily in the 2010 Conservative manifesto 'a society with much higher levels of personal, professional, civic and corporate responsibility; a society where people come together to solve problems and improve life for themselves and their communities; a society where the leading force for progress is social responsibility, not state control' (House of Commons Library, 2015). His speech in Liverpool that July claimed to set out 'real, practical steps that we are taking to help make the Big Society a reality'. Yet it came to very little. Very few of us who are truly passionate about civic power, community engagement and social entrepreneurship want to set these against public services; instead, we work with them, adding value. Volunteering is not an antidote for austerity. I will come back to the role of citizens more widely in chapter 16.

In 2004, the then DfES in *Governing the School of the Future* estimated there were 350,000 governor places across England's schools, of which 12% were unfilled, meaning that just over 300,000 citizens volunteered. This figure still tends to be quoted although, as I documented in chapter 7, the number of places on governing boards has fallen. There are now approximately 230,000 places of which NGA estimate almost 200,000 are filled. This NGA figure from survey work compares with about 175,000 named volunteers on GIAS (Get Information about Schools), which is likely to be an underestimate due to some failures to keep up to date. It is often said that school governance is the largest volunteer force in the UK, but in fact we are beaten to that title by charity trustees of the 180,000 registered charities, plus many more thousands of small unregistered charities.

The right people round the table

Despite introducing that phrase as one of the eight elements of effective governance, I am not entirely comfortable with its inference that there are some people who are 'wrong' for the role. But actually there are people for whom meetings and all that goes with them are the last thing they want to spend their limited spare time on. I need to be less squeamish about admitting that. It is not a judgement on their citizenship or their right to be heard on state education.

We have seen in chapter 7 that over the past 20 years there has been a move from governing bodies that appeared to be representative of stakeholders to ones where attributes likely to contribute to the board's competence are given priority. There is sometimes an assumption, particularly in some academic writing, that the shift towards more 'business-like' boards means that local voices and parental voices are less welcome, presumed to be non-professional. As the RSA report (with the same title as this chapter) stated: this is intellectually lazy and often untrue (Breslin, 2017). We have also seen a quiet revolution in appreciating more diversity on the boards.

Regardless of their route onto the board, governors and trustees are appointed or elected to govern in the best interest of pupils: that mission is the guiding principle, and other interests in conflict with this principal interest have to be minimised. There is a critique sometimes expressed by those supporting a stakeholder model that professional people recruited for their expertise will be detached from the school or trust; that being without a stake, as it were, there will be no interest in the mission. Apart from being rather condescending to those who volunteer, this is not borne out by NGA's extensive data on why volunteers put themselves forward. Some volunteers arrive with a loyalty, sometimes even affection, for the school, but others without a prior attachment become loyal through undertaking the role and learning about the institution. The skill is not to let that loyalty cloud your judgement.

Motivations to govern

NGA's annual surveys give a consistent picture of why people volunteered to govern: two thirds say that they do it to make a difference to children's lives, to serve their community, and to use their skills and experience. Research shows that governors rightly see themselves as working on behalf of the interests of the school as a whole, but that is often described as acting in the interests of its pupils. Place is also important to many volunteers.

Over half of respondents (58%) were motivated to put themselves forward by their interest in education, 37% had an existing interest in governance and 34% applied because a school was in need of support. Knowledge of schools playing a part was confirmed by a survey carried out by GovernorHub in 2022 which found only 9% of respondents said they had no knowledge of the school sector at all before they became a governor; 43% had some professional knowledge, having worked in the sector, another 43% had some knowledge from being a parent or carer of school-age children, and 20% had some knowledge through personal relationships with people working in schools.

Only 20% of respondents to NGA mentioned that wanting to learn new skills for their professional lives was a motivating factor, although the GovernorHub survey had a higher response of 36% when asked about new skills and experience. Once volunteers have the experience of governing, they often acknowledge the benefits to themselves – and the joy that volunteering can bring. Over the years, several studies have reported involvement in school governing can be a life-enhancing experience, including the suggestion that 'it would benefit all business people to be a governor for a period of time in order to provide a way of being more grounded in a wider social context and to communicate with a wider group of people' (Ellis, 2003).

Motive is also sometimes questioned by school staff with the suggestion that volunteers are drawn by the kudos of being a governor or trustee. There may be a tiny number who think that might be the case before they enter the board room, but even if the volunteering was entered upon lightly, the workload and responsibility is soon clear to see. The idea that governing brings public status with it in practice is laughable. Outside those involved, research shows it is a largely unknown or a misunderstood role. As part of NGA's visible governance campaign, we invested in lapel pins for our members to discreetly display that they were volunteering to govern and spread the word that more volunteers are needed.

There is potentially more of a risk of wanting status with larger MATs, but although there have been a few examples of chairs reminding others of their power, I genuinely have not seen that occurring to any extent. The amount of work and thought required dwarfs the status acquired; survey respondents are always clear that what keeps them governing is the outcomes for children and young people.

Routes to volunteering

NGA's 2024 survey found that having a child at the school (39%), being approached directly to take on a role (32%), working in education (26%) and a friend, relation or colleague mentioning the role (10%) were the main ways that respondents first got involved in school or trust governance. As I will cover later, there is much debate as to the role of employers, but they do not represent a major driver behind governor volunteering. For example, only 5% of respondents to the 2018 survey were encouraged by an employer to get involved in school governance.

How were you selected for your current governing role?	2016	2024
I was appointed by the governing board (often called co-option) or by trust members	39%	62% (including 9% by trust members)
2016: I was appointed by the LA 2024: I was nominated by the LA and appointed by the GB	13%	8% overall (13% in maintained schools)
I was appointed by the diocese/foundation body	11.5%	10%
I was elected by the parent body	18.5%	8%
I was elected by the staff	6.5%	4%
2024: Academy committee member/local governor appointed by the trust board	–	4%
Other/don't know	11%	3%

Table 10.1 How did volunteers come to be on a governing board?

'Other' included those confused as to how they came to be on the governing board, particularly for community governors in maintained schools who didn't initially recognise themselves as 'appointed' by the governing body.

Parent governors

Those figures underline that the number of spaces filled by parent elections have more than halved since boards were given the flexibility to reduce them, although many parents now volunteer to govern without being elected. But overall, the number of parents governing is lower than in the past. For example, a 2008 study found 71% of governors were originally involved in governance as a parent; this is enormous when you consider that some spaces were reserved for the headteacher, staff and local authority appointments.

In 2016, NGA found 44% of respondents had started governing as a parent in an elected place, with a large number commenting that they had since become a different type of governor, so it appears that the parent governor places provide an entry point for many who go on to govern long term. This was replicated by GovernorHub in 2022; while 18% were currently a parent governor, a further 21% had been in a previous role. That is what happened with me: I began many years ago as an elected parent governor, but I became a foundation governor as it was harder to find foundation governors than parent governors.

We have already seen that an average board size is nine members, so given that there is still a requirement of two elected parents on school-level boards, then the proportion of the respondents in this position should still be in the region of 20%. MATs can get round this by having two elected parents as trustees, but a cursory glance at GIAS suggests this does not often happen. Grandparents of children at the school account for about 4% of volunteers alongside other carers (1%).

A parent governor is not representing the views of other parents. Although their experience of being the parent of a pupil at the school and probably knowing other families provides them with an important additional lens, the governing board as a whole has the responsibility to seek out and listen to views of the wider parent body. This is not always clear to all and sundry; I would go as far to say it is one of the biggest misconceptions about boards as to whether those elected have representative roles. They do not: once a person is elected to a board, they are – as with everyone else – expected to use their own knowledge and judgement, not to second-guess their electorate. Elections are a tool to both provide legitimacy and obtain a diverse board coming from different perspectives.

Staff governors

NGA's membership was split about the value of staff governors, and I am too. It is a role where conflicts of interest are built in; so there are many things staff governors are prohibited from being involved with, such as: senior leader appraisal; pay decisions or reviews; staff restructuring; staff disciplinary; grievance or capability hearings; and exclusion or complaints panels (where they are reviewing their own headteacher's decisions).

It takes a courageous member of staff to stand up to their boss. Research in 2000 found almost one quarter of teacher governors felt inhibited by the presence of the head, and others noted teacher governors felt that there were conflicts of loyalty. Interviews also indicated that some chose to discuss potentially divisive issues with the headteacher before the meeting, but that way the whole board wasn't party to the information. This should be one of the biggest advantages of having a staff governor: hearing their perspective and sharing their understanding of the school.

Half of staff governors reported that they joined the board to develop skills for their professional life, but at the same time staff governors were – and still are – the least likely to take up any training for the role. They also often considered themselves in a representative role, when they are there to exercise their own judgement, and sometimes they struggle not to share confidential items.

In MATs, trust executives are no longer able to be trustees, and although there is no formal prohibition of them being local governors, that is poor practice. It can work with school staff on LGB, but an alternative would be to have a member of staff from another school within the trust. Of course, the whole LGB should make sure the whole staff team is consulted and listened to.

Foundation governors/trustees

Although the foundation appointments across the governance community make up approximately one in 10, they are of course concentrated in schools and trusts with foundations, most of which are appointed by the Church of England or Roman Catholic dioceses to preserve and develop the religious character and life of the school. Where it is the majority on those boards depends on the exact nature of the school and trust; for example, voluntary aided (VA) schools do have a majority of foundation governors.

Chairs of foundation schools often express frustration with the large number of foundation places, especially given falling numbers attending most churches, resulting in unfilled places or little notice being taken of other skills needed to govern. Church of England dioceses are often flexible with their faith requirements, whereas Catholic dioceses expect foundation governors to be practising Catholics. Several years ago we at NGA tried to open up a dialogue about this situation due to the numbers of reports we were receiving of problems finding candidates, but unfortunately there was a refusal to countenance any possible change to current constitutions or expectations.

There can be a further problem with foundation governors who are only interested in the religious aspects of the school. I once served at a VA school with a Catholic chair whose main interest was limiting sex education, and we had interminable but inconclusive discussions on this topic, despite an excellent and sensitive county council initiative. It would be healthier in terms of good governance to consider reform without undermining the Bishops' role. For example, having a committee of the governing board in Catholic schools and MACs (multi-academy companies) with associate governors and directors with the specific remit to defend the faith. This could reflect that of the Catholic inspectorate (Catholic life and mission, religious education and collective worship) and leave the governing board with fewer foundation members and more co-opted who are interested in the rounded education offer dealing with all the other aspects of the organisation and its sustainability. However, I cannot imagine that such a discussion would be countenanced by the Church.

Many Catholic dioceses have used the Bishop's mandate to insist that foundation governors support a diocesan strategy for all their schools to form MATs, often called MACs to distinguish its board from the diocesan trustees or sometimes now CMATs where the C is for Catholic. Foundations governors and academy trustees, or directors as the Catholic Education Service (CES) prefers to call them, are expected to uphold the Bishop's vision and expectations; this is not surprising when it comes to issues concerned with faith. Several years ago, I had a couple of conversations with the CES as to how far this stretched into secular matters and was told while all aspects of a Bishop's strategy should be adhered to, governors who failed to support academisation would not be removed. This was perplexing given many governors had come away from diocesan conversations with a different impression. In April 2025, *Schools Week* reported that governors of Catholic schools who opposed plans to join new mega MATs have been told by their diocese in South Yorkshire they 'should resign', while another diocese had apparently told its governors they could only pass compliance checks in the Catholic Inspection if they provided evidence they supported the next phases of the bishop's vision for three large MATs.

Employment

For many years, NGA's annual surveys showed that approximately half of respondents were in employment (of those, about two thirds were in full-time employment) with another 12% self-employed, 5% looking after a family and 30% retired. However, the number of retired has grown over the period from 28% in 2017 to the highest ever in 2024 at 41%. Although those in part-time employment has been fairly steady at 15%, the number in full-time work fell to 29% despite efforts to recruit younger volunteers.

Most governance volunteers are professional people. NGA's annual surveys confirm this. For example 83% in 2024: with 27% directors/managers, 34% educational professionals and 22% other professionals. This is replicated by the retired volunteers but with slightly more professional people (86%) due to more retired educational professionals (40%). Perhaps slightly surprisingly given the push for skills, this has always been the case. For example, a national survey of school governing bodies carried out by Keys and Fernandes in 1990 found 'lay' governors to be drawn from the middle class, highly educated sections of the population. The prefix 'lay' is now rarely used, which is pleasing as it suggests a lack of knowledge of a particular subject. It is also an unhelpful distinction given that about one third of those who volunteer are or were formerly educational professionals. A 1999 study by Scanlon, Earley and Evans again found 80% of governors and chairs were from professional or managerial professions, with a majority well educated and well qualified. In 2016, Andrew Wilkins concluded that those governing were an elite, but not properly defined; if I take that to mean not representative of the full socioeconomic spectrum, that's correct, but this is not a change from the time when there were more stakeholder places.

For several years, NGA ran a campaign called Educators on Board to encourage educationalists of all sorts to volunteer to govern in another school or trust rather than at their own, due to the conflict of interest that comes with being a staff governor. It is wonderful CPD, and it brings important experience and knowledge to the school or trust being governed as well as their own. Volunteering increases staff understanding of the skills, care and the challenges of governing well, and increases their respect for the role. It also puts them in a good position if applying for promotions, having accumulated experiences that can put them ahead of their peers; for example, of recruiting senior staff or being part of an appeal panel. All too often those being recruited to their first headship do not have sufficient knowledge or experience of governing, especially if it is limited to their own school or trust.

Support from employers

NGA surveys show the proportion of employed governors and trustees being given time off work to volunteer has fallen from 60% in 2015 to 41% in 2024. Of that time off given, 71% is paid. Few employees have their requests for time off refused (2–4%), but about one quarter of employees don't ask even though they reported needing time off.

Governors of maintained schools are legally entitled to 'reasonable' time off work for public duties such as school governance, although this does not have to be paid. The legislation has never been updated to include academy trustees. In the 2015 Conservative Party manifesto, David Cameron pledged to grant three days' annual volunteering leave to employees in the public sector and those working for large companies (firms with 250 or more staff). Before the election, Cameron described the policy as a 'double win', benefiting both the economy by fostering a more motivated workforce and society by encouraging engagement with charities, communities and school governorship. However, it was never enacted largely because businesses lobbied against it, but also because others in the Conservative Party didn't share Cameron's interest in the 'Big Society'.

What is particularly disappointing about this reduction in support from employers is that the arguments about the benefits of governing for professional development have been made for some time. A 2010 report of research carried out by the City of London Corporation found school governing to be the best voluntary activity for staff development. In 2018, when governors were asked by NGA whether the experience of school governance had provided skills that were valuable in their professional life, about 10% disagreed while 67% agreed. In 2021, a report titled *The Value of Volunteering* from Education and Employers and CIPD found that employers who support their staff to volunteer in schools and colleges reported employees to be more motivated and productive, and have a better sense of wellbeing.

The CBI (Confederation of British Industry) was a staunch supporter of volunteering in the schools and colleges for a considerable time, especially when Neil Carberry led their education team. For example, in 2013 their evidence to the select committee enquiry laid out the win, win, win: first, governing being a great development opportunity for employees, adding to their skills; second, boosting employee engagement and adding to a company's positive profile; and third, better governance meaning better schools, which in turn means better education outcomes and strengthening the country's skills base. In 2019, the CBI education and skills survey reported 31% of business supporting employees to govern, but since the pandemic employer engagement with schools and colleges has fallen from 94% in 2019 to 68% in 2022.

There has also been a large amount of work carried out by a range of organisations – such as Business in the Community; many chambers of commerce; Education and Employers; Governors for Schools (formerly SGOSS); and Academy Ambassadors – to persuade employers to support and encourage school governing. Yet this is often unknown in the wider school sector: it was often suggested to us as a new idea that employers should be lobbied to do more. This work needs to be relentless to have any impact: warm words from corporates are not always followed by action.

Going in at the top of employer organisations or businesses often didn't bring sustainable change. They are often based in London where the need for volunteers is less and they struggle to get the message to regional staff. A global chair of a financial services company has been involved for years in promoting employee engagement in schools, and when I happened to meet his North East regional director, she had not heard of the programmes he was promoting. When he was Education Secretary, Damian Hinds decided to work with the IoD (Institute of Directors) to recruit academy trustees, and despite the IoD producing a report, their campaign for volunteers produced very few recruits.

Just as corporates often say it is hard to get a response from schools, it is also difficult to find the middle manager or HR manager in a corporate who is going to make it their mission to support school governance. NGA produced a resource as part of its Visible Governance campaign for volunteers and prospective volunteers to give to their employers. It suggested a range of ways to champion the role, including volunteering days, a governor/trustee network and specifically encouraging up-and-coming younger staff.

The House of Commons education select committee (2013a) recommended that: 'Any potential barriers to the recruitment of effective school governors should be removed. We recommend that the Government review the current incentives for, and requirements on, businesses that release their staff for governor duties.' Yet absolutely nothing has happened.

Diversity of boards

School and trust boards have a diversity problem. This has been a concern for me ever since I joined NGA and began travelling round the country to governor conferences: entering the room immediately made one aware that the visible attributes, especially regarding age and race of volunteers, in no way reflected our communities. In NGA's early days we had so little capacity, I needed to find partners to make any sort of campaign work, and it was extremely hard to get anyone excited by the issue. I had a go in 2014 to stir up some interest in a campaign when the Inspiring Governance Alliance came together, but to no avail with the DfE saying it was not a priority.

Diversity, equality, inclusion and belonging was a topic I spoke about at events regularly, often with an emphasis on race. At the end of a keynote session at Lewisham, two Black governors came to thank me for raising the topic as white people tended to avoid it. This was helpful learning for me; an indication to keep campaigning.

I am not claiming credit for original thought here: I drew on evidence and research from other sectors and other countries. Making sure boards are not made up of 'people like us' has been an issue in many sectors. For example, as long ago as 2003, *The Tyson Report on the Recruitment and Development of Non-Executive Directors* from the London Business School encouraged companies to 'cast a wider net to build more diverse and effective boards' and a 2017 report by Clore Leadership into governance of arts organisations and museums expressed concern at the 'crushing lack of diversity at board level'. Corporates had to have a concerted campaign on Women on Boards to improve the dismal participation of women as paid non-executive directors with a target of 40%, a problem we don't have in schools.

Gender

Women, as with many voluntary activities, are well represented among those governing schools: women have made up between 59–63% of the respondents in the seven times NGA's annual surveys have asked about gender. Women are now governing in greater numbers than men in every type of school and trust. The number of women who are trustees of a MAT has been increasing over the past few years but are not yet at quite the same level of overrepresentation as in maintained schools. Almost three quarters (74%) of those respondents who are elected parent governors were female, so that will affect the MAT trustee split slightly.

For years, women have governed at slightly lower rates in secondaries than primaries, and this continued with 58% of those governing in secondaries in 2021 being women, compared with 65% in primaries. This may be in part due to the added kudos of governing at secondary level or possibly due to primary education being seen as largely the province of women, as is evident in the workforce. The percentage of female volunteers on special school boards had risen to 74%.

It is sometimes suggested that one reason that women are less likely to be appointed as senior leaders in schools and trusts may be because recruitment panels for headteachers and chief executives are made up primarily of men; given the predominance of female governors and trustees it seems highly likely that women will be well represented on those recruitment panels.

Female governors and trustees were just as likely to feel that they have the opportunity to develop and progress on their board (in fact 65% v 64%), and they had very similar reactions when asked about whether they had considered resigning: 72% women said 'no', as did 73% of men. For the first time in 2021, we asked respondents if they felt that their opinion is valued on their board: although female and male respondents are almost equally likely to 'agree', men are more likely to 'strongly' agree (75% v 67%.) Similarly, men are a little more likely than women to 'strongly' agree that they feel they belong on their board (72% v 63%).

Age

Boards are skewed to older volunteers and we are going backwards despite our attempts to recruit younger members. More than half of volunteers (53%) are now aged 60 or more, and this has been rising over the period from 2016 when it stood at 32%. Year on year, NGA's surveys have shown that just 1% of respondents are under the age of 30, and those under the age of 40 have reduced from 12% in 2015 to 7% in 2024. These numbers might not be 100% accurate as those with least time are least likely to complete a self-selecting survey, but such a fall is pretty telling. It is especially concerning as it corresponds with a time when both free recruitment services concentrated on targeting employees. Inspiring Governance reported that over 80% of their placed governors were under 50 years of age, with 45% being under 35 years of age.

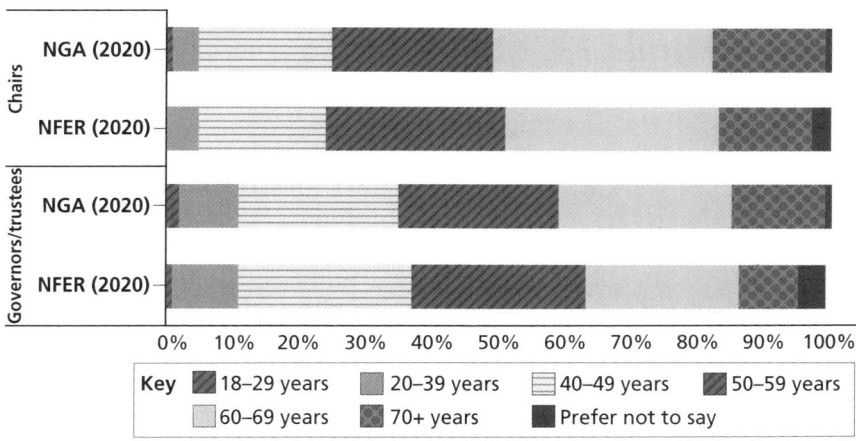

Figure 10.1 Age of governors/trustees in England in 2020.

Other sectors have the same problem. The Charity Commission reported the mean age of a charity trustee as 57 in 2017 but in 2025 it has risen significantly to 65 years. Over half of charity trustees (54%) are retired, compared to 22% of the population. Given those figures, I was feeling positive about the diversity of the board of the small charity I chair when – during the writing of this very chapter – the youngest trustee contacted me to resign as the birth of his second child meant he didn't have the time to contribute. I am holding my breath as another has just had her second baby.

More schools have been making efforts to attract alumni as governors; even where they have moved away, they will usually have family and friends locally, which means they bring useful knowledge and can still visit sometimes even if having to join online for some board meetings. There are two other groups who also tend to bring down the average age of a board: middle leaders from other schools, and parents, especially those of primary school children.

I was lobbied by a young member in 2016 who felt in need of peer support, and we joined her in piloting the Young Governors' Network, which still exists today for those under the age of 40. It moved online during the pandemic. I stayed away in the spirit of leaving younger people to get on with it, but they primarily talked about the same issues that older governors and trustees talk about – funding, relationships with the headteacher, how we understand what is truly happening in a school, pupils' welfare, whether a new school structure is important – but in an atmosphere where their views counted. We know that younger governors and trustees are less likely to feel that their opinion is valued (53% compared to 71% of over 40s) and that they are invited to participate in board discussions equally to others (57% compared to 71% of over 40s.)

For three years, Clare Collins, then NGA's head of consultancy, had the pleasure of working with some of Teach First's ambassadors who govern. Although these volunteers are busy teachers or have moved on to other demanding careers, often with young families, they made time for governance development. Teach First funded an impact report, but governing being a collective activity, it was difficult to isolate the effect of having an alumnus on board. However, Clare's analysis was that they were able to make a meaningful contribution and add value to a governing board, their energy and enthusiasm shining through. Their discussions were more generative than often is the case.

Ethnicity

The lack of ethnic diversity on governing boards is a long-standing issue. Black and minority ethnic groups in the UK (often now termed global majorities) are underrepresented on governing boards: only 5% of respondents to the 2024 NGA annual survey declared themselves as not white, and this is no more than in 1999. This is truly shocking, especially given the increase over this period in the proportion of the English population that is Black, Asian or minority ethnic. Finally, there was a small movement in 2025's survey with 7% of governors and trustees identifying as being from a minoritised ethnic background, and 91% identifying as being white. This is similar to the Charity Commission's 2025 report *Trusteeship: A Positive Opportunity*, which found 92% of trustees are white.

At one point I reported that all the work that has been done for the best part of a decade by all sorts of people and groups was producing some green shoots. When I looked at those recruited in the previous two years, the percentage of respondents who are not white almost doubled, and looking just at the previous year it was 15%. Over 30% of volunteers appointed through Inspiring Governance (the DfE-funded school governance recruitment service for eight years until 2024) were Black, Asian or from ethnic minority backgrounds, and Governors for Schools had a better result (40%) in 2024–25, along with 73% being under 45. There have been a few surveys with slightly higher responses, including GovernorHub's in 2022 with 8% identifying as not white; however, there have not been enough such results to justify me claiming sustained progress yet.

Of those that chose to disclose their ethnicity in 2024, 95% of governors and trustees surveyed identified as white, 1% of respondents identified as Black/African/Caribbean/Black British, 2% identified as Asian/Asian British, and 2% identified as being from a mixed or multiple ethnic background. The 2021 census data tells us 83% of the population in England over age 16 is white; 79% of those aged under 60 and 94% of those aged 60 and over.

Younger governors and trustees are more ethnically diverse, with 28% of volunteers under 30 and 10% of those under 40 identifying as belonging to an underrepresented ethnicity falling to only 2–3% of those 70 years and over (in 2025). While there is hope that with new volunteers the diversity of boards will improve, this is hindered by the underrepresentation of younger volunteers.

There are of course significant variations in and between regions, with the census showing London as the most ethnically diverse region with 54% white residents, while the North East and South West have the highest proportion of white residents (93% each). These differences are reflected in NGA's volunteer figures too.

Boards are missing potentially valuable contributors, and by including members with different ethnicities, the board and therefore the school gains access to new knowledge, resources and networks, and different perspectives and ideas.

This is also an issue of social justice. Growing up in Bermuda where I attended a state secondary school that was majority Black, I learned about racial injustice at a much earlier age than most white English people of my generation. I then arrived back in Liverpool, a city I grew to love but one with a horrendous involvement in the Atlantic slave trade. I went to an almost entirely white school on the edge of Toxteth, where the so-called race riots took place within hearing distance of my home as I finished my A-levels, giving me another graphic example of racism but in a different context.

The significance of these experiences was only brought home to me about five years ago when I turned up at the launch event for Professor Paul Miller's book on racism and education to find myself in a busy room as one of only three or four white people. I don't need to tell people from the school sector in England how unusual this is. Joining a table where a number of Black women, all educationalists, were talking about their arrival in cold, damp, grey England from the colourful, sunny Caribbean was something I could immediately relate to, having arrived at Runcorn station one foggy February evening without any winter clothes and being shocked by rows and rows of brick houses. Of course, my position as a white British young person was completely different, but there were points of commonality too.

What makes the level of progress particularly disappointing is that there have been efforts made by many people and organisations to raise awareness of this problem and the opportunity to govern over the best part of a decade. We began to work with a whole range of other groups committed to campaigning for more representation of Black, Asian and other minoritised ethnic groups, including the grassroots groups BAMEed and DiverseEd. In 2017, Sharon Warmington set up the Black Governors Network to help place Black African and Caribbean volunteers on boards; she underlined the issue saying: 'I've been around governance all of my working life but no matter where I've been I'm usually the only Black person in the room.'

Other protected characteristics

In 1999, one in 20 governors were disabled, increasing to 7% of chairs, and by 2022 7% of all NGA survey respondents identified themselves as having a disability. This is much lower than the census figure of 18% and an estimate that disability may now affect 24% of the UK population.

Just under 4% of NGA survey respondents in 2021 and 2022 identified as lesbian, gay, bisexual or a sexual orientation other than heterosexual, very similar to official figures for the population, with 6% preferring not to say.

Class is not a protected characteristic, and possibly much less talked about as a result, although a 2025 consultation on equality law reforms is considering socioeconomic protections. Research by James et al. in 2010 commented on the middle-class discourse of the board in the school sector. The Charity Commission reported in 2025 that 65% of trustees are above the national median for household income, down from 75% in 2017.

Continuing the argument for diversity

When Theresa May became prime minister, government departments were instructed to take an interest in diversity, and the argument we had been making about the importance of diversity of experience and background on a board in addition to a range of skills became mainstream. It was now broadly understood that there needed to be sufficient diversity of perspectives and approaches to enable robust decision-making and avoid groupthink.

By 2017, we had persuaded the DfE to include the diversity argument in its *Governance Handbook*: 'Having some people on the board… who come from outside the faith or ethnic group of the majority of pupils, can help ensure that the board has sufficient internal challenge to the decisions it makes and how it carries out its strategic functions.'

In 2018, we launched the Everyone on Board campaign with a focus on recruiting Black and Asian heritage volunteers at our summer conference with the support of the then Education Secretary Damian Hinds MP. It was welcomed with open arms and minds by our members; I can't remember any emails admonishing me for being 'woke' then, although a few of those appeared in later years.

The 2019 edition of the DfE's *Governance Handbook* was really rather expansive about diversity, even featuring in the foreword by the then Under Secretary of State for Schools Lord Agnew: 'As an ex-trustee, I recognise that the foundation of effective governance is based on the commitment, skills, knowledge and behaviours of a group of volunteers. However, I also believe that for a board to be effective it will need to consist of a diverse group of volunteers, from a variety of backgrounds, who each bring with them different perspectives and experience but who are there for the same purpose, to ensure they can provide the best education to their students.'

At the height of the Black Lives Matters movement, the national representative organisations in the sector met monthly to share our efforts. Public commitments had already been made by all of us in a national statement, the first year with the DfE and afterwards by the sector, coordinated by NAHT. In 2020, the Boris Johnson government decided to withdraw all funding for future equality and diversity projects, which included those increasing diversity in school leadership. The publication the following year of the badly researched report from the Commission on Race and Ethnic Disparities (CRED) was deeply unhelpful and ignored by most actively trying to make a difference to racism.

In 2021, NGA published *Increasing Participation in School and Trust Governance: A State of the Nation Report on Recruiting and Retaining Volunteers*. It made the thorough case for diverse boards as the sector lacked a publication that brought together all the arguments. We had attended many events and discussions on diversity by this point, and held some ourselves, but these had not been properly documented. We kept being approached by people who thought they had uncovered an unknown issue. As late as 2024 an academic threw this challenge at NGA.

I commend you to that NGA report, from which this matrix about the relationship between diversity and board performance (quoted by Howe and Curtis in their 2016 book *Difference Makers*, which brought together research in the field across a range of sectors and countries) bears repeating:

CHAOS	HIGH PERFORMANCE
High diversity	High diversity
Low alignment (to mission, values and strategic direction)	High alignment
Different individuals with their own agendas results in unproductive conflict	Open to new ideas and committed to a common purpose leads to innovation and improvement
INERTIA	**GROUPTHINK**
Low diversity	Low diversity
Low alignment	High alignment
Members have no real interest in what is going on	Everyone is on the same page but suspicious of other views from outside, and can stagnate with no new ideas or develop an illusion of invulnerability and take excessive risks

Table 10.2 The relationship between diversity and board performance.

The following year NGA had evidence that more boards had recognised this issue and were taking successful action. Many more boards (62% in 2022, compared with 37% in 2021) tried to recruit a volunteer from an underrepresented group and a significant majority of those (75%) were successful.

The challenge of volunteer recruitment

In 2004, the then DfES reported that of the 350,000 current governor places in England around 12% are unfilled, with the highest proportion of vacancies among community governors. While the average rate did not vary greatly between types of authority, many inner-city and disadvantaged areas have particular problems attracting and retaining governors.

Both the number of vacancies and governing boards finding volunteer recruitment difficult were at an all-time high in the 2023 NGA survey: over three quarters (77%) of governors and trustees reported it as a challenge compared with half in 2015. The 2024 data showed 44% of boards had two or more vacancies. In 2025, 39% of boards had two or more vacancies, compared with 31% in 2016, the first year we asked this question. Having a single vacancy is not a red flag, but over this nine-year period while boards have shrunk in size, the number of boards with three or more vacancies has increased from 10% to 15%. With a common board size now being nine members, this means a third of the board is missing.

Overall, the unfilled places can be estimated to be about 14% compared with 11% in 2010. The total number of seats across England has reduced over this time from the much quoted 300,000 to approximately 225,000 volunteers. This gives an estimate of 31–32,000 vacancies.

The increasing difficulty in recruitment is affecting all types of schools with MATs finding it a little more difficult: in 2024, 78% of MAT trustees and 80% of local governors found recruitment difficult, compared with 64% of SAT trustees and 75% of maintained governors. The survey data suggests in very general terms that most boards, whether maintained, MATs or SATs, tend to have a single vacancy, while the academy committees of schools within MATs are likely to have at least two.

This raises some interesting issues. First, SAT boards tend to be slightly bigger, but find it easier to fill those extra places. SATs are more likely than maintained schools to be secondaries, and the data also shows secondary schools find it a little easier to recruit volunteers, partly because of the greater size of their hinterlands.

Second, the slightly more onerous role of trustee is not proving harder to recruit to. This is especially interesting given that between 2011 and 2013 a large majority (84% to 88%) of respondents thought more school autonomy would make the role more challenging, and 60% thought that as a result recruiting suitable volunteers would become harder. In fact, a local governor on the academy committee is the least onerous role in terms of both responsibility and time but is reported to be the hardest to recruit. Volunteers want their time to be used well, and in some MATs, there is more work to be done to make these local roles clear and meaningful. I will come back to that in chapter 11.

The literature confirms that finding governors, especially parent governors, can be particularly difficult in areas of disadvantage. However, there tend to be increased challenges in special schools, with foundation governors, and in smaller schools (for example, in rural areas). There have always been regional variations, and in 2023 this was 86% of respondents in Yorkshire and Humber struggling with recruiting volunteers, compared with 69% in London. It is surprising to see even that many in London as for years the two recruitment agencies – Governors for Schools and Inspiring

Governance – have had more volunteers in London than anywhere else; even more than they could place.

Barriers to recruitment

The challenge of volunteer recruitment is longstanding: it has been noted in a myriad of research reports over the last quarter of a century, and it is not confined to school governors and trustees. Since Covid-19, it has been harder to recruit volunteers across the whole third sector, as not only did some people not return after the pandemic, but society across the piece changed its thinking in terms of how people are willing to spend their time.

Every report has identified two big barriers: a lack of time and a lack of awareness of the role. For some people, there is also a lack of confidence and even an alienation from the education system. Some governing bodies once appeared reluctant to take on potential governors who were not previously known to them, but this culture has changed in almost all cases.

Governing is not a well-known opportunity, described as 'overlooked' in the literature. NGA ran a Visible Governance campaign to try to combat the low profile, even within the education sector, let alone among the general public. The campaign launch week went exceedingly well, but it was closely followed by the pandemic, and we weren't able to generate quite the same buzz later on. It was originally envisaged as a one-year campaign, but it has now become part of NGA's ongoing repertoire, spreading knowledge of the opportunity to put back into the community and to learn from volunteering to governance. Our membership survey rated its importance as four out of five, relevant to recruiting more volunteers and helping governance to be included in the national education conversation. I wish it had made more of an impression.

Governing schools and trusts is largely a back-room activity, happening behind closed doors, out of sight with much confidential information, not something done in the glare of publicity. It is almost always invisible when it is working well, but very much in the spotlight when things go wrong. I have used the expression 'organisations with good governance do not fail' while being conscious that is a deficit vision. School and trust governance is in fact a force for good, not simply an insurance policy to pick up the pieces when things go amiss. Governing boards exist not just to stop things going horribly wrong: they are also there to help things go wonderfully right. We need to tell those stories better. NGA tries with its bi-annual outstanding governance awards, and in recent years a national school governor awareness day has been started.

In addition governance is a big ask, and it is obviously not for everyone.

Time taken to govern

Often, the story volunteers had been told about the commitment before applying to be a governor or trustee was very different from the reality of governing.

Research on the workload of governing boards paints a complex picture, but the overall message has been relatively clear: governors had a high workload and show considerable commitment. In 2005, the third of volunteers giving more than 21 hours per term seems low compared with 20 years later, and a 2007 study found almost half of the responding governors (46%) were contributing more than 100 hours a year, the equivalent of almost three working weeks. NGA has used a number of methodologies to get to the bottom of the time needed.

In 2019, survey respondents most commonly reported spending over 30 days a year on governance duties, equating to 2.5 working days a month. In the 2024 survey, a third of respondents reported spending rather less – between 10 and 15 hours – on governance duties a month, with a similar amount (31%) reporting spending fewer than 10 hours. NGA's 2024 *A Matter of Time* study, which used diary record, found the median to be 17 hours a month or 2.3 working days. So it is perfectly reasonable to say that the average governor donates half a day a week.

Chairs and vice chairs spend more time. The amount of time given by chairs varies considerably: the 2025 survey found that many LA-maintained governors in a chairing role spent between 10 and 15 hours a month on governance duties (33%) – much less time than in the NGA research diaries that reported 44 hours. This is a big disparity, but the difference in data collection should be noted – one relied on estimated time and one on recorded time. NGA carried out two pieces of research specifically on chair's workload. In 2016, the median total time spent on chairing a single school was 44 days a year (a little under one working day per week), and in 2020 *On Chairing a MAT* found the median to be just under 50 days a year. Regardless of board type, there is significant variation between individuals. To sustain their chairing role, those employed full-time tended to adopt tactics to reduce the time taken by the voluntary role.

Workload

A 2004 DfES survey reported that just over half (53%) of governors said that they had too much work to do. Headteachers in the survey also thought that the level of governors' accountability and workload was too high. NGA's surveys have given lower answers. For example, in 2024 22% of respondents found their volunteer role unmanageable, leaving a significant majority managing it given their other commitments. However, this just didn't correlate with the feedback we were getting the rest of the year from NGA members: perhaps a feature of those most time constrained was that they were less likely to complete the survey.

NGA's 2023 report *Taking Stock of Governance Workload: Ensuring School and Trust Governance is Sustainable* explored the issues through exit interviews with recently resigned volunteers and a staggering 2500 contributions on the pressure trustees and governors face. This research absolutely captured the zeitgeist. I don't think any other report we produced at NGA was read as widely.

It's not that there have been additional responsibilities added in recent years, but that the context in which governance is taking place – as with leadership – is more complex. Families are often under more stress, which brings more issues to the board table, often ones without a narrow education remit. Increasing numbers of complaints from parents add to the workload.

The introduction of trusteeship of large multi-school organisations, which might have been expected to create a greater workload, is not evident in our data. The legal requirements alone do not dictate governance workload. The time needed for governing boards to examine options for structural change, usually the move to join a MAT, isn't acknowledged sufficiently in the sector.

At NGA, we set ourselves the task of identifying responsibilities that could be removed from boards, and we came up with just one: exclusion review panels, an additional and very different type of task given to already overloaded volunteers. While holding school leaders to account for pupil exclusions is part of the strategic governance role, boards do not otherwise get involved with the cases or even the details of individual pupils, and it is time that exclusions are brought in line with this principle. The rising numbers of exclusions has added to pressures and should be removed. This proposal received support from many others in the sector including many parents who understandably perceive governors to be on the side of the school and the headteacher.

The hours and the relentless pressure have become too much for many, with a quarter of volunteers and a third of chairs considering throwing in the towel altogether. It was not just the amount of time required but also often the emotional toll. There was evidence board practice can be part of the problem, but improving board practice – while important and addressed by NGA – is not the whole solution. Systemic respect and support are required.

Research over time on school governance has established that boards tend to comprise core and peripheral governors. This core that is taking on more activities includes the chair, the vice chair and chairs of any committees; they tend to be older and less representative of the demographics of the local population. That core doesn't have decision-making responsibilities, and it is crucial to ensure the power still lies with the whole board.

Retention

Despite this workload, large numbers of volunteers keep governing. The 2020 NFER research found three quarters (77%) of survey respondents were planning to stay in their post for the next 12 months, but two thirds of interviewees identified that their board experienced retention issues. The most common reasons given for leaving were not having adequate time to give to the role (21%), a change in personal circumstances (15%) and finding the role too demanding given their skills (11%), but also 9% thought it was due to the board's ineffectiveness.

In 2022, GovernorHub encouragingly found 92% planning to finish their term of office, and nearly half (46%) aiming to do a further term. Among the 17% who didn't plan to do another role or term, nearly half (46%) are over 65, many noting that their age was a barrier to a subsequent term.

For NGA's 2023 report on workload, a number of people who had recently resigned were interviewed. Although their specific reasons for leaving the board varied, the conversations all reflected the issues raised by the quantitative work about the pressures of governance. Interviewees raised as the most important issues the additional roles they had on the board and its expectations, the time required, relationships with their governing board, the pressure of the mental load and the approaches taken by the headteacher/CEO, as well as the length of time spent on the board and their age. Chairs described the role following them home, with a work–life balance difficult to achieve due to being leaned on constantly because of their experience and seniority and the seriousness of the issues being raised. There were two other factors that came into play for some: the amount of training and development, and the practice of governance, including the failure to stay strategic.

In 2024, just over one third of respondents to NGA's survey were considering resigning, and in 2025 this was 26%. On a board of about nine members, this means generally two or three people, perhaps one more than you'd want to step down each year in an organised fashion so the board contains both new and experienced members. That mix is valuable; a fresh perspective from someone who doesn't know 'how things are done here' helps practice evolve.

Length of service

There has always been a range of long service and others who serve for a shorter period. Governors and trustees tend to be appointed for four-year periods. The annual surveys give a snapshot of the range of service.

	Involved in school/trust governance		On this governing board	
	2017	2024	2017	2023
Less than 12 months	11%	11%	14%	16%
1–4 years	28%	27%	38%	36%
5–8 years	18%	15%	21%	19%
Over 8 years	43%	47%	27%	29%

Table 10.3 Lengths of service in school/trust governance.

Very experienced governors and trustees who have served 10 years or more in the system have increased from an average of 25.5% in the first three years of the annual survey (2011–13) to 37% in the more recent three years (2022–24). I am pleased to see that a significant number of those with long service move to another school or trust. This has the advantages of preventing relationships of the first board from becoming too cosy and compromising the ability to challenge, and of also sharing experience around the system.

Unlike most other sectors, there are no term limits mandated for governors and trustees. These are generally thought to be good practice; for example, included in the Code of Governance for Further Education. NGA promoted the practice that no more than two terms (eight years) should be spent on a governing board, and up to six as chair. This was not embraced by all NGA's members who usually develop a great attachment to a particular institution. We have seen often that governors have a commitment to a particular place, and so serving elsewhere is not as attractive.

In the school sector, there seems to be slightly more long-service than among charity trustees who were found in 2025 to have a third of members serving between four and 10 years and nearly a quarter (22%)

for more than 10 years. I didn't push an introduction of term limits in my last years at NGA as, although the right thing to have in a mature system, the current position seemed too fragile. Enforcing the retirement of experienced governors and trustees would not sit well with such challenging recruitment: the latter is currently the more pressing problem.

In the early days of MATs there was a considerable turnover of trustees, particularly those brought in from outside; this may have been in part that there wasn't always a connection with the schools or their communities, which keep other volunteers governing. But some were surprised about how onerous the role was and felt keenly their lack of knowledge of the school sector (e.g. data, finances, the context in which schools are operating, the complex range of impacts). Their confidence and competence in their own field did not necessarily transfer with them, and their senior corporate jobs came first, meaning their attendance wasn't always good.

At the same time, we had the emphasis on recruiting for specific skills. Lord Nash and Lord Agnew, both with considerable experience of trusteeship, expressed their frustration that people from business were not necessarily making good trustees. In some cases, it was because their own employment came first and they were not attending regularly, but Lord Nash was also noticing that sometimes individuals with skills in a particular field – HR or finance – only contributed when those items were being discussed. I argued that these factors were exacerbated by the DfE's lack of expectation of induction. Both were adamant that businesspeople would not read more than two sides of A4 and it would feel patronising to be made to undertake training. This was a very strange stance to take in a sector that was all about knowledge and learning.

Multiple roles

About one fifth of respondents to the NGA survey in 2024 served on more than one board; this is slightly more than before the pandemic and more than at the time of Trojan Horse scandal. That increase could also be related to MATs using the same people to govern at different levels, even though this is not good practice, as we looked at in the last chapter. After the Trojan Horse reports the DfE stipulated – and still does – that no one should serve on more than two boards unless there are 'exceptional circumstances'. This rule is barely mentioned now, which is fairly incredible given Gove co-wrote in Policy Exchange's 2022 report *The Trojan Horse Affair*: 'Few issues posed as significant a concern to young people as Trojan Horse.' I will come back to that in chapter 15.

What keeps people governing?

Research by Phillips and Fuller (2003) summarised the findings of four annual surveys of governors from 1999 to 2002. The aspects of school governing that made it worthwhile just over 20 years ago are all very recognisable today:

- Involvement in the life of the school.
- Working with and supporting staff.
- Being part of and celebrating the school's success.
- Making a difference, seeing children benefit.
- Advocacy on behalf of the school.
- Their own development.
- Using skills acquired elsewhere to benefit children.
- Supporting and coaching other governors.

On the other hand, those aspects that were least worthwhile were:

- The amount and complexity of the paperwork.
- The annual parents meeting (now abolished).
- An unrealistic workload and responsibilities.
- Inadequate support for governing bodies.
- Central government interference.
- Problems with the LEA, the DfES and private contractors.
- Budgetary unfairness.

Punter and Adams carried out similar work in 2008 on aspects of governor retention, reporting the factors that made governors feel valued and wanting to stay in post were: being welcomed and accepted by the headteacher (84% of respondents), being welcomed and accepted by fellow governors (70% of respondents) and being invited to use their skills (63% respondents). Other significant factors were becoming involved in key tasks and being integrated with the work of the governing body. The aspects that frustrated governors and threatened retention were criticisms of the local authority and central government, and the inadequate level and complexity of school funding.

Inclusion and belonging

Creating a welcoming and listening board culture encourages volunteers to remain engaged and committed. NGA's 2021 participation report provides a pretty positive overall picture of inclusion on boards, for example, with only 4% of respondents saying that their views weren't always valued. Focus groups found that school and trust leaders were important in encouraging volunteers to participate in discussions, acknowledging their contributions and helping them feel valued and confident.

However, governors and trustees from ethnic minority backgrounds were slightly less likely to feel that they belonged on their board, that their opinion is valued by their board (71% of white volunteers strongly agreed that their opinion is valued compared with 50% Black, 55% Asian, and 58% mixed/multiple volunteers) and that they are invited equally to contribute to the board's discussions (70% white volunteers, 69% Asian, 58% mixed/multiple group and 55% Black volunteers). Things that made volunteers feel excluded included poor meeting practices, lack of access to impartial and free information, poor board dynamics and a lack of collaboration.

High-quality induction including buddying was confirmed as crucial in raising the effectiveness of governance and giving volunteers a confident start to their role, whereas their experience was very patchy. This was depressing given the many options now for induction. NGA also encourages annual conversations where the vice chair usually meets with all members of the board individually to hear their views of how the board is operating, any development needs, what could be done to improve the board's functioning and what else that volunteer could offer.

A number of interviewees were surprised at how formal the board meetings were in comparison with their workplaces. Some governors were much more comfortable with this than others. In one case, both the head and chair reported that everyone would be comfortable to speak, but a working-class parent governor said she had not previously attended formal meetings, and when she first came to the board it was 'quite daunting actually'.

Chairing boards

Apart from the relationship with the executive leader in chapter 4, I have said too little about the chairs of boards. They are another one of the eight elements of effective governance. But there's no point in reproducing NGA's *Chairs Handbook* where I do draw on the fairly extensive research on chairing. I shall just emphasise that the school and trust governance would collapse without competent chairs of boards.

Chairs have greater workloads than the rest of the board. An NGA report in 2020, *Chairing a Board: Developing Governance, Sharing Leadership*, aimed to raise the profile of the role and its importance, while also stressing the need for distributed leadership. To create a system that prevents those in full-time employment from leading boards would not be healthy.

Chairs are more likely than other members of the board to be older and white. Twenty-five years ago, they were slightly more likely to be in employment (66%) than today. In 1999, only 2% of chairs were Black, Asian or a minority ethnic groups, compared with 4% in 2022, still hugely underrepresented. The only positive finding was that Black, Asian and ethnic minority volunteers are more likely than their white colleagues to consider putting themselves forward to chair in future: 42% compared with 31%.

In 1999, just over half of all governors were found to be female, but only 36% of chairs. In 2003, The Education Network's study found very similar results, with 54% of all governors being female, but just 37% of chairs. So a quarter of a century ago women were already the majority of school governance volunteers, but significantly less likely to lead a board. Women on boards are now a little less likely to chair than men, but the majority of chairs overall are women. Thank goodness it is now fairly uncommon for a chair of a board to be called a chairman, as it was in a 1995 piece of research.

Women account for more than half of chairs of governors in every type of school; in fact more than 60% in maintained schools and at local governance level within MATs. Even in secondary schools, more than half of chairs are women, which was not quite the case six years ago. We saw the percentage of female chairs of MATs responding to the annual survey gradually increasing to reach 53% in 2021, but then fall in 2022 (the last year for which we have figures on gender) to 47% in MATs and 46% in SATs, compared respectively with 59% and 50% of other trustees being women.

When I'm asked what is the most important of the eight elements of effective governance, my answer is a good chair. They will ensure all the other elements are in place. That is much easier said than done. Just as I am contending that governance does not get enough profile across the sector, chairs also often fly below the radar: the role is not recognised as being as crucial as it is in practice. Having ministers with responsibility for the school system who had recently been chairs of trusts themselves changed that dynamic. For the record the system of school and trust governance would collapse if it were not for all the volunteers who bravely step forward – or often are thrust forward – to take on the chair.

Pay

While still a minority view, there has been a notable trend towards support for remuneration for the governing among the governing community from 28% in 2011 to 39% in 2024. Plus, we have seen already that many notable people outside the volunteers themselves every so often will make the suggestion, often repeatedly and forcefully, that school governance should be a paid role. Therefore, NGA did considerable work exploring this topic, first in 2015 and then again in 2023 and 2024. The workload report includes a detailed section on this debate, but the synopsis there is that there is not yet evidence that a transition to paid governance duties in the school sector will solve any identified problems, and it would bring new issues with it.

Governors and trustees have been able to claim reimbursement for their out-of-pocket expenses for many years. It is best practice to have an expenses policy and a culture of encouraging claims to be made easily; it is a way in theory of making governance inclusive and more accessible to those who cannot afford associated costs. However, in practice this often does not happen and uptake is minimal. Furthermore, expenses do not cover any loss of earnings.

Some suggest paying those who govern our schools and trusts would aid effectiveness of boards, but there is no substantial evidence for this. The benefits might include easier recruitment and greater board diversity. However, paying non-executive directors in the corporate sector has not achieved this with some describing the situation as 'self-perpetuating oligarchies' and identifying the need to broaden the pool of talent.

On the other hand, arguments against remuneration include altering the nature of the governance role and the motivations, building in a conflict of interest, and create another task for those with oversight of the school: the need for a contract of some sort and performance management. It would also bring a substantial cost to the public purse. In 2014, together with Bath University, NGA costed the amount volunteers gave to the system, and it exceeded £1 billion a year.

One way to reduce this amount would be to pay only the chair or the core of most committed governors/trustees. Although he's not the only commentator to have put this forward, this was a favourite proposal of Sir Michael Wilshaw when HMCI, who wanted to distinguish 'the two or three people who hold the most senior roles on the board, and who could be responsible for "cascading" training to other members'. But I must say, I disagree. Paying a couple of members would undermine the fundamental philosophy of the board being a team, changing their relationship with the rest of the board and potentially leaving others willing to do less.

Both the DfE and the House of Commons education committee have in the past supported the involvement of volunteers. I remain committed to the voluntary ethos, but have been interested to see the charity sector beginning to have this discussion too, primarily to achieve more diversity on boards.

In the charity sector, there is the option to seek permission from the Charity Commission to pay trustees; very few do and those tend to be very large charities. That option could be given to large MATs. I want to see the MATs with the largest budgets have to appoint trustees through the public appointments process which, although rather slower, brings more formality and should reduce the cronyism in the system. Those chief executives are extremely powerful people and the appointment of the board that holds them to account should be done at arm's length.

Powers are already in place to pay members of Interim Executive Boards (IEBs), which is a different job as its name suggests – and an executive one, which we will look at in chapter 15.

Conclusion

Citizens volunteer to govern schools and academy trusts because they want to put something back into the community and to help improve the education for local children. Governing schools can also be a hugely rewarding experience, with many enjoying being part of an educational community. It also can provide the development opportunity for a strategic leadership role with a profound purpose. By and large, the same people are volunteering as governed over the last quarter century or more, often professional people with management experience, but there are fewer of them doing more and a growing number of vacancies on boards. This is in part due to changes in broader society, particularly since the Covid-19 pandemic, with some people making different choices as to how they spend their time.

Volunteering remains a fundamental part of British life, and there is no evidence that paying for governance, with its significant price tag, would improve the number of people coming forward or the diversity and effectiveness of boards. Engagement as a school governor is one of the most popular forms of volunteering, and any move to abolish or undermine this participative spirit should be viewed with caution, especially when large parts of society are already sceptical about elites who are said to benefit from governance of public services.

The 2016 reaction to Nicky Morgan's proposal merely to reduce the places reserved for parents suggests removing school governors and academy trustees would not be popular. Any government serious about exploring alternatives would first need to commission a considerable piece of research. The small amount of international evidence available doesn't show us a better model. Our model in England is not only deeply entrenched; it provides a legitimacy that other options are unlikely to as I explore in chapter 16.

Payment is likely to change the motivations to govern and reduce the connection with localities, which is important to give the boards legitimacy. Paying for training and development time could be considered, particularly but not only for any training that is mandated. All boards must ensure they pay expenses so that people with limited resources or additional needs are able to take up the opportunity of civic leadership.

Having a board that holds diversity of thought, skill and experience is integral to good governance, as is aiming that the governing board is reflective of the community that it serves. Despite the widespread recognition that diversity should be central to the composition of a governing board, progress remains slow. The lack of ethnic diversity on many governing boards is a long-standing issue that is likely to reduce the knowledge of pupils' needs and undermine decision-making. Successful efforts have been made to proactively recruit to address gaps in race, background and experience, similar to addressing skill gaps. This will need to happen always and everywhere.

The biggest barrier to volunteering is that citizens do not know this opportunity exists. The generally low profile of school governing inevitably creates challenges for governor and trustee recruitment. In practice, most of the work raising awareness of the role and recruiting volunteers is carried out by the very same hard-pressed volunteers, with the help of their governance professionals, adding to the pressure and time required by a diminishing number of dedicated people. Government has a role in encouraging people to think of contributing. A marketing campaign is needed as there has been for other public sector roles.

Moreover, the DfE and the sector as a whole mustn't continue to push governance to one side in every conversation on every topic of importance and then expect individuals will spring up like magic to the rescue and stand up to the task without any support or gratitude. Appreciation (in both senses) of the role is missing from government reports, press releases and communications of all sorts, and from the general discourse around school leadership. This needs to change to render governance more visible and have support available when citizens stand up and be counted.

The workload of governance is a challenge when retaining volunteers in the sector, particularly those in full-time employment. The flexibility of that work and the amount of time employers will allow people to have off will have some influence on whether they can find the time to volunteer: given persuasion hasn't worked with most employers, the government is needed to make a difference. If this does not change, boards are going to continue getting older as retired people fill more places. In the meantime, boards could use more associate governor and trustee positions so that younger people can see how a board works.

There is only one significant policy change that would reduce workload without undermining the governance role and that is to remove governors from involvement in exclusion panels. The current situation is unsustainable, and a new approach is needed. Alternative proposals have been suggested, including the call from human rights charity, JUSTICE, in 2018 for the introduction of a new suitably qualified and experienced independent reviewer to replace volunteer panels.

Over 200,000 citizens being involved in holding our schools to account and acting as their ambassadors in the wider world is no mean feat. It is a movement of 'good people doing good things', as Damian Hinds MP described them to me when he was a Conservative Education Secretary. Lord Jim Knight, a previous Labour schools minister said in *TES* in 2012: 'By and large, school governors are great, but the governing bodies are not.' I liked this distinction at the time but more than a decade later the performance of boards has moved on, as we will see in the next chapter.

Despite all these warnings, it is important to record that the governance community generally remains an incredibly motivated and inspiring group. There's a lot of data in this chapter, and I hope this very straightforward conclusion has not been lost. This role requires celebrating and cherishing; the people who give so generously of their time and skills should be noted and cared for, not for sentimental reasons but as part of a hard-nosed approach to ensuring our children receive the education they deserve. I've circled back to governance being an essential element of a mature, well-functioning school system, and that means we need to ensure there is a supply line of good people volunteering.

11.
The state of school governance now

Very quickly during the first lockdown, most governing boards moved to online meetings. This was a tremendous adaptation achieved fairly efficiently and without much fuss, especially given that large numbers of governors and trustees had not used the technology before and not everyone was equipped at home. Governance professionals played an important role in supporting this change.

In her foreword to the October 2020 DfE *Governance Handbook*, Baroness Berridge, then Parliamentary Under Secretary of State for Schools, wrote: 'I have been impressed to see the governance sector adapt so quickly to virtual meetings, while continuing to discharge your core functions. Despite the challenges, you have continued to play a vital role in supporting school leaders to ensure that the needs of all learners, including vulnerable children and young people, have been met… So, thank you. I recognise it has neither been easy nor straightforward.'

In the summer term of 2020, NGA carried out a piece of small-scale qualitative research with Ofsted to investigate the decisions and actions of governing boards. *Governing in Unprecedented Times* involved virtual focus groups with governors and trustees in different types of schools and trusts across the country. We were writing it up over the summer break when there was still uncertainty, and rereading it now is a reminder of just what school and trust leadership were dealing with, often without timely or consistent national guidance.

Governing boards' involvement in decisions to partially reopen schools and, in oversight of risk assessments, to make sure children, staff and parents were safe weighed heavily on them. Their responsibility for the wellbeing of so many other people and the potential consequences of decisions felt enormous. There was an emphasis on the additional support they had given to school leaders during this time, which chimed with everything NGA was hearing via other routes. Chairs in particular were sounding boards for headteachers in often lonely positions, although less so in most MATs. In some cases, urgent decisions were made via the 'chair's action', and there were other amendments to governance practice made in some cases in terms of schemes of delegation, committee business, Covid-specific working groups and review of agenda items. Many governing boards continued to hold governors' panels and to recruit senior leaders even though this was not expected by the DfE, but some judged these issues could not be deferred without damaging the functioning of the school.

Despite a variety of views on many topics, when it came to determining the priorities for the return to school, there were two very clear front runners. The first priority was on pupil wellbeing and emotional resilience, and the second priority was learning loss, with special attention to disadvantaged pupils. Many participants felt the effects of the pandemic on emotional and social development and on academic outcomes would be felt for some years. I was told these findings were greeted with some frustration by HMCI who thought other things more important, but rereading the report five years later, the judgement of governors and trustees – especially given how little was known at the time – has held up. They were also thoughtful about how their longer-term strategy might be affected and were determined to come up with solutions that suited their pupils and their communities. They wanted to 'write their own narrative'.

The online legacy

At the end of the pandemic many governors were thrilled to be able to visit schools again and remake the connection. The option of online meetings remains; NGA's 2022 survey data showed one in five meetings were held virtually, with the remainder roughly equally divided between fully in person and hybrid. Committee meetings were slightly more likely to be online (25%) compared to 17% of full board meetings.

Many boards continue to use both online and face-to-face meetings, with the hybrid option often being less attractive given issues both with technology and the meeting dynamics. Even if they are audible, those on screen cannot always interject in the same way as those in the room, no matter how good the chair is. However, joining online does allow attendance from some who could otherwise not join due to travel or work commitments; this can be particularly useful for younger members of the board. They also provide the opportunity to recruit governors/trustees from further afield; for example, alumni who now live elsewhere.

Online meetings can be more efficient and more focused, but they are not conducive to all aspects of governing. In-person meetings are invaluable for the board to bond as a team and with leaders, building trust and rapport. Not only can meetings held in schools increase boards visibility and their knowledge of the school, the informal discussions before and after meetings help build relationships. Sharing a physical space can help people connect. The more fluid nature of communication that characterises meeting face-to-face encourages creative thinking and can lead to improved generative and strategic sessions. Researchers from Columbia Business School found that teams meeting online generated fewer ideas than those meeting in person, possibly because these sessions lack the energy and synergy of face-to-face interactions. Non-verbal communications – which are trickier to assess online – account for a large part of the meeting dynamic. Cultural anthropologists believe that gestures, posture and body movements help us make sense of up to 70% of conversations. Some surveys report that participants are 76% more likely to get distracted during remote meetings.

As someone who travelled far and wide across England before Covid-19 restrictions began, I missed the more informal conversations with members on the edges of events, seeing how the context is different in different places, listening to them relaying in their own words the ups and downs of governing. Much governance training and events have remained online, saving NGA staff and others lots of travelling time but losing some of the nuance of connecting in person.

National leaders of governance

It requires an expert to review, observe and evaluate a board's work. I had lobbied for National Leaders of Governance (NLGs) as soon as I joined NGA and had wanted it to be a paid role. It was decided that experienced chairs would instead be asked to volunteer further to mentor new chairs or those with challenges, and many did, some becoming consultants along the way.

In 2019 the minister announced a review of the DfE's system of leadership designations, and I served on the NLG review's advisory group. There was much consensus, with recommendations published in September 2020. The DfE understandably wanted to focus the role where need was greatest, and the NLG advisory group agreed that 'access to a highly effective cadre of experts in governance was of significant value, particularly for those governing in schools and trusts facing challenges'. This meant conducting reviews where governance was thought to be weak and coming up with a plan for improvement for the board, rather than acting as a mentor for the chair. NLGs therefore needed to be selected using different criteria, paid and quality assured with deployments, as they were called, and matched with the consultant's experience.

External reviews of governance (ERGs) are the most reliable methodology for assessing the quality of governance in schools and trusts, but only when conducted by experienced, quality assured, independent assessors. The DfE guidance updated in 2025 says, 'An ERG can identify areas for capability and capacity building for those involved in governance, improving board effectiveness. ... The review will examine the governance structure, operations and performance across the board.'

Even before I left in 2024, NGA had carried out more than 1000 ERGs, with numbers increasing every month and many more in trusts than maintained schools. Having established ourselves as a market leader for ERGs, we were delighted when this was in effect confirmed by the DfE with NGA's appointment after a competitive tender to deliver the reformed NLG programme in May 2021.

Speaking at the NGA's annual conference in November 2022, which coincided with the publication of the independent evaluation of the first year of the new NLG programme, the minister for the school system, Baroness Barran, said she was 'delighted' that trustees and school leaders interviewed 'really valued the quality, rigour and challenge that NLGs are providing', and that she was discussing with NGA how they would take forward the findings to ensure the programme continues to have a 'positive impact'.

The contract lasted for two years before being prematurely terminated in 2023 due to shortage of DfE funds. Having spent almost six months selecting and training the NLGs to cut it off at that stage was not the best use of funding. However, it provided a wonderful opportunity to analyse the performance of boards of all types across the country, and this we did in our own time, publishing *Charting the Course to Good Governance* in 2023 and *Growing Good Governance* in 2024. Here, I will summarise the findings that apply across single schools and trusts, but save the MAT-specific issues for the next chapter.

Charting the course to good governance

The first 200 ERGs carried out by NLGs for boards referred by the DfE or local authorities emphasised the interconnected nature of common challenges with one problem very likely to cause another. Recruiting people with diverse experiences, skills and knowledge to suit the needs of the board and the organisation was difficult. The lack of a targeted recruitment plan meant that the rate of individuals leaving could be faster than vacancies being filled. Board composition was found to be a challenge, including finding the right size to suit the needs and context of the school/trust: too big and decision-making became difficult; too small (often eight or less) and it lacked capacity and the comprehensive range of skills, experience and backgrounds, exacerbating governance workload and contributing to poor oversight.

Insufficient scrutiny of executive leaders was the second most common theme identified by NLGs. This was exacerbated by a lack of both objective reporting by executives and triangulation of sources. Meetings did not allocate sufficient time for questioning and scrutiny, with some boards having an overreliance on a few experienced governors or trustees. Unsatisfactory monitoring covered a range of issues including finances, with one fifth of ERGs finding inadequacies in financial oversight. Weak financial scrutiny often coincided with the lack of a board member with financial expertise.

Negative board culture was seen in a small but not insignificant proportion of ERGs where lack of shared purpose, tensions and weak dynamics affected decision-making and relationships between the board and leaders. Board members can act as a barrier or a distraction from the core focus of the board. Dynamics between the board and executive were at times influenced by workload and misunderstanding of roles, exacerbated when schemes of delegation are unclear. Failures in communication badly undermined governance, leading to confusion, duplication and non-compliance.

Almost a third of governors or trustees in the ERGs analysed were not involved in agreeing a well-defined vision and strategy, and therefore did not have a sense of ownership or understanding of what they were trying to achieve and were not monitoring progress against the strategy. Governance in these examples was often reactive and working in an uninformed way. A greater understanding of the governance role in the setting of vision and the related strategic direction was required, as for some was the allocation of resources to areas of highest need.

A small proportion of ERGs demonstrated poor identification of risk, or failure to identify and monitor mitigations. For example, falling pupil rolls was a commonly highlighted risk that did not always have planned mitigation that was regularly reviewed. Several boards failed to identify recruitment and retention of staff as a significant risk while others showed no evidence of monitoring or proactively addressing increasing staffing issues.

Some ERGs showed a deficit in terms of governance support and development activities that enhance board practices. Limited engagement with regular sector updates and training weakens board capabilities. As we saw in chapter 7, there is increasing recognition of the critical role governance professionals play, but a minority of boards still underutilise or undervalue the role.

Growing good governance 2024

A similar exercise with the next 209 ERGs along with progress reports carried out after six months took us up to the end of the NLG programme in October 2023. This report, building on the previous year's with some deeper analysis, provided a real state of the nation of the governance in England's schools and trusts, very much skewed towards struggling schools and trusts. There were no surprises. Weaknesses identified almost always concern their core functions of boards; while not ideal, this does have the advantage that they tally with the rest of NGA's development work and solutions. Apart from a couple specific to the MAT model, all the practice recommendations have been seen over the last 20 years or longer.

Yet despite this exercise not having turned things upside down, it has been a rich source of learning. There is value in validating and reinforcing what the sector should already know. It is significant fresh evidence that adds weight to the knowledge bank. Some aspects are showing more progress than a few other more stubborn issues, but overall we have a sound governance sector where boards take their development seriously. The report differentiated between boards of trustees and governing bodies and highlights the different challenges faced by different school structures: we will come back to the delegation and communication complexities within MATs in the next chapter.

There have been some real improvements over the last 15 years. Fiduciary functions are generally well managed with a good level of compliance and the prominent proportion of schools and trusts meeting statutory requirements in spite of intensifying pressures. Financial oversight and a firm grip on financial responsibilities were also positively reported even within this group of challenged boards. The basics of clear roles and professional support are also largely in place. There is far more recognition now of just how imperative it is to have the best governance professional you can get your hands on in post with the ERGs underlining how they often made the key difference in boards.

On the other hand, we are not quite where we need to be. Some boards were seen to be struggling to maintain a strategic focus, with a few still getting bogged down in operational matters. The first half of the 2020s brought hurdle after hurdle even after the pandemic was over, such as: the energy crisis; the cost-of-living crisis and increasing family poverty; industrial action; attendance and behaviour issues; funding restraints particularly regarding SEND; and falling rolls. Against this backdrop, some struggling boards have been in reactive mode with urgent issues dominating their discussions at the expense of strategy setting. Almost half of governing boards or boards of trustees examined by NLGs had not established a long-term vision and strategy that focused their work. The findings showed that a key barrier to developing a strategy is the headteacher or CEO failing to recognise the need for one.

Holding leaders to account also emerged again as a significant challenge in two thirds of the boards referred to NLGs. Over half were struggling to get the right balance and approach to the relationship and interactions between board and leadership, this being even more prevalent in maintained schools than trusts. Where holding leaders to account was identified as an issue, just over a quarter (27%) specifically noted major weaknesses in leadership engagement with governance as a culprit, often due to how and what was being reported to the board. Workload continues to strain board capacity, but leadership workload prevents some leaders finding the time needed to engage well with governance.

Stakeholder engagement was an area for development for just over one in five boards, with MATs struggling in this area most, marginally more than SATs, compared with fewer than one in 10 maintained school reviews. Stakeholder feedback was not being used effectively in holding senior leaders to account and in developing the ethos and direction of schools/trusts.

Making progress

During the NLG programme, 141 schools and trusts benefited from a progress review carried out three months after the initial ERG. Despite the relatively short timeframe, considerable progress was evidenced in more than nine out of 10 settings. These progress reviews seemed to be having a significant impact on driving improvement in governance practice due to the combination of boards being held accountable for delivering action plans and given ongoing support and guidance. The findings also emphasise the importance of reviews being carried out by an experienced and objective external reviewer, providing an independent perspective on the board's progress and offering constructive feedback and support. This follow-up helped to maintain momentum and challenge long-established ways of working where change was misunderstood or resisted.

Where little progress had been made on action plans, common barriers included no governance professional, who was essential in managing the activities and ensuring impetus, and a lack of board capacity, especially where different approaches to volunteer recruitment had not been adopted. Recommendations need to be owned by the whole board and to have realistic timescales. Volunteers' other commitments can prevent immediate change, but contributions that fit with availability need to be found.

Continuing to improve

As long as we accept that the commissioners – the DfE, the local authorities and dioceses – were pretty well able to identify schools and trusts where governance needed strengthening, the NLG programme provides definitive evidence that a significant majority of boards are governing well at any one time. But we also know that standards previously good can decline, both when there is no change in a board and it becomes cosy and complacent, but also when people – volunteers or senior leaders – move on and new people without any experience of governing take their places. The impact of this could do with some research; I hope that governance professionals provide some protection, but they are unlikely to fully mitigate the risks, especially if those joining have no training, and they do not benefit from all the learning of the past 25 years.

Induction training is not mandatory for governors and trustees of schools, whereas it is required for other crucial voluntary roles, such as magistrates and citizen advice volunteers. The call for mandatory induction training has consistently been made by the governance community over a long period: over 12 years in 11 surveys, an average of 94% of respondents support its introduction with over half of the total strongly supporting it. Although the demands of training contribute to the workload, it is notable that new governors have lower workloads than others.

It is ludicrous not to expect new governors and trustees to be trained on the fundamentals of their role, but how quality relevant training could be commissioned for all would need thought. It might be possible through a voucher scheme for each new governor/trustee registered on GIAS, but only if there was some form of quality assessment. Tenders for small amounts of funding are unduly bureaucratic. There were times when I wondered about the wisdom of asking the government to mandate training as it seemed to run counter to my efforts to get governing boards to take control in a bottom-up way. Mandatory induction training mustn't become a barrier to recruiting volunteers. It is perfectly possible to design and tailor different sessions for different structures; NGA has been doing this for some years. The induction process needs to be systematic and also expose them to the history, culture and vision of the organisation. Although some of us still prefer being in a room with other people, e-learning and online sessions make induction much more accessible.

I frequently fell into the trap of believing that we've talked about such and such for so long, we don't need to prioritise it anymore, only to find a couple of years later that same poor practice is beginning again. Some issues will be perennial; for example, the line between strategic oversight and operations as discussed in chapter 4. The sector has moved a long way since the Balarin et al. 2008 report that found over 60% of governors contributed to operational tasks. A reminder that 'governing is a thinking role, not a doing role' and they need to be 'eyes on, hands off' is usually enough to get back on track.

Governance will only remain sustainable by better sharing of the workload. Vice chairs in particular need to take more prominent roles: it would help if GIAS recognised the role. Any proposed changes in practice must put the workload of volunteers centre stage.

Moreover, we mustn't go backwards: the fundamentals need to be respected. In 2024, boards carrying out skills audits had fallen from its high point of 87% to 78%, and although changes should be made to the template used to improve it, abandoning the practice would be risky, especially given the need to not just recruit for skills but also for other aspects of diversity.

Committees

Committees and working parties with an effective scheme of delegation can reduce the burden on the full board provided it is a certain size, does not repeat what is done in the subgroups and care is taken to prevent overspecialisation by individuals. Large numbers of committees do not tend to add to efficiency. At NGA, we have for many years suggested two are sufficient when governing one school: one for resources and one for education. However, we did not have huge success in streamlining this way of working: there were 22% with one or two committees when we first asked this question in 2013, and this had only risen to 38% in 2019.

Taking this further, the model of handling almost all business at board meetings without committees has advantages. Almost always those of us who have experienced working in this way are convinced of its improved efficiency. No longer is there any need for committee reports to the full board with the danger of re-opening conversations and often saving work for senior leaders or governance professionals writing reports. Instead, all governors/trustees are present for all items as the conversation happens at the full board. This seems appropriate given all are equally responsible for all aspects of the organisation's activity, but it's also more inclusive. The percentage of boards adopting the practice of no committees rose from 2% in 2013 to 19% in 2022. The full board probably needs to meet more often, but this tends to reduce board time overall. This simpler model needs to be tried by others, especially smaller boards; committees are sometimes an area of unnecessary bureaucracy hung on to out of habit.

Self-review

It's clear from this study that most boards are now committed to their own continuous improvement, compared even with 10 years ago when Ofsted (2016) found two thirds of schools had not engaged in any self-evaluation of governance before being found to be less than good by Ofsted. NLGs found regular board self-evaluations to be embedded as commonplace, indicating a positive culture of reflection and a desire for development. This is higher than NGA survey data, which shows where there was a high point of more than half of boards (58%) having carried out a review each year before the pandemic, and almost all say it has been useful, but that has fallen in recent years. In 2025 just under half of boards (49%) had carried out some form of governance review in the past year, 40% a self-review and 9% an ERG, whereas you might expect it to be one in three.

This compared with fewer than one in 10 NLG deployments reporting there was no self-review. A lack of depth, quality and impact of self-evaluation did feature in other cases. It may amount to little more than a cursory tick-box exercise without critical reflection or a meaningful plan for action. Other boards conducted more thorough self-review but struggled to translate the findings into tangible improvements. A key factor influencing the effectiveness of self-evaluation was the level of engagement and ownership from the entire board.

Self-reviews don't provide insurance against poor practice. The most effective boards also sought input from stakeholders such as staff, parents and pupils, as well as drawing on external data and benchmarking. This helped to validate or challenge the board's own perceptions and identify blind spots. The ERGs highlighted the importance of using a structured framework or tool; it is crucial to use a self-review template that is based on experience and expertise, so no apologies for promoting NGA's, which has been tested, revised and evolved since 2012.

The 20 questions were originally developed for use by schools maintained by local authorities and single-academy trusts in 2012 by NGA and The Key under the auspices of the All-Party Parliamentary Group (APPG) on Education Governance chaired by Neil Carmichael MP who later became chair of the House of Commons education select committee. They caught on quickly, probably because of the APPG branding, and were cited by several witnesses, including the minister, as being another very useful tool in self-assessment during the 2013 select committee enquiry into governance.

The 21 questions for MAT boards were created in 2015 by NGA and the APPG in response to the growing number of schools in MATs and now include an additional 16 questions for self-evaluation of those at academy committee level (local governing bodies) to encourage MATs to review all layers of governance. They were downloaded almost 11,000 times from mid-2019 to November 2021.

All three sets of questions were updated in 2022 following an extensive consultation with over 300 governors, trustees and governance professionals, which included seeking feedback on how the questions had been used and had improved board practice and any areas not currently covered. The revised and restructured questions include a greater emphasis on board dynamics, culture and behaviours, and replaced multi-layered questions with shorter, focused statements for reflection. They are also disseminated by other organisations, referenced in the DfE's governance guidance and incorporated into many external reviews of governance. NGA's surveys over the last three years show that about two-thirds of self-reviews use the 20/21 questions.

Peer review

In 2014, NGA developed a peer-review model for three or four governing boards, but it did not take off. During the pilot, we discovered it did need at least light-touch facilitation by an external expert to prevent poor practice being adopted by others. Good practice needs to be spread from board to board, not just practice that feels familiar as it sits with current mindsets. Research would be useful to explore further what makes peer reviews of governance successful.

Boards do not generally even tend to observe other boards. This may be back to the issue of time and capacity, but it is also a cultural issue. Many boards are wary of being observed. This needs to change; we all need to be challenged to improve and avoid groupthink.

Preventing decline

This is hardly ambitious, but governance is central to preventing the decline of the organisation as a whole and in the case of schools the decline of outcomes for pupils. My evidence-based contention is most governing boards are performing well enough to do this, but there is still some shocking governance, and that is not confined to the most challenged schools. Given all the efforts that have been made to improve governance over the past 20 years, might decline be more of a risk?

At the time of writing, the DfE does not appear to have a strategy to improve governance or even to prevent its decline. After investing in volunteer recruitment and governance development, in their last couple of years the Conservative government removed all that piece by piece. The demise of the NLG programme leaves the sector without any quality assured governance expertise. The RISE teams put in place by the Labour government do not appear to have any role in governance.

Ofsted is not in its current iteration in a position to be relied upon to pick up problems with governance; they look at it very speedily and rarely report on it in any meaningful way. Ofsted is not the arbitrator of governance; slavishly doing what Ofsted requires is unhelpful and, when it comes to governance, unambitious.

As I covered in chapter 3 and since, we know the things that make a difference: a great chair, an independent governance professional, a lead executive who invests in building trust and reporting well, and high-quality training and support for governing boards. The latter I have barely mentioned until this point in the book, but it is very much woven throughout the history of English school governance.

Training, development and support

Back when English state schools were maintained by the local authority, training, advice and support was provided by local authorities, and over the last 15 years gradually fewer managed to provide a full range of governor services. However, many have survived by charging for services (usually termed 'traded service') or by outsourcing the work. As with all things, they range from the excellent to the very basic. In those areas where the training and clerking services provided are good, some academies buy them too.

Initially, as recorded by the education select committee in 2013, there were concerns that few quality alternatives were emerging to the training traditionally provided by local authorities, but there is now a lively market in school and trust governance support services. There is much choice, although some is possibly not the highest quality, and that is difficult to assess before signing a contract. Furthermore it is not a level playing field with marketing when commercial organisations have larger budgets.

In their report in 2018, Judge and Kashefpakdel found: 'Overall, interviewees felt that school governor training had improved and is more available. However, it was felt that whether governors undertake training greatly depends on whether a school governing board encourages it, the budget available for governor activity (which some interviewees highlighted was reducing in the current funding climate) and the geography of the school itself – i.e. how close the school was to credible providers.' This last point is no longer as valid as moving online during the pandemic gave some services a lifeline with training attendances increasing and gave boards much more choice.

By and large, it appears that the market has worked, but this contention probably needs testing by independent research, especially given that NGA played an increasing role in it. In particular, NGA's suite of e-learning, Learning Link, grew to become the market leader.

Governing boards used to be reluctant to spend money on their own needs, including professional clerking and training: this was referred to in a DfES report in 2004, and it came to the attention of the National College for School Leadership when together we carried out a set of regional events to test out the argument for the college's forthcoming support for chairs and boards. In its response to the select committee, the House of Commons education committee (2013) stated: 'Governing bodies who do not invest in improving their effectiveness by taking up training are making a false economy.' It is a concern that in the current tightened financial context that such bad habits may reassert themselves.

The House of Commons select committee in 2013 concluded that too many governors had not had suitable training and the government should require schools to offer training to every new governor. The government argued that this can be encouraged through Ofsted and that Ofsted would be resourced adequately in order to undertake an increased role in helping to ensure effective governance in schools. The inspection handbook published that year stated that in making their judgement on the effectiveness of governance, inspectors will look at how well governing bodies develop the skills of their members. The House of Commons education committee said, 'Ofsted will want to know that the governing body takes seriously their training needs and ensures that every governor who needs training receives training of a high quality.' This did happen for a time but has long since disappeared.

The DfE responded that:

> '…to address a market failure in the provision of training for clerks and to ensure there is a high quality benchmark in the market for governor training, we have doubled the investment we make in governance through NCTL. By 2015, this funding will enable NCTL [NCSL's successor] to:
>
> • Build on the early success of the leadership development programme to expand it to reach over 6,500 chairs, vice chairs and aspiring chairs;
>
> • Designate up to a total of 535 high quality chairs as National Leaders of Governance;
>
> • Develop and roll out a programme of training for 2,000 clerks to governing bodies; and
>
> • Develop and publish training resources and deliver high quality training for governors on specific key policy priorities including: understanding performance data, driving financial efficiency in schools, and developing new performance related pay arrangements for teachers.'

NGA was one of the half dozen providers of the clerks and chairs programmes, and the DfE funding dramatically increased the take-up of the training until it ceased in 2021. NGA continues to offer an updated version of those courses now at a price, and numbers, particularly of chairs undertaking them, are not nearly as high as when free to participants.

In 2023, the NLGs could conclusively see that ineffective practice correlated with a lack of engagement in training and opportunities to network. Weaknesses in oversight or skill deficits were often linked to a lack of training and development to support knowledge and understanding of how to discharge their duties. Conversely, there were examples of where active engagement had had a visible impact in how governors and trustees positively perform their core functions, such as picking up practical tips, asking area-specific questions and templates for effective monitoring visits, as well as better understanding their roles and responsibilities.

Decision-making

I have previously emphasised the importance of high-quality information and a conducive culture as pre-conditions for good decision-making. This is also the case in other sectors; for example, here is a recent example from the university sector that fits beautifully with all I have been saying.

Created by Hugh Jones, 2025

Figure 11.1 What is good governance is higher education?

While principles and procedure set the scene for good decisions, they won't guarantee them, as we saw in chapter 3. We are lacking in the education sector any published analysis of how good board decisions have been. We began discussing this just before I left NGA, and the DfE guidance updated in 2025 says, 'A review should consider the process and impact of decision-making.' The decision-making process has been assessed in the past, but the consequences of decisions have not been widely considered.

The starting point needs to be: just how many decisions do boards make? During my extensive reading and re-reading of school and trust governance literature I was very struck by a phrase used by Helen Young (2017) who carried out many board observations in the course of her research: 'busy but passive'. Are boards in practice really doing what people like me say they are doing: making decisions? If the answer is hardly at all, it means while governance is central on paper, in practice it may be making itself largely irrelevant. This is a challenge we need to get to the bottom of.

In professional settings, the ability to make good decisions depends on a mix of cognitive processes, experience and environmental factors. The quality of board decisions should be increased by being a collective endeavour with a variety of different minds involved. As well as being driven by their values, sound decision-makers balance analytical reasoning with intuition, using data while recognising when instinct is valuable. In NGA's *The Chair's Handbook*, I cover briefly the emotional intelligences needed to lead a board and the need to recognise the emotional reactions, displayed or not by board members, which influence their thinking. I also talk about who has the influence in and outside the meeting.

Psychological influences can either reinforce ethical decision-making or introduce hidden biases that undermine governance outcomes. Psychology, neuroscience and behavioural science explore how cognitive biases, heuristics (mental shortcuts relying on patterns, past experiences and intuition) and social influences shape governance-related decision-making. There is evidence showing how biases such as confirmation bias, anchoring (overreliance on an irrelevant piece of evidence), overconfidence, loss aversion, groupthink and fear of authority have been detrimental to both institutional governance and leadership decision-making, such as during the global financial crisis.

This is also relevant to the education and political academic critiques of the current system I've mentioned: i.e. it reinforces existing centralised power structures by incorporating both frameworks and behavioural nudges to steer compliance and raises questions about real organisational agency. Is ethical responsibility being fostered or decision-making manipulated? Although there are many academics who believe the latter, the practical evidence seems to be missing. I agree that there is a certain amount of performativity in the system. For example, as most boards are aware that – for very good reason – good questioning is necessary, this will be encouraged by the chair and the lead executive professionals and minuted by the governance professional. Even though this may be done for Ofsted's benefit in part, surely this is also a way of developing board practice, rather than anything more sinister or centrally controlled, and could become an authentic aspect of that board's behaviour.

It is almost impossible for a board to know that it has made 'the right' decision. Whereas the impact of operational decisions might be seen relatively quickly, boards are making decisions with longer-term results; some of the current members might not even be there when the outcomes become apparent. ERGs may only be able in the short-term to record recent decisions and include an in-depth diagnosis of current decision-making and its quality. This happens in some other sectors, and we need to adopt that practice in the school sector. Subsequent ERGs could then look at the decisions recorded at the previous review and consider whether the board, given hindsight, would make the same decision now, and if not, why not. For trusts, the AGM could usefully also have a conversation with trustees about the thinking behind their decisions.

The Committee for Standards in Public Life (2025) points out that 'public office holders are often required to make complex decisions, sometimes in ambiguous and fast-moving operational environments. In such circumstances, taking a step back and viewing problems through the prism of the public interest can help public office holders focus on what really matters.' They also point out that 'it is far easier to evaluate past decisions from the vantage point of knowing the outcome than it is to foresee problems in advance.'

Considering the impact of governance

A whole range of sources confirm that governing boards are very aware of their responsibility to promote high standards of educational achievement. For example, 99% of NGA survey respondents reported this in 2014. A few may argue that's evidence of the performative nature of governance, but most accept this as an important function. Governors and trustees are also concerned with the development of what's often called the whole child and the happiness of pupils.

A large majority of NGA's 2025 survey respondents felt 'that my governing board has made a positive impact on the strategic direction and outcomes of my school or trust in the past year': 88% of maintained schools governors; 87% of SAT trustees; 85% of MAT trustees and 78% of local governors within MATs. Nearly half (47%) strongly agreed. When asked where boards were having the greatest impact, financial oversight and resource allocation was the most frequently selected area (57%) across nearly every board type, region and school phase, apart from local governors in MATs who are less likely to have financial responsibilities. Half of respondents chose educational outcomes and curriculum oversight as there they had had impact; 50% also chose strategic planning and long-term vision; 41% chose pupil wellbeing and safeguarding; but only 28% chose staff recruitment, retention and wellbeing.

As Tim Brighouse and Mick Waters (2022) state, there is 'regrettably' a lack of research on the issue of whether governing boards 'have made a significant contribution to school improvement'. I have taken to heart their experience that they have rarely seen it. My experience is somewhat different in that I am aware of boards who have had to suspend or remove a failing headteacher and then often work with a new headteacher as the school improves. It may be one step removed from educational improvement, but that work is critical to the organisation's turn around and success.

Judging the quality of governing solely on impact on pupils might not be hugely helpful. Good pupil performance will reflect well on the governing body but perhaps inappropriately so. It is likely to judge governing boards in schools in disadvantaged settings harshly and those in grammar schools overgenerously. Sometimes governing boards in high-performing schools take their foot off the pedal, whereas those in more challenged communities have to concentrate all the time.

Even if a range of measures are being monitored, we really couldn't say with any sort of confidence that good governance leads to those improved experiences and outcomes for children and young people. There is a chain of so many actors and variables between the governing board and pupils that the cause and effect may never be proven. The literature in other sectors, some with simpler outcomes measures than schools, does not provide answers.

Some previously 'good' or 'outstanding' schools decline when trustees or governors have taken their eye off the ball, and that weak governance has not been identified by any part of the system. By that time, pupils are affected. That is why ERGs need to be embedded as an expectation.

Conclusion

Due to a heroic effort by those participating in governance it is in a far better state than it has been before: you don't just have to take my word for it. NGA had 400 independent ERG reports to draw on that showed the need to keep on keeping on with the fundamentals of governance. The next step of governance development in the sector is to analyse decisions that have been made to ascertain whether that requirement to make good decisions is being lived up to.

The sector can't be complacent. There are always new school leaders and new volunteers to induct well. Experienced governors and trustees need a bit more courage and curiosity to undertake peer reviews, or simply to observe another board while allowing themselves to be observed. I don't want to suggest this doesn't happen at all. Many chairs do play a significant role in the sector giving even more of their time to guide other chairs, such as the service provided by IGovS.

Over the last five years there has been no impetus from on high to improve governance: Ofsted had to all intents and purposes withdrawn from the arena and, with Lord Agnew's replacement with Baroness Berridge as minister for the school system, we no longer had a passionate advocate for governance in the ministerial team. She was much more interested in the growth of trusts and her successor Baroness Barran was soon overtaken by the RAAC (reinforced autoclaved aerated concrete) crisis.

DfE funding to support governance was cancelled, piece by piece; first the development programmes for chairs, future chairs and governance professionals, then the decision not to replace the academy trustee recruitment service, Academy Ambassadors, the NLGs in 2023 and the governor recruitment service, Inspiring Governance, in 2024. This left the government making no investment whatsoever in the almost quarter of a million volunteers who have oversight of our state schools in England. It beggars belief. The Labour government did not improve any of this in its first 18 months.

Schools and trusts have to use their general funds to subscribe to NGA and others for support, and the majority do, but there are still some who are loath to spend their general funding on governance. The case for funding for mandatory induction training should keep being made, especially while it is still so widely supported both among those who volunteer to govern and those who work with them.

It can be a challenge in many parts of the country to recruit volunteers. Giving the general impression that school governance is weak does not help that task, nor does it help the morale of the governance community. Of course, I'm not claiming every governing board in the land is excellent, but discourse based on ignorance detracts from the incredibly important role and what it takes to govern well. Unless you have governed at a school or trust that does not employ you, or you are a governance professional, you are unlikely to fully understand the time, complexity and judgement required. At NGA, we had the privilege of daily conversations with those that do, and the care taken to ensure governance is working well is humbling. The importance of working collectively to get school governance right should not be understated; there are so many people who came with us. We only knew what we knew because so many governors, trustees and governance professionals worked with us, trusting us to share their experiences. This really should not be forgotten. Practice was not laid down from on high.

Adaptability and resilience of the governance community was underlined by their role during the pandemic, quickly adapting to new situations and challenges presented by Covid-19. It was also needed to development a brand-new model of governance fit for purpose for MATs: the next chapter will look at where we have got to with this fundamental change.

12.
The state of MAT governance now

The move towards MATs has transformed the English school sector, introducing a very different form of school management and accountability. However, 23 years after the first eight academies were created in England, albeit as SATs, its institutional governance can't be described as immature any longer. In chapter 9, I covered all the early learning about governing a group of schools, and here I explore progress on those additional features.

In 2021, NGA updated the analysis with the publication of *MATs Moving Forward* and there had been some progress. Many MATs were now open and willing to talk about the challenges they encountered as they grew, bold enough to admit points of learning and mistakes made along the way, helping others who came afterwards.

There had been significant improvement in the clarity of roles within MAT governance and their maturity is evident in the dramatic improvements in achieving separation of personnel between layers. NGA's annual surveys recorded a reduction from 73% of members being trustees in 2018, to just 9% in 2024. Generally schemes of delegation (SoDs) have also improved. There is a danger that SoDs are now seen as debates of the past, when they continue to provide the spine of MAT governance and need to be regularly reviewed.

Trust governance professionals have increasingly played an important part in delivering higher expectations. In 2021, NGA's governance professional survey told us just 27% of lead governance professionals managed a team that clerked governance at the local tier, whereas the figure in 2024 was 88%.

In 2021, communication between the layers of governance still wasn't always as good as it needed to be to improve relationships and strengthen governance. The growth in size of many trusts necessitated constant reviews of governance structures. Over half of MAT trustees reported plans to increase the number of academies in their trust.

Local governance within MATs had resisted the suggestions of its demise, but practice remained patchy, and there was still an underlying concern about loss of voice. At NGA, Sam Henson and I decided we needed to do more to lay down the minimum expectations as that wasn't happening from the DfE or looking likely to happen.

There had been an increase in scrutiny and expectations on boards' financial governance duties. There has also been progress in the oversight of MATs by the DfE, with governance taking a more central part.

The issues identified in chapter 11 on the remaining governance practice shortcomings all apply to MATs. Both reports of NLG (National Leaders of Governance) reviews – *Charting the Course to Good Governance* in 2023 and *Growing Good Governance* a year later – provide evidence that the core functions of governance need attention in some MATs too. For example, in a quarter of MAT board reviews analysed, trustees were not effectively holding the CEO to account. Failing with the fundamentals isn't because the MAT sector is immature; effort always has to be made to make sure they are done well. Governing is difficult, as the then minister Catherine McKinnell MP confirmed at NGA's 2025 summer conference.

One institution

There remains a question with some MATs: has the group of schools become one cohesive organisation? NGA's 2024 research with over 1500 trust respondents showed that while 77% of local governors felt that the MAT adds value to the work of the school, only 30% of local governor respondents did not feel their school is part of one organisation. These figures underscore the need for boards of trustees to develop a MAT-wide vision and strategy as found wanting in chapter 11, but also to do more to foster a sense of belonging and shared purpose across all their schools. This is not simple: a MAT needs to develop its own identity while respecting each school's history, connections and context.

There is a delicate balance between central identity, authority and control, and individual school identity, needs, character and delegated decision-making. The latter will be set out in the SoD, but it is not just a legal construct, but also more importantly a component of the trust's values and culture. MATs must harness the opportunities of centralisation and at the same time empower localised leadership at school level. The trust-wide strategy should be owned and delivered by all.

In 2024 almost four out of five local governors (78%) agreed their voices were heard by executives and trustees. On the other hand, fewer than one in five local governors were invited to attend the MAT's AGM, so there is still some way to go in valuing the local perspective and creating belonging in this way.

The non-negotiables of each trust and the way it asserts central control vary hugely. Some MATs have been criticised for imposing a regimented way of doing things that allows little or no localised expression. In its 2022 White Paper *Opportunity for All*, the DfE under the last government emphasised that boards should 'anchor the trust's strategy in the needs of its schools, the communities they serve, and the wider educational system'. At the other end of the spectrum are the trusts that combine procuring some specialist services with delegation of much else to their schools. This may or may not be combined with collaborative practice that maximises learning from within their schools, tapping into the strengths for the benefit of all. Some MAT boards and executives have been forthcoming about the difficulty in establishing an identity and ambition that is broad enough to connect with multiple communities, yet specific enough to be meaningful. This tension will be a perennial challenge for MATs; it's built into the group of schools model.

Communication between layers

Effective two-way communication is essential. Improving communication across the MAT's schools and across the tiers of governance has been an aim for many MATs for several years. In 2025 only six out of 10 local governors reported that communication between the local tier and the trust board is effective and well managed, a drop from 71% in the 2024 survey and even below 62% in 2023. MATs with 11 to 20 academies reported the highest satisfaction with communication, possibly suggesting this could be an optimal size for effective communication, large enough to necessitate robust systems, but not so large that messages get lost in the scale and complexity. In the 2022 survey, almost two thirds of MATs had regular meetings of their local chairs with the chairs of the trust board.

Growing Governance reported that 17% of MAT boards referred to NLGs had weaknesses in their relationships or communication between tiers of governance. Managing the relationship between the trust board and academy committees was a key priority for most MATs. As well as communication, issues included a lack of clarity around their respective roles and responsibilities, insufficient focus on collaboration and inadequate reporting from academy committees to the trust board.

Evolution of executive teams

Trust boards need to be confident they have built the right executive team that complements their values and supports schools well, even though it will need reviewing if the MAT grows. There is much variation in the sector that has not been very well shared or documented. On the other hand the DfE rightly specified in the AFH (Academies Financial Handbook) the need for appropriately qualified financial staff as initially this has been slow to materialise, and the introduction of the chief financial officer and often also a chief operating officer once funding allows has made a significant impact.

NGA conducted research in 2021 that identified three trends:

1. Internalisation of functions: MATs increasingly bringing services in-house rather than contracting out to third parties.
2. Centralisation of functions: more responsibilities shifting from individual academies to the central team.
3. Specialisation of roles: moving from broader catch-all positions to specialised roles, such as HR expertise.

A significant minority of trusts felt they were 'making it up as we go along' when it comes to their central teams, and a majority expressed a lack of confidence and general uncertainty in handling this issue. As there has been no system leadership on this crucial issue, apart from the EFA on the financial side, the DfE could commission some research. *Schools Week* reported this was being scoped in 2023, but it has not appeared. Such work should not prescribe any particular approach, as these are clearly trust-level decisions, but understanding the options would be of benefit, especially as cash is extremely tight. In 2025 there is still not enough information and guidance from the DfE for trustees making decisions about restructuring executive teams and setting pay rates as MATs grow.

Executives are also the people who performance manage the headteachers, a fundamental but unexplored change. Many MATs have executive heads overseeing and supporting three or four headteachers, whereas as they grow this may become regional directors with more heads reporting to them. Confederation of School Trusts' (CST) 2024 survey reported school improvement is most frequently organised around central staff working across multiple schools (88%) or school-based staff working across multiple schools (67%). Just over half of MATs had directors of SEND, the likelihood increasing with size. Significant numbers employ subject specialists.

Staff have been known to question what exactly some executives do all day. It certainly is not plain to all in all trusts, whereas in others the value of central services alongside school improvement support is well understood and appreciated.

Stakeholder engagement

It was notable that the only significant area where the NLG programme found MATs struggling slightly more than maintained schools was with stakeholder engagement, and in 2022 just over half of local governor survey respondents felt that their MAT effectively engaged with parents and the wider community. This came as no surprise given the scale of many MATs and the lack of attention paid to this topic by the powers that be, but it is disappointing. As public services, all MATs should have some sense of place and put community and the role of schools within their communities at the heart of their vision and values. The DfE's trust quality descriptions state that is it the board that 'oversees strategic relationships with external stakeholders' underlining the non-executive role.

NGA ran a long but successful campaign to have stakeholder engagement built into the DfE's core functions of governance. From 2024 stakeholder engagement is one of the DfE's three defined purposes of trust governance. The local tier of governance should be commissioned to obtain and share local views with the board of trustees. Therefore, it is alarming that NGA's 2025 survey shows that local governance having a remit to engage with stakeholder engagement has fallen from 65% to 56%. CST's 2024 report found almost half of trusts were intending to focus on stakeholder engagement in the coming year. Boards often become overreliant on information from trust executives; this is a real risk when information coming from schools is always mediated by central teams.

Most MATs need to work harder at engaging with parents and the community. An Edurio 2025 report found that while families typically feel informed about what's happening in school, they don't always feel listened to or understood, nor do they fully understand how decisions are made. Trust boards and trust executives need to understand what stakeholders think, even though they will leave most of the engagement activities to local governors and school leaders. NGA's 2024 survey found that trust boards were less likely to hear from the local tier about stakeholder engagement in larger MATs. To add to that disconnect as MATs grow and expand into new towns or counties, the number of stakeholders increases and engaging with them would be a huge task. Executives of geographically dispersed

MATs cannot as easily achieve the necessary civic engagement in each place, but headteachers can continue to perform this important role.

The move to groups of schools must not come at the cost of removing the school's local connectedness and engagement with the place they are embedded. The information gleaned is essential to MATs as they seek to respond to local needs. Local governors themselves play a part in raising the profile of the MAT within the community.

Local governance

At the heart of the transformation to good MAT governance lies this essential yet often underappreciated component. In chapter 9 the case was made for local governance at academy level. By academy level I mean a committee for every large school, but if a MAT includes some small primary schools in the same locality, one committee can serve both or all three schools, mimicking small maintained federations. The schools need to be relatively close and governors need to be drawn from both school communities. The local tier does something the trust board can't – focus on one location and the schools there. This does not distract or detract from the trust board's role: hearing from all its places improves decision-making.

After NGA's 2019 *Moving MATs Forward* report, the value of strong local governance became increasingly apparent to the sector. For example, in 2021 CST produced guidance that stated 'the local tier of governance is absolutely essential to effective governance of a complex organisation in a multi-academy trust'. Although the initial reaction for some MATs when the first Covid-19 lockdown began was to cancel LGB meetings, most were reinstated online fairly quickly. Some trustees told us that during the pandemic they could not have managed their responsibilities with risk assessments without the contribution of academy committees who knew the staff, the premises and the community, but for others where the LGB's role was mainly educational, that wasn't as relevant in the beginning.

Understanding the full potential of local governance was not universal and for some time many MATs struggled with meaningful practice, leading to confusion, inefficiencies for heads and duplication of effort between volunteers and executives. NGA continued to write about local governance extensively, bringing experience and wisdom together in the thought leadership piece *MAT Governance: The Future is Local* by Sam Henson (NGA, 2022). Edurio also reported that only 43% of parents found the MAT's role clear, and that isn't improving. We were delighted when later that month, the DfE's White Paper, *Opportunity for All*, said, 'So that trusts continue to be responsive to parents and local communities, all trusts should have local governance arrangements for their schools.' This statement, lobbied hard for by NGA, spurred others in the sector to turn their minds to local governance, convinced of its continuation. The 2024 survey revealed that local governance exists in almost all MATs. Only five out of 1081 MAT respondents had no form of local governance, with 3% being unsure, down from 12% in 2021.

While NGA had been keen to help facilitate innovative approaches, the reality is this has not developed as we once imagined it might. NGA's model SoDs first published in 2016 had four variations (including an SoD allowing delegation to committee covering clusters of schools), but over the years as our knowledge of local governance in practice increased, this became just one template with room for amendment.

There has been experimentation by some MATs with a different approach often called cluster or hub committees over a larger geographical region. In some cases, they were an additional layer, which added bureaucracy, confusion on role and duplication without adding value. In larger MATs, cluster groups for heads and staff make sense as was documented in *Locality Matters* in 2023, one of the methods of collaboration, but there is no need to mirror that arrangement for non-executives. A link trustee for each hub could possibly work.

If hubs were part of the governance structure, hub committees more often replaced academy level committees, and the examples sometimes quoted no longer exist apart from a hub advisory board (HAB) model reported by the Plymouth Marjon University in 2025. The 31 schools in the MAT studied are distributed between five HABs, and despite the schools being fairly local, they seem to have lost the all-important knowledge of place and the connection with the community. Parents were generally disconnected from the process, when the MAT had hoped to improve engagement. A better model would be for each secondary school to have its own academy committee, and the primaries that are truly close to each other, as some are, could share an LGB. However, five schools is very likely to be too much to cope with by one committee even if nearby; a five-school MAT would not decide to carry out all its business in the board of trustees.

Talk about cluster/hub level governance instead of a local tier has surfaced again in the last two years, driven by the difficulty of volunteer recruitment. One would not decide to stop teaching English anymore if recruiting English teachers was a struggle; likewise, let's not remove an essential layer of governance because governors are not easily found. Unfortunately there hasn't been any public clarification from the DfE condemning this as a poor reason for undermining good MAT governance. The loudest voices in the MAT sector very much cry not to be straight-jacketed, which perhaps inhibits the DfE from being clear as to what is good practice. The mindset of 'there can be so many models' has given some boards and leaders an excuse not to engage fully, and it has caused genuine confusion for others. Doing things well should be the standard, not simply doing things differently.

Setting the standard

Based on NGA's extensive research and engagement with the sector, *The Future is Local* (NGA, 2022) contained a set of expectations to make local governance meaningful and effective.

1. Trust board visibility and accountability to the local tier with local governors invited to hear of the work of the trustees as a minimum on an annual basis through the AGM.

2. Two-way communication between trust boards and local tiers, including regular meetings with the trust board chair, vice chair and local chairs.

3. Clear scheme of delegation with roles and responsibilities understood by all.

4. Investment in professional governance support: there must be professional clerking of every academy committee and a MAT lead governance professional to guide and connect the work of local committees and the trust board.

5. Clear separation of people between governance layers.

6. Meaningful role for local governance in support and challenge, with no removal of the local committee simply for being challenging. There is a formal process for removing governors including an appeals process.

7. Academy committees/LGBs appoint their own chair and vice chair and can add to their membership.

8. The trust maintains a clear distinction between accountability through governance and accountability through line management (by executive leaders); the local tier is formed by local volunteers and executives do not attempt to control the conversation.

9. Local input in headteacher performance management and headteacher recruitment, usually by the chair.

10. Whole trust governance development plan that encourages governors to learn from schools outside their trust.

11. The local tier does not have its own committees – an academy committee/LGB is itself a committee of the trust board. A fourth tier of governance is unduly complicated and increases workload.

12. Local tier contributes to strategy setting and school improvement and is aware of the school's budget, the plan for expenditure and can make representations; for example, to resource leadership posts.

These expectations were trialled at NGA's MAT network with 130 attendees, a mix of MAT trustees, governance professionals and CEOs providing quick-fire reactions. They were almost entirely endorsed; the one least supported (with 38%) was the expectation that the local tier does not have its own subcommittees. This fits with the general reticence to move from the traditional maintained structure of committees and didn't deter us from continuing to say it is effective practice.

The thinking was further tested over the following year and confirmed in NGA's next paper, *Local Governance Here and Now*, which explored practice on the ground. Roughly three quarters of local governors report being heard by the trustee board in surveys since 2020. This question gives a good indication of how seriously local governance is being taken. On the other hand, only one in five local governors are invited to the AGM; this is a gap and should become standard practice.

NLGs in 2023 and 2024 were still identifying some outdated governance structures, which posed a risk to core governance functions, introducing duplication and inefficiency. It was especially likely to happen when the MAT first formed but also when a new school was integrated into the trust. Those early days of complex, long or historic SoDs leading to lack of clarity and duplication across governance tiers have not been entirely eradicated.

The 5Ss of local governance

The level of delegation and influence to the local tier in the early days varied widely, but NGA's *Local Governance Here and Now*, bolstered by annual survey results, found that local committees were carrying out similar core functions. These covered:

1. Standards.
2. Safeguarding.
3. SEND (special educational needs and disabilities).
4. Stakeholders.

The trend in recent years has been to consolidate this vital monitoring role irrespective of MAT size and nature. However, scrutiny is not the only benefit of academy committees; they can also support the head as well as challenge, develop opportunities to consult, and advocate for the school and the trust.

Considering the five mindsets – impact; fiduciary; strategic; generative; values and culture – those four Ss mean that there is naturally less of the fiduciary mode required, leaving more space and energy for the others. This also fits with the broader effort needed in school governance discussed earlier to move from the domination of compliance. Although there was understandably much concern that the role of local tier would be dumbed down given it doesn't tend to involve much decision-making, the conversation and ideas all centre firmly around pupils and their needs, which is what motivates most volunteers and what brings the joy to school governance. This couples well with the need to develop relationships with the staff and school leaders, supporting them and embedding a healthy culture.

In 2024, the NGA survey confirmed the prevalence of the 4Ss with a large majority of local committees engaged in the governance of safeguarding (89%), SEND (84%), standards (78%) and stakeholder consultation (65%). The 4Ss were styled as a minimum role, certainly not an exhaustive list. Their introduction was well received and widely appreciated as easily understood. Worryingly the level of delegation fell in 2025: safeguarding (84%), SEND (80%), standards (66%) and stakeholder consultation (55%). One third of local governors not looking at standards is a concern; I can see no good reason for eliminating any of the 4Ss, but standards is at the heart of a school's purpose.

Work with some Church of England academies suggested a fifth S of 'service' could be added for them to recognise their role in monitoring the Christian distinctiveness of the school, including collective worship, and in SIAMS (the statutory inspection of Anglican and Methodist schools, which explores whether a school's Christian ethos lives up to its foundation as a church school). Indeed, SMSC (spiritual, moral, social and cultural) could be added for everyone. SMSC has been an integral part of education in England for many years, but possibly less spoken about since it's become slightly hidden in the Ofsted framework within the category of personal development. It's surely time for SMSC to take its rightful place again.

I also toyed with adding a sixth S for 'staffing', particularly where there is a relevant trust strategic priority, such as staff wellbeing, but this could be incorporated under stakeholders, of which staff certainly are an important group. Strategy also begins with S! If I were involved in determining an SoD, I would want to consider sustainability too; even though the premises and carbon issues will usually be overseen by someone in the central team, there are the community, culture, curriculum, CPD and careers aspects of environmental sustainability that could be considered or at least monitored at school level.

Local governors will usually be involved in staffing panels, but it is arguable that as the employer, trustees should undertake staffing panels. Local governors are likely to be asked to make up panels for school complaints and exclusions. That can be soul-sapping and very time-consuming work. There really won't continue to be an appealing role if these tasks take a higher proportion of the time donated by volunteers.

In 2021, in *MATs Moving Forward*, we wrote that far more attention needed to be given to the role of the local tier of MAT governance, and how those volunteering locally can be used best to influence trust decisions and make a difference to the pupils in the school they govern. This isn't yet universal, but there is now a blueprint that just needs some concentrated effort. Adopting NGA's expectations with the 5Ss worked into the SoD is a win-win with the knowledge of the school and its community informing the board of trustees, and more than enough for local governors to get their teeth into. Governing at local level then remains a hugely worthwhile occupation. Support and challenge on these issues is fundamental to pupils receiving a good education.

The DfE regulatory review (2023a) sadly managed to water down the hard-won 2022 White Paper commitment to local governance with its conclusion: 'We recognise the importance of meaningful local and community engagement when building high-quality but we will not be prescriptive about how trusts achieve this. We are pleased to note the overwhelming majority of MATs now have local tiers; our focus is on ensuring all trusts engage as effectively as possible with their schools and local communities.' In other words, the expert group – most of them MAT chief executives – wanted no change even where practice was poor, and they did nothing else to spur on the improvement of engagement. This is typical of the resistance to change, almost on principle, seen on a number of occasions.

Mandate local governance

Getting local governance right is crucial to the long-term success of the MAT model: without it, effective and accountable governance is extremely difficult to achieve. Local knowledge has to be harnessed if MATs are going to live up to the rhetoric of serving their communities. At NGA we argued that the undefined remit of local governance was a blessing and a curse, on the one hand giving flexibility to harness the power of local voice in different ways, and on the other preventing the establishment of a basic set of requirements. NGA stepped successfully into that breach and there's not been disagreement about the expectations. The model is well and truly tried and tested, but the knowledge is not universal.

In some MATs there's a lack of time and energy devoted to developing local governance. The notion of flexibility in practice has not led to excellence through innovation; it has just provided a licence to push this issue down the priority list. Regulation or inspection shouldn't always be needed to ensure the right thing happens, but more than a nudge is needed to get the fundamentals for strong MAT governance everywhere. Even with the advice of governance professionals, the stakes are too high to leave to new executives and trustees, pressed for time, to work out for themselves.

Given local governance is now almost universal, mandating it would be barely noticed but would push the last few recalcitrant MATs to practise better governance and those who are mediocre to take it more seriously. It would also prevent unnecessary and sometimes interminable conversations about which model to use. Sharing a local committee between small schools close to one another fits the bill and doesn't need permission from on high. The mandate could possibly be introduced on a 'comply or explain' basis, although I am not convinced this is necessary; the additional flexibility provided would be at risk of again muddling the message and the practice.

There could be exceptions for very small local trusts and temporarily, where struggling schools require additional support, the equivalent of interim executive boards (IEB) in maintained schools. Those IEB members should be paid for their time, so it would be easy to distinguish from an academy committee.

This would need consultation and arrangements to take note of existing articles; for example, with the provision for foundation governors in faith schools, but I'm floating this as a starting point. Local committees could have:

- Between seven and 10 governors, none of whom are leaders or trustees of the same MAT (although of course the headteacher would attend).
- A minimum of two elected parent governors (or for a federated committee, one for each school) and a maximum of four elected places.
- An elected member of staff who is not a member of the leadership team.
- At least four others with connections to the community, including employers.

The local committee would choose its chair and vice chair from the group, and if no one wanted to take on the chair, the school could recruit a chair externally. The chair invites executive leaders or trustees to observe or present when the committee thinks necessary. They need to be independently minded, while of course signing up to the MAT's value and ethos. Volunteer recruitment would be supported by the trust governance professional, but decisions to co-opt made by the committee itself (apart from foundation governors). In NGA's 2025 survey, 76% of local governors said they recruit their own members (as opposed to 66% of trustees saying local governors did their own recruitment, but they are unlikely to be the same MATs).

Financial governance

Audited accounts are often quoted as a good transparency feature of the trust sector, and while this is true, it is a low bar. Apart from very small ones, charities registered with the Charity Commission have had to submit accounts for the past 30 years. It is also worrying to note that auditors do not seem to have been a force for uncovering dodgy practice in MATs; before ESFA regulation was tightened, many of the scandals came to light through whistle-blowing from staff.

Improvements in financial oversight may provide lessons on how to improve other aspects of MAT governance and regulation, although finances lend themselves much more to compliance and straightforward regulation than other aspects of education. Even key spokespeople in the MAT sector had to admit that better oversight from the ESFA (as it was initially) was necessary to bring rigour to financial management and governance. The *Academy Trust Handbook* (ATH) forms part of a trust's funding agreement with the Education Secretary, so the inclusion of a 'must' in it means compliance is contractually binding. There is no need to set regulations before Parliament.

Even small additions made to the ATH brought warnings from sector leaders that trust autonomy could be undermined, sometimes demanding explanation of DfE intent in terms of tightening the grip of Whitehall. NGA and many others were involved in much consultation about the content of each edition of the handbook, which has become absolutely key. While that sort of exercise will never please everyone, the officials tried very hard to get it right. There was a simplification exercise in 2022 to consider the ATH from first principles. All in all, we've ended up with a perfectly reasonable mechanism for ensuring there is no return to the extent of poor financial management and misuse of public funds of the early days.

Often the 'musts' added to the ATH had been good practice recommendations previously, but that hadn't been enough to transform practice. That should be a sobering realisation for those who argue most for freedoms and autonomy. Sometimes those freedoms simply give permission to ignore good practice. For example, a trust having a skilled governance professional was recommended until it was upgraded to being a must in 2020, as happened the following year for a risk register being regularly reviewed.

In 2023, a new requirement was added for boards to approach the DfE region when their most senior executive leader plans to leave the trust, whatever the reason for their departure, to discuss their structure and options, including plans for recruitment. Some branded this as 'micromanagement', but transparent succession and transition does need underlining in the sector. Remember also this person is the accounting officer, accountable to Parliament for the use of public funds and the delivery of a crucial public service. The expectation did not change the autonomy of the board of trustees. The cry of 'hands off our autonomy' perhaps needs to be used more sparingly.

Centralisation

The Kreston UK *Academies Benchmarking Report 2025* considered 79% of MATs to be fully centralised for finance, estates, HR, IT and procurement, although many still have data processors in each school. They also reported that the trend towards pooling income and/or reserves continues, with all sizes of MATs showing an increase; 37% of responders are pooling and a further 28% are considering it. This is significantly higher than CST's 2024 survey, which reported about 18% of MATs under 20 schools pool their general annual grant (GAG), while for trusts 20 schools and over, the rate of pooling is double that (37%), and a further 9% are considering it.

Pooling of resources over the years has proved controversial in some trusts, with *Schools Week* (Dyson, 2025) suggesting that it contributed to one MAT's decision to dissolve after 20% was held back from one school. Pooling funding has been the part of 'one organisation' that local governors are more resistant to. According to NGA annual surveys, the proportion of local governors agreeing that their school's resources, including reserves, should be shared with other schools in the MAT has been gradually rising over time to 62% in 2024, but then fell back again significantly in 2025 to under half (47%). Larger MATs face a slightly greater challenge in this area with 42% of local governors in MATs of 20+ schools even in 2024 disagreeing with resource sharing. The alternative tends to be called top-slicing, harking back to maintained days, charging each school for central services. The average top slice contribution identified by Kreston is in the range of 5.5% to 8.8% of GAG income in 2025, representing an increase from the 2023 reported range of 5.4% to 7.4%. There are also some outliers in charges, but knowledge of the services provided are needed to make comparisons.

Although rightly there have been calls for more transparency, there is little schools can do once they belong to a MAT: we are back to who has the power and who makes the decisions? Trusts centrally will decide how much to allocate to schools, and once the budget is set, it tends to be managed from the centre. For example, in the NGA survey, management of a school's budget was cited as a delegated responsibility by 53% of local tier respondents, in 2019 74% of MAT trustees said they expected local governors to monitor the use of the budget and by 2025 this has reduced to 35%.

Financial sustainability is a challenge in the school sector. Medium-term financial planning is crucial for MATs, albeit tricky without future funding figures, and the considerable cost of central teams must be considered carefully alongside their benefits. These are difficult decisions for trust boards to take as capacity in a central team can be increased to facilitate future growth, which may not materialise.

Executive pay

Pay levels for trust executives sadly have not been held in check by boards of trustees, in some SATs as well as MATs. Criticism of excessive pay in trusts has been rumbling for a long time. The House of Commons Public

Accounts Committee (PAC) began expressing concerns about pay when scrutinising the annual academies report and accounts; for example, after seeing 102 instances of 'trustees' being paid salaries that were in excess of £150,000 in 2015–16. Those trustees were all chief executives, and PAC commented in their March 2018 report that 'some academy trusts appear to be using public money to pay excessive salaries. If the payment of such high salaries remains unchallenged, it is more likely that such high salaries become accepted as indicative of the market rate. This could then distort the employment market in the sector for senior staff.' I think this has indeed happened.

The PAC urged the DfE to take action where pay was found to be excessive, but the DfE has had to admit it has very little power to make changes, and its influence has been remarkably unproductive in effecting change in pay levels. It began writing letters to trusts requesting justification for the salary, but admitted it didn't accept the justification in about two thirds of cases. DfE published guidance on setting executive pay in 2019 a year after NGA did, although several editions of both later, it is still useful to have both as their tone is slightly different, with the DfE version majoring on compliance and scrutiny. NGA set the bar a little higher with more of an emphasis on values, legitimacy and pay ratios. Performance-related pay is pushed by others, even though it is not generally welcomed in the school sector, and it is often assumed salaries should rise as more schools join the MAT. However, once a CEO is managing a team of half a dozen executives, their job is not that different day-to-day, whether they have 30 schools or 80; they are never dealing at a school level.

In 2020, the ATH mandated the publication of staff earning over £100k in £10k bands (including off-payroll workers). This is an example of transparency, even where it combined with some considerable press coverage, led by *Schools Week* over many years, failing to drive better practice. The justifiable coverage means the public see these high salary levels reminiscent of the private sector; it helps strengthen the perception that academies have been privatised, that their bosses are in it for themselves and that the academy model is expensive. One study that attempted to compare the local authority structure with the MAT one did conclude the latter was more expensive given the number of highly paid executives for smaller numbers of schools (Bubb et al., 2019).

There needs to be a change of tactic given the ongoing concerns about executive renumeration in some MATs and the resulting damage to public trust. The DfE needs to develop a recommended pay scale for chief executives and other executive posts in trusts, and if new posts are not found to be appointed within the range, then it may need to become statutory. Since 2023, trusts need to inform the DfE when their accounting officer is departing, and this gives them the opportunity to have the conversation about pay.

Although not usually able to join the Teachers' Pension Scheme (TPS), executives command very healthy pension contributions and access to the Local Government Pension Scheme. In the early days, confusion abounded as to who was entitled to the TPS, which is one of the best defined benefits schemes. I attended a roundtable meeting of MAT chief executives with Lord Nash and was astounded when they chose to use about a third of their hour with the minister to lobby for access to TPS. In the end, the minister said words to the effect of: 'You can go back to teaching if you want TPS.'

Academy trust governance code

A specific governance code for the sector was published in 2023 by a group of sector bodies including NGA, Catholic Education Service and Church of England Education Office, but led by CST and the Chartered Governance Institute UK. Its starting point was the charity code, but it ended up considerably longer. Despite its length it includes very little on local governance. The code may be useful for some trusts who want a more specific version or as a reference for governance professionals, but it is unknown how much it has been picked up and used to improve board governance. My experience of trying to affect practice taught me that self-review tools need to be easy to engage with; boards do not have lots of time to deal with yet more long documents.

The role of the DfE

We saw the Conservative government's attempt in 2016 to force full academisation fail. Although the government's aspiration remained the same, a schools White Paper in March 2022 tried a more subtle route with choice rather than compulsion. Nadhim Zahawi was Education Secretary when both the White Paper was published and a Schools Bill introduced in the House of Lords in May. Political upheaval across the UK government resulted in five education secretaries that year creating uncertainty around the proposed reforms and much else.

In summer 2022 the DfE reconfigured their regions group to bring together the functions working with trusts with the ESFA. It was broadly welcomed as many had experienced times when communication between the ESFA and DfE regions was poor. Over the years, trusts' experiences of interacting with DfE regional directors (formerly RSCs) and their offices were decidedly mixed, with some reporting very positive experiences alongside other negative views. At that time regional directors were described on the DfE website as 'responsible for delivering departmental policy, including commissioning academy growth and support and intervening in underperforming schools'.

The 2022 bill attempted to bring in a single regulatory approach to replace the existing messy mixture of regulation, contracts and related guidance such as the ATH. It was essentially a tidying-up exercise, part of the mission to persuade doubters that the MAT system was transparent, effective and competently overseen, but it did give the department more powers to intervene where necessary. The bill met a barrage of opposition and was abandoned, along with much of the White Paper, before it could make its way to the house of commons. The trust sector had successfully flexed its muscles, making it clear they wouldn't tolerate a different method of regulation.

The voices of MAT trustees, as opposed to chief executives, were almost entirely unheard, so NGA carried out a specific survey in August and September to inform the debate around the reforms. It underlined that trusts are diverse and those who shout the loudest are not always representative. Trustees were open to increased scrutiny and oversight of trusts; a majority (54%) agreed with the statement that 'the standards used to hold trusts to account should be more stringent, and trusts should be more transparent in demonstrating how they meet these standards' with just 21% disagreeing.

A DfE (2023a) review of regulation and commissioning aimed for a simple, proportionate regulatory strategy focused on the right risks and the right level of accountability, and better and more transparent commissioning decisions informed by a clearer articulation of what it means to be a high-quality trust. The review concluded 'that the current regulatory approach broadly provides the right safeguards, checks and balances against the most significant harms in the school system: abuse of children, financial fraud, and large-scale trust failure'. It said little about the quality of education being provided.

The report emphasised the need to be risk-based when delivering regulatory oversight, but it is not clear what changes would enable the DfE to do this well. At the time, the regions group aimed to engage on trust growth plans, performance and risk indicators, financial health and governance concerns. In terms of understanding the provision of good education, the DfE regions group has the same lagging national data as trustees but without up-to-date trust-specific intelligence. After the Covid-19 pandemic, the national attainment data was missing at the same time that they were without new inspection results, but how this affected DfE decisions hasn't been explored. I will come back to the DfE's ability to identify governance concerns in chapter 15.

The review did at least on paper deliver a more transparent approach to commissioning. NGA had long raised concerns with the DfE that some commissioning decisions lacked clarity, transparency and consistency, with some trustees describing them as 'arbitrary' or 'biased'. There had been a recurring theme reported to us over the years of RSCs having favourites, particularly in medium or larger trusts.

In order to build confidence in the department's decision-making, the DfE updated its guidance – *Commissioning High-Quality Trusts* – alongside quality descriptions under the five pillars of: high-quality and inclusive education; school improvement; workforce; finance and operations; and governance and leadership. The descriptions cover more than 30 high-level themes. They give an idea of what the DfE is looking at and are cited in the regional advisory board minutes. *TES* has been tracking the advisory board decisions, which tell us trusts are sometimes declined due to concerns about overstretch and insufficient capacity in school improvement, weak governance or lack of local presence. Smaller or newer trusts are often encouraged to partner or merge rather than expand independently. At the time of writing it is unclear whether the advisory groups are going to continue.

The Conservative government confirmed several times in their last couple of years that they wanted 'to reach a trust landscape with coherent geographical clusters, that preserves local choice for parents and benefits from the capacity of multi-academy trusts able to take on and turn around underperforming schools'. They expected trusts to 'grow in a way that supports strong geographical clusters, enabling school improvement, operational efficiency and local collaboration' (DfE, 2023a). The DfE says that its regions group is committed to considering strategic needs of the area as well as school-level characteristics. However, for many years they had been trying to persuade specific MATs to expand outside their region, and it may not have completely ceased, especially as many MATs are left without geographical sense.

Even as late as 2023, I was saying to the minister with responsibility, Baroness Barran, that more should be said by the DfE about how a MAT governs well, especially after their support for local governance had not been followed up since the White Paper, but the minister said, 'Ah but we can leave that to you.' I tried to convince a series of ministers the sector took more notice of them than NGA, but the 'self-improving' system was very much the dominant belief. I am unconvinced that external reviews of governance (ERGs) would have been taken up as much if the ESFA hadn't included them as good practice in the AFH.

Transparency was improved a little in the wake of the White Paper with more information placed into MAT performance tables, though they are not easy to use. This discussion should be continued alongside the discussions on the school report cards. The DfE also made more effort to share practice both at regional level and, for example, with national induction sessions for new chairs and chief executives. A regional strategy published annually might prove useful.

The 2022 creation of the regions group changed the nature of the role. Regional oversight by RSCs had been more narrowly focused on academies; approving conversions and free schools, monitoring trust performance and re-brokering individual academies. The new remit related to the whole-school system, including maintained schools and improving co-ordination with local authorities, covering safeguarding, SEND sufficiency and place planning. Regional directors are no longer simply academy regulators but have more of a role in ensuring system coherence. This stewardship of the region has been built on by the Labour government.

Another schools bill was before the House of Parliament at the time of writing with many – but not all – trust executives arrayed against the changes to trust regulation and oversight. It will be interesting to see whose power triumphs this time.

Growth

The 2022 White Paper's suggestion that trusts should grow to 10 schools (or 7500 pupils) without a doubt spurred further discussions with even some trustees who disagreed with the last government's vision reporting their board was seriously considering growth. The evidence paper published alongside it was not strong enough to convince everyone that joining a MAT was the best way forward for their school and pupils. On the other hand, additional funding pressures are leading some schools who hadn't joined a MAT to revisit that decision in the hope of becoming more financially sustainable. However, some – particularly SATs – reported that the financial savings were not presented to them convincingly by MATs.

MATs Moving Forward in 2021 reported that the smallest trusts (under six schools) were least likely to have grown: 63% of them had not, compared with 40% of 6–10 schools; 23% of 11–20 schools; and 20% of the 21–30 schools. Only 16% of those over 30 schools had not grown in the previous year.

NGA's 2022 survey of MAT trustees found they were not all convinced by the proposition that MATs should contain at least 7500 pupils or 10 schools. Trustees recognised the value of economies of scale, but also that many MATs served a particular area, which they might not want to expand beyond fulfilling a requirement for an arbitrary minimum size. Once again, I reiterated to the regions group the request from smaller trusts to be considered as a destination MAT, rather than the DfE going first to the easier option of the better-known, bigger MATs. There should be an opportunity to grow for small, strong trusts that want to, and I was assured there was.

In the last couple of years the average size of a MAT has grown further from about six schools to eight, but with an ever-growing range and again with the larger trusts likely to grow more. The percentage of 2024 survey respondents aiming to grow their MAT was 65%, a rise of 11 percentage points since 2019. Unsurprisingly, trustees in the smallest MATs were most keen to grow, with 43% of trustees of a MAT of two to five schools saying their trust was too small; yet again the survey also showed trusts already bigger than 10 schools were more likely to actually increase in size.

Both NGA's surveys and Kreston's annual reports confirm that more MATs seek to grow than actually achieve it. For example, 61% of Kreston's 2025 respondents expected their MAT to grow in 2024/25, and 83% in 2025/26, whereas in 2023/24 just over a quarter (26%) actually grew.

The momentum towards growth is likely to continue but possibly not at the same rate as before the 2024 general election. The new government has removed conversion grants and the Trust Capacity Fund, which is likely to slow down growth. It might also result in some challenging schools which MATs do not want to take on, especially if they have already had a number of poor Ofsted ratings and have been re-brokered between MATs previously. Those schools already existed, sometimes dubbed SNOWs – schools no one wants – or 'untouchable'. The new government has stipulated there will be investment in school improvement through the

RISE teams, so this may be more successful than the DfE regional group having only one structural solution at hand.

The 2022 White Paper had included a proposal that involved local authorities setting up MATs to attract more maintained schools. The DfE was giving the impression that local authorities would have a role in running the MATs. There was quite a lot of interest from local authorities before the DfE belatedly cancelled the pilot. Existing MATs didn't generally like the competition and many argued a conflict of interest. However, NGA objected because it was being sold on a misunderstanding of the MAT model: local authorities were only going to be allowed to nominate some founding members, not trustees. Furthermore, like every other MAT, once the trustees were in place they couldn't take into account another authority's views or position anyway. The whole enterprise was built either on economy with the truth or, as we have seen at other stages of the academy project, the regulator actually misunderstanding it.

Trust mergers

The number of MATs has fallen slightly in recent years as some merge. The number of mergers rose each year as conversation rates fell, leaving MATs needing to seek alternative plans if they were to grow. CST's 2024 survey found over a third of trusts exploring mergers. This consolidation has been most common in the more heavily academised regions as there are more options there.

Financial sustainability considerations also fuel these discussions. At first, mergers often involved SATs joining a MAT, but in the last couple of years they have increasingly been between MATs. Many exploratory conversations between boards of trustees do not lead to a merger as trust and relationships need to be established along with agreement on ethos and values. One of the biggest motivations for consideration of a merger is the departure of a CEO making it easier to rethink the most senior team and not to have two chief executives compete for the role.

A maximum size?

Large trusts represent a major change in school structure that has not yet received public acceptance. Some parents, including notably Sarah Vine (a journalist and Michael Gove's ex-wife), have objected to their children's schools being handed to a faceless organisation based somewhere else in the country.

Research would be useful as the size of trust has not been demonstrated to be a critical factor in ensuring the best education. The National Foundation for Educational Research (NFER) criticised the government's claim that large MATs can manage their finances more effectively than other types of structure, saying it was 'difficult to evidence'.

Scale providing efficiencies must be balanced against responsiveness and meaningful civic engagement, which require local understanding and connections. There is a risk that the model starts to creak under the strain of achieving both: a trust board simply can't process information from that many schools and the executives also risk adding less value to decision-making when they don't know the schools, the people who work there or the communities they serve. Apart from the headteacher, who has their fingers on the pulse of each and every school, and how are those vital signs relayed to trustees?

Moreover, if a MAT of that size begins to decline, the impact could be enormous. You can't compare the size of MATs with, say, hospital trusts: hospitals have a very different relationship to communities, much less significant, but despite that do not tend to straddle the country. You also can't compare MATs with local authorities as they have a very different set of roles.

Large trusts are a minority of the sector with 15% of academies in MATs with more than 30 schools, but increasing their size has been the direction of travel; for example, since the Covid-19 pandemic, the largest has grown by about 20 schools to 91 currently. This has happened not by design it appears, but in preference to strategically growing small MATs to a sustainable size.

The government should consider its vision for the MAT sector: would it be happy if more and more MATs merged to create more large trusts as is currently happening? NGA tried for some years to stimulate this discussion, but those leading large trusts have nothing to gain by shining light into this corner.

The government could put a cap on the size of a trust, taking into account the number of pupils as well as the number of schools, at least while some analysis was carried out. Large MATs wanting to help turn around schools would still be able to do so without them joining the trust, and at the same time the DfE could support those MATs below 10 schools to expand successfully.

Removing schools from trusts

Although an academy cannot seek to leave a MAT, they can be taken out of one MAT when Ofsted has judged they are underperforming and given to another identified by regional group. This is known as re-brokering and was the main route the DfE under the last government had within its gift for improving schools. Two-hundred and eighty, representing about 3% of academies in MATs, were moved to a different MAT in 2023/24, similar to 275 in 2022/23. However, only 11% of those re-brokered, up from 7% in 2022/23, attracted grant funding to deal with the financial challenges of taking them on. The total grant funding was £2.87 million, up from £1.36 million in 2022/23, which suggests more MATs are struggling financially.

It is time now to consider introducing into the system a carefully designed route for a school to leave a MAT in specific situations. This proposal works most easily in a system where local governance is mandatory. Legislation could be introduced to permit the LGB to vote to leave the MAT if they believed it was in the best interests of pupils. The school would stipulate its requested destination. Sam Freedman, former special adviser to Gove, in his Institute for Government publication *The Gove Reforms a Decade On* argued that this 'vote would then be subject to authorisation by the regulator to prevent vexatious or frivolous attempts to leave'. I understand Freedman's caution, but there is also a danger that the regulator has a bias against change.

Power in the system has become centralised in the DfE, and therefore if we want this to be a move towards more bottom-up power, as both Freedman and I do, requests can't be refused at every turn. It may be that the local authority within which the school seeking an exit is situated would be a better arbiter. Kenneth Baker, former reforming Education Secretary, has railed against the power of the regional directors.

Freedman also qualified it with: 'It is important that this should only happen if there is a strong case young people would benefit from a move, rather than simply because an individual school did not agree with difficult personnel or finance decisions taken by the MAT.' If this was included, benefits would need to be interpreted broadly, and I would want to add cases where MATs have made promises before a school joined that have been broken. Past cases might be difficult to evidence, but NGA has been frequently told that the MAT said something different before they joined. There will of course be some issues where it is good for a trust to change its approach, but under the current system the school has no route to challenge.

This would allow more innovation in the system. Re-brokering doesn't have to be centred on failure as it has been. This measure could also allow a group of schools to leave as a cluster to form their own MAT. I introduced a MAT education director to Lord Nash to advocate for a group of schools to separate from a struggling, widely dispersed MAT. She was persuasive, focusing on the added value of her local knowledge and connections to the improvement of the cluster, as opposed to executive time wasted travelling long distances to an area where she didn't add that value. Nash referred it to the RSC, but no change came of it.

Umbrella trusts could be re-examined as potential suppliers of shared services, should a cluster of schools want to detach itself from a MAT but have the option of buying in the services, hence keeping the efficiencies of scale for procurement but not needing it to be linked to the ethos and culture of education and decision-making. This could potentially provide the benefits of size while reducing the consequences of a decline in leadership or governance.

Collaboration outside the MAT

Collaboration has been increasingly promoted. For example, David Carter as schools commissioner took every chance to encourage it between MATs and with the wider sector. After the 2022 White Paper's proposal to introduce a collaborative standard, the regulatory review watered this down to a mention in the trust quality descriptions: 'Works collaboratively with schools, trusts, local authorities, dioceses, parents and other civic partners to ensure the delivery of statutory functions and acts in the wider interests of the local community' (DfE, 2023c).

CST's 2025 survey reported 61% of trusts support other academies, 68% support maintained schools and 36% support other trusts. This represents considerable commitment. It could be formalised with a DfE expectation of MATs with capacity supporting underperforming schools outside the trust. CPD and specialist services developed by MATs can be shared with other schools and trusts.

An all-MAT sector?

As of June 2025, 62% of pupils attend academies: 83% of secondaries, 44% primaries and 49% special schools are academies. Just over half of state schools (51%) are academies, although the number in MATs is still just below the half-way mark, given that 4% of schools are SATs.

We have passed the year by which the Conservative government originally thought all schools would be academies, and without a doubt their ambition did convince some governing bodies who did not want to be left behind to convert. The 2022 schools White Paper included the proposal to create a 'stronger and fairer' system by making it fully, or almost fully, MAT-based by 2030.

It is highly unlikely that this current Labour government, or even another of a different complexion, will mandate the academisation of the remaining 49%. Some assume the drift into MATs will continue even though there has been a change of government to one disinterested in school structures, and at the time of writing a White Paper is awaited. The 2025 NGA survey shows that over half of maintained schools and SATs have considered joining a MAT in the past year. A quarter of respondents reported deciding not to go ahead, but 15% plan to join a MAT in the near future, slightly more maintained schools than SATs. Decisions to wait and see may be influenced by the ambiguous evidence of impact and the fact that conversion grants have disappeared. However, financial insecurity may well continue as a driver to join a MAT.

Many – probably most – commentators suggest it would be best to have a single system, but NGA's survey of MAT trustees in 2022 found only about half (51.5%) of respondents supported the aim of a fully academised system by 2030. Some argued that it was necessary to move past the 'fragmented' and 'inefficient' mixed economy in place; but others were sceptical as they didn't want schools joining them without commitment to the group. There was also an emphasis on the importance of listening to governing bodies who best understood their school's context and challenges.

Inspections of MATs

Ofsted introduced MAT summary evaluations (MATSEs) in 2018 to give 'an accurate and balanced understanding of the contribution that trusts make to the school system, to highlight areas of strength that may be disseminated more widely and to provide an insight into any weaknesses' (Ofsted, 2023b). They carried out fewer than 30 on a range of MATs, pausing for Covid-19 and again in 2023 due to lack of resources. A narrative report without a grade followed the exercise, which included visits to schools and was generally accepted by the sector. MATs subjected to them seemed to find the feedback useful.

The themes Ofsted gave MATs credit for are unsurprising, very much reinforcing what is expected of a MAT. Effective central services allow school leaders to concentrate on improving teaching and learning. Consistency of approach on safeguarding, polices and systems across the schools was praised, as is having a framework for curriculum, which then gives schools room to amend and make their own. MATs were commended by Ofsted for enabling schools to retain their individual characteristics and for being a MAT that schools are proud to belong to.

A trust-wide vision guiding decision-making is expected alongside a clear delegation structure. Ofsted identified local governance as a common area requiring improvement, including understanding of their role. The importance of strong self-evaluation, good understanding of strengths and weaknesses, and good use of data and evidence to monitor and focus support were consistent themes. As well as curriculum development, assessment practice and school improvement, MATSE letters covered the success – or otherwise – MATs were having with SEND provision, pupil attendance, behaviour and exclusions, and support for disadvantaged pupils.

Investment in staff development was a major strength of successful trusts, as was fostering collaboration between their schools, which surely should be taken as read. On the other hand, Ofsted reported that MATs needed to collaborate more with other trusts and schools.

Ofsted has repeatedly called for MAT inspections to be introduced for years. Its 2023 review of the role of MATs in school inspection found that 'trust leaders and inspectors highlighted that inspection at school level does not hold the trust sufficiently accountable or attribute enough credit to the trust's work'. The 2012 National College for School Leadership's fellowship commission had recommended MAT inspection, as has everybody who's considered it since.

It was therefore not a surprise when the 2024 Labour manifesto included MAT inspections. However, apart from the welcome abolition of overall grades, their first year of government was dominated by strife over reform of school inspections. Ofsted has limited resources, but it would have been far more productive if time had instead been given to the development of MAT inspections. In January 2024, the House of Commons education committee has expressed its frustrations at the delay and recommended that 'the Department must authorise Ofsted to develop a framework for the inspection of MATs as a matter of urgency and set out a plan for building the appropriate expertise and capacity in this area'. The 2025 spending review has given Ofsted an extra £20 million in 2026–27 to allow this to be implemented.

So many of us, including such people as former Labour schools minister Lord Knight, have warned that Ofsted's current inspectors do not have the relevant experience to be able to carry out trust inspections, and that inspections would need to be designed carefully. NGA's survey of MAT trustees in 2022 gave a clear majority (63.5%) in favour of the inspection and grading of trusts, although many trustees stated that if it was to work in practice this would require improvements to Ofsted.

MAT inspection must not be a summary of inspection of its individual academies or the outcomes of their pupils, but needs to demonstrate whether the added value that being part of the trust is meant to bring is being delivered. Governance and leadership will need to be central to MAT inspection, and I am aware of the additional but unavoidable focus that would mean for trustees. An entirely new inspectorate workforce will be needed to carry out the inspection of MATs, assuming their focus will be on inspecting the trust's performance regarding governance, leadership, and financial and resource management, as well as school improvement and staff development.

MAT inspections could use the DfE's trust quality descriptions, although an updated version, with collaboration and inclusion extended and local governance included. As I will expand on in chapter 14, the expectation of system leadership would be rarely met if judged in any way robustly, and it could be replaced by a focus on the MAT's interest in and leadership of place, reinforcing the importance of their schools' role within their local communities and the broader locality, often now labelled their civic contribution. Using the descriptors would provide consistency and eradicate the need for a large piece of work developing yet another new framework. A discussion would take place with inspectors about the impact of the MAT's work as well as its strengths and weaknesses.

Given the diversity of MAT structures and ethos, even if inspectors were recruited from within the trust executive workforce, they would need specialised training to be able to effectively evaluate trust-wide performance. An inspection team would need to include experience and expertise of each of the five (or six) pillars of the descriptions. Inspections of their schools could happen only if the MAT inspection raised questions.

I have concluded that inspection is the way to make some executives sit up and take notice. This is counter to everything I believe about how a healthy system should work, but it made a difference back in 2012 with single school governance, and it will make a difference with MATs too.

Alongside that, I hope there will be other changes to reset the culture of accountability.

Conclusion

Progress has been made, particularly in codifying good governance practice and building MAT capacity. How to govern a MAT is now known: harder to do in practice than on paper, but experimentation is no longer required. There is now much practice to learn from, and as I set out in part A, as with other sectors, it is the people, their understanding of the role and responsibility, their commitment, their behaviours in and outside meetings, and the strength of their relationships among the board and with senior executive leaders that make the difference. Good governance fundamentals are not tick-box exercises that can be confined to the archives; they need to be constantly reflected upon. I am happy to be held in future to my prediction that they will not go out of fashion and be replaced by something new and shiny.

Ultimately, the success of the MAT model will depend on its ability to balance collective direction, central expertise and common systems with responsiveness to local needs and contexts. Empowering local governance and harnessing local knowledge and community connections is key to achieving this balance. The system needs people in the community who care for and advocate on behalf of the local school and the interests of its pupils. The case for the local tier of governance has been made and there is almost universal support: so let's stop debating this and bake it in. We must not let the difficulty of volunteer recruitment – which has been with us forever – push us backwards to a less meaningful, less relevant model.

More than nine out of 10 MATs have returned to the tried-and-tested model of one committee per academy, and another 6% have some local committees that cover more than one school. This overwhelming preference for one model should not be seen as a failure of innovation but as the system having improved its understanding of good MAT governance and thus reaching the next state of its maturity. There are clear signals from the 2025 NGA survey that the practice of local governance may now be going backwards; without a doubt it is not progressing as it should be, given all the knowledge and guidance available. Stakeholder engagement is also not receiving the attention it should despite it now being one of the DfE's three functions of governance.

Some MATs have improved their governance through bitter experience, learning from their own missteps and those of others. Just as governance is a collective endeavour, so was compiling this understanding of what works. A body of knowledge has been carefully marshalled and painstakingly documented; it deserves to be acknowledged, shared and built on, not overlooked or even belittled. A belief that no one else among all the thousands practising or advising on governance has had the interesting thoughts you might be having now suggests arrogance, rather than any respect for what has gone before and been learned. We must keep that curiosity, fine tune, scour the governance universe for change, update and listen to 'new' ideas, even if those ideas are not new to everyone.

We are over the period of trial and error brought on by Gove's cavalier approach. Hard work, primarily by volunteers in large numbers, has ensured good MAT governance is perhaps not yet commonplace but certainly familiar. It has been known for influential, powerful people to make the case that trust governance was worse than we knew it to be, often in a throwaway fashion; very few of them went out of their way to really educate themselves. The improved state of MAT governance hasn't been officially acknowledged by the powers that be in public, but in private conversations with both officials and ministers it was made clear to us that there was no longer a fear of imminent catastrophes as had haunted earlier ministers. Sadly though, the response was then to push governance further down the list of priorities, rather than make a clear public statement.

The development of trust governance professionals has played an important role in establishing better practice and protocols at institutional level. However, without NLGs, there is no longer a recognisable cadre of MAT governance experts, and I am concerned that the DfE will not have sources to draw on for advice. They certainly don't have the in-house expertise to diagnose when governance is slipping, and therefore the equivalent of NLGs needs to be reinvented. Regulation of the fiduciary side of governance much improved over the life-time of ESFA, and in these straitened times – with resources limited both within regions group and schools – it is an open question whether the DfE remains able to oversee the existing number of trusts.

The change of government provides an excellent opportunity to reassess the evolution of MATs to date and how that might continue. MATs are far from being a uniform sector; they are diverse in many ways: size, ethos, geographic spread and how much control they retain at their centre. Although there had never been a political statement that a system dominated by large MATs is the end goal, that would appear to be the direction of travel, albeit at a very slow pace.

The current government should adopt a strong narrative about the importance of human-sized trusts with geographical sense that enables collaboration, support and connection, avoiding isolation and optimising regional networking. DfE regional directors need to adjust their decision-making accordingly to be more proactive and coherent in supporting the growth of smaller trusts. This would be well received by the majority of the sector and by parents (at least those that noticed!). This is the time to pause the growth of the very large trusts while the missing rounded discussion is had about their role and the risks they bring. The sector grew rapidly at times, without any sort of roadmap, lacking a strategic plan, verging on the chaotic, and now needs a vision of the end point.

The stakeholder input into the last government's regulatory review underlined that for many leaders, 'the strength of the academies system stems from pairing freedoms with clear incentives and support from government' (DfE, 2023a). These beliefs have never been stress tested, and furthermore we know that some MATs are run with much central control rather than extending freedoms to individual school leaders. The benefit could be more simply that the group of schools provides resilient collaborative structures that allow teachers to develop their prowess and provide more career opportunities for all staff. More research is needed to better understand the relationship between MAT size and structure with educational outcomes, sustainability and legitimacy. This is not the time for complacency; as we will see in the next chapter, funding is the biggest growing challenge faced by governing boards.

The voices of the chief executives are loud, with much power and influence in the sector held by the individuals leading the largest trusts. The recruitment of their boards needs to move to the public appointments system, out of reach of the charges of cronyism. Each time change is suggested to the current regulation system there is a revolt by trust executives. However, all NGA's work with trustees showed that those governing MATs are far more open to increased scrutiny than is often claimed. Many positively ask for a pay framework for executives. The government needs to get a grip of excessive pay as sadly self-regulation has not prevented the top end of these public salaries becoming out-of-keeping with public sector values and ethos.

The stakes are high. The decisions made by MAT boards have a profound impact on the educational experiences and life chances of millions of children across England. The importance of ethical, values-driven leadership and governance has never been clearer. Building cultures of transparency, integrity and inclusion – which are reflected in the decisions made – must be at the heart of MAT governance. Those governing MATs with good leaders do not always realise that this is not the case everywhere. This takes us back to a central purpose of governance to broaden the power base and ensure the voices of all can be heard. There is considerable room for improvement on engaging stakeholders.

By getting governance right, we have the opportunity to create a more equitable, high-performing system that truly serves every child, regardless of their background or circumstances. A model has developed, overcoming the initial lack of preparation or understanding by the coalition government. Evolution has been piecemeal and has not kept pace with change. As MATs are responsible for the education of more and more pupils, the time is right to mandate good governance practice and to review the architecture of the English school system.

Part D:
The bigger picture

13.
The challenges for boards

NGA's annual surveys, which take place in the first half of each summer term, have provided a tremendous record. Since 2018 with numbers varying from just over 3000 to 6864 in 2020 during the first Covid-19 lockdown, respondents have been asked about the challenges facing their schools.

The effect of the pandemic is very clear in Table 13.1. The 2020 responses were given during the first lockdown, whereas a year later shows a clear difference with pupil wellbeing featuring as the biggest challenge and the only time premises makes it into the ranking until 2025. The 2021 inclusion of the recruitment of high-quality leaders rather than other staff may be because boards, and especially chairs, had much more contact during the pandemic with school leaders than with other staff and were very aware of the strains on leaders.

Another crucially important duty of governing boards is ensuring that their school or trust is a safe environment for pupils. Safeguarding is sometimes talked about in terms of compliance, but it is much more than that, driven by the organisation's culture and ethos. Again the effect of pandemic on the wellbeing and safety of some pupils was recognised, with almost three quarters of governors and trustees reporting an increase in safeguarding concerns in 2021.

	2018	2019	2020	2021	2022	2023	2024	2025
1	Balancing the budget	Balancing the budget	Balancing the budget	Pupil wellbeing	Balancing the budget	Balancing the budget	Balancing the budget	Balancing the budget
2	Attracting and retaining staff	Staff wellbeing and workload	Staff wellbeing and workload	Use and maintenance of premises	Attainment of disadvantaged pupils	Attendance	SEND	SEND
3	Staff wellbeing and workload	SEND	Broad and balanced curriculum	Attracting high-quality leaders	Staff wellbeing and workload	SEND	Attendance	Staff wellbeing and workload
4	SEND	Attracting and retaining staff	Improving attainment	Balancing the budget	Improving attainment	Staff wellbeing and workload	Staff wellbeing and workload	Falling pupil numbers
5	Improving attainment	Pupil wellbeing	Pupil wellbeing	Behaviour and exclusion	SEND	Attracting high-quality staff	Attracting high-quality staff	Attendance
6	Attainment of disadvantaged pupils	Improving attainment	SEND	SEND	Post Covid-19 recovery	Energy costs	Falling pupil numbers	Managing and improving premises

Table 13.1 Top challenges for their schools reported by governors and trustees in NGA's annual surveys.

'Broad and balanced curriculum' only appeared in the top challenges in the academic year that the revised Ofsted framework with its emphasis on curriculum was introduced. From 2022 NGA has also asked about the school's or trust's strategic priorities: 'ensuring a broad and balanced curriculum' and 'attainment' took the top two spots for priorities until 2025 when SEND became the top priority. In 2023 pupil attendance entered the top priorities list at the number-three spot, knocking out pupil mental health and wellbeing. The other two spots for priorities are taken each year by 'making best use of resources' and 'staff wellbeing and workload'.

The 2025 NGA survey underlines the crisis in the SEND system, which has been waiting for reform since 2019 when then Education Secretary Gavin Williamson announced a review to consider rising costs and demand, inconsistencies in provision, parental dissatisfaction and tribunal rates. Almost two thirds of governing boards name SEND as one of their three top challenges, an almost three-fold rise from 22% in 2023 and over half (53%) making it a strategic priority in 2025. Governing boards reported growing difficulties in accessing funding (84%) and securing education, health and care plans (67%) for children who need them.

SEND is worthy of far more space that I have given it in this book: we are awaiting a White Paper, and I hope that in the months following my putting this to bed there will be progress made by the Labour government. Likewise I have not given special schools the attention they deserve here; the tension of capacity of both special and mainstream settings versus appropriate environments and excellent teaching will continue to be at the heart of debates about the best education for children and young people with SEND.

The number of survey respondents allows NGA to consider regional disparities, but the variation is not nearly as significant as I initially expected. The data can also be cut by structure (maintained; SAT; MAT), but that again shows very little variation in challenges and priorities. However, that is not the case for phase as seen in Table 13.2. In secondary schools 'attracting high-quality teaching staff' and 'behaviour and exclusions' feature in the top four challenges in both 2023 and 2024, whereas for primary schools only 'falling pupil numbers' enter the top rankings for the first time in 2024. It had already featured the previous year in London.

Primary					
2023		**2024**		**2025**	
Balancing the budget	57%	Balancing the budget	67%	Balancing the budget	73%
Support for pupils with SEND	29%	Support for pupils with SEND	41%	Support for pupils with SEND	68%
Attendance	27%	Attendance	29%	Falling pupil numbers	27%
Staff wellbeing and workload	24%	Falling pupil numbers	25%	Staff wellbeing and workload	24%
Secondary					
2023		**2024**		**2025**	
Balancing the budget	39%	Attendance	42%	Balancing the budget	59%
Attendance	35%	Balancing the budget	40%	Support for pupils with SEND	51%
Attracting high-quality teaching staff	30%	Attracting high-quality teaching staff	39%	Attendance	35%
Behaviour and exclusions	30%	Behaviour and exclusions	32%	Behaviour and exclusions	20%

Table 13.2 Governors and trustees' top four challenges for their schools in NGA's annual survey by phase from 2023 to 2025.

School funding

Not only do funding constraints consistently take the number-one spot for challenges for boards, but the proportion registering it as a top challenge has increased from 40% in 2020 to 68% in 2025, the highest in the survey's history and a full 23 percentage points above any other challenge. The last time we saw anything like this was in the lead-up to the introduction of the national funding formula (NFF) in 2018/19. In the few years before that we could track the tensions rising in the governance community as balancing budgets became increasingly difficult. The Institute of Fiscal Studies (IFS) calculated there to be an 8% reduction in real terms in the total spending on schools between 2009/10 and 2017/18.

Governors and trustees resented taking the decisions needed to balance the budget: redundancies, often starting with teaching assistants, increased class size, reduced pastoral support, reduced extracurricular activities, reduced spending on buildings and maintenance, reduced school opening, and reduced qualifications or subjects on offer. At that point secondary schools, especially sixth form provision, were generally more affected than primaries. For example, in 2018 over two thirds of governors and trustees reported that subjects on offer in the sixth form had been reduced. Schools subject to redundancies within the last year rose from 20% in 2012 to 60% in 2019.

In the few years before 2019, governing boards' concerns about inadequate provision for pupils with SEND had been growing as the number of pupils with needs grew. At the same time available resources were not keeping up and a range of services for vulnerable children were being cut or overwhelmed. In 2019 only 17% of respondents were confident that funding pressures could be managed without any adverse impact on the quality of education provided, and many identified SEND as a priority area for any additional funding from the government.

NGA hasn't been an organisation that shouts a lot. Only once to date in its 19-year history has NGA held a lobby of Parliament specifically for governors and trustees. That was in 2019 when there was a coordinated coalition from all directions – unions, headteachers, parents – to raise awareness among MPs of the shortfalls in school and college funding and their consequences. Boris Johnson did announce increased school funding shortly after he became prime minister that summer. This is an example of democratic accountability in action.

The driving force of the NGA campaign *Funding the Future* was the increasing number of governing boards saying they were unable to manage funding pressures without negatively impacting pupils' education. They got on with attempting to balance budgets with much work being done with senior leaders to explore the best use of resources, but reducing the experience of children and young people was not the reason they had volunteered.

The additional three-year settlement took the heat out of the situation for a time, but some costs, such as energy, began to spiral upwards, and primary schools began to lose pupils due to the lower birthrate. Although the reduction in pupil numbers could provide an opportunity for a per-pupil funding increase, it is much more likely the funding will be used for other areas of stress, particularly the overwhelming demand for SEND provision. In 2025 IFS predicted that given the continued rise in the number of pupils with special needs, 'the best schools could hope for is a real-terms freeze in mainstream school funding per pupil' (Sibieta, 2025). Overall, the DfE's total budget will increase to £109.2 billion by 2028, equivalent to an annual average real-terms increase over the next three years of 1.5%, lower in percentage terms than most other departments but the fourth largest increase in cash.

Financial sustainability

In 2025 nearly a third (30%) of NGA's survey respondents reported that their school or trust was unable to balance income and expenditure without drawing on reserves, while a further 11% required a licensed deficit from the local authority or a loan from DfE.

There are deep-seated concerns from governing boards that financial viability is becoming more precarious. For example, in NGA's 2025 survey only 16% of schools and trusts perceived themselves as financially sustainable in the medium to long term, a fall from 19% in 2024. This frightening level of fragility may not come to pass, but we do know for certain that in the last few years the number of schools and trusts needing to draw on reserves to balance the in-year budget has grown. Sixth forms are again particularly underfunded, and this can affect the breadth of the offer. Competition for pupils often results in less collaboration and innovation than would benefit young people.

In 2024 only 28% of MAT trustees reported that their trust was sustainable without major change; this compared with 23% of SAT trustees and only 15% of maintained governors. Maintained schools are heavily primaries, so likely to be facing falling rolls; but even taking that into account, the MAT structure is slightly less vulnerable. Yet even for many of them the future is uncertain on the current trajectory.

It has always been known that small standalone schools are expensive to run, and although the NFF provides some mitigation, it's not enough to ensure the continuation of all. This is a controversial area; closing village schools is deeply unpopular with the residents, but there is an issue of equity if those pupils are subsidised at a far greater rate than those in the next town. The DfE and Ofsted use fewer than 150 pupils to define a small school. There are about 4000 mainstream schools in England with fewer than 150 pupils, mostly rural; just over half of those have fewer than 100 pupils and a few hundred have fewer than 50. The average spend per pupil in a primary is £6700, whereas – due to fixed costs – a school with 100–149 pupils is likely to be in the range £7500–£8500 per pupil, a school between 50 and 100 pupils in the range £8500–£10,500 and those with under 50 up to and even over twice the average cost per pupil. There are many good community arguments for preserving schools under 100 pupils, but not for that level of educational added value. It would be good to investigate the possibility of top-up funding from community development pots, especially for the very smallest. Many small schools aren't as remote as might be imagined, and many have parents choosing to drive some distance for what is perceived to be a nurturing environment.

Financial efficiencies

NGA's survey from 2020 to 2025 asked what strategies are being used to achieve a balanced budget, and the top responses are staff restructures, reviewing contracts for services, greater collaboration and looking at opportunities to generate income.

The school resource management adviser (SRMA) programme was piloted in 2017/18. Over the next three years almost 1000 institutions had an SRMA review, and the total identified savings across all deployments had reached £303 million (ESFA, 2021). However, not all those benefits were realised in practice. As so much of a budget is spent on staff costs, it is unsurprising that more than half of the recommendations are about optimal deployment of staff. Some controversial recommendations have had media coverage but generally school leaders value the advice. A few case studies have been published over the years, but it is ridiculous that the DfE has not published a full 'lessons learned' report as NGA did from the NLG reviews.

We don't want capable volunteers to walk away because the cuts required to balance budgets are just too dispiriting. The most soul-destroying task I had to do as a school governor years ago was to chair a panel to confirm the redundancy of a teacher I admired; they were devastated at having to leave the school. I held it together during the panel but once home I wept. The teacher was snapped up by another school while we reduced the deficit a little. Governing can be emotionally challenging as well as intellectually.

School buildings

During the earlier funding crisis NGA began recording the reduction of spending on buildings and maintenance of premises. For example, over a third (35%) of respondents had already reduced it in 2018, the second most common response to financial constraints. It was predicted this lack of investment in buildings could lead to more costly work in the future.

In 2025 the National Audit Office (NAO) reported a maintenance backlog 'has increased steadily' in recent years to at least £49 billion across key public services of which £13.8 billion applied to schools. The NAO cited several reasons, including historic underinvestment, cost increases and inflationary pressures, and many buildings reaching the end of their intended operational life.

The Labour government has committed to increasing the school rebuilding programme, as part of its 10-year infrastructure strategy. IFS said the increase in school capital spending overall equated to a 7% real-terms increase, which reversed real-terms cuts since 2015.

Staff responsibilities

Even though the responsibility of an employer is not listed by DfE guidance as one of their key functions, boards rightly tend to act as though it is. Governors and trustees report that staff recruitment is more challenging in secondary than primary, and more challenging in London and the South-East, and usually least challenging in the North-West. As is well documented, national targets for attracting people into teaching have been missed for many years, some subjects more than others. Schools are then in competition with each other; the ability to successfully recruit a science teacher usually comes at the expense of another school. The pay of classroom assistants has been so comparatively low that recruitment difficulties have grown, a subject that doesn't get as much priority as those governing think it should.

Workforce survey shows in 2010 almost three quarters (74%) of new teachers stayed five years after qualifying, compared with 67% by 2023. NFER (McLean and Worth, 2025) tells us the reasons are too little pay, too much workload and too limited flexibility. There is also much evidence that the relationship with your manager is an important factor in decisions to stay or go. Another reason for boards to ensure knowledge of good people management and professional development is being fostered, and a people strategy developed.

Since 2014 just about a third of NGA survey respondents say they find it hard to attract a lead executive. In 2024 29% of respondents said their lead executive/headteacher had left in the past two years, almost half of them to retire. Even though attracting a lead executive is not high in the list of concerns, some governing boards have been known to 'over pay' because they fear that their headteacher or chief executive might be 'poached' or choose to move to a larger school or MAT. Catholic schools face an additional issue as their leaders must be practising Catholics.

The challenge of ensuring equality, diversity and inclusion (EDI) applies throughout the institution, but school and trust leaders are not as diverse as even the teaching population, let alone the school community. There is also the issue of gender pay gap so well tracked by National Association of Headteachers. NGA and ASCL (the Association of School and College

Leaders) have produced free e-learning resources that focus on the governing board's role in ensuring EDI.

Staff wellbeing and workload

Staff workload and wellbeing has through the years featured as a governing board concern and priority. Teacher wellbeing in England has been a subject of increasing interest, with the DfE under the Conservatives establishing three working groups on marking, planning and data management in 2016. That was also the year I contributed to a book called *Managing Teacher Workload*. In 2021 the DfE published an Education Staff Wellbeing Charter, which over 3000 schools signed up to. The Labour government has continued the work by publishing a conversation guide for workload and wellbeing.

I served alongside my job share Emma Balchin on the DfE's workload reduction taskforce, which was supposed to make final recommendations to government, Ofsted, and school and trust leaders by the end of March 2024. However, it was overtaken by the general election; without any funding attached, it became impossible to make meaningful headway. For example, many of us had wanted to provide more time for teacher PPA (planning, preparation and assessment) and professional development. Flexible working was also a topic much discussed.

Academic research has explored factors influencing teacher satisfaction and retention, various aspects of teacher mental health and the effectiveness of wellbeing initiatives. School-level initiatives embedded within supportive cultures prove more effective than tokenistic interventions that do not attempt to address the root causes of stress. There is some evidence that better teacher wellbeing is associated with better student wellbeing and improved quality of teacher–student relationships.

Staff development

Research by the Wellcome Trust and Education Datalab showed that teachers are much more likely to stay if their confidence and skills are boosted by high-quality continuous professional development (CPD). Labour leader Sir Keir Starmer in 2023 announced plans to work with schools to deliver 'teacher training entitlement, including backfilling roles so that teachers at every stage of their career can be released for training' (Martin, 2024). It was slightly overshadowed on the day by a protest by two young climate activists asking about the Green New Deal but has become part of government's opportunity mission. I will return to the importance of investing in professional development in the next chapter.

Disadvantage

As the NAO and many others have reported, the gap in children's attainment between the poorer and others had been narrowing before the Covid-19 pandemic, which then had a detrimental impact. The gap at age 5 widened in 2023/24 to 4.7 months, up from 4.6 months a year before and 4.2 months pre-pandemic. The attainment gap for those finishing primary school narrowed slightly from 10.3 months to 10.0 months in 2023/24 but remains larger than pre-pandemic lows. The gap continues to widen for key stage 4 and fewer are participating post-16 than at any point since 2019, leaving more than one in five disadvantaged young people out of education or training.

The Covid-19 pandemic also changed attitudes towards school attendance and for some that sense of belonging as well, resulting in less learning for some pupils, often the most disadvantaged.

Pupil premium introduced by the coalition government, although largely frozen by the Conservatives after the Liberal Democrats left government in 2015, played an important part in concentrating the minds of leaders and governing boards on strategies to reduce the gap. The story up to 2018 is told in NGA's report *Spotlight on Disadvantage*. In 2023 the Sutton Trust found that 41% of school leaders used pupil premium to fill gaps in their budgets, up from 33% in 2022.

The premium in 2024/25 stood at £1515 in primary; £1075 in secondary; £2630 for looked-after children; £350 for service children; and £570 in early years. The Labour government has begun to increase the early years rate and needs to continue to do that given its crucial period for improving vocabulary and closing the gap more generally.

The pupil premium was a topic where the DfE during coalition times did try to spread good practice in a number of ways, such as awards winners and Sir John Dunford as Pupil Premium Champion with a 10-point plan. The lessons were not always clear; at an NGA conference in Newcastle we had two award-winning headteachers, one of whom said their success was as a result of engaging the community, while the second had protected the children from their own community as much as a school could.

The DfE requires schools to publish a premium statement agreed by governors, which some leaders consider overly bureaucratic, while others think it is key to the decision-making process. In 2023, the DfE looked at a sample of 400 schools and found that 80% had published a 2022/23 statement and a further 11% had a 2021/22 statement that covered 2022/23

(Verian, 2025). The DfE does not assess the quality of statements, nor does it have a systematic way to monitor compliance and follow up with schools. However, a DfE-commissioned evaluation report in 2025 found that 'overall, schools were positive about the impact of premia funding on school and trust strategies. … Around nine in ten schools (89%) and trusts (90%) agreed that having the pupil premium and recovery premium meant disadvantaged pupils had access to a wider range of support than they would otherwise.' Almost all MATs were supporting their schools with developing the premium strategy, but most decision-making on how to spend premium was exercised at school level.

The Education Endowment Foundation (EEF) set up by the government in 2011 to improve the educational attainment of the poorest pupils in English schools provides evidence and guidance that is well used by leaders and governing boards. However, its scope is somewhat limited by what is measurable, how small effects can be and restrictions on the type of intervention covered. I unsuccessfully tried to persuade the EEF to broaden their areas of interest; my previous work at Child Poverty Action Group and Citizens Advice had given me connections with those who research interventions in other aspects of socioeconomic disadvantage.

Poverty at home has been recognised for many years in academic research as being the strongest statistical predictor of how well a child will achieve at school. Explorations of variations in school pupils' exam results at age 16 in England have shown consistently over time that only around one tenth of all variations can be accounted for by factors relating to schools (Mortimore, 1997). Background factors of poverty, race and class were shown to dominate all other factors in influencing attainment.

Schools still can and do make some difference. Teachers are the most important school-based factor and really good teachers matter the most for pupils from low-income families because they don't necessarily have other resources to fill in the holes. But our lack of success in narrowing the gap should make us consider again from first principles how to focus support and funding. Some advocate for all the pupil premium to be spent on improving teaching, whereas others argue for filling a few of the holes that poor families cannot.

The DfE doesn't have a definition of disadvantage, so NGA set about coming up with one, led by Fiona Fearon, head of policy and research. I have up until now been speaking about pupils on pupil premium, but Figure 13.1 provides a widened consideration, and NGA has material to support work with each of the five groups.

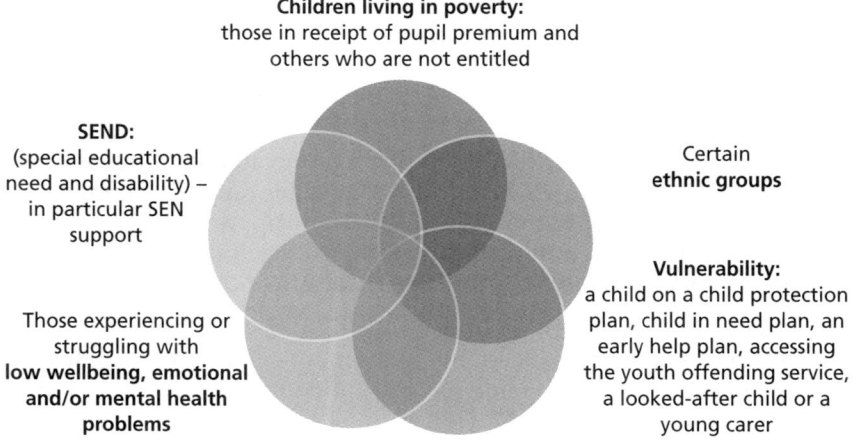

Figure 13.1 Five pupil groups facing educational disadvantage.

Families under stress

Schools are seeing families under pressure from the cost-of-living crisis, rising poverty, the risk of homelessness and rising mental illness, all of this at a time when many other public services and third sector support have withered. School staff have found themselves on the front line, often spending large amounts of time trying to support families and children. Many longstanding NGA members are telling us that they have never before seen this level of pressure on schools.

In 2018 almost half of schools in NGA's annual survey provided additional services for families in need, including washing school uniforms, meals outside of term time, food banks and emergency loans, 38% of schools were providing financial support with purchasing school uniforms. In 2025 more than half (51%) of respondents reported an increase in the additional support their schools provided to pupils and families in the past year. As with previous years, the most common forms of support were second-hand uniform provision (76%), wraparound care before and after school (64%), and breakfast provision (56%). Notably, in one year there was a five percentage point increase in the number of schools offering meals outside of term time.

Just over a quarter (26%) of respondents reported that their school had adapted to this shift and saw the additional services as part of the school's role. ASCL coined the phrase that schools have become the '4th emergency service'. It is important to distinguish between school buildings hosting other services and any sort of requirement for teachers to take on roles of other professionals; not only is there the extra workload, but also they are trained to teach children, not in other disciplines.

There is a further repercussion of the changes in wider society on the work in classroom. The 2025 Kindred[2] School Readiness Survey found one in three children starting in reception in 2024 were deemed not school ready by teachers compared with 90% of parents believing their child was ready. A quarter of children joining reception were not toilet trained, a third don't respond to simple instructions, 30% cannot communicate their needs and a quarter lack basic language skills. Half (49%) of teachers said the problem had worsened since 2023. Teachers report losing 2.4 hours per day supporting children who are not ready for school.

Just over two thirds of children achieve the good level of development as assessed against the EYFS (early years foundation stage) profile, but for girls on FSMs (free school meals) this is 60% and boys on FSMs it's 43%. The government has set a target of 75% school readiness by 2028.

Environmental sustainability

Climate change is another problem that faces us all, this time not just in Britain, but across the planet. The work of the Intergovernmental Panel on Climate Change and our own Climate Change Committee makes it absolutely clear that action needs to be a priority. The DfE updated its Sustainability and Climate Change Strategy in December 2023 with an expectation that a senior sustainability lead would be appointed and climate action plans in place for each school by 2025.

NGA launched its Greener Governance campaign at the end of 2021, in large part inspired by young people's voices and to coincide with COP26 in Glasgow, the first UN Climate Change Conference to formally spotlight education as a driver of climate action. COP26 hosted a joint summit of education and environment ministers and agreed global commitments to climate education.

We promoted a six Cs approach to environmental sustainability – culture, curriculum, campus, community, CPD and green careers. The most common action schools and trusts are taking include embedding environmental sustainability into the curriculum; providing outdoor learning; energy saving measures and solar panels; and reducing waste.

In May 2022 41% of schools/trusts reported in NGA's survey they had taken action on environmental sustainability; and in May 2023 this had increased to 64% of respondents. It has since flatlined, with 61% of respondents saying in 2025 their school or trust had taken practical action on environmental sustainability following board discussions. There is significant support available from a large range of experts from Climate Ambassadors to Let's Go Zero advisers to the National Education Nature Park run by the Natural History Museum. Lack of funding can be a barrier, but there is also much that can be done that reduces costs or attracts grants funding.

Conclusion

The challenges faced by governing boards will come as no surprise to anyone working in the English school sector as they very much chime with the wider literature and commentary. They provide a summary of the ebbs and flows of the state of the nation's schools currently coming to a crescendo with funding constraints and increasing SEND.

The subject that hasn't got the space it deserves in this chapter is the wellbeing of young people. Those governing have always spoken to me about it, as well as attainment, and parents are also clear that although they care about their children's achievement, their happiness is paramount. As Bridget Phillipson, the Education Secretary said in 2024: 'The most recent data shows 1 in 3 fifteen-year-olds don't feel they belong in school. ... Achieving and thriving – the two pillars of our plans for pupils – are not in opposition.'

Discussions around board tables are not widely known, and I hope this data has helped illustrate the scope of what those on the accountable body of the school or trust must understand. They are responsible for an institution's conduct, its budget and its offer, and they are saying in large numbers that they are unhappy with the decisions they are having to make because of funding constraints. These are not generally people who are out on the streets making a fuss; they are carefully combing through governing board papers and asking questions of school leaders behind closed doors, quietly forming part of the glue that keeps our state schools running.

They govern in the interests of pupils, current and future. Their vested interest is the mission of the school or trust, and their voices add richness to the discussion. Although participating in its stakeholder working groups, NGA has been left off the Improving Education Together (IET) group chaired by the Education Secretary. IET is described as a meeting of government, unions and organisations representing employers. NGA has always been part of the STRB (School Teachers Review Body) process for consulting on pay. Fewer than one in 10 of NGA's 2025 survey respondents are satisfied with the government's performance, the same as in 2023.

The sector is fragile, but so are others. At its best, governance at all levels should be generative, asking questions, poking about in the dusty corners and then posing ideas that may lead to solutions. Brilliant schools are an absolute necessity, but they are insufficient on their own to secure a young person's flourishing in the here and now and after they leave school. Those of us in the education sector, whether governors, leaders or policymakers, need to be brave enough to think differently in the interests of young people and their future, but also the future of our country, its economy, its cultural and civic life, and even the planet. I will come back to how we could work together to improve life in our communities.

14.
Improving schools

When there is so much literature about improving institutions and organisational change, it did seem strange when I entered the school sector to find none of that knowledge was in common parlance. Instead, school improvement was often spoken about as various schemes largely developed by those outside schools and sold to schools; a pick-and-mix approach. There still is a significant industry of that sort, some not-for-profit and some commercial. They vary from single consultants to global giants.

I couldn't understand why bespoke CPD wasn't at the heart of improving teaching and learning. This might have been in part because HR and even 'management' had a bad name within schools; it seemed to be associated with disciplinaries when things went wrong, rather than a force for good. Appraisal seemed to be an exercise largely of looking at targets, often numerical, rather than a primary focus being a dialogue about development. Even line management and regular one-to-ones with the individuals managed seemed an alien concept, something I rarely heard discussed among senior leaders.

In 2016 David Weston, then chief executive of the Teacher Development Trust, chaired a Teachers' Professional Development Expert Group for the DfE with developing standards for CPD, and there has since been some change with putting professional development at the centre of school improvement.

School by school

In chapter 4 I looked at the importance of the whole school or trust culture for improvement with leaders articulating the narrative. Boards need to ensure there is capacity for the professionals to work together with peer coaching and in triads to improve subject knowledge and classroom practice, and to broaden the pool and harness the intelligence of networks.

A single school is too small to be your entire professional development community, and that is why federations and MATs have an advantage.

I had been struggling with whether there was some magic I was missing on school improvement because I haven't been a school leader, so I was reassured to read a piece by Annette Montague (2025), chief education officer of Greenwood Academies Trust in *Schools Week* entitled 'School improvement is too human to be codified', emphasising the need to bespoke the work to the school and people in that school, and she warns against taking eyes off that focus while obsessing about the need to scale up improvement.

I am also very aware that I'm not considering the holistic discipline of organisational improvement including its non-teaching functions. That is very much the business of the Institute of School Business Leaders who have in recent years been investigating the relevance of 'operational excellence' to the back-office functions of schools and trusts. The DfE's SRMAs (school resource management advisers) can also be useful when considering improvement on the financial management side.

Professional development

CPD will vary from person to person, but the philosophy is now less about attending conferences and courses and more about school-based, peer-to-peer activities in which development is fused with routine practice. Professional development really does become a continuous, pervasive process that builds knowledge and confidence, rather than an occasional activity that is sharply distinguished in time and space from the classroom. The government funds an entitlement, the Early Career Framework, for all early career teachers to access professional development during their first two years. The average teacher in England spends only four days on CPD per year, compared to a global average of 10.5 days. Finding and affording teaching cover for CPD remains a barrier.

Having said CPD isn't about courses; there are many professional courses, some a part of the golden thread developed by the DfE and others developed independently by organisations such as the Teacher Development Trust, Forum Strategy and the Chartered College of Teaching. The NPQ (national professional qualification) in middle leadership in 2022 was replaced with three new NPQs: on leading teacher development; leading behaviour and culture; and leading teaching (covering responsibilities for leading teaching in a subject, year group or key stage). Significant DfE funding was provided to NPQs post-Covid, and even though much of that has now been removed, they are widely taken up. The interim evaluation report for NPQs in 2024 gives an overall positive picture, even with those interviewees who had not engaged with the reformed NPQs being 'generally passionate about CPD in their school and highlighted the non-NPQ training they were taking part in… Factors identified as being influential in leading to these impacts were high-quality facilitators and their ability to contextualise learning, the role of coaching and mentoring, as well as the opportunity to meet other leaders, share practice and create networks of support' (CFE Research, 2024).

Role of leadership

A central task of leadership is to help improve employee performance. In the case of schools, this has been summarised in leadership literature in a number of ways as 'school leadership improves teaching and learning, indirectly and most powerfully, by improving the status of significant key classroom and school conditions and by encouraging parent/child interactions in the home that further enhance student success at school' (Leithwood, Harris and Hopkins, 2020). Or alternatively as 'creating energy, building capacity, meeting and minimising crises, securing and enhancing the environment, seeking and charting improvement, and extending the vision of what is possible' (Brighouse and Waters, 2022).

In 2020 the NAHT published its *Improving Schools* report, in which the School Improvement Commission, of which I was pleased to be a part, concluded that: 'It is leaders, together with their governing boards, who create the conditions in which teachers can develop and thrive.' This is not contentious, but it is not universally seen.

Support inside or out

Unless it has got to the stage of an intervention, leaders will generally decide whether there is knowledge and capacity inside the school or trust. MATs are more likely to have capacity and expertise internally, but that is not universal. Evidence to the education select committee from the DfE showed extraordinarily high rates of sponsor approval: only 25 out of 704 applications to become a sponsor had been declined (3.6%) as of November 2014. The bar was not high for deciding there was the wherewithal to improve another school, so it is unsurprising that the success rate of MATs varies.

Ofsted's report on stuck schools in 2020 found that the schools had received much school improvement advice from too many different sources, and it rarely had the intended impact. School leaders commented on a poor match between the problems of the school and the advice on offer. Advice and support were perceived to have a greater impact when they were built into the school or MAT's strategy and delivered internally with oversight by people who knew the school.

Leaders perceived that the quality of the advice itself was often lacking with the external advisers, including the DfE schemes with designated NLEs and Specialist Leaders of Educations (SLEs). There is now an accreditation scheme for those providing school improvement support to schools. It's been built by the Association of Education Advisers (AoEA) influenced by research, rooted in practice, and tested across systems. As Les Walton, its founder, said at their 2025 annual summit: 'Real change doesn't wait for permission. It doesn't always come from the top. Often, it emerges from the middle – from the everyday influencers quietly shaping the future of our schools. ... It's built around a "continuous improvement circle" – one that supports professional learning and reflection, rather than compliance.' This is a much-needed development shaped by a very welcome philosophy.

Local authority support

In NGA's survey in 2011 three quarters (76%) of respondents thought that their school improvement partner had been an important resource and they wanted to retain their services, and the same number agreed that cuts to local authority services had had, or were likely to have, an adverse effect on their school. This was repeated in 2019 when 65% of all respondents, not only maintained schools, said they had been badly affected by the reduction in local authority services including school improvement support.

In many local authorities, but not all, there is little in the way of a school improvement service left. This should be reinvested in, but realistically this is unlikely to happen given the SEND expenditure. However, the amount of coordinating some local authorities are still involved with is possibly underestimated.

Peer review

Peer support networks have always been important despite having to balance collaboration with the competitive pressures of a quasi-market. More formal schemes of peer review tend to choose review partners from outside the local area. They also have to be credible with thorough challenge and an expectation of improvement, not taking the easy route of endorsing another's current practice.

Teaching school alliances

TSAs existed for a decade from 2011 and represented both a collaborative venture for the many schools that provided expertise to the alliance and a source of CPD and school improvement support for other schools. At their height TSAs covered the so-called 'Big Six': ITT, CPD, school-to-school support, SLEs, succession planning and research in locally responsive ways. For example, in 2015/16 TSAs provided support to 41% of schools rated as 'requires improvement' or 'inadequate', which added up to 1091 schools.

SLEs were phased out as the NPQs were reformed, and TSAs were replaced in 2020 by 87 larger teaching school hubs, which concentrate DfE resources on teacher training, NPQs and the ECF, moving away from the broader school improvement remit of TSAs.

RISE

The government's new regional improvement for standards and excellence (RISE) teams working with DfE regional directors began work in 2025, although the support will be fairly limited, targeted and matched to needs. There has been some concern that this confuses accountability if the regulator becomes involved in improvement; they are generally limited to compliance and intervention if the performance is not as expected. However, I think it remains clear that accountability remains with the accountable body – be that the board of trustees or the local authority – but this can be another source of help for those who are struggling.

MAT-led system

There is a fairly widespread view that MATs have the potential to facilitate significant improvement in the school system. However, understandably trusts are generally focused on what they can do to improve the education provided by their own schools, rather than the experiences of young people outside their schools. This is incentivised by the competition for pupils. As we saw in chapter 12, although collaboration is much stronger between schools within a MAT given its legal status as a single organisation, there are examples of collaboration with others outside their trust. We don't want to have replaced insular, isolated, individual schools with insular, isolated, individual trusts.

If the expertise built up within MATs is to be extensively harnessed for the good of all pupils in all schools, this requires a change in mindset for many MATs. I am unconvinced that it would be achieved without expectations from the DfE such as:

- Schools, including those within MATs, are active participants of area-based partnerships carrying out school improvement activities and liaison with other local public services.

- MATs with capacity support underperforming schools outside the trust (some already do).

- CPD and specialist services developed by MATs could similarly be shared with other schools and trusts.

MATs are different from each other as well as from single schools; what works in one might need to be applied differently in other contexts.

Collaboration

We have a problem with language: 'network', 'cluster', 'partnership' and 'collaboration' are used interchangeably. I am going to largely stick with 'network' and 'partnership' to suggest a bit of size as opposed to a couple of schools or trusts working together on peer review or school improvement support. A 'network' suggests bottom-up whereas a partnership is more likely to be mandated or encouraged top-down. Sometimes these coincide where voluntary collaborations that schools have initiated have then utilised government-backed initiatives to bolster existing partnership activity. Both however should enjoy horizontal governance of their own, an important element that is currently in short supply. The sector has largely accepted that groups of schools with common formal governance structures of the vertical kind – MATs and federations – are single organisations, within which staff collaborate, although some research still conflates this with collaborations between separate institutions.

It seems self-evident that learning from other institutions helps improve practice; few dismiss the notion of professional dialogue leading to school improvement despite the paucity of evidence as to how collaboration between schools best promotes improves student outcomes or provides other benefits. International evidence shows that the world's best-performing educational systems sustain improvement by establishing collaborative practices around teaching and learning and developing leadership. They also include a mediating layer between the schools and the centre, which is a little more complicated here in England where there is not one clear layer but a menu of options, many of which charge fees to sustain their organisations, such as NGA, and in many cases also to make a profit. This is an added complication that some intelligence that might have been shared between partners now has a price attached to it.

The House of Commons education committee concluded in 2013 that 'given the high level of enthusiasm for school collaboration, it is striking that definitive evidence of its impact is lacking'. Despite this, the committee's report was strongly in favour of collaboration: 'School partnerships and cooperation have become an increasingly important part of a self-improving school-led system. We believe that such collaboration has great potential to continue driving improvement to the English education system. The diversity of structures and models already in place is a strength and proof of vitality. Schools should be able to adapt models of partnerships and cooperation that suit their needs within a legislative and policy framework that is as non-prescriptive as possible.'

They noted that collaboration has most impact 'where more effective schools have paired with less effective schools to help them to improve... and where the number of schools involved has been limited'. This refers to what I have called school improvement support rather than broader networks or partnerships. There have been many different forms of top-down funded partnerships over the years, some of which are Investments in Education Action Zones, Beacon Schools, Excellence in Cities, Leadership Incentive Grants, Network Learning Communities, City Challenges, Teaching Schools and Research Schools.

The current school system does not always promote or enable networking, yet many networks exist. NGA's 2025 *Creating Connections* report shows the variety and that informal networks dominate but with local authorities still playing an enabling role in many. They exchange knowledge, experience and best practice across teaching, leadership and operations, joint professional development, and shared resources such as facilities, staff and equipment. This reduced duplication, increased access to specialist facilities and equipment, and was considered more cost-effective than other options. This is encouraging and suggestive of an appetite for schools to work together despite the competitive conditions in which they operate.

A further advantage of local networks is that they do not need to wait for a diagnosis provided by inspection. They can make use of practice-led diagnosis mediated by feedback loops generated by user input, data and peer contribution.

Networks that work

Years ago I was working with HM Treasury who were trying to find out what made partnerships work in some places and not others. They discovered three critical things: a couple of very committed leaders, trust and clarity of purpose. I was surprised capacity wasn't a fourth, but the argument was these committed leaders created the capacity, the focus and the enthusiasm.

A number of educational studies analysed by Armstrong, Brown and Chapman in 2021 also identified leadership, in terms of establishing clear goals, coordination and the sharing of responsibility, as central to collaborative practice between schools. Relational factors, including high levels of trust and clear communication, and contextual features such as history, geography and any pre-existing culture of collaboration, also appear frequently, ensuring deep and mature collaboration. Networks are underpinned by trust and shared knowledge but are susceptible to complacency or exclusivity when relationships become comfortable.

The most frequent barriers to the initiation, effectiveness and sustainability of interschool collaboration cited in the literature are: threats to school autonomy; perceived power imbalances between schools; the additional associated workload; difficulties in establishing shared objectives and common goals; the lack of funding; and the existence of a quasi-market. Leaders have to be committed to the work, and this may be limited by changes of staff.

NGA's *Creating Connections* report notes that perceived divisions between school types can create barriers to networking with a 'them and us' mindset, particularly inhibiting collaboration between academies and maintained schools. Respondents also identified staff capacity and funding constraints as key obstacles, resulting in inconsistent engagement. Differences in size, setting, ethos and priorities may make aligning goals difficult. It was suggested meaningful collaboration can be difficult to start or maintain without some facilitation, and it could be useful if the DfE endorsed collaboration beyond the MAT model.

It is sometimes said that governors and trustees are not supportive of partnership work as they want the concentration to be on their own school or trust and are not convinced there will be benefits. However, research has found governors to be predominantly supportive of the concept of networking and interested in its governance, although they were concerned about the implications for their workload. There is also valuable networking of governors themselves, often in the form of local governance associations. However, without local authority support (and therefore being reliant on volunteer coordination), local governance associations have proved difficult to sustain with the number of them falling dramatically since 2010. A few have survived by increasing membership fees to cover a training and support offer.

The local area

Dame Christine Gilbert (2017) has argued that area partnerships provide the opportunity to 'shape a different model of professional accountability that motivates and inspires teachers, as well as incentivising system-wide collaboration'. She leads the Association of Education Partnerships (AEPA) alongside Baroness Estelle Morris. These partnerships exist in a minority of local authority areas, about 30, and they have grown up in different ways depending on the local context. All have significant involvement of experienced school leaders.

In terms of governance, the partnerships tend to have some form of executive officer, overseen by a board made up of school leaders, local authority officers and other (often high-profile) educational stakeholders from the region, sometimes with an independent chair. The partnerships are typically funded through a combination of income generated from membership and subscription fees, and specific commissions sourced either from the government or the local authority. There hasn't been much discussion of the potential conflicts of interest caused by traded services.

There is not unanimous agreement about the scope of area partnerships, but without any upwards accountability to the DfE, they enable schools to nurture forms of lateral accountability where, as professional peers, they can support improvement in less formal ways. The area partnership is likely to have a range of services from CPD to improvement advisers to sell, and these need to be considered locally owned. There can also be a broader agenda of supporting collective efforts to increase community cohesion, mitigate the effects of poverty and improve support for vulnerable families and young people.

To build on the principles of what works, the development of area partnerships should be underpinned by a clear purpose and led locally by coordinating groups made up of school leaders and educational professionals working with other community stakeholders, drawing on local intelligence and setting their own agenda.

Trusts are expected to work collaboratively with other trusts, other schools, local authorities, dioceses, parents and other civic partners, and act in the wider interests of the local community; this is included within the trust quality descriptions and the *Academy Trust Handbook*. While many MATs are actively engaged with local authorities and other local services, it is not universally practised. It may be this therefore needs to be mandated. It was generally seen that during the Covid-19 pandemic work with local authorities both at DfE regional level and with many MATs improved, but those relationships and networks have not all survived. Feedback was often that local MATs would engage whereas larger MATs with just one or two schools in the area do not. Sometimes it is sufficient that the trust empowers their local headteachers to engage, but they need to be encouraging of the endeavour.

My experience of working with Christine Gilbert on the Knowsley Commission showed me that while the six secondary heads met together, there was no leadership from or interest in the place by the four different MATs involved, each at the time with just one school in the area.

In a couple of years' time almost half of England will undergo a significant local governance reorganisation to create unitary authorities. Often people's idea of a locality is considerably smaller than current local authority areas; they will not necessarily coincide with what public service providers need to plan strategically.

Scaling from local to regional

Evidence from New York, Boston, Ontario and Singapore – as well as nearer to home in London – shows that schools can make faster progress when improvement efforts are coordinated and steered at a city or sub-regional level. The London Challenge ran from 2003 to 2011 but has not been drawn on enough given its generally accepted success.

The London Challenge had impact for a range of reasons: clear moral imperative to close attainment gaps across the capital; schools had a voice; and its Keys to Success programme used data to group families of schools and pinpoint the schools most in need, placing them at the centre of bespoke matched support. Rapid cycles of experimentation, evaluation and feedback ensured that proven strategies were refined and scaled, with expertise moving round the city. Boroughs like Tower Hamlets and Hackney were key partners, not sidelined. Their involvement in planning and delivery helped sustain momentum and legitimacy. London identity and pride, such as the idea of being a 'London teacher' or 'London leader' was cultivated through CPD, Teach First, chartered status and shared goals, creating a sense of belonging and professional esteem.

The London Challenge invested heavily in leadership development. National and Local Leaders of Education and teaching schools delivered one-to-one mentoring, coaching and peer reviews. The London Leadership Strategy offered structured pathways from middle-leader training through to headship development. By building local capacity and embedding collaborative networks, the initiative shifted the centre of gravity towards school-led improvement underpinned by transparent use of data. It transformed London's secondary and primary outcomes into a sustained success story.

There were also some helpful external factors: London was booming economically, its ethnic minority communities had a positive ethos for school and learning, and there was political support.

Other city challenge programmes in Greater Manchester and the Black Country modelled on London Challenge had mixed results. Key reasons for their more limited impact include: shorter timescales; weaker local civic ownership; less coherent delivery with fragmentation and variable capacity; tighter budgets and less flexibility; and the lack of Tim Brighouse's unifying and galvanising leadership.

National networks

I have worked in a number of professional sectors; none of them are neat and tidy when it comes to their national organisations. The addition of the Chartered College of Teaching filled an important gap in the school sector, and there is a good range of unions and other representative bodies. There are also subject associations that don't always have the seats they deserve round the policymaking tables.

The Foundation for Education Development (FED) has attempted to make changes to bring more of the development of education policy outside the political process, carrying out a number of consultations. Rather than waiting for the DfE to take the initiative, FED set up a National Education Assembly designed to give all education stakeholders a meaningful input into national education policy, practice and strategy.

Language of school improvement

One reason why school improvement perhaps holds a mystique is the language used. 'Self-improving system'; 'school-led' and 'system leadership': I am unconvinced these are adding value. I am not even sure a self-improving system is a thing: it might look as though there is one because all the individual organisations are getting better at what they do. I don't think we need this jargon to tell us that teachers and schools learn from each other and from research so that effective practice spreads, and it's helpful when the best schools and leaders share their expertise with other schools so that all schools improve.

There has been much said about system leadership, although there seems to be two slightly different interpretations. For example, for Professor David Hopkins, 'system leaders' are those headteachers who are care about and are willing to work for the success of other schools as well as their own; and for Leora Cruddas, they are those who act on, rather than just in, the system. The former is a good thing but not really commensurate with such a grand title, and the second is fairly rare, and will almost always come about through networks or partnership work, either local or national. The term seems to cover an initiative that has a positive impact on more than one institution, but these are highly unlikely to redesign the system. System leadership suggests something bigger: improvement that encompasses all schools, not just the chosen few, the lucky few.

Conclusion

We now have a sector that knows each institution is in the business of improving itself and has a board that knows it is accountable for that. The headteacher or executive leaders will also feel accountable for the institution's performance and the pupils' outcomes, but that should be a much more nuanced conversation between them and the board (in the first instance, the chair, as I discussed in chapter 4).

Education has many facets, many debates, and there has been a tendency to overcomplicate school improvement. I think we might be coming to the end of this period. In the last few years there have been many steps towards embedding CPD. The system and people in it are less likely to get hung up on lots of initiatives, big ideas and fads. Instead, much more attention is being paid to developing and retaining the people who work in schools. That clarity doesn't make it easy: it takes effort, perseverance, time and tailored support.

Schools can call on all sorts of others for support and expertise: that does not alter this fundamental overall accountability. Some of those arrangements will be paid for and there will be some expectations laid out. Other teachers, leaders and schools will be sources of support and development. The focus on MATs and MAT growth has sidelined collaborations outside trusts a little over the past decade, but there is much to learn from the history of collaborative work in the sector, including from the London Challenge. Now is the time for schools and trusts to brush that off and take it forward; many have been without making a big deal of it or taking much credit for it.

In order to aid a system that values evidence-based professional accountability coordinated at the local level, the heavy reliance on external accountability should be rebalanced towards an investment in the professional capital of teachers and school leaders. I will return in chapter 17 to how collaboration outside institutions and across regions could be embedded into the sector.

15.
Who governs the governors?

This is a neglected question. The only time I can really remember oversight of those who govern being talked about to any extent was during the Trojan Horse crisis. That was a unique situation but with some more generally applicable lessons that I will came back to, but let's first look at how the system should work.

Web of accountability

As we saw in chapter 2, governing boards are part of that web; as the accountable body for their institution, they are subject to those other six dimensions:

1. Legal.
2. Inspectorates, audit and scrutiny.
3. Peer and professional accountability.
4. Media.
5. Accountability to users.
6. Democratic and social accountability.

Those last two I am covering in the next chapter.

Although the word autonomy has been thrown about with gay abandon over the past 20 years, it is correct that maintained schools and trusts (but not always their schools) have a large amount of decision-making devolved to them. A question however arises as to how truly self-governing an institution can be in a system that is highly regulated. Governing boards should – and I think in very large part do – know how they fit into the web in relation to auditors, Ofsted and the regulator. Mature governing boards understand their role is a part of the national managerial accountability mechanism, but also see governance as local civic participation, which adds value to schools' work.

Boards are both governing others and being governed by local authorities and/or the DfE. They understand the power dynamics and that the decisions they make must be compliant with the law. They should carry out their duties in those other three mindsets of governing: the strategic, the generative, and values and culture. Governing boards are there to be proactive, not simply obey a higher law. Some academics portray them as puppets being controlled by government rather than using their own judgement; this is a crude caricature. The system does shape what boards consider but creativity and courage can empower boards and their institutions to work in different and better ways. Here I am looking at what could and should happen when governance doesn't work well.

The government has made it clear for many years that 'the responsibility for taking action to improve outcomes lies with the accountable body – that is governing board of the academy trust (single or multi-academy trust) or the governing board of maintained schools. But when a maintained school or an academy trust is failing to improve a school that has been identified as failing or coasting, it is important that RSCs, acting for the Secretary of State and exercising her powers as set out in the academy's Funding Agreement, are able to take action to secure rapid improvements' (House of Commons Education Committee, 2016).

Ofsted

We have seen that different chief inspectors (HMCIs) have given different priority to identifying the strengths and weaknesses of governance. NGA produced two research reports on practice with the 2019 Ofsted framework: *A View from the Board: Ofsted's New Education Inspection Framework* in 2020 and *School Inspection: A View from the Board Two Years On*. They make it very clear that the new framework led to the role of governance being diminished within the inspection process, including an analysis of over 800 published reports finding very few substantive mentions of the quality of governance. They were thus of little or no use as a spur to development.

The 2020 report gave me the opportunity in the foreword to repeat: 'The level of influence [the inspectorate] is currently given is unhealthy. It should not be Ofsted that is determining your work, but the knowledge and the experience of the profession, developed by the school leadership and overseen by the governing board. Governors and trustees have a role to play in reducing the heat and the stress currently created by an inspectorate seen to be all-powerful. We need to help build a confident, knowledgeable, wise cadre of school leaders who look to the governing board first and foremost for their accountability.'

Ideally the inspectorate should be able to ring a warning bell on poor governance practice before the education of children has been seriously affected. However, the 2019 iteration of inspection coupled with the decision to no longer recommend ERGs (external review of governance) left Ofsted providing very little specific information on poor governance, let alone any sanction or recommendation of remedial action. This was a backwards step after the work under the previous HMCI on governance in schools with declining standards. Instead, governance was only targeted for intervention after an inspection when leadership and management was judged to be requiring improvement or special measures.

Whistle-blowers

The Audit Commission reported in 2012 that a high proportion of whistle-blowing reports come from schools, with the observation that risks increase with more autonomous governance structures and periods of change, as was occurring with academisation. (As an aside, the commission, another player in the accountability web, was disbanded in 2015. The coalition government claimed that 'rather than being a watchdog that champions taxpayers' interests, it has become the creature of the Whitehall state' (Pickles, 2010) while its outgoing chair argued that the commission had played its part in assisting in the 'very significant' impact of local authority improvement in the previous decade. We have lost the body that provided system-wide oversight of local government performance, value for money and governance, and the fragmentation of its role has led to less consistent scrutiny, especially in areas like education, housing and social care, and loss of both coherence across public services and profile.)

Since whistle-blowing legislation was introduced in 1998, employees have been encouraged to come forward with disclosures of dangerous or criminal behaviour, without fear of reprisal or dismissal. Arguably the need to speak out against such activity is especially pertinent to the education sector, which deals with young and vulnerable people to whom there is an overriding duty of care. But whistle-blowing remains a sensitive, almost taboo, subject that is accompanied by a great deal of confusion and fear of repercussions. Protect's research in 2023 shows staff in education are willing to raise concerns, but too often they are ignored and retaliated against. More still needs to be done to ensure schools and trusts react in the right way to whistle-blowers and their concerns.

Although there are no documented cases, I am aware of a few occasions where whistle-blowers have tipped off relevant bodies about governance concerns. It can be difficult for staff to work out where to take those concerns and then for the concerns to be taken forward formally if staff are unwilling to go on the record.

Removal of individuals

How governing boards are held to account varies according to whether they govern a school maintained by local authority or an academy trust. There are some similar principles for removing individual governors and trustees: usually the institution who appointed them is also the route for removing them. For example, dioceses have the right to remove foundation governors or trustees and have policies laying this out. They are rarely used in practice but have been mentioned when needing to bring governors into line.

There is also a level of peer accountability with processes whereby boards can remove an individual in certain circumstances. This presents a conundrum: a judgement needs to be made as to whether the one or two considered 'the awkward squad' are preventing the board from functioning well or whether they are the ones who are on to something. For example, the leadership of Holland Park School after years of parental complaints and staff whistle-blowing had been ignored finally came to be investigated due to the persistence of a couple of trustees, who others considered to be difficult. There were also two red flags that weren't taken seriously enough by the DfE: the close relationship of the longstanding chair with the headteacher, coupled with his excessive pay.

Disqualification

Trustees as company directors can be banned – disqualified – if they don't meet their legal responsibilities. They will be seen as unfit in a number of instances including allowing a company to continue trading when it can't pay its debts and not keeping proper company accounting records. Unfitness (with no allegation of dishonesty) means incompetence of a high degree. Various bodies, including the Insolvency Service and Companies House, can apply to have a director or former director disqualified.

As well as being banned from company directorship or the running of a company for up to 15 years, there are other restrictions, affecting other public offices, and also the status of solicitors, barristers and accountants. I have met both lawyers and accountants who have stepped down from boards of trustees because they felt that their fellow trustees and senior executives were not up to the mark, and they couldn't risk their own professional reputations. In one case I was told the board of trustees was skewed towards educationalists resistant to taking advice from non-educationalists.

Trojan Horse

This affair in 2013/14 was hugely controversial with contested narratives and concerned ways to obtain the control of schools. An anonymous letter purporting to provide tactics on how to ensure state schools became Islamic in nature began two inquiries with slightly different scopes, one commissioned by the DfE and the other by Birmingham City Council. The findings from those inquiries made it clear that the issues experienced in a few East Birmingham schools did not amount to extremism nor 'a systematic plot to take-over schools'. The reports also raised some big questions, such as how schools, including academies, are overseen and the role of faith and worship, which I expected to be followed up by the DfE, but were not.

It was found that a small group of connected activists attempted to use the role of school governor or academy trustee to replace headteachers and subvert the school ethos to emphasise the differences between cultures, rather than fostering tolerance and equality. In fact, considering the media frenzy at its peak in the summer term of 2014, little was changed by the DfE in the short and medium term to prevent determined groups of likeminded individuals seeking the power of governance. The few minor changes – for example, the recommendation not to govern in more than two settings – were barely promoted. Tahir Alam, the chair of trustees, at the centre of the group is to date the only volunteer disqualified in the school sector.

Anyone interested in a full discussion with many perspectives can read *The Birmingham Book: Lessons in Urban Education Leadership and Policy from the Trojan Horse Affair*, to which I contributed a chapter on the lessons for governance, and I am happy to share on request the contemporaneous briefing I wrote.

A register

After Trojan Horse and the 2016 White Paper, a register for governors and trustees – and more recently governance professionals – was incorporated into Get Information on Schools (GIAS), which has been of much use. Although the historical entries on GIAS have a limited use, there is still no easy way for recruiting boards to discover who has been removed from a governing board.

Maintained schools

Local authorities (LAs) have statutory powers for maintained schools allowing them to issue warning notices, remove governors, suspend budgets, set up Interim Executive Boards (IEB) and recommend academy conversion where necessary.

Warning notices can be triggered if standards are unacceptably low, leadership is ineffective or governance has broken down. The LA must set out specific concerns and a timeframe for improvement. If the governing body fails to act, the LA can escalate intervention, often by appointing additional governors with relevant experience or replacing the entire board with an IEB. An IEB is thus an intervention to remove failing governance and a school improvement mechanism of last resort.

Interim executive boards

An IEB is as its name suggests: a hybrid between governance and executive action for a set period of time, or you could term it 'governance plus'. It has the strategic role of the governing body it replaces, but also operational jurisdiction needed to achieve rapid improvement, whether of education or other aspects of the school's functioning. IEB members really should be paid as they are performing an executive function; this is not just an NGA view but one from a range of powerful commentators from Sir Michael Wilshaw as HMCI in 2012 to the House of Commons education committee.

A local authority must get the permission of the DfE before installing an IEB, and this can be time-consuming which is really unhelpful in these urgent situations. There needs to be a review carried out to see the impact of this process, and consideration of reducing that to a duty to inform, or possibly consult over a 10-day period. The DfE could check that the local authority has been through the required stages, which include a consultation with the governing body and the involvement of the diocese or foundation for their school.

There is very little guidance for IEBs; NGA did a short piece of action research several years ago to begin to fill the gap. We found IEBs were most successful when they comprised four or five experienced members independent of the school, usually two external educationalists alongside an experienced chair, a finance expert and an HR expert. We didn't proceed with the work for a number of reasons, including that local authorities were not tending to use them as often because it was resulting in an academy order being made. Depending on the time the DfE took to find an appropriate MAT, the IEB sometimes made significant improvements, but the structural intervention almost always proceeded anyway.

Use of intervention

Both the public accounts committee and the education select committee have queried the lack of intervention in failing schools by some local authorities. It was pointed out in 2019 that 42 local authorities had not appointed an IEB since 2006, and 45 had not issued a warning notice since 2009. Sometimes local authorities preferred to avoid taking action under the legislation because they feel it undermined their relationship with the school and wanted to bring about improvements through persuasion and co-operation. The DfE considered that they should take a co-operative approach for a more limited time period before using their formal intervention powers. The Conservative Education Secretary imposed IEBs directly on a number of occasions, but generally as part of 'the rapid transformation of many poorly performing schools into sponsored academies'.

The National Audit Office published a report – *Academies and Maintained Schools: Oversight and Intervention* – in 2014, finding that of all formal interventions, IEBs were associated with the highest rate of school improvement. Almost half of schools receiving formal intervention improved, but IEBs had the strongest correlation with positive Ofsted outcomes.

Members of academy trusts

Members of the academy trust are its guardians, holding the trust board to account for the effective governance. They have a limited and distinct role, one that is quite often misunderstood; despite the NGA producing guidance since 2018, many trusts have struggled to define the role, continuing to interpret it incorrectly. For a considerable time this uncertainty was perpetuated by the DfE failing to produce guidance; Sam Henson and I had a discussion with the governance unit advising on this annually and then little happened, some of which was unhelpful.

The DfE likened the trust membership to company shareholders, despite charitable companies not having shareholders, whose liability is limited to the number of shares they have bought. The members of academy trusts have a liability limited to £10. Furthermore, shareholders are paid a dividend, while academy trusts are not-for-profit organisations, where members volunteer with no monetary award. We worked hard to get that comparison out of the DfE governance guide, only to find it popping up in the *Academy Trust Handbook* (ATH).

The DfE also mistakenly adopted my expression of being 'eyes on, hands off', which applies to governing boards for members in both the *Governance Handbook* and *Academies Financial Handbook*, which led to many members hovering around and even sometimes attending trustee meetings. Even though it has now been removed by the DfE, some other organisations continue to use it. Members are not 'super trustees', and new myths can develop that need to be busted. The DfE used to specifically refer to skills and expertise that members should have, but in its latest iteration this has been replaced by a better description of the role.

Members do hold some considerable power, such as agreeing and amending the articles of association, appointing the majority of the trustees and dismissing them all, regardless of who appointed them. Their role is minimal when the board of trustees is performing well but must swing into action when governance is failing. If this works well, that intervention should happen before the trust and its pupils decline. Members' main business comes at the AGM and initially an AGM wasn't required; it is in later model articles. The agenda of that AGM should include either a report from an external review of governance (ERG) or in the intervening couple of years a self-evaluation. This does not happen in the majority of trusts, and perhaps requiring trusts to submit the minutes of their AGM to the DfE might improve practice.

Innovation

For a sector that prides itself on innovation, there has been very little innovation in the membership model. Some trusts have failed even to extend their membership to five individuals, the DfE's recommended number. For a decade I have been encouraging trusts to extend their membership to include any parents or community groups who opt to join, and occasionally I heard whispers of this happening, but couldn't track down actual examples. This expansion would demonstrate a real willingness to be accountable more widely.

In 2025 ULT, the largest MAT, gave every school a vote at its parent company AGM through its local governing body. This is very welcome in terms of providing another route for local voice, but it is a model that keeps the power and decision-making at trustee board level. It also illustrates how diverse the trust sector is as it is not a route open to most MATs.

The Department for Education

The boards of trustees are held to account for underperformance by the DfE through their regional director. I am not convinced that their offices have either sufficient knowledge or capacity to provide secure oversight and intervention, especially after the cancellation of the National Leaders of Governance (NLG) scheme. Furthermore, in 2025 the grounds for DfE issuing notices to improve were restricted so that governance is no longer always considered.

Regional directors have shared their dilemma that they need to strike a balance between giving trusts the time and support to improve and take decisive action when necessary. It can be difficult for them to ascertain when that line should be crossed. However, intervention in MATs by the DfE is limited, and this needs to be reconsidered from first principles by a review that does not give the advisory power to the trusts who are being regulated.

Conclusion

In the move to a MAT-dominated sector, once again we see that neither membership nor intervention when governance fails were properly considered when the system began. Some of the trust governance catastrophes seen to date might have been more rapidly dealt had the DfE had the power of intervention. As MATs grow, taking responsibility for the education of more and more pupils, the effect of governance failure on pupils and staff is likely to be greater. This risk needs to be addressed in the system. In chapter 12 I proposed a more rigorous and independent form of appointment of trustees for larger MATs, but that in itself does not solve the problem of poor performance in office. IEBs are a useful option for maintained schools; perhaps the equivalent is required for boards of trustees.

Widening the membership franchise would be a real breath of fresh air in system. Membership is currently lacking in transparency. Even local governors don't tend to be invited to the AGM. But throwing the door open to a wide range of others who have an interest in the trust's schools for information would be quite a revolution, but even better if that involved some real transfer of power to those who really own our schools, as I explore in the next chapter.

16.
Who owns our schools?

I don't mean literally own the buildings, though that also has many players and much complexity in its answer, made more complex by academisation. The initial conversion legislation in 2010 did not deal with this question well enough and regulations had to be passed in 2012 to formalise land transfer. Funding agreements were also amended to prevent non-educational use after one of the early academy scandals involved the Durand Academy Trust using land for other activities. Payments from a leisure centre continued to be paid to the executive head, Sir Greg Martin, after his retirement, and he became chair of governors at the school. There were court challenges, and the Charity Commission became involved to ascertain what pay-off from the leisure business was reasonable when Greg Martin had to leave this role too. This case underlines the fundamental need for good governance to restrain an executive who has become too powerful and driven by things other than the mission of the trust.

Here I want to consider the broader question that concerns two of the dimensions of accountability:

- Accountability to users: in particular parents and carers, and ensuring voices are heard.
- Democratic and social accountability.

Other top-down dimensions may seem much more powerful; indeed they have been given pride of place and therefore risk disciplining powers controlling – or at the very least steering – those who make devolved decisions. Now is the time to change that balance.

Governing boards are not the owners; they are the custodians, the guardians, the stewards of the trust or school they govern. Often school leaders say 'we are legally accountable to the government but really we are foremost accountable to our communities and their children'. That must be right but not enough action follows this to make it true in practice. Concern about the other dimensions of the accountability web push these to the periphery. There is too much emphasis on 'upward' accountability. We need to ensure that both the architecture of the system and the practice of schools recognises the public ownership of our taxpayer-funded schools.

The rhetoric for almost 30 years from governments of all political persuasions has been of devolution of power to the people from central and local governments. This has supposedly been brought about by decentralising reforms shifting powers away from politicians and civil servants, often termed 'bureaucrats' rather than public servants, to schools, local communities and citizens. For example, the 2016 White Paper used the typical phrase 'empower local communities, putting children and parents first', while at the same time failing to make any changes that achieve this. When the 2022 White Paper did appear to be taking tentative steps in that direction, they were quashed by a regulatory review group including many of the powerful, primarily MAT, executives.

Participation of citizens matters for two reasons. We live in a democracy and participation provides legitimacy, securing a wider agreement to the contract between the public and schools. Secondly, it adds to learning of both the individual institution and the wider community. Practical wisdom and different lived experiences add another dimension and perspective to professional expertise. I am back on the topic of Callaghan's speech of half a century ago: teachers and school leaders don't alone have the right to determine entirely what citizens, also other people's children, learn and how they are treated at school.

My thesis may well be challenged by those who say: 'It's outcomes that matter.' For example, Graham Stuart MP, then chair of the education select committee, said at a joint NGA and BELMAS (the British Educational Leadership, Management and Administration Society) event in 2014 that he was 'less interested in democratic accountability than in quality'. These concepts should not be mutually exclusive, although there is likely to be some creative tension when defining quality. The power to govern under democratic rule should not be reserved exclusively for experts and professionals; it should be tempered by the views, experiences and even political opinions of the people.

Accountability to users

There are levels to being held to account through engagement with stakeholders. The first is for schools to provide routes to listen to experience and concerns, then there's a more participatory level where advice is sought from stakeholders and lastly there's the handing over of some decision-making power. Forum Strategy has been promoting this philosophy of putting users and the community into the driving seat with a local focus and shared responsibility.

Ensuring that the voices of pupils, parents, staff and local communities are heard and reflected in decision-making remains a persistent challenge. (Parents covers other carers, often grandparents, and guardians.) Innovative approaches to stakeholder engagement are still needed. In all the years of work at NGA with senior leaders as well as governors and trustees, the importance of the contribution of local people, community links and parental engagement was almost universally appreciated. Yet so little progress has been made.

I appreciate I have barely mentioned pupil voice, but for the record it is also underexplored and underpractised, despite the existence of pupil councils. Student governors, who feature in some other educational governance, would also be worthy of consideration at the top end of secondary schools.

Engagement with users

Guidance from the DfE makes very clear that it expects mechanisms are in place for communication with parents and that governing boards show how decision-making has been influenced by parents' views. For many years I lobbied the DfE to consult parents more and kept being disappointed that, despite its warm words, the DfE lacked interest in consistently championing parental engagement. The DfE has a most peculiar stance towards parents, quoting the need for the system to keep them informed, but then failing to make any efforts to communicate themselves and sometimes even displaying an underlying distrust of them. ParentKind has filled that gap on providing some parental views at a national level.

NGA's annual surveys tell us about four in five boards see the results of a parent survey and three out of five monitor the findings from pupil and staff surveys. Given the emphasis on staff workload and welfare, I am surprised all boards aren't asking to see staff survey results. Also worryingly, governors' and trustees' meetings with staff have reduced quite substantially, as have focus groups with parents and pupils, and meetings with parents and student councils, the latter, for example, dropping from 71% in 2016 to 42% in 2024. This may be due to the workload of governance discussed in chapter 10, but ways to reverse this need to be found.

Research by Baxter and Cornforth (2019) found the same challenges of MATs when aiming to connect with the school communities they serve as NLGs did in chapter 12, revealing that the failure to implement fundamental processes such as communication strategies are leading to fragmentation and feelings of disconnect.

As we discussed with culture, accountability requires bodies to be approachable and to make it easy for people to raise issues with them. Of course engagement must be genuine and meaningful. Sometimes it is seen as a public relations activity seeking to secure support for decisions to all intents and purposes already made. During the Covid-19 pandemic often school–parent relationships strengthened as parents appreciated the efforts staff were making to provide learning for their children. However, it also had the effect of changing the deal between school and families as touched on in chapter 13.

There isn't one voice for any stakeholder group, and managing the differences can be time-consuming. Some public sector organisations, particularly with elected representatives, have more experience than schools of managing to balance the needs and interests of different residents.

There are other mechanisms that can be used, such as a larger and permanent council of stakeholders. Some boards of public bodies and some ombudsmen have advisory groups in place for hearing directly from the users of their services, which enhance executive and non-executive understanding of how the public experience aspects of their service and bring a good source of constructive challenge.

Transparency

Openness is one of the Nolan principles, and any work on ethical leadership promoted the importance of transparency. In the school sector we perhaps do not give enough thought to what we should be putting into the public domain. By contrast, local authorities work in a much more open way with most papers published and a large majority of decisions – including the agreement to the annual budget – made in public meetings.

Given that schools are not as open, we need to be sure that it's not self-serving, not defensive of the institution. Against that backdrop, there are some items the DfE expect schools to publish, such as pupil premium statements. These are dismissed by some leaders as onerous, but they provide a structure for a governance conversation. The introduction of the pupil premium by the coalition government raised the profile of the attainment gap and concentrated minds on how to close it. The DfE argues it is also information for parents, but very few will find and read it. That is where transparency is limited; it has not fuelled parents with enough information to be armchair auditors.

Decisions taken by the DfE, and sometimes governing boards too, leaves parent bodies feeling that they are kept in the dark. This lack of transparency was raised also by ex-minster Robin Walker MP, who criticised the lack of transparency with the regional director's decisions concerning academies. One of the most infamous concerned Downhills School in 2012 when Education Secretary Michael Gove sacked its governing body and replaced it with an IEB before transferring the school to a MAT. Hundreds of parents and supporters attended a protest meeting at the school in Tottenham, including local MP and former pupil David Lammy, complaining about the lack of consultation and information provided. Its standards improved after joining the MAT. Others may be less dramatic, but when a school is moved into a MAT or is re-brokered between trusts, the general response is that there is little or no meaningful consultation of parents.

The role of the governing board

Those who volunteer to govern are active citizens who are working to secure another's rights. Governing boards make the decisions under the oversight of either the local authority or the DfE, but they do it on behalf of others. Participatory democracy is a model of governance where citizens actively shape and take decisions through ongoing, direct involvement in policymaking, budgeting and institutional oversight. It's not just consultation. The sheer numbers of volunteers required for school governance resulted in what Professor Ranson (2011) called the 'largest democratic experiment in voluntary public participation', more than other public institutions. This clearly is the business of governing boards, but it also suggests an ethos of inclusivity that attempts to include diverse voices (as we discussed in chapter 10).

Some academics appear to write about a golden age of participation and governance democracy that is no more; serving volunteers might find that a trifle dismissive. Indeed it is often researchers who extol wide participation without having much of any participation within their methodologies. Wilkins (2016) argues that 'parents have been divided: those with or without the privileged knowledge and skills for school governance'. Grek (2013) used 'expertocracy' to describe those being given power because of their technical knowledge and understanding of data, and this could be applied to that former group of governors. There is some danger of this but most school-level boards, as opposed to MAT boards of trustees, will welcome and support parents who do not come from the professional class. Parents from disadvantaged communities are more likely to develop the confidence to become members of the governing body when they have been involved in the life of the school.

A study by PWC in 2007 highlighted the importance that headteachers gave to governing bodies being representative of their local communities, and this is something we continued to hear: again it adds to the board's legitimacy.

It is also arguable whether governing boards act as deliberative democracy; this does not work if it's focused on compliance, rubber-stamping executive decisions or dominated by technical data at the expense of broader experience. The *Chair's Handbook* contains much on how to deliberate well and take decisions collectively, but discussing well among themselves is only half the story.

Boards have the power to make some crucial decisions, but they need to do that by taking other voices into account. Dialogue between governors and the governed is an important means of democratic accountability. At times governors and trustees can be the conduit between the professionals and the public, but more often they need to assure themselves that leaders have appropriate structures and arrangements in place to listen to the stakeholder voice. A public space should be created so that citizens can help shape services.

Visible governance
Even though board meetings remain a secret garden accessed by the headteacher or executive lead, and sometimes by other senior leaders (often to make a presentation), it is crucial that other staff are aware of who the governors – and trustees – are. Estelle Morris, the former Education Secretary, makes a compelling case for governors noticing teachers.

Visibility of governance also gives legitimacy and suggests accessibility and approachability. The MAT structure undermines the visibility and transparency of schools to others, and it is important that local governance is used to combat this.

Elected governors
We have seen that once on the board, no governor has a representative role; they govern in the best interests of pupils. It is not their role to represent a stakeholder group. However, the sheer fact of elections and the

perceived representative role of those parent and staff governors provides a legitimising factor for the board, an authority in its community. Elections also prevent a board becoming a self-perpetuating oligarchy at risk of groupthink. Those disposed to governance by clique must not have that option. Parents and staff bring a perspective and knowledge that other governors and trustees may not.

The importance of that was seen in 2016 when then Education Secretary Nicky Morgan proposed removing the requirement for elected parent governors in academy trusts. Before its publication, I had written a rather long defence of parent governors which on the surface was well received, and I was told the proposal wouldn't be going ahead. However, it was only dropped for maintained schools, so immediately NGA began a 'Keep Parents Governing' campaign on seeing the White Paper.

Parents, especially on Mumsnet, responded with hundreds of critical posts, arguing that removing parent governors would undermine democratic accountability and disconnect schools from the communities they serve. Parents expressed concern that governance would become dominated by 'yes men' or corporate-style boards with little understanding of pupil needs or local context. Many defended the value of lived experience and commitment over formal qualifications.

It was mainly parents, alongside governors, who made a lot of noise about the loss of connection with academy trusts and contacted local MPs: they didn't want their schools taken over by remote trusts. The strength of opinion possibly took the education establishment by surprise.

When Nicky Morgan failed to defend the policy, she quietly dropped it along with much else in the White Paper. It is a rare example of grassroots parental activism influencing national education policy, and it emphasised the role of parent governors as a symbol of ownership and warned the DfE not to allow the centralisation of MAT governance without community input.

Community accountability

One of my early jobs after graduation was as a community worker, and having championed working with stakeholders most of my career whenever I have had the opportunity, I understand how difficult it can be to get right. Rising complaints from parents and the changing contract between families and schools accelerated by the Covid-19 pandemic has make it harder, but also more important. We are living in precarious political times where many citizens, particularly those with lower incomes, feel abandoned by the powers that be and often also by the professional classes.

Schools have a crucial role to play in fostering understanding and helping any divisions within their community to heal. In fact, they are still under a legal duty (maintained schools through legislation and academies through funding agreements) to promote community cohesion. It was defined by the Cantle Report as: 'A society in which there is a common vision and sense of belonging by all communities; the diversity of people's backgrounds and circumstances is appreciated and valued; similar life opportunities are available to all; and strong and positive relationships exist and continue to be developed' (Home Office, 2022).

This is a neat illustration of the current power of Ofsted to shape the accountability mindset of the sector: after community cohesion was removed in 2011 from Ofsted's remit, it has barely been discussed. There is also the bigger conversation as to whether a focus on community cohesion is a distraction from the core business of educating children. I am arguing that it is part of schools' civic responsibility, and working in partnership locally could add value. Community cohesion is very relevant to England entering 2026.

The role of trust members

The current trust structure of membership aims to ensure good governance, but that by its very definition should include listening to stakeholders. This top level of trust governance overseeing the board of trustees is ripe for providing a direct route back to citizens, both users and taxpayers. A minor tweak would be to invite them to the AGM, but a more meaningful change is to dramatically increase the number of members. Both would provide much-needed transparency, and the invitation to the AGM should be non-negotiable. The second is much more radical as it would transfer some power. Over the many years I have encouraged trusts to consider this, there has been no appetite for this level of change, even from those arguing for more community engagement. At the same time surveys show we have parents feeling disenfranchised from MATs they see as distant from their communities.

Those with the power do not give it away lightly. Extending membership would not only change the balance of power slightly but would introduce that missing element of democracy back into the academy system, arguably more directly than local council elections. Although a radical suggestion on paper, in practice if all – or even much – is well, there will not be a disruptive revolution, rather one that gives people a sense of belonging and the say they are entitled to. In fact, systems do need disruption every so often as power tends to settle, and the big trust executives have been in place for long enough now to have become a powerful elite. That dynamic between the institution and those served need to be opened up more.

There have been concerns expressed to me about the potential capture by parents who are angry with their school; if an issue has been handled badly to such an extent that there are a significant number of people willing to come to the AGM to express their opinion or vote in a particular way, this provides an incentive for schools, including local governors, to take it seriously at an earlier date. It may not be immediate as it requires trust to be built over the years, but providing a public space, a forum, for views to be aired is part of that. If there is going to be capture from a group, it is likely to be middle-class capture, so an AGM could not be the only means of participation, but it may be the right one at trust level complementing a whole range of opportunities at school level.

In the charity sector we are used to being accountable to members at AGMs; at NGA we produced a more accessible annual report in addition to the audited accounts. In 2013 the Charity Commission observed in written evidence to the Academies Commission that the model charitable company membership provisions for academies are relatively narrow, generating concerns about representation and stakeholder influence. This is not difficult to correct.

The education academic literature some time ago identified three roles for maintained governing bodies (as they were then) – managerial, bringing local information to decision-making and democraticising – and since the move to academies, particularly MATs, has been strenuously criticised for covering only the first. However, with trustees concentrating on that first, meaningful local governance providing the local context and some legitimacy, we can then use the member layer to provide some of the third: democracy.

Conclusion

As the school sector has become more and more entrenched in rendering account to Ofsted and the DfE, it has downgraded the voices of others. Most schools have not lost connection with their communities and local places; they are very much part of the local architecture and, with the cuts in other public services, one of the most visible. However, the system does not value or reward that work of engagement. This needs to change.

The English school system over the past 20 years has prioritised performance with a nod to direction, vision and most recently culture, but without due thought to voice and legitimacy, those other principles of governance I introduced in chapter 1. There is a suggestion from some quarters that much of the establishment, often styled as the elite, has lost touch with the little people, the many citizens in many parts of the country, particularly disadvantaged areas. The aftermath of the Grenfell Tower fire eight years ago brought into terrible focus the distance between those who make the decisions and those who live with the consequences. There are some indications that we could be in danger of that happening in the educational world, when in fact schools have an important role to play in healing the divisions, and many are already engaged in that way.

At the very least a public space must be created to ensure citizens can speak to communicate their claims and protests and where all voices are welcome and heard. Systems of governance acquire authority if they are perceived as legitimate; that is, if they have wide support. Consent continually has to be tested and reaffirmed. To take this a step further, many of us support the principle of subsidiarity that decisions made nearest the ground are likely to be more sound. A more devolved system would work better: I will come back to that in the next chapter.

Citizens also need to know that they are welcomed as governance volunteers and by participating in other meaningful ways with the school. MATs need to take decisions about their own role in the civic contribution: is this work devolved to school level where the networks exist? Especially as MATs grow, executives have less locus in this work; they are unlikely to know all the key actors in each locality. It is absolutely not downplaying the importance of meaningful civic engagement, but acknowledging that most often contributions have to happen locally. Central trust staff can support school leaders to engage locally, ensuring enthusiasm and capacity is real.

17.
Governance of the system

Where does all of this leave the power and decision-making in the system as a whole? Governing boards are responsible for outcomes, conduct and sustainability of individual institutions while central government remains responsible for outcomes from the whole system and value for money. So far, so clear.

We saw in chapter 13 that when working to address the challenges of disadvantage, headteachers are becoming 'community connectors', as a 2025 study by Sim and Major termed them, and in chapter 16 we saw that parents and communities require a greater say. In chapter 14 we saw that the drivers of better education for pupils had begun to shift to a school improvement model focused on professional development; however, other powerful actors may not yet have recognised this as they continue with a very top-down accountability system, which causes fear and may inhibit innovation. We need to reconfigure the system without much disruption, distraction or distress to devolve more power and decision-making.

I would have liked to adopt the approach that Hood and McInerney took some years ago with their model of no one being responsible for more than one function. That never did quite work for the DfE, who have oversight of all things educational, but that's in the nature of its role as regulator and the Education Secretary's responsibility and accountability. The buck stops there.

Combining ESFA into the regions group earlier in 2025, putting all the DfE's regulatory function in one place, was the right move for clarity and efficiency. It has been suggested by some such as the Confederation of School Trusts (CST) that an independent regulator could be set up to be accountable to Parliament for academy trusts. I think that would create confusion about roles and add duplication into the system, and parliamentary accountability methods are usually more symbolic than robust. It would also not appear to be in line with current government thinking, given, for example, the abolition of NHS England.

On the other hand, some fear that the current structure has outsourced responsibility and accountability to a range of other players, some of whom are privately owned. In fact, almost all those many other players tend to supply services to schools or trusts, so that is a procurement and contractual relationship and doesn't involve any transfer of power or decision-making.

Jonathan Slater, former Permanent Secretary at the DfE, has pointed out the 'consequence of academisation is that it does concentrate political power very much in the hands of a very small number of people in Westminster, supported by an increasing number of civil servants … I think it's more centralised than it should be' (Whittaker, 2022). The power base includes No. 10 and HM Treasury more than is necessary.

We have lived through a period of great centralisation of power. I don't know who did the counting, but it is often said that when LMS (local management of schools) was introduced in 1988, the Education Secretary had 250 powers and she now has over 2500. This is unhelpful, but now it is not the time to fight that particular battle given the other bigger challenges acting against providing the best possible education schools can. We need to find another meaningful route for the devolution of power.

HMCI has assumed a disproportionate power, and I hope by privileging more horizontal accountability, the confidence of school leaders will increase and this will in turn diminish Ofsted's. I am not proposing any change of structure for Ofsted as an organisation, but I would ensure HMCI was the person who ran the inspectorate, rather than each HMCI designing a new inspection framework. This job would fall to an advisory group who would make recommendations for any change to the Education Secretary. I am sure they would be making a better fist of it than Ofsted has been over the last couple of years. Secondly, the HMCI needs to be held to account – like any chief executive – by the Ofsted board; Dame Christine Gilbert exposed their poor governance with her excellent report, and I have every confidence that as the newly appointed chair she will ensure it carries out its responsibilities.

A messy set of school structures

At the time of writing, we are waiting to see what the Labour government's vision is for the architecture of the school system in England, knowing that structures are not important to them. That is understandable, given the many other crucial issues, in particular the SEND crisis, the education of pupils facing other disadvantage, secondary teacher supply and I would add insufficiency of funding.

There's a long list of commentators who've expressed concerns about continuing to have a dual system: trusts and maintained schools. It superficially sounds attractive to have a single system, but the problems of the dual system are not well explored. And actually, it is significantly more than dual: within both the maintained and trusts sector there are many structures. Having a trust-only system would not provide us with a uniform system given their range of sizes and shapes. There would still be a couple of thousand individual trusts – currently 2262 – without any formal links.

Even more often the system is described as 'fragmented' but usually without solutions attached. We are all on a quest for coherence, but without a clear diagnosis of what exactly causes or results from the incoherence. While trust autonomy has provided the opportunity to do some things differently (although again we don't entirely understand what), it has also contributed to the unsticking of the system. Collaboration between schools within trusts has been privileged at the expense of broader collaboration across the system. Further research needs to be done to ascertain just how much it is autonomy that leads to school improvement, as opposed to collaboration and learning from each other. All appear to be supportive of the ambition to reduce fragmentation, but as discussed elsewhere, due to the geography of MATs, connected localism cannot be achieved by bringing all schools within MATs.

It is argued that the dual system is more expensive; that sounds plausible, but again I haven't seen definitive evidence, and it would be difficult to quantify. Structural conversions are also costly and time-consuming. Some 2019 work commissioned by the Local Government Association showed the executive tier within MATs to be an expensive addition to the system, especially when the number of trusts is taken into account, each with a necessary executive team.

A variety of school types is very much par for the course in England and has been for a very long time. We would not have started from here. Yet while a single system would be tidier and easier for DfE and other organisations like NGA currently producing two sets of guidance, it would be extremely hard to achieve. We have learned that forcing everyone to restructure is doomed, and probably more than the DfE can cope with anyway.

There have been a couple of suggestions of alternative structures for all schools, but none of them I have seen provides all the answers, and indeed some make no legal sense. Furthermore the energy, goodwill, time and money it would take to achieve anything near to that is currently better used on other more significant problems, particularly in the next few years when we need to support the government's mission of ensuring fairness and opportunity for all children. Now is not the time to initiate yet another round of distracting structural reform. However, I have suggestions.

Maintained schools

Primary schools should be positively encouraged to form federations to provide a little more capacity and collaboration. To effect change, a message from ministers would help as well as support from local authorities. If the federation were to have a foundation, it would have almost all the advantages that academies do without having to leave the maintained family of schools to which most schools left are very committed. The MAT option is of course available to them.

Very small schools

Very small schools of whatever structure should be able to apply to a community development fund to support their continued existence rather than expecting to be further subsidised by other primaries from school funding, as is the case now.

Trusts

My proposed cap would prevent very large MATs from expanding further, and schools would be given the right with regional director permission to leave a MAT to exist as a smaller MAT in a geographical cluster, enabling local partnership working. Backroom services could still be provided using an umbrella trust model to deliver to smaller MATs and federations and maintain efficiencies. The division of very large MATs into more geographically focused ones could be considered by trust boards; experience tells me this is most likely to happen when a CEO is due to leave.

When the time is right, the relationship between academy trusts and central government should change from guided by a series of individual, but highly similar, contracts to a set of regulations that apply to all. This would require significant consultation and may be seen by some, including those with vested interests, as a reduction in academy freedoms, but this need not be the case.

Working together at local level

There's a general feeling that there needs to be 'glue' to stick everything together in this disjointed system. But who provides the glue and who wields the glue stick? The answer is not a change of school structure, but an increase of trust. It is about how those many schools and their staff work together with each other and other civic players. We need to persevere with local and regional partnerships. Loic Menzies in 'Mapping the way to educational equity' takes the same approach, and I commend his succinct conclusion, which provides 12 insights for taking forward the complicated issues leaders are faced with.

The localities model is the future. It may be that in addition to their institutional duties, governors could engage more broadly in communities to help tackle the obstacles to learning that occur outside the school gates. I hesitate to recommend that when I am so very well aware of their existing workload. However, it may be that the reduction of duties of local governors within MATs combined with an obligation on trusts for community engagement leads in that direction, and that would be beneficial. Bringing school governance out of the board room and extending the role to community leader is daunting, but surely it would be worthwhile to spend more time considering how needs of children and families could be better fulfilled with less time on structural change.

MATs on the map

The civic landscape is not built to deal with the existing vast range of MAT shapes and sizes, and even with my proposals to limit the most extreme outliers, there are no simple solutions to making this chaotic pattern work with other services. It is a lesson that the eight DfE regions, which existed from 2014 with much criticism, were reshaped in 2022 to fit with the nine standard government regions.

In theory very large and dispersed MATs might have the capacity to engage with partners at regional level, but the practicalities are difficult as most relevant partnership work is carried out at a sub-regional or very local level. Navigating many different local landscapes – local authorities, health services, community organisations, demographics, local challenges – requires a level of local knowledge, relationship-building and communication channels that are extremely hard to maintain from outside the area and yet are crucial to the success of networks. Smaller and medium sized MATs should be able to make connections and build strong relationships with other players in their local authority areas. They know the places and the people, both those they are serving and those in other public services.

Remember that most MATs are still small and medium sized. They grew out of a locality and many took a decision not to extend themselves beyond certain boundaries. In the early days many NGA members took to calling themselves community MATs to distinguish themselves from chains. They were a different creature. It was also a signal about their ethos; they were not trying to build an empire but serve the locality.

There has been much said about MATs leading – or just acting – civically. But the reality doesn't always live up to this rhetoric. I am sure many MAT leaders would positively want to make an impact outside their schools' gates, but the MAT world was not designed to facilitate an additional level of relevant connections, and the unplanned shape that has emerged does not lend itself to this work. The examples offered by MAT advocates often involve community or place-based networking, which may more often be within the headteacher's domain. There is no shame in accepting that while MATs act as a catalyst for connections between their own schools, it is the school who acts as a catalyst for much of the civic activity.

Local authorities

Despite the role of local authorities in education diminishing with the growth of the academy sector, they retain important legal responsibilities as well as local democratic legitimacy. Trusts often argue that local authorities have too great a conflict of interest to manage their duties well, while some schools are maintained; these will need to be managed, but remember the DfE also has a combination of legal duties plus the oversight of academy trusts. Rarely do I hear that conflict being called out even when some funding and partnership possibilities were limited to academies only.

I have not written enough about the role of local authorities in either the history section or the current time. As well as supporting school improvement where maintained schools are underperforming, the crucial wider roles of local authorities include:

- Ensuring sufficient school places, including planning for falling rolls and demographic shifts.
- Coordinating admissions for maintained schools and overseeing fairness across all schools.
- Statutory duties for SEND provision, safeguarding and fair access protocol (even for academies).

- Supporting vulnerable children, including excluded pupils and those with SEND.
- Managing home-to-school transport, especially for SEND pupils and those in rural areas.
- Championing educational excellence for all children in their area.

They also influence early years and childcare planning, and often act as partnership convenors, bringing together schools, trusts and other partners. Local authorities know the wider social and service infrastructure of a place. They also have a scrutiny function, but capacity has resulted in education not often being the issue under examination. The recent celebration of Tim Brighouse's legacy underlined how leadership from local authorities can be transformational.

The government has acknowledged that local authorities are essential in bridging gaps between national policy and local delivery. For example, the government is widening slightly the role of local authorities as regards admissions; they have respected the autonomy of trusts as their own admission authorities. This will need to be kept under review as the system on in-year moves is very difficult for parents. There needs to be more parental voice in the admissions system.

NGA's 2024 annual governance survey asked those governing in MATs about the roles local authorities should play. On protecting vulnerable pupils, 78% agreed LAs should oversee safeguarding and child protection while 62% said LAs should review pupil exclusions in academies. Opinion was split on admissions, with half (51%) saying LAs should control them, going further than the government.

Complaints

At the time of writing the DfE is reviewing the complaints system, which is overdue. The increase in parental complaints, particularly vexatious ones, is creating unsustainable levels of work for school leaders and governors with multiple routes open for the same or similar complaints. While it is incredibly important institutions learn from complaints and that parents and other citizens have a route for redress, the system has to be manageable for all concerned. It could be that new single agency, perhaps a specific ombudsman, is needed.

Working together at regional level

The Blunkett review of 2014 recommended independent regional Director of School Standards (DSS), and despite their performative title, he wanted to build on the success of the London Challenge. At that time there were not as many academies, and the DfE's regional commissioners were at the start of their eight-year existence. I would keep the DfE's regional directors acting on behalf of the Education Secretary as the regulators of academies, making the decisions about interventions and re-brokering in MATs.

I also want sub-regional independent appointments called something like an education partnership director or commissioner or chair working with not only trusts and maintained schools, but also other early years and FE providers. The RISE teams and possibly also the SRMAs (school resource management advisers) would be attached here and not to the DfE. The DfE should not get involved in school improvement itself, whereas sub-regional education expert teams could offer a range of support alongside local authorities and dioceses. They would bring a range of advantages a civil service team can't: educational experience; local knowledge; smaller geographies allowing better building of relationships with key players; and alignment with civic structures. They would have a remit to join up with other public services and those working to improve social cohesion and reduce poverty. This is likely to improve responsiveness as it would be easier to spot emerging issues across the area. They could convene civic partnerships where there are gaps and coordinate multi-agency collaboration to tackle systemic barriers faced by disadvantaged children.

They would play an important role in providing that glue needed to prevent fragmentation and would have greater legitimacy as seen 'of the place' but also 'of the sector' rather than 'distant bureaucrats'. There would need to be a debate as to how they would be appointed and held to account. Would this be by both the DfE and the local authorities within the sub-region, or could that vertical governance be done away with? Could the current area-based education partnerships provide a model? Their intelligence would no doubt be of use to the DfE's regional director when making their decisions, but partnerships would need to be independent and able to speak truth to power.

Conclusion

As a governance geek I have often felt I've been letting the side down when I made the case that people and relationships are more important than structures; it has certainly caused eye-rolling from some quarters. My inability to come up with a lovely architecture was a failing, and I was a little shocked when I saw my musings set out in *About Our Schools*. I needed to do better!

Having spent the last year rereading and reading more widely, I have not changed my mind. I am now loud and proud: the glue required is not primarily structures. It is relationships bound by trust in its wider sense. We just need to make sure that the structures don't prohibit that relationship-building. It would be neat and tidy to have all schools within one structure, but we are now very likely to have a dual system for the foreseeable future, so we need to make that work. The proposed sub-regional partnerships should help those all-important relationships flourish.

Bridget Phillipson, Education Secretary said to *TES*: 'Overall, we need to move to a system that is more rooted in partnership and collaboration … [The system] has become fragmented, and we need to find ways of working together to deliver better life chances for our children'(Severs, 2024). She repeated this philosophy in the early years policy paper a year later, broadening it to include others involved in giving children the 'best start in life': 'We want to see health, children's and family services, nurseries, childminders, schools, charities, and businesses connecting and collaborating to deliver this shared mission' (DfE, 2025).

Continuing to pretend place is not important to the school system is untenable, and minimising partnerships serving that place is absurd. The shape of the system is a muddle and does not align with real life. We need to agree on some boundaries and put effort into working across them, but not slavishly. Anyone who has examined the situation comes to the same conclusion as the House of Commons education committee (2017): 'the Government encouraged trusts to expand too quickly over too large geographical regions'. This needs to be reversed.

My approach for building a less fragile future comes back to the role of trust that I began with in part A with Professor O'Neill's Reith lectures. So many voices have coalesced around this. The time is now!

18.
Onwards, upwards and outwards

Good governance must be ethical, effective and accountable, and to achieve that needs care, commitment, lots of dialogue and holding many things in the balance.

Governing is an art. Not everyone will be good at it or have the patience for it; having to subsume your own passions and strongly held opinions into the team's and taking accounts of others' views is not for everyone. Governing is both harder and better than is often suggested by commentators. I hope I've been able to dispel the myth that school and trust governance is frequently weak. I am not complacent: it's a work in progress and always will be. The same well-documented fundamental issues pose difficulties in practice. More boards need to be cognisant of all five mindsets of governing: the fiduciary; the impactful; the strategic; the generative; and values and cultures.

The sector has in the end adapted well to structural changes. It took much longer for the responsibilities granted by the seismic change of Local Management of Schools (LMS) from 1988 to embed than might have been expected; the partnerships between the executive and the non-executive required much navigating, and to a lesser extent still do in daily practice today.

The depth and breadth of the academic research for about a quarter of a century allowed me to tell the recent history. Although it may be invidious to name names as there are so many who have written in this field, I found the work of Professors Stewart Ranson, Chris James, Peter Earley and Toby Greany and all their colleagues most compelling as they marry the theoretical with a great understanding of the practice. We are now missing a body of academic work of this nature on current governance, even with BELMAS doing what it can to encourage researchers. I do hope others will emerge to take up this study and make a career out of it. There is so much to look at.

By comparison to the post-LMS period, the move to widespread trusteeship has been achieved more quickly and generally well with the support of governance professionals. This was critical as more autonomy for trusts and the growth of MATs meant the performance of governing boards was even more pivotal. Without good governance the risk of trusts failing was greater, and we went through a period of dramatic failures before more emphasis on ethical leadership was established.

At the same time, the sector had to develop the new model of governance required for MATs. I use the singular there purposefully: I provided the evidence that there is one model for trust boards informed by local governance used by almost all MATs. Furthermore, if practised well, it stands the test of good governance, including the accountability requirement, providing meaningful engagement for local stakeholders. This model has taken much time, experimentation and reflection to get to: there really is no need to reinvent wheels. But a lack of mandate can suggest that local governance is optional, and new players – whether trustees or leaders – without the knowledge and or possibly the inclination for challenge may look to water it down. In a healthy system this should not be able to happen.

Recruiting volunteers is hard; although it always has been, it is harder now than in 2010. Concerted effort with support from your governance professional is usually successful when tapping into all sorts of networks, professional ones, local ones, anywhere where civic-minded people, people who care, congregate. We must continue to encourage people from all walks of life, all backgrounds, all ages, all races to come forward so that boards are as diverse as they can be. This work will never cease: it can't be thought of as a chore but as a way of getting to know the highway and byways of the community better.

School and trust governance is an exercise of participative democracy, one of the most significant in England and Wales, involving just under a quarter of a million people. Even if we could afford to pay them, which we cannot right now, there is no evidence that this would improve the quality of governance. By definition it would reduce the involvement of citizens motivated by wanting to give back to the community and supporting the flourishing of the young people.

Give governance the respect it deserves

The school accountability web is daunting with its multiple dimensions, but in order to diminish the power and fear of Ofsted, let's turn it upside down and inside out and shake it round a bit. Until governance is understood and fully embraced by leaders in the sector, it's unlikely we'll be able to oust Ofsted from its overbearing presence. Senior leaders truly need to believe that after professional accountability, governing boards are the first line of accountability in schools and trusts. None of us are in the business of disregarding accountability or lowering expectations, and we shouldn't be cowed into retreating when the powers accuse us.

Reshaping accountability with governance at its heart gives back power not just to governing boards but also leaders. More confident school and trust leaders will in turn work with teachers and other staff to provide the best learning environment possible for children and young people. Rebalancing the system to one where trust in the profession registers on the dial of accountability requires the role of institutional governance to be embraced. If the sector and its professional leaders are ambivalent, no amount of process design and quality frameworks will lead to change.

Governance needs allies – with some courage and enthusiasm – to change the culture, to change their habits of thought and taken-for-granted beliefs that influence how they think, talk and act. That change requires the people in the sector to proactively use their soft power to persuade and illustrate through their own example. Reclaiming professional accountability and taking pride in accountable governance, both upwards to boards and outwards to communities, go hand in hand.

This doesn't require a wholesale paradigm shift in accountability, but a healthier repositioning of its seven dimensions: legal; inspections and audit; professional and managerial; governance and culture; accountability to users; transparency and the media; and democracy. Democracy understandably doesn't feature much in practitioners' thinking as its influence on weekly practice seems minimal. By contrast, it is lionised in the theoretical literature without any suggestion of how it does – or could – shape and improve the education of children and young people.

This middle way should respect that central and local government's approach is anchored in democracy, giving them the right to set levels of ambition and articulate priorities as part of holding services to account, but not be limited by this. Although of course governing boards are required to work within the accountability system they are part of, there is much more room for manoeuvre than is often taken. Schools – and those who lead them – are restrained and constrained by government frameworks. Let's not continue to encourage the powers that be to develop more. Let's instead empower ourselves – those who govern, the profession and the communities – to engage in dialogue to thoughtfully draw up the parameters and priorities of local provision. Trusts can build that into their DNA by developing their own democratic accountability through the mechanism of trust membership. Across the sector we need to find better ways of making sure communities can influence education and the schools that provide it.

Invest in governance. The spreading of governance literacy across the sector will happen so much more effectively if there is funding attached, and if high-quality training is readily available. The market for governance development is wide and varied – and NGA is a big player in it – so conflict of interest klaxon, I cannot be objective when I conclude that there is a lot of choice and that the quality of some offers is high. But with funding as tight as it is, money allocated to each volunteer and each senior leader would ensure this happened. Governance for leaders should not be left to the array of leadership programmes that exist while there are unanswered questions about their content. A bespoke entitlement should be designed. Mandatory induction training for first-time governors and trustees also needs to be instituted: it is supported by almost all volunteers.

Do we need further structural reform?

The multiplicity of structures is untidy, but in the English sector we are used to the untidiness of structures and diversity is often lauded. We can make it work. The alternative proposal of compulsion would meet the same fate as it did in 2016. Some governing bodies of maintained schools will continue to take decisions to join a MAT with financial security. The political rhetoric against maintained schools has been debilitating in the building of trust and has acted against collaboration between schools unless within a MAT. The 'more in common' refrain is appropriate to adopt.

I've shown that changes to governance arrangements in the last two decades emerged as an afterthought, the unintended or misunderstood consequences of other changes when governance should have been a first-order education policy consideration. It led to muddled thinking and muddled governance practice. Governance of a group of schools has now been untangled but will need continuous effort to ensure we do not go backwards. Furthermore, the size and shape of those groups have developed without an eye to what is best for the system as a whole. This should not be ignored.

Whatever change is proposed in future needs to be tested against the governance question: who has the power, who makes the decisions, how do other players make their voices heard, and how is account rendered?

The system today with its multiplicity of different forms largely results from decisions of individual unconnected governing bodies up and down the country, characterised by commentators as the Wild West. It is the perfect time to take stock. Should the direction of travel continue to be bigger and bigger trusts, which means fewer and fewer trusts? This gives more power to those trusts and acts to lessen the voices of others. A much healthier, more accountable system would cap the size of MATs and split any national trusts into smaller regional MATs. There would be the option of retaining umbrella trusts to link all their now independent regional or local MATs with the provision of backroom services.

Pride of place

Despite all the changes to the ways schools are grouped together and governed, it is the individual schools who are at the heart of communities, educating our children. Whatever the legal structures, schools are very likely to remain the bedrock of the system and civic activities will take place largely at local level by those connected with schools. This is not going to change, and it is that school connection that gives those actors legitimacy. Yet the current system does not acknowledge the importance of place for those who attend school, those who work in schools and with schools, and those who volunteer to govern schools. Continuing this is untenable and it misses an important driver of improvement.

So much is said about the need to collaborate outside one's own institution, but there is no privileging of local collaboration in the system; quite the opposite. By failing to incorporate horizontal governance or accountability, the system is missing a crucial element for improvement. This would not be difficult to build into the accountability system by a combination of two changes. Report a version of the school report card at local level, which may have the added advantage of aiding local democracy, and then interrogate those local cards with leaders when inspecting trusts and schools. This is unlikely to affect parental decisions as they will generally be interested only in their own school's score, but it should spur on the development of productive local networks and the sharing of excellence across the locality.

A few years ago, it was suggested we could be entering the era of network governance: that's an overstatement. Institutional governance with its legal standing cannot be disregarded or overridden, but there should be a stronger emphasis placed on building capability across the system with a sense of common endeavour for the common good. Doing this well and bringing people along with results relies on the same skills and behaviours required by boards combined with the professional knowledge acquired from cooperation between schools in MATs. The importance of all children, not just those being educated without our 'own' school or trust, provides a collective mission.

A flourishing future

Schools are very significant institutions in our society. That they are securely governed is of vital importance. I was struck reading the conclusions of Chris James and his colleagues after three studies from 2010 to 2013: 'An important outcome of our research has been the resilience of school governing – a consequence in large measure of its collective nature, capability to respond and adapt to changing circumstances, and the commitment of those involved. The current challenges facing school governing bodies are likely to seriously test those qualities' (James et al., 2013).

Despite different contexts, different structures and different evidence, this uncannily encapsulates my conclusion 12 years later. Governing boards have achieved more than standing the test of time; those challenges have – for the most part – been addressed wisely, thoughtfully and for now sustainably. In partnership with the profession and its leaders, governors and trustees have done well, navigating all that has been thrown at them including a pandemic and funding levels that leave much to be desired. There are fragilities in the school system; governing boards are the safety net.

The fact that school and trust governance in England by and large functions well is entirely due to citizens across the country in very large numbers coming forward to do their civic duty. Almost all offer their time because of a passion for their local school and for the current and future lives of children and young people. It's a marvellous thing, but it's not the equivalent of making pumpkin soup for the school Halloween fair. It is a fundamental part of the web of accountability. Governors don't own our schools, but together as a board they are their custodians.

Your governing board values the school and the trust, its people and its place in the community. I'm remembering the stories of three highly effective, committed chairs who have been dealing with difficult situations, in each case governance doing its job and preventing a school imploding.

No one else hears those stories as we protect the schools we are overseeing. They have been taken for granted, largely without thanks while thanking their headteachers and executives. This is not good enough.

Optimism is one of the seven virtues from the ethical leadership framework. It is always people that make the difference. Their sense of mission, their values, their commitment, their knowledge and their skills are the source of hope. Good people will keep coming forward to teach, to lead and to govern, and they need to be supported, developed, inspired and empowered. They don't need to be given a road map, but they do need to understand who has the power, who is making the key decisions and who needs to be listened to.

My visits around the country sustained me in my role as chief executive of NGA for so long, meeting the people who cared and wanted to make a difference. My analysis and conclusions set out here come from the evidence, but also from being passionate about voices being heard and a belief in collective wisdom and public service. They also come from being 'other' in the school system, and it took writing this book for it to dawn on me that this wasn't a problem, but a strength, just as it is a strength for most of those who govern schools and trusts. Although it was tiresome to have to spend my time litigating over and over again why governance needed to be in the room and then often failing to be taken seriously when I made it into the room, it needed to be done. It was my privilege to lead that argument for 14 years, and it is now over to others. I hope this book may provide a record of progress, some sector history and a call for change that could really make a difference.

Thank you and good luck: may your voices be heard, your knowledge recognised, and all power to your very many elbows.

'We are only trustees for those who come after us.'

William Morris, as quoted on a plaque in my home town.

Addendum: a new White Paper: Every Child Achieving and Thriving

Just before this book was due to go to press, the long-awaited White Paper was published by the Labour government in February 2026. A significant part of it relates to children with SEND (special educational needs and disabilities) being able to attend their local mainstream school and have their needs met by highly trained teachers, leaders and support staff; there are many people better qualified than I to unpack. However, there are a number of this book's themes included too:

Accountability measures: it is good to see some thought going into this, both the school profile and the reform of Progress 8. Embedding collaboration into the standards required of trusts is very welcome – four years ago it was quietly dropped after lobbying by executives; this time it is more likely to stay the course.

Moving more schools into trusts: this is very much 2022 revisited (see chapter 12). Similar strategies are mentioned. The change of language is unhelpful; there are many forms of trust in the sector and school trust is undefined. It appears to mean MAT, perhaps because Labour party members are often still antagonistic to academies.

Once again local authorities setting up trusts is suggested as a way forward, but as I covered on p. 284, this made little sense and last time hit the cutting room floor. Local collaboratives and partnerships are many and varied, but do not generally comprise only maintained schools, so can't be 'deepened' by moving into a single MAT.

An emphasis on locality is very welcome, alongside an acknowledgement that the school, not the MAT, is the child's anchor. The warm words of previous governments on parental engagement are repeated, but encouragement has not produced the sea change needed.

The locality narrative is not reflected in the structural proposals. Disappointingly, the DfE is privileging scale over geography. Since I wrote the main text nine months ago, more MAT executives have been raising concerns about a system of dispersed trusts. The government's ideal of 'trusts rooted in their communities' is rhetoric.

The consultation on making local governance in MATs compulsory (as I discuss on p. 274) is the saving grace. Again in the 2022 White Paper the last government supported local governance for all MATs, but the review group composed mainly of powerful trust executives made sure it didn't see the light of day. Most trustees know good MAT governance requires the intelligence and views from local governors.

Our country is divided with many citizens feeling unheard and let down by a distant overpaid establishment. In the school sector decision-making has been centralised over the past 15 years; we need to acknowledge and counteract that. We do need a system rooted in place, accountable to local people, and worthy of public trust. Therefore, local governance cannot remain optional. It helps provides legitimacy. The consultation promised this time must be open to all and I very much hope the outcome will be different in 2026.

Select bibliography

This bibliography is not the sum total of all that I have read on the topic of governance, leadership and school improvement over the years, but if you wish to know more, the references of the listed publications should take you to most of what I have read in the last three years.

Key guidance: the place to start for practice

ASCL, ISBL, LGA, NAHT and NGA (2022) *What boards and headteachers should expect from each other and what MAT boards and chief executives should expect from each other.* Available at: www.nga.org.uk/knowledge-centre/what-boards-and-leaders-should-expect/

DfE (2025) *Academy trust handbook 2025.* Available at: www.gov.uk/government/publications/academy-trust-handbook/academy-trust-handbook-2025-effective-from-1-september-2025

DfE (2025) *Academy trusts: governance guide.* Available at: www.gov.uk/guidance/-governance-in-academy-trusts

DfE (2025) *Maintained schools: governance guide.* Available at: www.gov.uk/guidance/governance-in-maintained-schools

NGA (2023) *Governing a multi academy trust: A handbook for trustees.* Available at: www.nga.org.uk/knowledge-centre/governing-multi-academy-trust-handbook/

NGA (2023) *Welcome to governance: A guide for new governors and trustees of single schools.* Available at: www.nga.org.uk/knowledge-centre/welcome-to-governance/

NGA (2024) *The chair's handbook: A guide for chairs of governing boards of schools and academy trusts.* Available at: www.nga.org.uk/knowledge-centre/the-chairs-handbook-paperback/

NGA, ASCL and ISBL (2025) *The three strands of leadership: Building strong schools and trusts through education, business and governance leadership.* NGA.

NGA, ASCL and NAHT (2025) *Being strategic: A guide for governing boards and headteachers in single schools* and *Being Strategic: A guide for multi academy trust boards and CEOs for MATs*. Available at: www.nga.org.uk/knowledge-centre/strategic-guide-boards-leaders

Part A: the fundamentals

Academy trust governance code (2023) Available at: https://atgc.org.uk/

Adams, J. (2001) 'School governors – non-executive directors?' *Education Today*, 51(1), 31–35.

Adams, J. and Punter, A. (2008) 'Finding (and keeping) school governors: The work of the School Governors' One-Stop-Shop.' *Management in Education*, 22(4): 14–17.

Association of Colleges (2013) *Creating excellence in college governance*. Association of Colleges.

Association of Colleges (2024) *Further education code of good governance*. Association of Colleges.

ASCL (2019) *Navigating the educational moral maze: Final report of the Ethical Leadership Commission*. ASCL.

Barker, R. (2009) *The Walker Review of corporate governance – an assessment*. Institute of Directors.

Bishop, K. and Camm, G. (2023) *Board Talk: 18 Crucial Conversations that Count Inside and Outside the Boardroom*. Practical Inspirational Publishing.

Brighouse, T. and Waters, M. (2022) *About Our Schools: Improving on Previous Best*. Crown House Publishing Ltd.

Browne Jacobson (2016) *Accountability, regulation and leadership in our school system: Exploring a ten year vision*. Browne Jacobson.

Buck, A. (2018) *Leadership Matters 3.0: How Leaders at All Levels Can Create Great Schools*. John Catt Educational.

Buck, A. (2020) *The BASIC Coaching Method: All You Need to Know to Coach with Confidence*. Cadogan Press.

Chait, R. P., Ryan, W. P. and Taylor, B. E. (2005) *Governance as Leadership: Reframing the Work of Nonprofit Boards*. John Wiley & Sons.

Charity Commission for England and Wales (2023) *Annual report and accounts 2022–23*. HC1458.

Charity Governance Code (2025) *Good governance helps charities achieve their goals.* Available at: www.charitygovernancecode.org/en

Clapham, A. (2024) *Undiminishing School Governance: Investigating 'Governance Maturity Theory' for School Governing Bodies.* Journal of Education Policy.

Committee on Standards in Public Life (1995) *The seven principles of public life.* The Committee on Standards in Public Life.

Committee on Standards in Public Life (2023) *Leading in practice.* The Committee on Standards in Public Life.

Committee on Standards in Public Life (2025) *Recognising and responding to early warning signs in public sector bodies.* The Committee on Standards in Public Life.

Committee on the Financial Aspects of Corporate Governance (1992) *Report of the Committee on the Financial Aspects of Corporate Governance (known as the Cadbury Review).* Gee Publishing.

Crowe, J. (ed.) (2013) *The State of Accountability in 2013.* Centre for Public Scrutiny.

Davies, G. (2024) *Getting the most from every public pound – a blueprint for value for money.* National Audit Office (keynote speech transcript).

DCSF (Department for Children, Schools and Families) (2010) *The 21st century school: Implications and challenges for governing bodies: A report from the Ministerial Working Group on School Governance.* Department for Children, Schools and Families.

DfE (n.d.) *National professional qualifications framework review.* Available at: www.gov.uk/government/groups/national-professional-qualifications-framework-review

DfE (2010) *The importance of teaching: the schools White Paper.* Available at: https://assets.publishing.service.gov.uk/media/5a7b4029 ed915d3ed9063285/CM-7980.pdf

DfE (2017) *A competency framework for governance: The knowledge, skills and behaviours needed for effective governance in maintained schools, academies and multi-academy trusts.* DfE.

DfE (2018) *Principles for a clear and simple school accountability system.* DfE.

DfE (2020) *Headteachers' standards: report of the review.* Available at: www.gov.uk/government/publications/headteachers-standards-report-of-the-review/headteachers-standards-report-of-the-review

DfE (2024, updated July 2025) *Academy trust governance guide - Guidance on strategic leadership and the governance of academy trusts.* Available at: www.gov.uk/guidance/-governance-in-academy-trusts.

DfES (2004) *Governing the school of the future.* DfES Publications.

Drucker, P. F. (2001) *The Essential Drucker.* Harper.

Dunne, P. (2021) *Boards: A Practical Perspective* (2nd edn). Governance Publishing.

Earley, P. and Creese, M. (2000) 'Walking the tightrope? The role of teacher governors.' *School Leadership and Management*, 20(4): 475–487.

Earley, P., Evans, J., Collarbone, P., Gold, A. and Halpin, D. (2002) *Establishing the current state of school leadership in England.* DfES Research Report RR336.

Ellis, N. (ed.) (2016) *Managing Teacher Workload.* John Catt Educational.

Fishel, D. (2003) *Boards That Work: A Guide for Charity Trustees.* Directory of Social Change.

Forde, E. (2024) *Herstory: A Leadership Manifesto.* Cadogan Press.

Garratt, B. (2010) *The Fish Rots from the Head: Developing Effective Board Directors* (3rd edn). Profile Books Ltd.

Gillen, S. (2022) *Building Better Boards: How to Lead and Succeed in a Changing World.* Bloomsbury Publishing PLC.

Hill, A., Mellon, L., Laker, B. and Goddard, J. (2016) *The one type of leader who can turn around a failing school.* Available at: https://hbr.org/2016/10/the-one-type-of-leader-who-can-turn-around-a-failing-school

Hinds, D. (2018) *Secretary of State speech at the National Association of Headteachers Conference.* Available at: www.gov.uk/government/speeches/secretary-of-state-speech-at-the-national-association-of-headteachers-conference

House of Commons Children, Schools and Families Committee (2009) *School accountability.* The Stationery Office.

Hudson, M. (2017) *Managing without Profit: Leadership, Governance and Management of Civil Society Organisations* (4th edn). Directory of Social Change.

Hutchinson, J. and Crenna-Jennings, W. (2019) *Unexplained pupil exits from schools: A growing problem?* Education Policy Unit and National Education Union.

Knights, E. (2018) 'Whistleblowing in schools.' In: *Protect 25 years: speak up stop harm.* Protect.

Lancashire, S. (2023) *Reflections on Being the CEO.* Cadogan Press.

Le Grand, J. (1997) 'Knights, knaves or pawns? Human behaviour and social policy.' *Journal of Social Policy*, 26(2), 149–169.

Leithwood, K., Harris, A. and Hopkins, D. (2020) 'Seven strong claims about successful school leadership revisited.' *School Leadership & Management*, 40(1), 5–22.

NAHT Accountability Commission (2018) *Improving school accountability.* NAHT.

NGA (2018) *Taking headteacher appraisal seriously: A report on the current headteacher performance appraisal landscape in English schools.* NGA.

NGA (2020) *A view from the board: Ofsted's new Education Inspection Framework.* NGA.

NGA (2021) *Paving the way for ethical leadership in education: Pathfinder schools and trusts.* NGA. Available at www.nga.org.uk/news-views/directory/ethical-leadership-in-education-campaign

NGA, ASCL and ISBL (2025) *The three strands of leadership: Building strong schools and trusts through education, business and governance leadership.* NGA.

O'Neill, O. (2002) *Reith lectures: A question of trust.* BBC. Available at: www.bbc.co.uk/radio4/reith2002/

Pain, M. (2019) *Being the CEO: The Six Dimensions of Organisational Leadership.* John Catt Educational.

Ranson, S. (2003) 'Public accountability in the age of neo-liberal governance.' *Journal of Education Policy,* 18(5): 459–480.

Roberts, C. (2025) *Wisdom in school leadership: Introducing the Framework for Ethical Leadership in Education.* Impact, Chartered College. Available at: https://my.chartered.college/impact_article/wisdom-in-school-leadership-introducing-the-framework-for-ethical-leadership-in-education/

Roberts, C., Ethical Leadership Commission (2019) *Navigating the educational moral maze: The final report of the Ethical Leadership*

Commission. Available at: www.ascl.org.uk/Our-view/Campaigns/Ethical-Leadership

Rosen, M. (2010/11) *The annual report of Her Majesty's Chief Inspector of Education, Children's Services and Skills.* Available at: https://assets.publishing.service.gov.uk/media/5a7d5ae5e5274a3356f2bb75/Ofsted_20Annual_20Report_2010-11_20-_20full.pdf

Scanlon, B. and Sneider, S. (2011) *The Board Game: Survival and Success as a Company Board Member.* LID Publishing.

University of Stirling, Cardiff University and Birmingham University (2021) *Processes and practices of governing in colleges of further education in the UK: Uncovering the complexities of governing.* University of Sterling.

Walker, D. (2009) *A review of corporate governance in UK banks and other financial industry entities: Final recommendations.* HM Treasury.

Waslander, S., Pater, C. and van der Weide, M. (2010) *Markets in education: an analytical review of empirical research on market mechanisms in education.* OECD Education Working Papers No. 52, OECD Publishing.

Whittaker, F. (2018) 'Hinds to "clarify" roles of RSCs and Ofsted to ease schools' confusion', *Schools Week*, 10 March, [online]. Available at: https://schoolsweek.co.uk/hinds-to-clarify-roles-of-rscs-and-ofsted-to-ease-schools-confusion

Whyatt, M. (2002) 'How business-like are we?' *Cadwyn*, (Spring, 3). University of Wales, Swansea.

Wilkins, A. and Mifsud, D. (2024) 'What is governance? Projects, objects and analytics in education.' *Journal of Education Policy*, 39(3): 349–365.

NGA's annual surveys

Throughout the book I have drawn on the data from the Annual Governance Surveys, the results of which were published by NGA (for the first six years only in its magazine *Governing Matters*), but also often covered in the sector press.

2011 NGA Governing Matters – *The true state of governance*, September, pp. 27–28.

2012 NGA Governing Matters – *The temperature of governance*, September, p. 21.

2013 NGA Governing Matters – *Annual survey of governors*, September, pp. 20–21.

2014 NGA Governing Matters – *Annual survey of governors and trustees*, September, pp. 28–29.

2015 NGA Governing Matters – *The 2015 survey of governors*, September, pp. 20–22.

2016 NGA Governing Matters – *Who governs our schools?*, September, pp. 14–15.

2017 NGA with TES – *School governance in 2017.*

2018 NGA with TES – *School governance in 2018.*

2019 NGA with TES – *School governance 2019.*

2020 NGA – *School governance 2020.*

2021 NGA – *Governance volunteers and board practice: School and trust governance in 2021.*

2021 NGA – *Governing in a multi academy trust: School governance in 2021.*

2021 NGA – *Priorities, resources and people: School and trust governance in 2021.*

2022 NGA – *Governance volunteers and board practice: School and trust governance in 2022.*

2022 NGA – *Governing in a multi academy trust: Trust governance in 2022.*

2022 NGA – *The priorities and challenges facing our schools: School and trust governance in 2022.*

2023 NGA – *School and trust governance – the here and now: An interim report from NGA's 2023 annual governance survey*, July 2023.

2023 NGA – *Annual governance survey 2023*, September 2023.

2024 NGA – *Annual school and trust governance survey*, July 2024.

2025 NGA – *Annual school and trust governance survey*, July 2025.

I also had the whole back catalogue of *Governing Matters* at my disposal, recent editions of which are online, but older copies would have to be requested.

Part B: the recent history

Academies Commission (2013) *Unleashing greatness: Getting the best from an academised system*. Pearson and RSA.

ACEVO (2013) *Realising the potential of governance: The report of the ACEVO Governance Commission.* ACEVO.

Adonis, A. (2012) *Education, Education, Education: Reforming England's Schools.* Biteback Publishing.

Balarin, M., Brammer, S., James, C. and McCormack, M. (2008) *Governing our schools: The school governance study by the University of Bath.* Business in the Community.

Baroness Smith of Malvern. (2024) *Mainstream free schools.* Available at: https://questions-statements.parliament.uk/written-statements/detail/2024-10-22/hlws150

Baxter J. (2016) *School Governors: Policy, Politics and Practices.* Policy Press.

Baxter, J., Cornforth, C. and Stansfield, A. (2017) *Structures, strategy and stakeholder communication: Three key challenges for the public leadership and governance of education in England.* Presented at the 2nd Public and Political Leadership conference, 6–7 Apr 2017. The Open University.

Benn, M. and Downs, J. (2016) *The Truth about Our Schools: Exposing the Myths, Exploring the Evidence.* Routledge.

Bernardinelli, D., Rutt, S., Greany, T. and Higham, R. (2018) *Multi-academy trusts: do they make a difference to pupil outcomes?* UCL IOE Press.

Bird, S. (2002) *Governance matters: LEA support for school governors.* The Education Network.

Bradley, A. (2015) *Focused inspection of Collaborative Academies Trust.* Available at: https://assets.publishing.service.gov.uk/media/5a74d0f040f0b61df4778ba2/Focused_inspection_outcome_letter_Collaborative_Academies_Trust.pdf

Breslin, T. (2017) *Who governs our schools? Trends, tensions and opportunities.* RSA Action and Research Centre. Available at: www.breslinpublicpolicy.com/wp-content/uploads/Who-governs-our-schools_-Tony-Breslin.pdf

Browne Jacobson (2019) 'Academy trusts – the role of members', *EdInfluence* (Podcast, series 2, episode 4). Available at: www.brownejacobson.com/insights/edinfluence-podcast-series-2

Cabinet Office (2008) *Excellence and fairness: Achieving world-class public services.* Cabinet Office.

Callaghan, J. (1976) *Towards a national debate.* Speech at a foundation stone-laying ceremony at Ruskin College, Oxford, 18 October.

Camden, B. (2015) 'University sponsors quiet over promised academy support', *Schools Week*, 6 March, [online]. Available at: https://schoolsweek.co.uk/university-sponsors-quiet-over-promised-academy-support/

Carmichael, M. et al. (2015) *Building Better Boards: An Opportunity for Education.* Wild Search.

Carter, D. and McInerney, L. (2020) *Leading Academy Trusts: Why Some Fail, But Most Don't.* John Catt Educational.

Davis, A. (2016) 'Toby Young: running free school was harder than I thought', *The Evening Standard*, [online]. Available at: www.standard.co.uk/news/education/toby-young-running-free-school-was-harder-than-i-thought-a3241746.html

DCSF (Department for Children Schools and Families) (2010) *The 21st century school: Implications and challenges for governing bodies: A report from the Ministerial Working Group on School Governance.* DfE.

Dean, C., Dyson, A., Gallanaugh, F., Howes, A. and Raffo, C. (2007) *Schools, governors and disadvantage.* Joseph Rowntree Foundation.

Deem, R., Brehony, K. and Heath, S. (1995) *Active Citizenship and the Governing of Schools.* Open University Press.

DES (1977) *A new partnership for our schools: (the Taylor Report).* HMSO.

DfE (2010) *The importance of teaching: The schools White Paper.* Available at: https://assets.publishing.service.gov.uk/media/5a7b4029ed915d3ed9063285/CM-7980.pdf

DfE (2014) *Do academies make use of their autonomy?* Research Report RR366, DfE.

DfE (2016a) *Educational excellence everywhere.* Cm 9230.

DfE (2016b) *Clerking competency framework: The knowledge, skills and behaviours required to provide professional clerking to the governing boards of maintained schools, academies and multi-academy trusts.* DfE.

DfE (2016c) *Multi-academy trusts: Good practice guidance and expectations for growth.* DfE.

DfE (2024, updated July 2025) *Academy trust governance guide: Guidance on strategic leadership and the governance of academy trusts.* Available at: www.gov.uk/guidance/-governance-in-academy-trusts.

DfES (2004) *Governing the school of the future*. DfES publications.

DfES (2005) *Higher standards, better schools for all: More choice for parents and pupils*. Cm 6677. The Stationery Office Limited.

Dingle, R. (2000) *Effective governors – effective schools? A study of governor effectiveness and its association with school effectiveness*. University of Newcastle, EdD thesis.

Dunford, J. (2016) *The School Leadership Journey*. John Catt Educational.

Dyson, J. (2025) 'Failing schools all improved after academisation – despite protests', *Schools Week*, 31 January, [online]. Available at: https://schoolsweek.co.uk/failing-schools-all-improved-after-academisation-despite-protests/

Earley, P. (2003) 'Leaders or followers? Governing bodies and their role in school leadership.' *Educational Management & Administration*, 31(4): 353–367.

Earley, P., Evans, J., Collarbone, P., Gold, A. and Halpin, D. (2002) *Establishing the current state of school leadership in England*. Research Report RR336, DfES.

Education Funding Agency (2013) *Final notice to improve: E-ACT Academy Trust*. Available at: www.gov.uk/government/publications/financial-notice-to-improve-e-act-academy-trust

Farrell, C. M. and Law, J. (1999) 'The accountability of school governing bodies.' *Educational Management & Administration*, 27(1): 5–15.

Freedman, S. (2022) *The Gove reforms a decade on: What worked, what didn't, what next?* Institute for Government.

Gann, N. (2016) *Improving School Governance: How Better Governors Make Better Schools* (2nd edn). Routledge.

Gove, M. (2012) *Michael Gove on FASNA's first twenty years*. Available at: www.gov.uk/government/speeches/michael-gove-on-fasnas-first-twenty-years

Greany, T. and Ehren, M. (2016) *Written evidence to Education Select Committee inquiry into the performance, accountability and governance of multi-academy trusts*. House of Commons.

Greany, T. and Scott, J. (2014) *Conflicts of interest in academy sponsorship arrangements: A report for the Education Select Committee*. London Centre for Leadership in Learning, Institute of Education, University of London.

Harwood-Smith, G. (2008) *Thinking ahead: Exploring the strategic role that headteachers and governors carry out in partnership*. NCSL.

House of Commons Committee of Public Accounts (2015) *School oversight and intervention*. House of Commons.

House of Commons Committee of Public Accounts (2018a) *Converting schools to academies*. House of Commons.

House of Commons Committee of Public Accounts (2018b) *Academy schools' finances*. House of Commons.

House of Commons Education and Skills Committee (2006) *The Schools White Paper: Higher standards, better schools for all: First report of session 2005–06*. HC 633-I. The Stationery Office Limited.

House of Commons Education Committee (2013a) *The role of school governing bodies: Second report of session 2013–14*. The Stationery Office.

House of Commons Education Committee (2013b) *School partnerships and cooperation*. House of Commons.

House of Commons Education Committee (2013c) *The role of school governing bodies volume II oral and written evidence*. Available at: https://committees.parliament.uk/work/2247/the-role-of-school-governing-bodies/publications/

House of Commons Education Committee (2015) *Academies and free schools: Government response to the committee's fourth report of session 2014–15*. The Stationery Office.

House of Commons Education Committee (2016) *The role of Regional Schools Commissioners: Government response to the committee's first report of session 2015–16*. House of Commons.

House of Commons Education Committee (2017) *Multi-academy trusts*. House of Commons.

House of Commons Education Committee (2024) *Ofsted's work with schools*. House of Commons.

House of Commons Public Administration Select Committee (2003) *On target? Government by measurement: Fifth report of session 2002–03*. The Stationery Office.

Hutchings, M. and Francis, B. (2018) *Chain effect 2018: The impact of academy chains on low-income pupils*. The Sutton Trust.

James, C., Brammer, S., Connolly, M., James, J. and Jones, J. (2010) *The 'hidden givers': A study of school governing bodies in England.* CfBT Education Trust.

James, C., Brammer, S., Connolly, M., Fertig, M., James, J. and Jones, J. (2011) 'School governing bodies in England under pressure: The effects of socio-economic context and school performance.' *Educational Management Administration & Leadership*, 414–433.

James, C., Brammer, S., Connolly, M., Spicer, D. E., James, J. and Jones, J. (2013) *The chair of the school governing body in England: roles, relationships and responsibilities.* CfBT Education Trust.

James, C., Goodall, J., Howarth, E. and Knights, E. (2014) *The state of school governing in England 2014.* University of Bath and NGA.

Jones, J. and Ranson, S. (2010) 'Reconfiguring the governance of schools in England.' *Management in Education*, 24(1): 7–13.

Judge, D. and Kashefpakdel, E. (2018) *Governing our schools 10 years on: What has changed in school and trust governance?* Education and Employers.

Kogan, M. (ed.) (1984) *School Governing Bodies.* Heinemann.

Lane, G. (2013) *How Different Governments Have Weakened Local Government and Democracy: An Insider's View.* IRIS Press.

Leithwood, K., Harris, A. and Hopkins, D. (2020) 'Seven strong claims about successful school leadership revisited.' *School Leadership & Management*, 40(1), 5–22.

Local Government Information Unit (2010) *Academies Act 2010: A concise guide.* LGiU.

Lord, P., Wespieser, K., Harland, J., Fellows, T. and Theobald, K. (2016) *Executive headteachers: What's in a name?* NFER, NGA and TFLT.

McCrone, T. et al. (2017) *Defining and collecting metrics on the quality of school governance: a feasibility study.* DfE research report DfE-RR681, NFER and NGA.

McCrone, T., Southcote, C. and George, N. (2011) *Governance models in schools.* NFER.

Menzies, L., Baars, S., Bowen-Viner, K., Bernardes, E., Theobald, K. and Kirk, C. (2018) *Building trusts: MAT leadership and coherence of vision, strategy and operations.* Ambition School Leadership.

Millar, F. (2018) *The Best for My Child.* John Catt Educational.

Morgan, N. (2016) *'Educational excellence everywhere': Academies.* Available at: https://hansard.parliament.uk/Commons/2016-05-09/debates/1605097000001/"EducationalExcellenceEverywhere"Academies

Munby, S. (2019) *Imperfect Leadership: A Book for Leaders Who Know They Don't Know It All.* Crown House Publishing.

National Audit Office (2014) *Academies and maintained schools: Oversight and intervention.* NAO.

Nash, J. (2014) *Lord Nash speaks about the power of unlocking academies.* Available at: www.gov.uk/government/speeches/lord-nash-speaks-about-unlocking-the-power-of-academies

National College for School Leadership (2012) *Good governance: Proposals from the 2012 Fellowship Commission.* HMSO.

NFER et al. (2020) *School and trust governance investigative report.* DFE-RR997, DfE.

NGA (2013) *The road to federation: Governing bodies that consider joining federations and multi academy trusts.* NGA.

NGA (2015) *The move beyond effective: Key themes for local authority governor services from the 2013/2014 school improvement inspections.* NGA.

NGA (2019) *Moving MATs forward: The power of governance.* NGA.

NGA (2020) *Putting a price on effective clerking: A report considering the pay and remuneration of clerks to governing boards across England.* NGA.

NGA (2021a) *NGA insights: Central leadership teams in multi academy trusts.* NGA.

NGA (2021b) *School and trust governance professionals: 2021 and beyond.* NGA.

NGA (2024) *Governance professional perspectives: Charting progress and potential in an evolving landscape.* NGA.

NGA and NCSL (2011) *Leading governors: The role of the chair of governors in schools and academies.* National College for School Leadership.

Ofsted (2001) *School governance: Making it better* (HMI 281). Ofsted.

Ofsted (2002) *The work of school governors.* Report from HMCI. Ofsted.

Ofsted (2011a) *School governance: Learning from the best.* Available at: www.gov.uk/government/publications/school-governance-learning-from-the-best

Ofsted (2011b) *Leadership of more than one school: An evaluation of the impact of federated schools.* Ofsted.

Ofsted (2016) *Improving governance.* Available at: https://assets. publishing.service.gov.uk/media/5a804e05ed915d74e33f9a88/Improving_ governance.pdf

Punter, A. and Adams, J. (2010) *Governors mean business: School Governors' One-Stop Shop volunteers: Their contribution and added value to schools in England.* University of Hertfordshire.

Punter, A., Adams, J. and Lang, J. (2003) *Governors recruited from the business community by the School Governors' One-Stop Shop.* University of Hertfordshire.

PWC (2007) *Independent study into school leadership.* DCSF Research Report RR818A.

Ranson, S. (2008) 'The changing governance of education.' *Educational Management Administration & Leadership,* 36(2): 201–219.

Ranson, S. (2011) 'School governance and the mediation of engagement.' *Educational Management Administration & Leadership,* 39(4): 398–413.

Ranson, S., Arnott, M., McKeown, P., Martin, J. and Smith, P. (2005a) 'The participation of volunteer citizens in school governance.' *Educational Review,* 57(3): 357–371.

Ranson, S., Farrell, C. Peim, N. and Smith, P. (2005b) 'Does governance matter for school improvement?' *School Effectiveness and School Improvement,* 16(3): 305–325.

Rosen, M. (2010/11) *The annual report of Her Majesty's Chief Inspector of Education, Children's Services and Skills.* Available at: https://assets. publishing.service.gov.uk/media/5a7d5ae5e5274a3356f2bb75/Ofsted_20 Annual_20Report_2010-11_20-_20full.pdf

Scanlon, M., Earley, P. and Evans J. (1999) *Improving the effectiveness of school governing bodies.* Department for Education and Employment.

Statutory Instrument 2000 No. 2122 The Education (School Government) (Terms of Reference) (England) Regulations. HMSO.

Staufenberg, J. (2021) *Ministers urged to rule on governance board conflict issue as trustees resign in protest.* Available at: https://schoolsweek.co.uk/ ministers-urged-to-rule-on-governance-board-conflict-issue-as-trustees-resign-in-protest/

Stuart, G. (2013) *Call for more support to help school governing bodies improve*. Available at: https://committees.parliament.uk/committee/203/education-committee/news/181331/role-of-school-governing-bodies--substantive/

Thomson, P. (2020) *School Scandals: Blowing the Whistle on the Corruption of Our Education System*. Policy Press.

Whitty, G., Power, S. and Halpin, D. (1998) *Devolution and Choice in Education: The School, the State and the Market*. Open University Press.

Wilce, H. (2009) 'Time for change: How a young woman plans to shake up the school system', *The Independent*, 12 November, [online]. Available at: www.independent.co.uk/news/education/schools/time-for-change-how-a-young-woman-plans-to-shake-up-the-school-system-1818636.html

Wilkins, A. (2016) *Modernising School Governance: Corporate Planning and Expert Handling in State Education*. Routledge.

Wilkins, A. (2017) 'The business of governance: Corporate elitism in public education.' In: Gunter, H., Hall, D. and Apple, M. (eds.) *Corporate Elites and the Reform of Education*, pp. 161–176. Policy Press.

Wilshaw, M. (2016) *Focused inspections of academies in multi-academy trusts*. Available at: https://assets.publishing.service.gov.uk/government/uploads/system/uploads/attachment_data/file/506718/HMCI__advice__note_MAT_inspections____10_March_2016.pdf

Part C: governance now

Agnew, T. (2019) *Salaries of top academy bosses to be fair, proportionate and justified*. Available at: www.gov.uk/government/news/salaries-of-top-academy-bosses-to-be-fair-proportionate-and-justified

Association of Education Advisers (2025) *Advising on Governance in Education*. Critical Publishing.

Balarin, M., Brammer, S., James, C. and McCormack, M. (2008) *The School Governance Study*. Business in the Community.

Breslin, T. (2017) *Who governs our schools? Trends, tensions and opportunities*. RSA Action and Research Centre. Available at: www.breslinpublicpolicy.com/wp-content/uploads/Who-governs-ourschools_-Tony-Breslin.pdf

Breslin, T. (2021) *Lessons from Lockdown: The Educational Legacy of COVID-19*. Routledge.

Brighouse, T. and Waters, M. (2022) *About Our Schools: Improving on Previous Best*. Crown House Publishing Ltd.

Bubb, S., Crossley-Holland, J., Cordiner, J, Cousin, S. and Earley, P. (2019) *Understanding the Middle Tier: Comparative Costs of Academy and LA-Maintained School Systems*. Sara Bubb Associates.

Chartered Governance Institute (n.d.) *The competency framework for governance professionals*. Available at: www.cgi.org.uk/qualifications-training/competency-framework/

City of London (2010) *Volunteering – the business case*. Corporate Citizenship.

Committee on Standards in Public Life (2025) *Recognising and responding to early warning signs in public sector bodies*. The Committee on Standards in Public Life.

Dewes, I. (2024) *Neoliberal Crises and the Academisation of the English School System: Why Governing Boards Choose to Join Multi-Academy Trusts*. Palgrave Macmillan.

DfE (2015, updated 2025) *External reviews of governance: guide for schools and academy trusts*. Available at: www.gov.uk/guidance/external-reviews-of-governance-whats-involved#full-publication-update-history

DfE (2022a) *Opportunity for all: Strong schools with great teachers for your child*. DfE.

DfE (2022b) *The case for a fully trust-led system*. DfE.

DfE (2023a) *Academies regulatory and commissioning review*. DfE.

DfE (2023b) *Commissioning high-quality trusts: How the Department for Education's Regions Group takes decisions about the creation, consolidation and growth of academy trusts*. DfE.

DfE (2023c) *Annex A – trust quality descriptions* and *Annex B – trust quality evidence*. DfE.

Dyson, J. (2025a) 'Brighton trust to close after "GAG pooling" controversy', *Schools Week*, 20 January, [online]. Available at: https://schoolsweek.co.uk/brighton-trust-to-close-after-gag-pooling-controversy/

Dyson, J. (2025b) 'RISE support trust refused new schools over "not strong enough" outcomes', *Schools Week*, 24 November, [online]. Available at: https://schoolsweek.co.uk/rise-support-trust-refused-new-schools-over-low-outcomes/

Ellis, A. (2003) *Barriers to participation for under-represented groups in school governance*. DfES research report RR500.

Freedman, S. (2022) *The Gove reforms a decade on: What worked, what didn't, what next?* Institute for Government.

GovernorHub (2022) *The missing pool of talent on school governing boards*. The Key.

Haslewood, B. and Jackson, I. (2025) *Parent experience report*. Edurio.

House of Commons Education Committee (2013) *The role of school governing bodies: Government response to the committee's second report of session 2013–14*. The Stationery Office.

House of Commons Education Committee (2024) *Ofsted's work with schools*. House of Commons.

House of Commons Library (2015) *The voluntary sector and the big society*. Briefing paper 5883.

House of Commons Public Accounts Committee (2018) *Academy schools' finances*. House of Commons.

Inspiring Governance (n.d.) *Inspiring governance: history and achievements*. Available at: www.educationandemployers.org/inspiring-governance-achievements/

James, C., Brammer, S., Connolly, M., James, J. and Jones, J. (2010) *The 'hidden givers': A study of school governing bodies in England*. CfBT education trust.

Jenavs, E., Haslewood, B. and Goffin, J. (2025) *National school trust report*. CST and Edurio.

Judge, D. and Kashefpakdel, E. (2018) *Governing our schools 10 years on: What has changed in school and trust governance?* Education and Employers.

JUSTICE (2019) *Challenging school exclusions*. JUSTICE.

Knight, J. (2012) *Do-gooder governors must now do better*. Available at: www.tes.com/magazine/archive/do-gooder-governors-must-now-do-better

Knights, E. (2016) 'Some school leaders are taking us for fools – we need to stand up to them', *Schools Week*, 7 January, [online]. Available at: https://schoolsweek.co.uk/publish-appropriate-levels-for-super-head-pay-recommends-government-committee/

Kreston (2025) *Academies benchmark report 2025.* Kreston UK.

McInerney, L. (2015) 'Publish appropriate levels for "super-head" pay, recommends government committee', *Schools Week*, 7 January, [online]. Available at: https://schoolsweek.co.uk/publish-appropriate-levels-for-super-head-pay-recommends-government-committee/

National Leaders of Governance (NLG) advisory group (2020) *Recommendations on NLG reform.* DfE.

NGA (2016) *A question of time: How chairs of governing boards spend and manage their time.* NGA.

NGA (2019) *Moving MATs forward: The power of governance.* NGA.

NGA (2020a) *Time to chair? Exploring the time commitments of chairs of multi academy trusts.* NGA.

NGA (2020b) *Chairing a board: Developing governance, sharing leadership.* NGA.

NGA (2021a) *MATs moving forward: The power of governance.* NGA.

NGA (2021b) *Increasing participation in school and trust governance: A state of the nation report on recruiting and retaining volunteers.* NGA.

NGA (2022a) *MAT governance: The future is local.* NGA.

NGA (2022b) *Updated 20 and 21 questions for governing board self-evaluation.* Available at: www.nga.org.uk/news-views/directory/nga-publish-updated-20-and-21-questions-for-governing-board-self-evaluation/

NGA (2022c) *School inspection: A view from the board, two years on.* NGA.

NGA (2022d) *The schools system: The voice of MAT trustees.* NGA.

NGA (2022e) *Career pathway for governance professionals.* Available at: www.nga.org.uk/news-views/directory/free-access-gov-professional-career-pathway/

NGA (2023a) *Charting the course to good governance: Common challenges: A thematic analysis of External Reviews of Governance by National Leaders of Governance.* NGA.

NGA (2023b) *Local governance here and now: Exploring practice on the ground.* NGA.

NGA (2023c) *Taking stock of governance workload: Ensuring school and trust governance is sustainable.* NGA.

NGA (2024) *Growing good governance: Exploring the legacy of the NLG programme.* NGA.

NGA and Ofsted (2020) *Governing in unprecedented times.* Ofsted.

Ofsted (2016) *Improving governance.* Available at: https://assets. publishing.service.gov.uk/media/5a804e05ed915d74e33f9a88/Improving_ governance.pdf

Ofsted (2023a) *How multi-academy trusts are involved in school inspections.* Available at: www.gov.uk/government/publications/how-multi-academy-trusts-are-involved-in-school-inspections/how-multi-academy-trusts-are-involved-in-school-inspections

Ofsted (2023b) *Summary evaluations of multi-academy trusts.* Available at: www.gov.uk/government/publications/multi-academy-trusts-summary-evaluations/summary-evaluations-of-multi-academy-trusts-for-1-april-2023

Phillips, J. and Fuller, M. (2003) *Governing body responsibilities – four years on: The load is still too great but some attitudes are changing.* NAGM.

Punter, A. and Adams, J. (2008) *Adding value to governance.* SGOSS.

Scanlon, M., Earley, P. and Evans J. (1999) *Improving the effectiveness of school governing bodies.* Department for Education and Employment.

West, A., Wolfe, D. and Yaghi, B. (2023) 'Governance of academies in England: The return of "command and control"?' *British Journal of Educational Studies*, 72(2): 131–154.

Wilkins, A. (2016) *Modernising School Governance: Corporate Planning and Expert Handling in State Education.* Routledge.

Young, H. (2017) 'Busy yet passive: (Non-)decision-making in school governing bodies.' *British Journal of Sociology of Education*, 38(6): 812–826.

Part D: the bigger picture

Ainscow, M., Armstrong, P. W., Hughes, B. C. and Rayner, S. (2023) *Turning the tide: A study of place-based school partnerships.* Staff College, The University of Manchester.

Armstrong, P., Brown, C. and Chapman, C. (2021) 'School-to-school collaboration in England: A configurative review of the empirical evidence.' *Review of Education*, 9(1): 319–351.

ASCL, NAHT, NGA and WomenED (2021) *Closing the gender pay gap in education: a leadership imperative.* With updated figures here: www.naht.org.uk/News/Latest-comments/News/ArtMID/556/ArticleID/2662/The-gender-pay-gap-in-school-leadership

Baxter, J. A. and Cornforth, C. (2019) 'Governing collaborations: How boards engage with their communities in multi-academy trusts in England.' *Public Management Review*, 23(4): 567–589.

Brighouse, T. and Waters, M. (2022) *About Our Schools: Improving on Previous Best*. Crown House Publishing Ltd.

Bubb, S., Crossley-Holland, J., Cordiner, J. Cousin, S. and Earley, P. (2019) *Understanding the middle tier: Comparative costs of academy and LA-maintained school systems*. Sara Bubb Associates.

Cameron, D., Munby, S. and Waters, M. (eds.) (2024) *Unfinished Business: The Life and Legacy of Sir Tim Brighouse – a Tribute and a Call to Action*. Crown House Publishing.

CFE Research (2024) *Emerging findings from the NPQ evaluation: Interim report 2*. DfE.

Children's Commissioner for England (2021) *The Big Ask, The Big Answer*. Children's Commissioner.

Cooke, G. and Muir, R. (2012) *The relational state: How recognising the importance of human relationships could revolutionise the role of the state*. IPPR.

Cousin, S. and Greany, T. (2022) *Developing a new locality model for English schools: Literature review update*. Nottingham University.

Crossley-Holland, J. (2023) *The role of MATs in localities*. LocalED.

Cruddas, L. (2025) *New Domains of Educational Leadership*. Hachette Learning.

DfE (2023) *Sustainability and climate change strategy: Our progress so far*. DfE.

DfE (2025) *Giving every child the best start in life*. Available at: www.gov.uk/government/publications/giving-every-child-the-best-start-in-life/giving-every-child-the-best-start-in-life

Diamond, C. (ed.) (2022) *The Birmingham Book: Lessons in Urban Education Leadership and Policy from the Trojan Horse Affair*. Crown House Publishing.

ESFA (2021) *School resource management adviser programme – 3 years on*. Available at: www.gov.uk/government/news/school-resource-management-adviser-programme-3-years-on

Gilbert, C. (2012) *Towards a self-improving system: the role of school accountability*. National College for School Leadership.

Gilbert, C. (2017) *Optimism of the will: the development of local area-based education partnerships.* UCL Institute of Education.

Gilbert, C. (2024) *Independent learning review for Ofsted.*

Greany, T. (2018) *Sustainable improvement in multi-school groups.* UCL Institute of Education/University of Nottingham, DfE.

Greany, T. and Earley, P. (2022) *School Leadership and Education System Reform* (2nd edn). Bloomsbury Academic.

Forum Strategy (2023) *In practice guide: pure accountability.* Available at: https://forumstrategy.org/in-practice-guide-pure-accountability/

Freedman, S. (2022) *The Gove reforms a decade on: What worked, what didn't, what next?* Institute for Government.

Grek, S. (2013) 'Expert moves: International comparative testing and the rise of expertocracy.' *Journal of Education Policy,* 28(5): 695–709.

Home Office (2002) *Community cohesion: A report of the independent review team chaired by Ted Cantle.* Home Office.

Hopkins, D. (2024) *Unleashing Greatness: A Strategy for School Improvement.* John Catt from Hodder Education.

House of Commons Education Committee (2013) *School partnerships and cooperation.* House of Commons.

House of Commons Education Committee (2016) *The role of regional schools commissioners: Government response to the committee's first report of session 2015–16.* House of Commons.

House of Commons Education Committee (2017) *Multi-academy trusts.* House of Commons.

James, C., Brammer, S., Connolly, M., Spicer, D., James, J. and Jones, J. (2013) 'The challenges facing school governing bodies in England: A "perfect storm"?' *Educational Management Administration and Leadership,* 27(3), 84–90.

Kindred[2] (2025) *School readiness survey.* Available at: https://kindredsquared.org.uk/school-readiness-survey/

Leithwood, K., Harris, A. and Hopkins, D. (2020) 'Seven strong claims about successful school leadership revisited.' *School Leadership & Management,* 40(1), 5–22.

Martin, M. (2024) *Whitehall 'must not dictate' teacher training entitlement.* Available at: www.tes.com/magazine/news/general/teacher-training-entitlement-must-not-be-dictated-whitehall

McLean, D. and Worth, J. (2025) *Teacher labour market in England annual report 2025.* Available at: www.nfer.ac.uk/publications/teacher-labour-market-in-england-annual-report-2025/

Menzies, L. with Quilter-Pinner, H. (2023) *Improvement through empowerment: Helping our teachers and schools be the best they can be.* Institute for Public Policy Research.

Montague, A. (2025) 'School improvement is too human to be codified', *Schools Week*, 4 February, [online]. Available at: https://schoolsweek.co.uk/school-improvement-is-too-human-to-be-codified/

Morrish, A. (ed.) (2025) *Beyond Belief: Why School Accountability Is Broken and How to Fix It.* Hachette Learning.

Mortimore, P. (1997) 'Can effective schools compensate for society?' In: A. H. Halsey, H. Lauder, P. Brown and A. Stuart Wells (eds.) *Education: Culture, Economy, and Society*, Oxford University Press.

NAHT (2020) *Improving schools: A report of the School Improvement Commission.* National Association of Headteachers.

NAO (2025) *Government building maintenance backlog is at least £49 billion, spending watchdog says.* Available at: www.nao.org.uk/press-releases/government-building-maintenance-backlog-is-at-least-49-billion-spending-watchdog-says/

NGA (2018) *Spotlight on disadvantage: The role and impact of governing boards in spending, monitoring and evaluating the pupil premium.* NGA.

NGA (2020) *A view from the board: Ofsted's new Education Inspection Framework.* NGA.

NGA (2025a) *Creating connections: An exploration of school collaborations.* NGA.

NGA (2025b) *Widening the lens on disadvantage: The governing board's role in tackling educational disadvantage.* NGA.

Phillipson, B. (2024) *Bridget Phillipson's speech to the Confederation of School Trusts.* Available at: www.gov.uk/government/speeches/bridget-phillipsons-speech-to-the-confederation-of-school-trusts

Pickles, E. (2010) *Eric Pickles to disband Audit Commission in new era of town hall transparency.* Available at: www.gov.uk/government/news/

eric-pickles-to-disband-audit-commission-in-new-era-of-town-hall-transparency

PWC (2007) *Independent study into school leadership*. DCSF Research Report RR818A.

Ranson, S. (2011) 'School governance and the mediation of engagement.' *Educational Management Administration & Leadership*, 39(4): 398–413.

Severs, J. (2024) *Bridget Phillipson on her plan for the quiet revolution of education*. Available at: www.tes.com/magazine/analysis/general/bridget-phillipson-interview-quiet-revolution-education

Sibieta, L. (2025) 'What the spending review really means for schools', *Schools Week*, 12 June, [online]. Available at: https://schoolsweek.co.uk/what-the-spending-review-really-means-for-schools/

Sim, A. and Major, L. E. (2025) *Heart of the community: A study of the Reach Foundation's Cradle-to-Career Partnership*. University of Exeter and South-West Mobility Commission.

Tian, M. (2025) 'Embracing complexity: Rethinking education inspection in England.' *Educational Review*, 77(5): 1500–1516.

Tian, M. and Diamond, C. (2024) 'OfSTED from within: Inspectors' views on challenges and future direction.' *Educational Management Administration & Leadership*.

Verian (2025) *Pupil premium and recovery premium evaluation*. DfE.

Walton, L. (2025) 'How we'll transform school support from the ground up', *Schools Week*, 13 June, [online]. Available at: https://schoolsweek.co.uk/how-well-transform-school-support-from-the-ground-up/

West, A. and Wolfe, D. (2018) *Academies, the school system in England and a vision for the future*. Clare Market Papers No. 23. Education Research Group, Department of Social Policy, and London School of Economics and Political Science.

Whittaker, F. (2022) 'Academies system has given politicians too much power, says ex-DfE boss', *Schools Week*, 7 February, [online]. Available at: https://schoolsweek.co.uk/academies-system-has-given-politicians-too-much-power-says-ex-dfe-boss/

Wilkins, A. (2016) *Modernising School Governance: Corporate Planning and Expert Handling in State Education*. Routledge.